SHAMBHALA DRAGON EDITIONS

The dragon is an age-old symbol of the highest spiritual essence, embodying wisdom, strength, and the divine power of transformation. In this spirit, Shambhala Dragon Editions offers a treasury of readings in the sacred knowledge of Asia. In presenting the works of authors both ancient and modern, we seek to make these teachings accessible to lovers of wisdom everywhere.

The COMPASS
of ZEN

禪羅針盤

Zen Master Seung Sahn

COMPILED AND EDITED BY *Hyon Gak Sunim*

PREFACE BY *Maha Ghosananda*

FOREWORD BY *Stephen Mitchell*

SHAMBHALA
Boulder
1997

SHAMBHALA PUBLICATIONS, INC.
4720 Walnut Street
Boulder, Colorado 80301
www.shambhala.com

© 1997 by the Kwan Um School of Zen

16   15   14   13   12   11

Printed in the United States of America

⊗ This edition is printed on acid-free paper that meets the American National Standards Institute z39.48 Standard.

♻ Shambhala Publications makes every effort to print on recycled paper. For more information please visit www.shambhala.com.

Distributed in the United States by Penguin Random House LLC and in Canada by Random House of Canada Ltd

Library of Congress Cataloging-in-Publication Data
Seung Sahn.
    The compass of Zen/Zen Master Seung Sahn.—1st ed.
        p.   cm.
    ISBN 978-1-57062-329-5 (pbk.: alk. paper)
    1. Zen Buddhism.   I. Title.
BQ9266.S47   1997   97-14070
294.3'927—dc21   CIP

CONTENTS

4. Zen Buddhism

Conclusion

PREFACE

SHAKYAMUNI BUDDHA always gave very important teachings about karma, or the law of cause and effect. He laid down this law very simply in the Four Assurances: "This holy life of practice of Dharma, if lived—and should there be a heaven after all—is paradise, and will assure the student's long enjoyment of it. If there is no world beyond, at least in this very life the one who follows Dharma will be truly free from hostility and affliction. If the law of karma is indeed effective and true, then people who do no ill cannot suffer. Even if the law of karma is not effective, however, still their life of purity will always gain for them the praise of their intelligent fellow men and women, and bring happiness in this life." These are the Four Assurances of the Buddha. If anyone accepts the teachings of the Dharma they will obtain the fruit of these Four Assurances. These Four Assurances are for all students of the Buddha.

I first came to America on October 10, 1980. My country was having a terrible conflict. I came to do peace work here and to assist at the World Conference on Religion and Peace, being held under the auspices of the United Nations and U. N. Church for Peace. Cambodia was having many problems from war and civil strife, and many people were dying. But nobody seemed to notice. When I arrived I had no place to stay, and almost no resources. Very soon after coming here, I met Zen Master Seung Sahn. Later I learned that he was the seventy-eighth patriarch in the Zen lineage from Bodhidharma and the Buddha, a great master from Korea, but at that time I saw only a humble monk. He gave me a place to stay and helped me do my work when none would let me in or support me. Almost no one was interested.

I was worrying very much how I could bring attention to the situation in my country. But even though we did not know each other at that time, Zen

Master Seung Sahn immediately took me in. Still, I worried a lot. He said, "You are a monk, so you shouldn't worry."

"Why?" I asked.

He told me, "You are a monk, so you already have four million dollars!"

I could not believe what he was saying. It sounded a little crazy to a Theravada monk. "What do you mean?"

"Since you are a monk, any temple in the world is your home, so you already have one million dollars. Also, you will always receive clothes from your students, so that's two million dollars. For your whole life, many people will always give you food so that you can practice and teach other people the Dharma—that's three million dollars. Next, everybody will give you medicine when your body is sick: that's four million dollars. All you have to do is practice and teach other people the Dharma. It is very simple. You are a monk, so you are also a millionaire. Why should you worry? Ha ha ha ha!"

Zen Master Seung Sahn is my great teacher and very best friend. When I was in New York he gave me shelter, food, medicine, and clothes. He showed me real lovingkindness. He even asked me to give teachings from my tradition to his own students in his Zen center, where I lived. He let me stay as long as I liked, to spread the Dharma in the United States and to help my own country. I will never forget this.

Don't know. Go straight. This is Zen Master Seung Sahn's life and his teaching. If we do this, then we have no problems; when we have no problems, there is no tension. We always have tension because of problems: problems of the past, and problems of the future. But when there is no problem, there is no tension.

Everything about Zen Master Seung Sahn is Zen teaching. He is always here and now, in the present moment, in all his actions. This is very, very rare. When he is sitting, standing, walking, eating, talking, listening, and working—every moment, his life is always very clear. That is why he is such a great master. His teaching is clearly visible in every moment, in all his actions—verbal, physical, and mental. He has always been this way, ever since I met him.

Zen teaching embraces all teachings, including the Theravada. The Eightfold Path of Right Understanding, Right Thought, Right Speech, Right Action, Right Livelihood, Right Practice, Right Mindfulness, and Right

Meditation are all found in Zen, as you will see in this book. So are the Four Noble Truths. Therefore we all follow the great Zen Master Seung Sahn as our master, teacher, and friend.

Let it be so.

With deep respect and gratitude,

SAMDECH PREAH MAHA GHOSANANDA,
Supreme Patriarch of Cambodian Buddhism

Providence Zen Center
Cumberland, Rhode Island
April 24, 1997

FOREWORD

ZEN MASTERS are notorious for letting their eyebrows fall out. Because of their great compassion, they plunge into the weeds of relative truth. They prescribe medicine, then prescribe antidotes for the medicine, then prescribe antidotes for the antidotes, until the finally unconfused student, overwhelmed by such love, says, "That's it. Thank you so much, but I'm perfectly well now."

The truth is beyond words. "You should let go of all teaching," the Diamond Sutra says, "even the Buddha's teaching." Why so many words then? The great ninth-century Zen master Yang-shan said, "In my shop I handle all kinds of merchandise. When someone comes looking for rat shit, I'll sell him rat shit. When someone comes looking for gold, I'll sell him pure gold." Pure gold means that there *is* no gold: there's nothing to sell, nothing to buy. In fact, it's time to close up shop, take the customer by the hand, and go out for a drink.

> A monk asked Ma-tsu, "Why do you teach, 'Mind is Buddha'?"
> Ma-tsu said, "To stop a baby from crying."
> The monk said, "When the crying has stopped, what then?"
> Ma-tsu said, "Then I teach, 'Not mind, not Buddha.'"
> The monk said, "How about someone who isn't attached to either?"
> Ma-tsu said, "I would tell him, 'Not beings.'"
> The monk said, "And what if you met a man unattached to all things: what would you tell *him*?"
> Ma-tsu said, "I would just let him experience the great Tao."

Zen Master Seung Sahn is a born teacher, an astonishingly adept and fertile inventor of skillful means. In the early days, just after he came to America, he would change his slogan every few months. One month it was "Only go straight," which he would repeat so often that it seemed to be the theme song of the whole universe, even in the depths of our dreams. Then, two months later, it was "Just do it" (this was long before some hotshot at Nike came up with the phrase). Then it was "Don't check other people's minds." You get the idea.

But all these marvelous teaching devices, and all the many teachings you will find in *The Compass of Zen,* are variations on a single theme. Zen Master Seung Sahn has said probably a million times, "I brought just one teaching to America: Don't-know mind." That's all you need to know: Don't-know.

Of course, if you're in the market for rat shit, he will sell you the finest quality pellets, and if you want to take an extended tour through the weeds, he will be an excellent guide. The Great Way and a dozen side paths: all are present in *The Compass of Zen.* However lost it may get you, it always points to true north, because it issues straight from the great bodhisattva heart of Zen Master Seung Sahn.

STEPHEN MITCHELL

EDITOR'S PREFACE

O NE SPRING DAY in the early 1970s, a young Zen student named See Hoy bounded up the front steps of a Los Angeles Zen center. He went in the front door, adjusted his *rakasu*, and seated himself with the other students getting ready for evening *zazen*. Soon it was his turn for *dokusan* interview. When the bell was rung, he entered the interview room and bowed to the teacher, the great Kozan-roshi. Then he seated himself for *dokusan*.

After he presented his koans, the interview was finished. Before leaving, See Hoy pulled several rolled-up sheets of typing paper from under his *rakasu* and flattened them out on the floor in front of Kozan-roshi. "Roshi," he said, "A few days ago someone gave this to me to study. They said it would clarify certain things about Buddhism and Zen practice. I want to know what you think." The fifteen-some pages contained line after line of Chinese characters, handwritten with obviously great energy. Each line was accompanied by a line of neatly typed English translation underneath. After flattening out the document for a few moments, he lifted it up with both hands and offered it to Roshi, who merely placed the document behind him and then rang the bell, signaling the end of the *dokusan*. The student bowed and left.

For the next several weeks, Roshi said nothing to See Hoy about the curious homemade document. Then one day, at the conclusion of their regular *dokusan*, Roshi reached behind him and pulled out the document. This time, instead of being rolled up, as he had received it, the neatly printed document was meticulously folded in half, its rolled edges carefully smoothed out. He opened it up and looked at the front page.

For several moments, Roshi did not say anything. His eyes scanned the page from top to bottom. Then he cleared his throat. "This is good, very good. Where did you get it?"

"It was given to me by the Korean Zen master Seung Sahn the last time he was in Los Angeles," See Hoy replied.

"Hmmm." There were several more moments of silence. "This is all you need to know about Buddhism. Not a single word more or less."

"Then should I study it?"

"Yes, by all means. Studying this will certainly clarify your understanding of the teaching."

Years later, when See Hoy received Dharma transmission and became a Zen master, he recounted the story of how *The Compass of Zen* had deepened his appreciation of Buddhist teaching at a time when he was just a young student trying to find his way among the plethora of dharma teachings available to him in Los Angeles in the early 1970s. Although the document was small in size, he once said to an international group of Zen students sitting a three-month intensive meditation retreat that *The Compass* had clarified his sense of the bone—the core or essence—of the Buddha's teaching more than any other sutra he had ever read.

The meditation scene in America in the late 1960s and 1970s was wide open. There were many accomplished Asian masters teaching. New meditation centers representing all the major Eastern spiritual traditions were springing up like mushrooms after spring rain in all the major cities and near many college campuses. Among the heirs of the 1960s, there was an explosion of interest in shared life in semimonastic communities. And there was a tremendous outflow of new books presenting many different approaches to meditation and the path to enlightenment.

This somewhat dizzying array of spiritual opportunities was a boon to many who were growing weary of the dominant spiritual traditions of the West. Yet the very number of opportunities created an atmosphere where the teachings could be had all too easily; the line separating clear teaching from ineffective teaching was not always obvious. America was becoming the spiritual shopping mall it is today, its shelves overstocked with spiritual products. As Zen Master Seung Sahn also said about the situation in America at the time *The Compass* was written: "America was like a department store. There were many, many great masters and teaching styles. But who was giving the Buddha's true teaching? How could meditation students find their way through this department store? That was not always clear, and many Western students didn't understand the Buddha's original teachings. Many people were following a wrong way. So *The Compass of Zen* appeared."

The Compass of Zen is a distillation of the core of the Buddhist teaching by an enlightened master of considerable renown. It was prepared by Zen Master Seung Sahn in the early 1970s to clarify his Western students' grasp of some of the most essential principles in each of the three main Buddhist traditions. Not intending it to substitute entirely for sutra readings, Zen Master Seung Sahn devised *The Compass* as a complementary way for Western students of meditation to find their way easily among the various traditions without having to wade through the technical points of major sutras. As he once said, "*The Compass of Zen* only presents the bone of Buddhism. The teaching flesh of Buddhism is all different. Nowadays in the West you can find Hinayana flesh and Mahayana flesh and Zen flesh. There is Chinese and Tibetan and Korean and Japanese and Thai flesh. But underneath all of this, what is the *bone* of the Buddha's teaching?" The awesome job of *The Compass* was to present this bone in a simplified but not overly reductive manner.

The Compass of Zen was not intended just for Zen students. According to Zen Master Seung Sahn, it was initially prepared with two purposes in mind: first, to clarify the bone of Buddhist teaching for anyone interested in understanding correct teaching; and second, to broaden the perspective of his own Zen students, that they might not remain conversant only with Zen-style teaching. It is said that this Zen master took great pains to remind his students to keep a very wide view of the Buddha's teaching, and not let themselves be compartmentalized in their use of expedient means and just view the teachings in terms of Zen's means. When someone asks him, in one of the talks from which this book is derived, why he, a Zen master, would present the teachings of Hinayana Buddhism and Mahayana Buddhism, he replies, "Go home and look in your medicine cabinet. How many medicines do you have there? Only one?" He encourages his students to keep this view: to understand the bone of Hinayana teaching and Mahayana teaching just as they would understand the bone of Zen.

For over twenty years, *The Compass* was used within the Zen lineage established by Zen Master Seung Sahn in the West, the Kwan Um School of Zen. Initially the thirty-one-page root text was used by beginning students as a clear and simple map of the Buddhist teachings. It was also used to train dharma teachers and to test students during kong-an interviews. Although widely known within the Kwan Um School of Zen, it was seldom circulated outside the sangha. As the years passed, students began to ask the Zen master to comment on various subjects in the text. Zen Master Seung Sahn delivered several long series of talks on *The Compass*, beginning at the 1977 Dharma Teachers' Yong Maeng Jong Jin, held in Providence, Rhode Island. In these talks he provided more detailed explanations of various aspects of the Buddhist tradition.

The present text is a compilation of several series of talks that Zen Master Seung Sahn has given on *The Compass of Zen* since 1977. It is composed of lectures he gave at the Providence Zen Center (April 1988), Lexington Zen Center (May 1988), Hong Kong Zen Center (March 1993), Seoul International Zen Center at Hwa Gye Sah Temple (Winter Retreat, 1993–1994), Singapore Zen Center (Spring 1994), and Dharma Zen Center, Los Angeles (December 1995). This text also includes material translated for the first time from talks that Zen Master Seung Sahn delivered on *The Compass of Zen* in his native Korean. Those talks were originally published in two books in Korea, *Mountain Is Blue, Water Is Flowing* and *Moon in a Thousand Rivers*, and translated by the editor exclusively for use in this text. Lastly, the present text includes material delivered by Zen Master Seung Sahn on various related subjects during his daily question-and-answer sessions with Zen students at the Seoul International Zen Center, Hwa Gye Sah Temple, from 1994 to 1996.

One of the most fascinating qualities of this particular Zen master is his extraordinarily spontaneous and almost limitless energy. For those fortunate enough to have attended the talks from which these pages are derived—or at least to have seen the videos—it is immediately apparent that there is something operating here beyond the reach of mere genius. It is unbounded enlightened wisdom. *The Compass of Zen* lectures, like all of Zen Master Seung Sahn's dharma speeches, combine a pure, enlightened wisdom with a grasp of the texts that is almost scholarly at times; a delivery at times serious, and at most others, well, hilarious. All along, the central point—the bone—is the same: How do we wake up and help this world, from moment to moment? This text attempts to preserve the spontaneous quality of Zen Master Seung Sahn's verbal delivery, since the delivery is as much an example of his unique teaching style and expedient means as is the material itself.

The present text makes no pretense to being an academic treatise. It makes no claim to render any kind of scholarly veracity vis à vis texts or traditional modes of expression. Like the author who has delivered these talks, *The Compass* is an uncompromising pointing at original nature that does not rely on polite expression. *The Compass* treats the tradition and its teachings from the standpoint of purely enlightened insight, and doesn't worry so much about convention. This is the way a Zen master teaches.

Finally, something must be said about the use of the term *Hinayana* ("small vehicle") rather than the term *Theravada* ("way of the elders") to refer to early Buddhism. There is no pejorative intent here. The use of this term has been considered at some length. In his original written outline of *The Compass of Zen*, as well as in the talks on which this book is based, Zen Master Seung Sahn uses the term *Hinayana* as the traditional term to refer to Buddhist teaching before the full flowering of Mahayana Buddhism. To most readers the term *Theravada* suggests a living tradition of Buddhism with its roots in Southeastern Asia rather than the original, historical period of Buddhism and the teachings associated with it. Additionally, the teaching of Zen—and of this Zen master in particular—emphasizes complete nonattachment to language as a primary means of liberation from the suffering caused by our conceptual minds. It is in keeping with this spirit that the usage of the term *Hinayana* is maintained.

Included at the end of this text is a section setting forth ten essential kong-ans (Chinese: *kung-an;* Japanese: *koan*) which Zen Master Seung Sahn has chosen to represent the entirety of the seventeen hundred Chinese and Korean kong-ans used in China, Korea, and now the West. In "The Ten Gates," the author distills the most essential "point" of each kong-an in detail, not through the usual opaque poetic commentaries or academic and etymological hodge-podge, but through a direct and meticulous exposition of the nature of the kong-an itself. This section of the text could well stand alone as a significant milestone in the history of Zen teaching and its transmission to the West. It lays out a use of kong-ans that is meticulous in the expression of the kong-an itself and—especially—a rigorous teaching which demands from moment-to moment a meticulously intuitive and spontaneous application of the kong-an to changing situations in everyday life. That can be seen most clearly in Zen Master Seung Sahn's delineation of the correct function of subject and object in kong-ans and everyday life. Such a meticulous application represents a revolutionary adaptation of traditional "mountain" kong-an practice to the myriad situations of contemporary life in modern society.

It has taken exactly four years to assemble the current versions of this compass from an array of textual sources, in Korean, Chinese, and English. In that time, I have been blessed with the assistance of an international assembly of bodhisattvas spanning three continents. Special mention must be made of the guidance of Venerable Zen Master Dae Kwang, Abbot of the Kwan Um School of Zen. Zen Master Wu Bong (Centre Parisien de Zen—Kwan Um) and Stanley Lombardo, JDPSN, professor of classics at the University of Kansas, advised in the final stages. Thanks are also in order to Ven. Do Mun Sunim, JDPS, of Seoul International Zen Center; Ven. Hyang Um Sunim, JDPS, Su Bong Zen Monastery; Ven. Mu Sang Sunim, Dharma Zen Center, Los Angeles; Ven. Chong An Sunim; Ven. Hae Tong Sunim (Lee, Jae-Gyun); Ven. Myong Do Sunim; J. W. Harrington, of the Kwan Um School of Zen; Kim, Yong-Hyon, of Konghang-Dong, Seoul; Lee, Hyon-Yong, of

Paris and Seoul; Kim, Ji-Eun, of Georgetown University and Apkujong-Dong, Seoul; Park, Song-Chol, of Dongguk University, Seoul; Lee, Mun-Gyun; Kim, Tae-Ok; and Lee, Jong-Hoon. Prakash Shrivastava (Mu Soeng), of the Barre Center for Buddhist Studies, and Richard Streitfeld handled this material in its earliest stages. Dyan Eagles, president of DharmaCrafts, contributed generously and invaluably, as always. And to Venerable Zen Master Seung Sahn: unspeakable gratitude beyong any measure.

Lastly, this book is offered to the memory of the late Zen Master Su Bong (See Hoy Liau), who until his death in July 1994 worked hard to see this teaching come to print. A short time ago, as a young Zen student, See Hoy Liau held this same *Compass of Zen* in his hands; three years ago he suddenly died a young Zen master. Where did he go? Now you are holding a compass in your hands. It is hoped you use this compass to find your own way where he went and where we all must go.

HYON GAK SUNIM
(P. Muenzen)
Diamond Hill Zen Monastery
Providence Zen Center
Cumberland, Rhode Island
August 1, 1997

THE COMPASS OF ZEN

INTRODUCTION
Where Are You Going?

A LONG TIME AGO, the world was a very simple place. Nowadays this world is very complicated. The main reason for this is that there are too many human beings living on this planet. The human population has increased far too rapidly. In 1945 there were some two billion people living in this world. Through thousands and thousands of years of human history, only two billion people appeared on earth, and that was enough. Compared to today, people's minds were relatively simple and clear. But in just the last fifty years since the end of the Second World War, three billion more people have appeared, and now human beings have become very complicated. Today there are nearly six billion people in the whole world, and some scientists say that in the next thirty years another three billion people will appear. These facts are directly connected to the sudden increase in the amount of suffering that humans and other beings are now experiencing. Let's look at this more closely.

Nowadays humans live more closely together, so their relationships have become more complex. Their desire for material things becomes deeper and stronger. Their thinking is more complicated, their lives are more complicated, and consequently there is much more suffering than ever before. Even the *kinds* of suffering in the world have become more complicated as humans come up with new weapons and new ways of hurting each other. Human beings not only make each other suffer. Nowadays, we bring much more suffering to all of the other beings in this world. We hurt the air, the water, the grass, the trees, everything. Human beings cut down whole forests, and take away the green belt. We pollute the water, the air, and the ground. Human beings always say they want freedom, but actually they are the number one dictators in this world.

So nowadays it is very important that human beings wake up. They must soon attain their correct job. Why do you *live* in this world? What are you *doing* in this world? When you are born, where do you come from? When you die, where do you go? Everybody says, "I don't know." That is a human being. Human beings think that human beings are very clever animals. But despite all their intelligence, if you look closely at what has happened in the world you see that human beings are actually the stupidest animals, because human beings don't understand human beings. A dog understands what a dog should do, and cats understand what cats should do. All animals understand their job and only do it. But we don't understand our correct job and correct way in this world, and instead we live only for ourselves. So meanwhile time passes, everybody gets old and dies. When you die, where do you go? Despite all their intelligence and cleverness, human beings don't understand the answer to this very important question.

If we want to understand ourselves and help all beings get out of suffering, we must first understand where this world's suffering comes from. Everything arises from our minds. Buddhist teaching shows that everything comes from primary cause, condition, and result. This means that some primary cause, when it appears under a certain condition, will always produce a certain result. So what is the reason for so many human beings appearing in this world, and what is the result of it? Why is there so much suffering, and why does it seem to increase every day? Perhaps the most important reason for such a dramatic increase in the amount of suffering in this world is the increase in the amount of meat-eating that humans do. Before World War II, human beings did not eat so much meat. In Asia, people have always generally eaten meat only on special occasions, perhaps only twice a year, on one of the major holidays. Nowadays Asians eat meat sometimes several times a day. The same has been true in the West for generations. This century has seen a very big increase in the amount of meat-eating on the planet. But how is this connected to the dramatic increase in suffering all over the world?

For centuries, if a man wanted to eat meat, he went into the forest and shot maybe one or two animals with bow and arrow—*piitchhuu!* Then he went home and ate it with his family. This animal died. But there was some kind of relationship between the animal and the person who killed and ate it. Their karma was somewhat clear. When the animal died, it could perhaps understand a little of what was happening: "Oh, this man will eat me! Maybe next life I will get him!" So the karma was very simple: it was only between this one man and this animal. It could be resolved between them and eventually brought back to a balance through the simple operation of cause and effect. In the twentieth century, however, human technology has grown up too quickly. Many special guns and techniques have been created to kill a greater and greater number of animals. Every single day, millions and millions of animals are routinely and mechanically slaughtered all over the world just to satisy human beings' desire-minds. Now one machine can kill many, many thousands of animals very quickly. Only one man pushes a button in a factory, maybe far away from the animals. When these animals die, many consciousnesses are suddenly and violently released from their dying bodies. These animals' consciousnesses then wander around and around and around, looking for a new body. Where they go, they don't understand.

The Buddha taught us that everything comes from primary cause, condition, and result. When so many millions of animals are killed this way every year, some of their consciousnesses are inevitably reborn as humans. Perhaps only 0.00001 percent become human beings, but that is still a lot of humans that have some kind of animal consciousness operating inside them. If you look at humans in this world nowadays, you see that while they may all have human faces and human bodies, their consciousnesses are not completely human. Some people have dog consciousness, some have cat consciousness. Others have rabbit consciousness or snake consciousness. Cow minds, pig minds, chicken minds, lion minds, tiger minds, and snake minds are all mixed together. Most people live with perhaps five or ten percent of our original human consciousness functioning inside them, and the rest is some animal consciousness controlling their mind. Instead of having the original human capacity for love, cooperation, and compassion, people nowadays only fight with each other and with this world. They cannot do correct to-gether-action with other human beings.

This is not to say there is something wrong with animals. But when you look at this world you see that animals tend to act together only with their own species, and don't like other animals. Dog-minds like dog-minds; they do not act with cat-minds. Snakes and lions and rabbits do not get along with each other. A snake-consciousness only follows other snake-minds, and has no compassionate action that can connect it with the suffering that some-one else is experiencing. Birds also don't like other species of birds, so they make groups of their own species and fly around together in these groups. If somebody attacks one of them, often the whole group will attack back. That is the nature of this animal-mind. The political situation in the world today is the same. We now live in a world filled with many smaller countries and political and ethnic goups—many with private militias—all fighting each other. Children become involved with guns and other forms of violence at earlier and earlier ages, doing things to other human beings which were unheard of just ten or twenty years ago.

This all comes from having too much animal consciousness dominating our minds. Nowadays, many, many human beings are like this. They have some kind of animal consciousness inside, so there is a great deal more suffering because they cannot connect their consciousness to human life in a crowded world. Most people only look after their own interests. There is a greater tendency for some fighting-mind to appear. They only follow their own particular ideas and opinions, no matter what is going on around them. Something is out of balance, so naturally suffering appears.

I had one student in America in the 1970s who owned several exotic pet snakes. She loved these snakes very, very much. She would carry them around on her neck wherever she went. Many people were afraid of them, but she was very natural with these snakes. They would even sleep in her bed at night. One day, she came to the Zen Center. I asked her, "Will you sit the three-day retreat this weekend?"

"No," she said.

"Why?"

"I cannot find someone to take care of my snakes. I love my snakes very much. But no one can take good care of them while I am at the Zen Center. So I cannot do meditation."

So I said to her, "You are no problem. You come to the Zen Center and do strong practicing. You can bring your snakes. I will talk to the housemaster and we will give you your own room. Then you can sit meditation and take care of your snakes. Do you like that?"

She was very happy: "Oh, yes. That's wonderful!" Then she came to the Zen Center and sat the retreat.

On the first day of the retreat, this woman's brother called the Zen Center. He was very anxious. "Is my sister there? Is my sister there? Our mother just got very sick. She is in the hospital, very far away. We must go to see her as soon as possible."

But instead of being sad for her mother, this woman got very angry! "No, I cannot come. Who will take care of my precious snakes while I am gone? Maybe if I go away they will die! Maybe someone will feed them the wrong things. Snakes are very temperamental, you know. . . ." She gave her brother this kind of strong speech. But he was not surprised. He already knew her mind for many years. He only hung up the phone.

Several days later, one of the snakes got sick. It was not eating its food and only lay in the corner. The woman suddenly became very, very worried. She stopped coming to the meditation sittings and made a lot of phone calls to the local animal doctors, looking for someone who truly understood snakes. Finally she left the retreat to take her snake to the doctor. She would not leave the retreat to see her mother in the hospital, but when her snake was suffering, her mind was immediately and deeply disturbed. This is very interesting.

So this woman's consciousness felt more for her snakes than for other human beings. She showed more compassion for her snakes than for her own mother! The behind-meaning of this is that this woman's consciousness was part human, but part snake. She could not do so much together-action with human beings, but she related quite easily and automatically with the snakes' situation. She did not have very much compassion for anything but them. That's very crazy! But nowadays many human beings are somewhat like this, and so it is not considered crazy anymore. So that is a very interesting story.

Animals' consciousnesses are not good and not bad. But human beings have many strong ideas and desires, so having some animal consciousness inside is not so good, because they cannot control it. When an animal is hungry, it eats. When it is tired, it sleeps. That is very simple! But human beings eat, and are still not satisfied. Even though their stomach is full, they still go outside and do many bad actions to this world: they kill animals for fun or decoration. Somebody catches fish for sport. Then everybody is clapping: "Ah, wonderful!" They laugh and smile and shake hands. The humans are very happy, patting each other on the back and taking pictures. It is considered to be a very successful day. But look at this fish. He is not happy, you know? The fish is flapping around—he's suffering! "Where is water? Where is water? Please, I want *water!*" They are laughing, and the fish is suffering and dying, right in front of them. Most humans cannot connect with the great suffering which is right in their midst. This kind of mind is quite usual nowadays. And that is *not* wonderful. The mind which lives like this has no compassion for the suffering of this world.

Human beings also kill animals not just for food. They take the animals' skin to make shoes and hats and clothes. And even that is not enough. They take these animals' bones to make necklaces or buttons or earrings. In short, they kill many, many animals in order to sell the animal parts for money. Because of these desires and this strong animal consciousness, human beings fight with each other, and destroy nature. They do not value life. So now this whole world has many problems: problems with the water, problems with the air, problems with the earth and food. Many new problems appear every day. These problems do not happen by accident. Human beings *make* each and every one of these problems. Dogs, or cats, or lions, or snakes—no animal makes as many problems for this world as human beings do. Humans do not understand their true nature, so they use their thinking and desire to create so much suffering for this world. That is why some people say that human beings are the number one bad animal in this world. Some religious traditions call this kind of situation the "end of this world."

That is only the end of the current human consciousness. Original human nature does not have this problem. In Buddhist teaching, rather than call this the "end of the world," we say that everything is now completely ripe. It is like a fruit growing on a tree. At first a blossom appears on the branch. As time passes this blossom produces a small bud, and the blossom drops away. The bud gradually matures into a fruit which swells and swells as time passes. The fruit is green at first, but over time the side facing the sun starts to turn a beautful color. At this point, only one side is colored, while the other is still greenish. More time passes, and the whole fruit is now a very wonderful color. The fruit may have a beautiful form and beautiful color, but there is still no smell, because the fruit is not yet ripe inside. As a little more time passes, however, the fruit becomes completely ripe.

Up until this point, it has taken a long time for this to develop from blossom to bud and fruit. For many months all of the tree's energy has gone up from the roots and down from the leaves gathering energy from the sun, and has gone into producing the fruit. This process has taken place over a long period, up to a year of change and growth in the tree and blossom and bud and fruit.

But now the energy flowing from the tree into the fruit is cut off. From this point on, once the fruit has become completely ripe, the changes in the fruit start to happen very, very quickly, just in a matter of a few days. Its form is not so good anymore, and its color is also not so good. But inside there is a very, very sweet taste, and the fruit begins to smell very strong. It is beginning to be overripe. Soon a few spots appear on the fruit, tiny black dots indicating that the fruit is "turning." After a few more days, there are many, many spots on the fruit. Once these spots appear on the fruit, the process of rotting cannot be slowed or stopped. The fruit becomes rotten just a few days after becoming ripe. When it becomes rotten, it cannot be eaten. But inside, this fruit has seeds. When the fruit has become completely rotten the seeds reach maturity.

The current situation in the world is like this fruit. Many, many centuries of human development made this fruit. For a long time, this single blossom was only belief in some God or outside power. Then the fruit appeared and developed. But only one side ripened at first; only one side had a good color and good taste, while the other did not. This was the emergence of capitalism and communism in this world. Then recently the changes in this fruit have started to happen very quickly. Communism disappeared, and now the whole fruit is the same color. The fruit has become ripe, and has just one color and taste now: *money*. Nowadays, there is no longer any ideology for separate belief. This whole world only wants money, and everyone's energy is going very strongly in that direction. This world has no true way—there is only the taste of money. Already many rotten spots have appeared: places like the Middle East, Rwanda, Yugoslavia, North Korea, even now in America, Russia, China, and Japan. Since the communist world broke apart, we see the emergence of many smaller groups and nations, all fighting each other. There is also the spread of many private armies and the routine buying and selling of weapons of mass destruction.

So this fruit has grown over a long period of time. But once it becomes ripe, it rots very, very quickly. When any fruit becomes rotten it cannot be eaten. However, inside this fruit there are seeds. These seeds are now ready: they can do anything.

So human beings must soon wake up and find their original seeds, their original nature. But how do we return to our original nature? Around twenty-five hundred years ago, the Buddha had a very good situation. He was a prince named Siddhartha, and had everything he wanted. But he didn't understand himself. "What am I? I don't *know*." In those times in India, the Brahman religion of Hinduism was the main religion. But Brahmanism could not give him the correct answer to his questions about the true nature of life and death. So Siddhartha abandoned the palace, went to the mountains, and practiced various spiritual austerities for six years. He found the Middle Way between self-indulgence and extreme asceticism. Early one morning, while meditating under the Bodhi tree, he saw a star in the eastern sky. At that moment—*boom!*—the young prince Siddhartha got enlightenment. He woke up, and became a buddha. He attained I. This means that the Buddha attained the true nature of a human being without depending on some outside force or religion or god. That is the Buddha's teaching.

Nearly every single human being living in the world today does not understand what they are. The Buddha was simply a man of great determination and try-mind who taught us the importance of resolving just that point.

Before you die, you must attain your direction. You must attain what you are. If you read many sutras, or chant to Amitaba, that will help you somewhat. That is not good, not bad. But why do you read many sutras? Why do you try this Amitaba Buddha chanting? So it is very important to make your direction clear. The Buddha taught us the importance of finding our true direction in this life. "What am I? I must attain my true self—this is the most important thing I can do." If you attain your true self, then you attain your correct way. When you are born, where do you come from? When you die, where do you go? Just now, what is your correct job? Everybody understands this body's job. Some people have lawyer jobs, or doctor jobs, or truckdriver jobs, or nurse jobs, or student jobs, or husband jobs, or wife jobs, or child jobs. These are our bodies' jobs, our *outside* jobs. But what is your true self's job? The Buddha taught us that for life after life after life, we must walk the Great Bodhisattva Way and save all beings from suffering. In order to save all beings, it is very important that you first save yourself. If you cannot save yourself, how can you possibly save other people? So this is why we must attain our true self, our true nature. This true nature cannot be found in books or conceptual thought. A Ph.D., no matter how wonderful, cannot match the power of even one moment of clear insight into our own true original nature. And the most direct path to that experience is meditation. That is a very important point.

Correct meditation means understanding my true self. The path of this begins and ends by asking, "What am I?" It is very simple teaching, and not special. When you ask this question very deeply, what appears is only "don't know." All thinking is completely cut off, and you return to your before-thinking mind. If you attain this don't-know, you have already attained your true self. You have returned to your original nature, which is mind before thinking arises. In this way you can attain your correct way, and you attain truth, and your life functions correctly to save all beings from suffering. The name for that is "wake up." That is the experience of true meditation.

Why is this book called *The Compass of Zen*? Buddhist teaching reveals that this world is an ocean of suffering. Everyone is born, suffers, grows old, and dies. We are reborn, we suffer, we grow old, and then we die. Every single being is reborn over and over and over again. Because of our desires and attachments, we have been doing this since beginningless time. The Sanskrit name for that is samsara—everything is always going around and around and around. The Sino-Korean characters for that are *go hae*, or "ocean of suffering." The Buddha taught that we must take a boat across this ocean of samsara, a ship of wisdom or *"prajna* ship." But like every ocean-going vessel, this ship needs a compass.

Let's say that you want to take a ship from Los Angeles to Korea. On board you have stowed plenty of food and clothing and medicine. These are necessary for your body to stay alive. But how do you find your destination on this journey? The most important thing to be clear about is your direction. If your direction is not clear, you will wander for years and years all over the ocean. You will be easily lost. In the meantime, perhaps you will run out of food, or get stranded on some island. So more than anything else on your journey, your direction is most important: "How can I find Korea? How do I get there? Where is Korea?"

To find your correct direction, you need a compass. If sailors have no compass, then even though they may have a very good boat, good maps, and excellent weather, they will not perceive clearly their correct direction. They will certainly lose the way and not reach the destination. But when you use this boat's compass correctly, you can find your true way. Then you can perceive that actually your true way is always right in front of you.

So if you want to understand your true self, you must practice meditation. Only keep this question very deeply: "What am I?" Don't *knowww*. . . . But there are many kinds of teachings you can follow along the way. There is Tibetan Buddhist teaching, Chinese Buddhist teaching, Korean Zen, Japanese Zen and *Namu myoho renge-kyo*; there is Vipassana, Transcendental Meditation, and Clear Light Meditation. There is Pure Land practice, Tantric Buddhism, and esoteric Buddhism. There are many, many kinds of teachings, especially nowadays in the West. What is a clear teaching, and how does it function? How does it point directly to mind? How does it help us find our correct way, truth, and a life that functions spontaneously and compassionately for all beings? That is the point of making this compass: to help you find the true bone of the Buddha's teachings in the three major Buddhist divisions.

There is an old saying in the East: "For a heat sickness, use hot medicine. For cold sickness, use cold medicine." Human beings suffer from speech-and-thinking sickness, so sometimes speech-and-thinking medicine can help them. That is why we have this *Compass of Zen* teaching. If you do not attach to the speech and words in this *Compass*, and only keep a don't-know mind, completely cutting off all thinking, then the speech-and-thinking medicine on these pages can help you find your correct way. You can find for yourself the bone of the Buddha's teaching. But if you attach to speech and words, even the Buddha's speech will take you straight to hell. So what follow below are many kinds of wonderful teaching words: there are Hinayana words, Mahayana words, Zen words, Chinese words, Sanskrit words, also Korean words, Japanese words, American words, and Polish words. There are true words, false words, good words, and bad words. Sometimes there are no words. There are many, many kinds of words. If you want to attain your true self, then don't attach to any of these teaching words. If you say that Hinayana Buddhism is correct Buddhist teaching, you will have a problem. If you say that Mahayana Buddhism is correct, you will have a bigger problem. And if you say that Zen is correct teaching, you will go straight to hell like an arrow. Don't hold this *Compass's* speech. Only perceive what it is pointing you to, and then you can just *do* it.

The most important thing you can do is to learn how to keep a great question very strongly: "What am I?" By keeping this question with great determination, what appears is only "don't know." There is no thinking. There is no longer any speech or words, because all thinking is completely cut off. The name for that is "don't know." Another name for it is true self, or true nature. It is sometimes called enlightenment and *satori* and *kensho*. But originally, this point has no name and no form. If you attain that, you attain Hinayana Buddhism, you attain Mahayana Buddhism, and you attain Zen. You attain that Hinayana, Mahayana, and Zen are all the same point. "What am I?" That point's name is "don't know."

So, I hope that you read these words but don't become attached to them, then only go straight *don't know*, try, try, try for ten thousand years nonstop, get enlightenment, and save all beings from suffering.

ZEN MASTER SEUNG SAHN,
Man of Dok Seung Mountain

Hwa Gye Sah Temple
Sam Gak Mountain
Seoul, South Korea
1 August 1997

1
Buddhism

The Purposes of Buddhism

佛教　目的

First attain enlightenment,

上 求 菩提

then instruct all beings.

下 化 象生

M ANY CENTURIES AGO, the Greek philosopher Socrates used to walk through the streets and marketplaces of Athens, teaching his students. He would say to them, "You must understand yourself! You must understand yourself! You must understand yourself." Then one day a student said, "Sir, you always say we must understand ourselves. But do *you* understand *your* self?"

"No, I don't know myself," Socrates replied. "But I understand this 'don't know.'" This is very interesting teaching. Buddhist practice points at the same experience, because most human beings pass through their lives without the slightest sense of what they are.

We understand many things about this world, but we don't understand ourselves. So why do human beings come into this world? Why do we live in this world? For love? For money? For respect or fame? Do you live for your wife, husband, or children? Why do you live in this world? If someone asked you these questions, you might very well answer, "I live for my children. I live to earn enough money for them, or maybe just to have a good life." Most people think like this. They live only for their family, for some fleeting social respectability, perhaps to enjoy art or to get some powerful position. Everyone wants to have a good situation for themselves. If you look at this world very closely, it is easy to see that most people eat and sleep and live merely for their own personal happiness. Yet these things are not the real purpose of human beings' life. They are just temporary means for living in the world. If human beings cannot find out who they are, how can they ever be truly happy?

The Buddha came from a royal family in India some twenty-five hundred years ago. He was a prince, named Siddhartha Gautama. He had a very good situation. In the palace he had everything he wanted: good food, good clothes, many beautiful women, a high seat, and a very good position. He was the son of the king, and someday he would inherit a powerful kingdom. That's very wonderful! But inside, Siddhartha was very unhappy, because he could not understand who he was. He could not understand life or death. He was deeply saddened that all beings must eventually get sick, grow old, and die. This gave him a big question about his own nature and the nature of all beings. "What am I? I don't *know*. . . ." At that time in India, the Brahman religion of Hinduism was followed by nearly everyone. But Brahmanism could not give the young prince the correct answer to his burning question. So he was even more unhappy. "Why do human beings come into this world? Why do we eat every day? What am I?" He ate food, but there was no taste. Heard music, but it gave him no pleasure. The beautiful palace became like a prison.

One night, Siddhartha left the palace. He left his family, his beautiful wife, and his infant child, cut off all his hair, and became a monk. Then he went to the mountains. For six years he practiced very, very hard. "What am I? *Don't know* . . ." He courageously kept this question with one-pointed determination. Then one morning, while sitting in meditation under the Bodhi tree, he saw the morning star in the eastern sky. At that moment—BOOM!—Siddhartha and this star completely became one. He realized his true substance. He realized that his mind was the universe—infinite in time and space—and the whole universe was nothing other than his own mind. He realized there is no life and no death. Nothing ever comes or goes. We say that he woke up and attained his true nature. He completely attained human consciousness: he saw that when ignorance appears, mind appears. When mind appears, desire appears. When *any* kind of desire appears, life and death, coming and going, happiness and sadness all appear. By completely keeping a don't-know mind one hundred percent—only go straight, *don't know*—the Buddha saw how to completely stop this endless cycle. He attained complete liberation from the eternal round of birth and death in which all beings trap themselves. He completely attained his correct way, he attained truth, and he attained the correct kind of life he should lead. The name for that is *enlightenment*.

But this truth that the Buddha attained was a very high-class realization. How could he make it function to help this suffering world? When he got enlightenment, the Buddha perceived all sentient beings being born, suffering, and dying; being born again, suffering, and dying; being born, again suffering, and again dying in an endless round of torment. He saw billions upon billions of beings caught in the beginningless cycle of birth, old age, sickness, and death, wandering around and around and around and around, nonstop, only following their desire, anger, and ignorance. The name for this is samsara. "I want this. I want that. I like this. I don't like that." When he attained enlightenment, the Buddha perceived every sentient being in a terrible state of suffering. It was a condition to which they had become so accustomed that it seemed normal. How would anyone ever believe what he had seen? "How can I teach this to other people?" he thought. It was like a man with a very high-class Ph.D. trying to teach little children what he'd learned: how would they ever understand? Sentient beings were so controlled by their desire minds, and so attached to their suffering way, he wondered if anyone would ever connect with this teaching. Sutras say that for several moments the Buddha doubted whether he should attempt to teach this. Perhaps people would have laughed at him, or worse, killed him for his heretical insight. The Buddha saw all this too. He could have stayed in this nirvana, his enlightenment, a state of infinite stillness and bliss, and never come out.

But the Buddha had profound compassion for sentient beings. He got up from his seat under the Bodhi tree, he left the stillness and bliss of nirvana, and he went into the contentious cities and towns to teach human beings. He left his "good situation." He did not attach to stillness and quiet. He did not attach to his bliss. He did not stay in nirvana, a state where there is no suffering or life or death. The Buddha returned to the noisy, fractious world to save all beings from suffering by showing them that it was possible to completely attain their own original nature, just as he had done. His enlightenment experience was not for him alone. That is a very important point. The characters for that are *dae ja, dae bi*: Great Love and Great Compassion. The Buddha attained enlightenment, which means that he attained his great function and the function of all beings. This was the beginning of Buddhism in this world.

So in general terms Buddhism means the teachings of the historic figure named Shakyamuni Buddha. But exactly what is Buddha? Buddha is really not special. The word *buddha* comes from a Sanskrit verb that means "to wake up." If you attain your mind, you attain your true self, and you wake up from your suffering dream. An eminent teacher once said, "Mind is Buddha; Buddha is mind." If you attain your mind—which means, if you attain your true self—then you become Buddha. So Buddhism's teaching simply means that Shakyamuni Buddha attained himself. He completely attained his own mind, which means he attained all beings' minds. And he attained the correct *function* of this mind, which is to help all other beings. That is a very important point.

So Buddhism is very simple: just ask yourself, very deeply, "What am I?" Only *don't know.* . . . The Buddha sat for six years only keeping a don't-know mind. The great Zen patriarch Bodhidharma sat in a cave in Shaolin for nine years, also keeping only don't know. So I ask you, who are you? When you were born, where did you come from? When you die, where do you go? If you attain these questions, then you attain your true self, and you become the very highest of animals. But if you don't understand, then it's the same as being a cat or a dog or any other kind of animal. Books cannot give you this attainment. Money cannot obtain this understanding. Even Buddha or some kind of god cannot give you this realization. This is why correct meditation practice is very important: How can I attain my true self, and completely attain truth and a correct life?

There are many paths that one can follow in order to attain this point. We have many religions and spiritual ways. But actually there are just two kinds of religion in this world: subject religions and object religions. Following an object religion means believing in some kind of god or some power or opposite being outside yourself. It means believing in some kind of power that controls this world and controls human beings. People think that if they believe in this god or power they will get something: they will get happiness or some good feeling. Maybe they will get special energy or magic powers or holiness. Perhaps they will go to heaven. Some practitioners of these traditions say they want to "become one" with this god, and may use some meditation practices to do this. But this is still making some object to become one with, so that is an object religion.

Buddhism is a subject religion. It seeks direct insight into the very nature of existence itself, beginning with insight into the nature of our being. "What am I?" "What is this 'I,' and where did it come from?" "When I was born, where did I come from? When I die, where will I go?" When you just ask yourself these questions, at *that* point all thinking is completely cut off. Inside and outside completely become one. Also subject and object completely become one, because without thinking there is no subject or object. When you ask that question—"What am I?" "Only don't *know* . . ."—then you, the universe, and everything—BOOM!—completely become one. So Buddhist teaching always points directly to the nature of your mind. "Human beings are like this, and this, and this. This is how suffering appears, and this is how you can take it away." It does not depend on books and learning. It does not rely on some god or outside power who will somehow answer these questions for us. The whole body of Buddhist teaching shows how, by asking this question—"What am I?"—you will attain don't know, which is your true nature, your true self. Buddhist teaching is always pointing you to a direct experience of your true nature so that you will actually attain the correct way, and truth, and a correct life. So you can see how the teaching of the Buddha is not really a religion at all; Buddhism is a path.

The purpose of Buddhism is, "First attain enlightenment, then instruct all creatures." These are like the two wheels of a cart. You cannot go anywhere without both of them together. If you completely disregard ordinary people, you cannot find your way. But if you don't make a strong effort to understand yourself, you cannot become a buddha. So this is why we say that enlightenment and helping all beings are like the two wheels of a cart. Riding them together, we reach the land of Buddha. Even if you study the eighty-four thousand sutras of the Buddhist Tripitaka, if you don't understand yourself, and cannot carry it out by helping other people in your everyday actions, all that understanding is utterly useless. At the moment your body dies, even a hundred Ph.D.'s will not help your true self find its way. An eminent teacher said, "One action is better than ten thousand thoughts." That is the same point: Great Love, Great Compassion, and the Great Bodhisattva Way mean attaining how our minds function correctly to save all beings from suffering.

To attain the purpose of Buddhism, first you must attain enlightenment: you must attain truth, and you must attain your innate *prajna*, or wisdom. You must attain your correct way in this world. Then you must save all beings from suffering. Saving all beings from suffering is our true job as human beings. Because when you attain your true self, you attain universal substance. This means that you actually attain that this whole universe and you are never separate; you and all beings are not separate because everything in the universe is actually the same substance. So you attain this whole world's situation: many, many beings are suffering very badly, all the time. And they are all not different from your own mind. This is a very interesting experience. The Buddha taught that in all of our numberless previous rebirths, every single being, no matter how small, must have been our father or mother at least once. By experiencing this view, what can you do? If you keep this don't-know mind always and everywhere, your true job appears very clearly right in front of you. Attaining my true self simply means that from moment to moment I keep a correct situation, correct relationship, and correct function in this world. I function clearly in this universe to save all beings. So getting enlightenment and teaching other beings are *not* two things, because when you return to your mind before thinking arises, at that point, everything completely becomes one. At that point, how could you *not* help all beings? Your correct situation, correct relationship, and correct function appear clearly in front of you. Helping other beings is enlightenment's correct *job*—it is really not all that special. That is the true purpose of Buddhism.

The Divisions of Buddhism

佛教 分類

Hinayana Buddhism

小乘 佛教

Mahayana Buddhism

大乘 佛教

Zen Buddhism

禪(宗)佛教

BUDDHIST TEACHING can be divided into three main teaching traditions: Hinayana Buddhism, Mahayana Buddhism, and Zen Buddhism. But Buddhism is actually not Buddhism. It is not some "thing." Buddhism simply means attaining a direct perception of reality, just as it is. A long time ago, someone asked Zen Master Joju, "Why did Bodhidharma come to China?" In other words, he was asking, "What is the meaning of Buddhism?" Joju replied, "The cypress tree in the front garden." And a monk once asked Zen Master Ma Jo, "What is Buddha?" He replied, "No mind, no Buddha." So originally, there was no Hinayana Buddhism, no Mahayana Buddhism, and no Zen Buddhism. Buddhism is just a name for the path of attaining our true selves and helping all other beings. But that is very difficult for many people. So the Buddha appeared in this world, got enlightenment, and taught us for forty-five years. First he taught Hinayana Buddhism. He taught the Four Noble Truths, that all life is impermanent, that therefore life is suffering, and how to get out of this suffering. He taught dependent origination and the practice of the various insights.

As his students' minds developed, he started to teach what came to be called Mahayana Buddhism. This is the path of emptiness. It is sometimes called the Great Bodhisattva Way. I vow not to enter the infinite stillness and bliss of nirvana until the last sentient being is released from suffering. And finally, when his students were completely ripe, he taught Zen. Twenty-five hundred monks assembled at the Vulture's Peak to hear the Buddha give a dharma speech. But he did not open his mouth, and only sat there, not moving. Several minutes passed. His students gazed intently at the Buddha, wondering if something was wrong. "Maybe our teacher is sick today . . ." "When will the teaching begin?" Finally, he picked up a single flower and held it aloft. But nobody understood. Everybody looked around, still waiting for him to talk about Dharma, still wondering when he would start teaching. Only one student, Mahakashyapa, smiled broadly from the far back of the assembly—"Ahhhhh!" Then the Buddha said, "I transmit my true Dharma to you," and gave Mahakashyapa transmission, making him the Buddha's first successor in a lineage that continues to this day. It was a transmission without words and speech, a transmission directly from mind to mind. So the teaching style of Hinayana Buddhism, Mahayana Buddhism, and Zen are completely different. Their techniques are different. But the direction and purpose are the same: How can we wake up and help this world?

Hinayana Buddhism teaches that when thinking appears, "I" appears. When "I" appears, then the whole world is divided into pairs of opposites. René Descartes said, "I think, therefore I am." That is the same point. If you have "I am," you also have "I am not." Existence and nonexistence, life and death, good and bad all come from this opposites thinking. This thinking also makes suffering. So Hinayana Buddhism teaches that when mind appears, Dharma appears. When Dharma appears, name and form appear. When name and form appear, then like and dislike, good and bad, coming and going, life and death, happiness and sadness all appear. The Hinayana view calls this realm which we all inhabit a "suffering world." All life is suffering, and suffering is life: samsara. Hinayana Buddhist teaching explains that we are living in this impermanent world, this suffering world, and it shows how we can get out of it. This suffering world is created entirely by our own thinking. Through this teaching we are shown how to go from this opposites world of life and death to attain the realm of the Absolute, or nirvana. In nirvana there is no life and no death; no coming or going; no up or down. It is a state of complete stillness and bliss. Attaining the completely void state of nirvana is the ultimate goal of Hinayana Buddhist teaching.

Mahayana Buddhist teaching begins at this point of emptiness and nonself, where Hinayana teaching leaves off. It shows how we can begin with the experience of emptiness to attain "complete world." This means that if your mind is complete, then everything is always complete, complete, complete. The sun, the moon, the stars—everything is complete. Suffering is complete. Happiness is also complete. What is not complete? A famous poem says, "One by one, each thing is complete. One by one, each thing has it." If you keep this mind [hits the table], that point has no inside or outside. It has no subject or object. [Hits.] You are the universe; the universe is you. We sometimes call that the Absolute. [Hits.] The Absolute means "complete."

This "complete world" means truth. When your mind has cut off all thinking, there is no thinking. No thinking means there is no "I." When there is no "I," then your mind is clear like space, which means your mind is clear like a mirror. It only reflects all things that appear in front of it exactly as they are: the sky is blue, the tree is green, a dog is barking, "Woof! Woof!" Sugar is sweet. When you see, when you hear, when you smell, when you taste, when you touch—everything, just like this, is truth. That is, we say, "complete world."

So attaining that this world is complete means completely attaining truth. However, the Buddha showed that we cannot stop here. True, everything is complete, just as it is; everything is truth. The sky is blue: that is truth. Sugar is sweet: that is truth. The wind is blowing through the trees outside right now: that is also truth. But we must take one more step: if you attain truth, then how do you make truth *function* correctly to make your life correct? Another way of saying it is, how do you help other sentient beings? Mahayana Buddhism means perceiving that all things are empty, and then from this fundamental experience of emptiness, attaining how this truth can help all beings, life after life. We sometimes call that Great Love and Great Compassion, or the Great Bodhisattva Way. From moment to moment my life is only for all beings.

Then what is Zen Buddhism? Zen never talks about absolutes, or the opposites world. It doesn't try to explain emptiness, truth, or complete world. The practice of Zen never explains *anything*. Zen simply points directly at our mind, our true self, so that we can directly attain enlightenment and help all beings. So there is no emphasis placed on language or learning in Zen—there is simply the practice of meditation. Zen teaching never checks the opposites world, it never checks the Absolute, and it never talks about complete world. All Zen teaching simply points to your mind, just this moment. What are you *doing* now? Zen teaching always returns us to what we can call "moment world." This moment is very important. In one moment, there is everything. In moment, there is infinite time and infinite space. [*Hits the table loudly with his stick.*] In moment there is the true way, and truth, and correct life. [*Hits the table loudly.*] In moment! In this one moment, there is everything [*hits*], and in moment there is nothing [*hits again*]. So if you attain moment, you directly attain everything. That is Zen Buddhism. There is no mind [*hits*], no Buddha [*hits*], no God [*hits*], nothing! [*Hits.*] But there *is* mind [*hits*], *is* Buddha [*hits*], *is* God [*hits*], *is* everything! Experiencing that is Zen Buddhism.

So each of the three main Buddhist traditions just uses different techniques to approach the same experience. Let's say you don't understand a watermelon. You never ate watermelon before. If you asked a Hinayana Buddhist to teach you what a watermelon is, you would be told that a watermelon starts from a seed, this little black seed that is planted in the ground. And then it sprouts, and becomes a little plant. Soon a vine appears. This vine grows and grows and grows. Some little flowers appear on the vine, and then from the flowers a fruit starts to grow. And it gets bigger and bigger and bigger, until it turns into this large, roundish fruit. Then perhaps someone eats it, or it rots and the seeds go back into the ground. And the whole cycle starts over again: seed, sprout, vine, bud, blossom, fruit; seed, sprout, vine, bud, blossom, fruit; seed, sprout, vine, bud, blossom, fruit. It is constantly going around and around and around. Another name for this is the Twelve Links of Dependent Origination. A watermelon seed, and then the fruit, and the seed, and the fruit—around and around and around, nonstop. This kind of teaching is primarily concerned with a consideration of time, or with something changing over time.

Mahayana Buddhism, though, is not about time. We can say that Mahayana Buddhism is primarily concerned with space, or "form." So if you're asking a Mahayana Buddhist about a watermelon, then maybe they would say, "Well, a watermelon has this green skin, with bands of dark and light green color wrapping around it. It can be fairly heavy. If you're in the West, a watermelon looks like a long, stretched-out football; if you're in Korea, it's shaped like a soccer ball. Watermelons are hard on the outside and soft on the inside. The watermelon is red on the inside, if it's ripe, and it also has these little black seeds. The red part of the watermelon is sweet, but the white part isn't so sweet, and the green part is somewhat sour-tasting." A Mahayana view is concerned with what the form is, what the truth of the watermelon is. A Mahayana Buddhist may also explain how all these characteristics—the color, weight, taste, and form—are all ultimately empty. Zen has a very simple and direct teaching style. Zen means that if you want to understand what a watermelon is, you take a watermelon, get a knife, and cut the watermelon. Then you put a slice into your mouth—*boom! Your* experience! Words and speech and books and learning cannot deliver this point. Even if you read one hundred books about watermelons, and hear one hundred lectures, they cannot teach as well as one single bite. "What is a watermelon?" *Boom!*—"Ahhh! *That's* a watermelon!" Then you *attain* watermelon, and this attainment is forever. This is why Zen teaching is described as "Not dependent on words and speech, a special transmission outside the Sutras, pointing directly to mind; see your true nature, become Buddha." Understanding a watermelon doesn't need words and speech—even a child understands this! This is the manner of Zen teaching.

The Structure of Buddhism

佛 教 構 成

The Precious One
which is the Buddha → the object of faith → emotional

〇佛 寶　　　信仰的　　　情的

Departing from pain
and attaining pleasure → samadhi → beauty → faith

離苦得樂　　　定　美　信

The Precious One
which is the Dharma → philosophical → intellectual

〇法 寶　　　哲学的　　　知的

Going from ignorance
to enlightenment → *prajna* → truth → understanding →

轉迷開悟　　　慧　真　解

The Precious One
which is the Sangha → ethical → mental

〇僧 寶　　　倫理的　　　意的

Putting an end to
evil and practicing good → *sila* → good → practice

止惡修善　　　戒　善　行

聖

holiness
moksha
liberation

解脱

GENERALLY SPEAKING, human consciousness is composed of three parts: emotions, intellect, and will. Every kind of pain or pleasure comes from our emotional nature; understanding comes from our intellectual nature; and action comes from our will. But how do we make these three function harmoniously to help this world? That is a very important point. So Buddhism also has three medicines for human consciousness. These medicines help human beings take away their thinking sicknesses which make suffering so that we can return to our original nature. The name for these medicines are Buddha, Dharma, and Sangha. We also call them the Three Treasures.

Time, space, and cause and effect, make this world. They are the strongest forces in the life of nearly every human being. Yet none of these things actually exists: they are all created entirely by thinking, as we shall see later. So how, then, can they exert such a powerful influence over us? Human beings' minds are composed of emotions, intellect, and will. These are called the three clouds, because if you cannot control your emotions, intellect, and will, or they do not function harmoniously, they cloud over your true self. The imbalance of emotions, intellect, and will deludes us into believing that time and space exist; you are controlled by cause and effect. Then you lose your way in this world. This causes more suffering for yourself and for others. Because of these three clouds, Buddhism has the Three Treasures of Buddha, Dharma, and Sangha.

The Treasure of Buddha

Then what is Buddha? *Buddha* is derived from a Sanskrit root verb which means "wake up." This is another way of saying "attain your true self." When you attain your true self, you become Buddha. But Buddha is not something special, and it is not something outside·you. Buddha means that if you attain your true self, you attain your own mind. An eminent teacher once said, "Mind is Buddha; Buddha is mind." So how can you attain your true self? The function of the first of the Three Treasures is to connect our emotional experience with spiritual practice and the search for enlightenment.

At first, when you begin practicing, you only believe in Shakyamuni Buddha and in his teaching. "I love Buddha. I want to become like Buddha." This is your *emotions* connecting to Buddhism through the Treasure of Buddha. As you continue practicing, your thinking settles down and becomes less complicated. This lets you see that you can actually balance your thinking and emotions as your mind becomes clearer. When you balance your thinking and emotions in this way, you can take away suffering and get happiness. As a result, your mind is not moving as outside conditions constantly change. You can see clearly, hear clearly, smell clearly, taste clearly, sense touch clearly—everything is *beauty*, just as it is. Then you can believe that the sky is blue, the tree is green, a dog is barking, "Woof! Woof!" You can believe in everything. One day, as Zen Master Un Mun was coming out of the outhouse, a monk asked him, "What is Buddha?" In that instant, the Zen master was looking at a long wooden stick, which was used to clean out the outhouse, hanging up to dry in the sun. So when the monk asked him, Un Mun replied, "Dry shit on a stick." That is all. Perceiving that truth is the same point. This is moment-to-moment life. We call this the Treasure of Buddha.

In the Treasure of Buddha, *beauty* means that when your mind is not moving, everything is beautiful, because everything is truth. But this kind of beauty does not come from the outside appearance or attractiveness of things. I was teaching in Paris several years ago when somebody at the Zen Center invited me to see an exhibition of paintings in a very high-class museum. There were many interesting works of art. But one important picture was hanging alone on a large wall. From across the big room, you could not tell what this painting was all about. As I walked up to it, this picture soon became clear—it was two old, worn-out socks, with holes in them, hanging in a big gilded frame! The socks were all dirty. But that was considered to be the best picture in the whole exhibition. Everybody in the museum was saying, "Waahhh, that's number one, you know?" Someone told us that the museum paid a great deal of money to acquire that picture.

But who would possibly want these dirty, worn-out socks hanging in an expensive frame in a high-class museum? What do these socks mean? What is their inside-meaning?

The inside-meaning of this picture is that some human being did a lot of walking in these socks. The person put a lot of energy and effort into them. With time passing, these socks became worn and full of holes—they showed a lot of suffering. So this picture of old socks is making a very important point: this picture teaches us something about a human being's life. The socks are just as they are. They are pieces of the ordinary, everyday life that most people ignore. So although the socks are very dirty, the meaning they convey is very beautiful. "What is Buddha?" "Dry shit on a stick!" Zen Master Un Mun taught the same point that these socks convey. But since it is not their appearance itself that is considered to be beautiful, where does this beauty come from?

True beauty comes from our not-moving mind. In Sanskrit, it is called *samadhi*. That means deep meditation, unmoving. Samadhi is simply our pure, original nature. If your mind is not moving, everything is beautiful, just as it is. If your mind is moving, however, then even if a beautiful picture, beautiful landscape, or other beautiful things appear in front of you, this view quickly changes in your mind, and it does not seem so beautiful. Everyone has experienced this at least once. For example, when you are very angry, or sad, or depressed, then even the melodious chirping of birds right outside your window sounds noisy and irritating. Because you attach to feelings or outside conditions, when these feelings or outside conditions change, then your mind is constantly changing, changing, changing. You lose your center. With this kind of mind, even a beautiful landscape may seem sad and ugly. Delicious food doesn't interest you. "I don't like that!" So the most important thing is to keep a not-moving mind, from moment to moment. Actually that is the true meaning of samadhi. It means having a mind that is not moving, whether sitting, standing, lying down, driving a car, talking, anything. When you keep a strong not-moving mind in any activity, you can perceive the true beauty of this ordinary world because you can see things exactly as they are. You can digest your understanding so that it becomes wisdom.

A not-moving mind gives rise to *faith*. When your mind is not moving, you can spontaneously believe in this world's beauty. You can believe that this whole world is already truth. The name for that is faith. So, unlike other religions, believing in Buddha as an *object of faith* actually means believing in your true self. Faith means simply believing in your true self, your original nature: you are already Buddha! Then you can believe your eyes, your ears, your nose, your tongue, your body, and your mind. You believe the trees, the sky, Buddha, God—everything! Someone once asked me, "Soen Sa Nim, do you believe in God?"

I said, "Of course!"

The person was very shocked. "You are a Zen teacher. How can you possibly believe in God?"

"I believe my eyes, ears, nose, tongue, body, and mind—why not believe everything? I believe this green tree, the blue sky, a barking dog, the smell of incense—why not believe in Buddha or God?"

So, you can believe *in* everything. Believing in everything means realizing that you and everything are never separate. [*Hits the table.*] *That* point. You and the universe are not two things, and never separate. Let's say a husband and wife both believe in their true self. Then even though the husband's and wife's bodies are separate, this mind always becomes one so actually they are never separate. If you believe in your true self, then you can believe in everything: you and everything already become one. The name for that is faith. Many religions teach that God and I are separate things. I am here and God is over there. In this kind of situation faith means having to believe in something apart from you that you cannot see. This is how most people live with faith. We call that an object religion because it makes some object and believes that that object exists through faith. This is not a complete teaching.

But as we said before, Buddhism is a subject religion: it has no subject and has no object. Actually it is not even a religion. So an eminent teacher said, "Mind is Buddha; Buddha is Mind." That is all. Having faith in Buddha is just a way of showing you how to believe in your own, true original nature. You are Buddha, Buddha is you! When you see, when you hear, when you smell, when you taste, when you touch—everything is truth, everything is beauty, everything is Buddha, just as it is. With a not-moving mind, even shit is beautiful! Why not? When this experience becomes clear for you, your true way appears clearly right in front of you. So the Treasure of Buddha means from moment to moment keeping a not-moving mind in any condition and any situation.

The Treasure of Dharma

Buddha taught that all suffering comes from our minds, from thinking. We human beings have too much understanding. If we have too much understanding, we have too many problems. If we have only a little understanding, then we have only a few problems. But if we completely keep don't-know mind, then everything is no problem. Strongly keeping only don't know means returning to primary point, to our mind *before* thinking arises. Thinking makes understanding, and all of your understanding is merely somebody else's idea. If you don't completely digest this idea, then for your whole life you are only following someone else's way. For example: Somebody says, "The sky is blue." Another person says, "The tree is green." But this sky never said, "I am blue." The tree never said, "I am green." Human beings say, "The sky is blue. The tree is green." Once, a very long time ago, somebody told you, "The sky is blue." And ever since, you have carried this idea around with you. A dog never says, "The sky is blue." Cats never say, "The tree is green." A dog also never says, "I am a dog." Cats never believe they are cats. Human beings make everything, and then they fight over it. Their view is a mistaken view. They make color, size, shape, time, space, names and forms. Human beings make cause and effect, life and death, coming and going. Originally these things do not exist. All this comes from thinking; our thinking *makes* everything. It is only somebody else's idea. Americans have an American idea: they say "dog." But Koreans have a Korean idea: they don't call it a dog, but say it's a *gye*. Which one is correct? To be absolutely sure, go ask a dog, "Are you a dog?" He will have an interesting answer. So if we want to digest all our understanding to make wisdom, we must first return to our minds *before* thinking arises. That point has no name and no form. Some people call it mind, or nature, or substance, or God, or self, or Buddha, or soul, or spirit, or consciousness. But originally that point has no name and no form because it is already *before* thinking, so opening your mouth to call it anything is already a big mistake.

Human beings' intellectual side is very important for their lives. Descartes said, "I think, therefore I am." That is a human being. Originally, thinking is not good and not bad. But everybody becomes attached to their thinking, so they have a problem. Everybody believes that their own thinking is correct and that other peoples' thinking is not correct. This is the major cause of suffering in this world. How do we make our thinking and our mind *function* correctly to help others? That is a very important point.

We must learn how to use our thinking correctly if we want to understand this world. So our intellect is very, very important when we're practicing, if we can use it clearly. Everybody has some lingering attachment, something they want. "I want this," "I want that." "Maybe if I smoke this cigarette I will feel better." "Just one more drink, then I'll quit." Sometimes we are not aware of them, even after a few years of practice, but we usually have some strong mental habits that continually obscure our way. And often they do not appear for a long time. When we're practicing, and suddenly this lingering attachment appears, if our intellect is not functioning correctly, we can just follow this desire-mind, which becomes apparent to us as some kind of seemingly harmless feeling or impulse. But if our intellect is working correctly, and our cognition is clear, then we can perceive the cause and effect that will result from blindly following this feeling. "Ah, that's just my feeling. That feeling is empty, you know? If I follow that feeling, it will only lead to suffering. It will not help my mind, not help my practice, not help my life." We can really still perceive what this world is, in truth, even though we have some strong desire or some feeling. The feeling does not control us, because our clear cognition perceives the cause and effect that will come from following it. So this intellect is very important. Some people call it "correct view."

The Buddha taught that ignorance causes suffering. But what is ignorance? Ignorance simply means not perceiving that this world is impermanent. However, if you only understand this conceptually, that is merely an intellectual view, and it cannot help your life. If you haven't attained your true self, you don't truly understand what is life and death. So it is very important that you take away ignorance in order to get enlightenment. How do you do this? First you must digest your understanding. When you truly digest your understanding, then "the sky is blue" becomes yours. "The tree is green" becomes yours. Over time, your understanding is becoming true wisdom. Your ignorance is changing as your mind opens. When you completely digest your understanding, we say you get enlightenment. Wisdom appears by natural process as you continue practicing, digesting your understanding. This is how Buddhist teaching connects with our intellectual side. That is the function of Dharma—the Treasure of Dharma.

The Treasure of Sangha

Sangha is the ethical side of practice, which means cultivating a correct life. Some people call it morality. Correct life comes from our will, our center. This means we try to take away bad habits and follow a good way that only helps all beings. If your center is not moving, then it is possible to live clearly and correctly for the welfare of others. We sometimes call that correct direction. That is the Buddha's basic teaching—from moment to moment keeping a correct direction in your life that only helps other beings. "Why do I do this?" "Why do I want to do that? Is this action only for me, or for all beings?" Sangha helps keep us pointed in the direction of attaining enlightenment and helping other beings.

To keep a correct direction, we need some basic guidelines for our life. These guidelines, or precepts, always keep us pointed in the direction of saving all beings from suffering. In Sanskrit, this kind of practicing is called *sila*. Precepts mean living a correct way, or Dharma, because the actual meaning of *Dharma* is "true way." So, a correct way is a correct life that from moment to moment helps all beings. It is very simple! When people formally commit to Buddhist practice, they "take refuge" in the Three Treasures of Buddha, Dharma, and Sangha. There is a ceremony where they take the Five Precepts that were established by the Buddha himself. These precepts urge us to refrain from taking any life, lying, stealing, engaging in sexual misconduct, or consuming intoxicants. These Five Precepts are common to all Buddhist traditions. They simply guide us toward keeping a clear mind and living a correct life. Very few can live a correct life on their own, so we must have these precepts to guide us. When the Buddha was about to die, his students gathered around him. Quite naturally, the monks were concerned about who would lead them after his passing into nirvana. One monk asked him, "Who will teach us when you are gone?" The Buddha replied, "Let the precepts be your guide."

Precepts are not special. They are simply natural rules that help our practice; that is why we call them Dharma. For example, in springtime, there are many flowers on the trees, so in the autumn we can harvest many fruits. If the blossoms do not appear on the trees in spring, we cannot get any fruits. That is a rule of nature. Spring comes, then summer, then fall, and winter. The four seasons always revolve around and around and around. That is this world's Dharma. In the winter there is lots of snow. That is also Dharma. If it snows one summer, we will have a big problem! Maybe there is snow in South America when it is summer in the United States. But in North America if snow appears during summertime, that is not correct. So this rule or law of nature simply ensures that the natural world always functions correctly. One springtime there are no flowers: everybody knows that is not correct! In autumn there is no fruit for harvest: that is not correct! For the whole winter there is not one flake of snow, but only blazing sunshine: that is also not correct! "Strange weather—this winter there hasn't been any snow!" Ha ha ha ha! That is a rule. Winter, snow; spring, flowers; summer, hot sun; fall, fruits appear. Nature has its own precepts, and these natural precepts are always the same. Nobody questions these rules.

However, human beings cannot keep rules. One precept says that if we want our meditation practice to bear fruit, we shouldn't take any intoxicants. Many people say, "Why not? I like that drink. I like cigarettes. I am free!" Then somebody may even tell them, "But doing that is bad—that cannot help your body, it cannot help your mind, it cannot help anything!" "I don't care! I don't care about my body! I am free!" Ha ha ha ha! Then they wonder why their meditation practice isn't strong. They wonder why their health is bad and their mind is not clear. So this kind of "freedom" creates a problem: people don't keep certain natural rules, so they make a lot of suffering for themselves and for others, because they cannot keep a clear mind. The trees don't make suffering. Water doesn't make suffering. Everything in this world is not causing itself suffering. Even a dog or cat doesn't make so much suffering and checking. All animals only follow their situation, which means they follow their natural precepts. If they don't keep these precepts, they cannot survive. If they cannot get food, they cannot eat. If they do not hibernate, they don't survive the winter. If they don't act according to their nature, they die. So they only follow their situation.

But human beings are very interesting. Human beings are the smartest animals, yet they make the most suffering for themselves and this world. This is simply because most human beings cannot follow their situation. We are attached to some idea about freedom, so we cannot follow even those rules that are intended to help us. We have a *broken* situation. Human beings only think about "my" feeling, "my" condition, and "my" situation. This feeling is often not in harmony with the way the universe runs, so it is a broken situation. Having a broken situation comes from not keeping their natural rules, or precepts. Human beings only want a good feeling, a good time, a good situation. This is only desire. But these come from where? You must decide something, and only *do* it, from moment to moment. If you can practice in this way, using the precepts as your guide, your mind-energy becomes clearer and stronger. As your mind gets stronger, then a good situation doesn't move you, and also a bad situation doesn't throw you off. You can digest your experience and make it correct, from moment to moment. But if you cannot digest your experience, then when a bad situation appears, "Ah haa!"—you get suffering and cannot function clearly for others. When a good situation appears, "Ahhhhh," you feel some happiness, perhaps lose your direction and stop practicing so much, and then get suffering when this good situation changes. So your mind is always moving as outside conditions change.

The most important thing is to keep your correct direction for all beings, regardless of whether you have a good situation or a bad situation. Don't attach to a good situation; don't attach to a bad situation. But always perceive how to make a bad situation or a good situation correct, so that you can *use* whatever situation you are in only to help other beings. Then a *true* good situation appears: *true* good feeling, *true* good condition, and *true* happiness. That is already Great Love and Great Compassion, the Great Bodhisattva Way.

It cannot be emphasized enough that the Buddhist precepts are not meant

for ourselves, to make our own lives peaceful. In Mahayana and Zen especially, precepts are used solely so that we can help other beings. There is a
very famous story of a monk who became the National Teacher to the emperor of China because of the great compassion he showed in keeping the
precepts. A long time ago in China, there was a monk named Hae Chung.
He was a very poor and simple monk who renounced even temple life to
follow a wandering existence in the mountains. Hae Chung always helped
other people. He was known for his kind and compassionate spirit and his
extraordinary love for even the smallest beings.

One day, Hae Chung was on his usual begging rounds. It was late autumn,
and because he lived far in the mountains, Hae Chung had been collecting
many provisions to endure the winter in his simple cave. Once the winter
snows came, he would be unable to leave the steep crevice for food or extra
clothes, so he worked hard to obtain his necessities as soon as possible. His
feet were by now swollen from all the distances he had traveled. Begging
bowl in hand, and loaded up with food, medicine, provisions, and a new
winter blanket, Hae Chung finally made his way back into the mountains
and began the long ascent through the wide, windy valleys.

When he was about halfway to his cave, Hae Chung was set upon by a
fearsome gang of thieves. The five brutish men surrounded him, brandishing
clubs and knives. "Look what we've got here," they said. "Hey, old monk!
What are you carrying?"

"Oh, just some things for the winter . . ."

"You're a beggar," they said. "Well, we're beggars too. So why don't you
just hand over all that stuff right now? Ha ha ha ha!" They all laughed very
hard while tightening the circle around Hae Chung. Several of them grabbed
him by the shoulders.

But Hae Chung was not afraid. His eyes were only filled with sadness for
these men, trapped by their karma. "No problem," Hae Chung said. "Take
it all." The thieves grabbed the money he'd begged. They took his only food
for the winter. They even took his medicine and the only blanket he had.
And they didn't stop there. Seeing that he would put up no resistance, the
thieves proceeded to take all of Hae Chung's clothes. In a few minutes, he
was completely naked. They were afraid that perhaps he would run down to
the village after they left to report them to the police before they could get
very far. So they had to prevent him from doing this. Seeing as he was a
monk, the robbers could not kill him . . . The robbers realized that Hae
Chung was a very peaceful monk, so they forced him to lie on the cold

ground, face up. Then they tied his wrists and ankles to the earth with the tops of the long grasses that grew wild in the mountains.

"Ha ha ha ha!! This stupid old monk couldn't hurt a thing," they said. "Even to save his own life! What a fool! Ha ha ha ha ha!" They stood around him, laughing all the while, and then headed off back down the mountain, carrying every one of Hae Chung's things on their backs.

Now these grasses were not strong, and Hae Chung could easily have uprooted them and pulled himself free. But he strongly followed these precepts. "The Buddha taught we cannot kill any life," he thought to himself. "So I also will not kill these grasses." He only lay there, facing the sky. It was very, very cold!

The next day, he was awakened by the dull rumbling of horse-hooves coming up the valley. It sounded like there must be an army coming! "What is happening?" he thought. It was none other than the emperor himself, out hunting with a retinue of ministers and his top general. When the emperor saw this naked old monk lying face up in the grass, he was incensed. In the East, such displays of nudity were a grave offense even among common people. But to display one's private parts to the emperor himself was simply unthinkable.

The emperor flew into a mighty rage. "General!"

"Yes, sir!"

"Do you see what I see?"

"Yes, sir!"

"Kill him immediately! Do you understand?"

"Yes, sir!" The general galloped right up to Hae Chung, his mighty horse practically stamping the monk to death as he dismounted and unsheathed his great broadsword. "You have offended the emperor, and the penalty is death!" As the general raised his sword, he saw that Hae Chung was not scared. Instead his eyes were calm and clear and full of compassion.

"General, please wait! It's no problem if you kill me," Hae Chung said. "But first untie this grass. I might struggle as I die, and I don't want to tear out this innocent grass and kill it." The general stared down at him—he could not believe his ears. The old monk's eyes were filled with passionate concern. "Please, General," Hae Chung said. "Untie the grass." This general had killed hundreds of men in battle as if it were nothing, and it had never moved his mind. But Hae Chung's calm face and compassionate speech pierced his mind like an arrow. He was struck motionless and lowered the sword. He could not kill the old monk.

Instead, the general knelt down on one knee and asked the monk, "Why do you care so much for this worthless grass?"

"The Buddha taught that we should not kill any life," Hae Chung said. "So I will not kill even this grass. It is simply the Buddha's teaching."

When the emperor saw them talking, he grew livid! "General! That's not correct! Why are you talking? You kill him or I will kill you!" But the general was also not afraid. He slowly walked up to the emperor and recounted his conversation with the old monk. Upon hearing the monk's teaching, the emperor was struck with amazement. "Oh, he said that?" This speech hit the emperor's mind very strongly, because the emperor had spent the last several days hunting in the mountains with his court. He was carrying many dead animals back to the palace for mounting. "I have killed all these animals for sport, yet this poor monk would not kill even a blade of grass to save his own life!"

The emperor approached Hae Chung. He saw the old monk's face was calm and even joyful, despite all the commotion around him. He asked Hae Chung how all this had happened to him. When Hae Chung explained the robbery, the emperor was even more deeply moved, and thought to himself, "This monk stayed all night in the bitter cold just so that he wouldn't have to pull up this grass and kill it. What compassion . . ."

"I am worried, Your Highness," Hae Chung said. "Please untie the grass, or it will die."

"Oh, yes, yes . . ." Despite his high status, the emperor himself bent down and slowly undid the grasses. Not only that, he gave Hae Chung his coat and ordered a courtier to hand over his pants! "I am sorry, venerable Sunim," the emperor said. "Here I have been hunting for three days. I have killed many animals, for prize and for sport. And yet you would not kill so much as a single blade of grass to save your own life! Please teach me! Come with us back to the court." Hae Chung accompanied the emperor back to the palace and became the National Teacher for all of China.

So precepts are not merely rules to limit our actions. Most people, especially in the West, tend to think of them as limitations. Actually, precepts mean correct direction. If you follow these precepts, you attain goodness. Correct action appears by itself: you don't need to check inside or outside. From moment to moment it is possible to just do it, because these precepts have already pointed out the way to our correct job of helping all beings.

Then you can believe in your true self one hundred percent. One name for that is freedom; another name is holiness. This is also called "become Buddha." You can live with no hindrance: your mind is empty, so your actions are also empty. Only *do* it, with no hindrance. That is the Treasure of Sangha.

So as we see, Buddhism has a very clear teaching structure: Buddha, Dharma, and Sangha. The Chinese characters for this read *sam bo*, the Three Treasures. There are three dimensions to the Three Treasures: they are the *original* Three Treasures, the *form* of the Three Treasures, and the *true* Three Treasures. Let's look at these a little more closely. The *original* Three Treasures are the historical figure of Shakyamuni Buddha; the actual teachings of Dharma that he personally spoke some twenty-five hundred years ago in various parts of India, before any sutras appeared; and the original gatherings of monks and laypeople who heard and followed his teaching while he lived—the original Sangha. So these three are the *original* Buddha, the Buddha's *original* Dharma speeches, and the *original* Sangha of people who heard and followed his teaching. In Chinese characters, we call that *jin che sam bo*, "the original Three Treasures."

But now some twenty-five hundred years have passed since the original Three Treasures appeared in this world. Now we have *sun jun sam bo*, or "form of the Three Treasures." Since the original Buddha, original Dharma, and original Sangha have disappeared, what is the *form* of the Buddha, Dharma, and Sangha that we see today? Every temple has a Buddha statue. In Chinese and Korean temples, the Buddha statue is gold. In many Sri Lankan and Thai temples, there is a white Buddha. In Japanese temples, the Buddhas are not painted so elaborately. This gold or white or plain Buddha is the *form* of Buddha—it represents the original Buddha in some kind of material form. Today we have as many as eighty-four thousand sutras. These are the written records of the Buddha's teaching, his dharma speeches. There are also many books with teaching and events from the lives of the eminent teachers. This is all the *form* of the Dharma that he originally delivered. And originally, Sangha meant only those people alive at the time of the Buddha who heard his teachings and put them into practice, but today there are many, many Buddhist communities throughout the world. There are Cambodian sanghas, Vietnamese sanghas, Sri Lankan sanghas, Chinese sanghas, Korean sanghas, Japanese sanghas, Tibetan sanghas. Also nowadays many new Buddhist sanghas appear in the West: the American sangha, the Canadian sangha, the Polish sangha, the German sangha, the French sangha, the

Russian sangha, the Spanish sangha, the Lithuanian sangha. This is the Buddhist Sangha, the *form* that we see today of the original Sangha. Taken together, these are called *sun jun sam bo*, the *form* of the Three Treasures.

But the *original* Buddha, Dharma, and Sangha have all disappeared. And the *forms* of the original Buddha, Dharma, and Sangha that we see today are all very different, from place to place, from country to country, and from temple to temple. Then what is *true* Buddha? What is *true* Dharma? What is *true* Sangha? In Korean and Chinese characters, we call this *il che sam bo*, which means "become-one Three Treasures." Your pure mind *is* Buddha. When your mind light shines clearly from moment to moment, that *is* Dharma. And when your mind functions with no hindrance in any situation, that *is* Sangha. So, Buddha is your pure mind, Dharma is your clear mind, and Sangha is your no-hindrance mind spontaneously functioning from moment to moment for the sake of all sentient beings.

This is all very wonderful speech, these beautiful words. But what really is a pure mind? What is clear mind? What is a no-hindrance mind? A long time ago, somebody asked Zen Master Joju, "What is Buddha?" Joju replied, "Go drink tea!" Another time, someone asked Joju, "What is Dharma?" "Go drink tea!" "What is Sangha?" "Go drink tea!" In Chinese characters, we call this *shil yong sam bo*, which means the *actual* Three Treasures. If you drink tea with a clear mind, then in that moment, you become actual Buddha, actual Dharma, and actual Sangha. This is a very simple, everyday mind. Joju answered many kinds of questions with "Go drink tea!" If you don't understand this you must go drink some tea, right now. If you don't like tea, you can drink Coca-Cola or a milkshake. Ha ha ha ha ha! Either way, you will attain Zen Master Joju's true teaching. You will attain the highest teaching of the Buddha and all the eminent teachers. Then you will attain the *actual* Buddha, Dharma, and Sangha. It is very clear.

Finally, in our root text it says that the Treasure of Buddha means beauty, the Treasure of Dharma means truth, and the Treasure of Sangha means morality, or goodness. The Sino-Korean characters for this are *jin song mi*. But how are beauty, truth, and goodness connected to Buddha, Dharma, and Sangha? What kind of beauty are we talking about here? What is the relationship between beauty, truth, and goodness? Everyone has seen beauty contests on television. Many women come together and are judged to see who is the "best." The panel of judges gives points for each woman's beauty, or *mi*. But they look only at the woman's face and body. If her face and body are beautiful, and her actions are graceful and correct, then this woman wins the contest. But true beauty and real truth are not only how our body and face appear: true beauty and truth are found in our mind. What does our mind look like? What kind of thinking do we have? What kind of actions come out of our minds? Usually our minds are filled with many kinds of ignorant thoughts, many likes and dislikes, and this makes the mind seem ugly. But if you practice hard and gradually take away ignorance, you get enlightenment. Then wisdom appears: that is true beauty and truth.

Everybody already has goodness, or *song*, in their mind. It is already present, and needs no special cultivation. One way to see this easily is by going to a movie. Most movies are about some fight between a good man and a bad man. At some point in the movie the good person is getting beat pretty badly—perhaps he or she is about to die. It looks like the bad man is going to win after all. That's no good! So while the good guy is being beaten, every single person in the movie theater is thinking, "No good! That's no good! Get up! Get the bad man!" If the good character and the other innocent people in the movie suffer a lot because of the bad man, then everybody who is watching the movie feels upset. Everybody in the theater has the same mind, a mind that feels for the good guy and the suffering of innocent people. Nobody wants the good person to lose or die. Then when the movie ends, of course the good person nearly always wins, and so everybody goes home with a good feeling. Why is this always so?

The anxiety we all experience during these kinds of scenes is because of the goodness we already have in us, all the time. Every human being is the same. "Get up! Get up! Get the bad man! Hit the bad man!" This mind appears. The common reaction that everyone has is proof of human beings' innate goodness. We want good to prevail. We want to see justice. This goodness is not necessarily something special that results from years of arduous spiritual practice—it is our true nature, always shining and bright. Our true self is nothing other than this spontaneous goodness, this vastly compassionate nature that always wants to help all beings. We carry it around with us all the time. My self and all beings are not different and never separate. We all have the same substance: since I certainly don't like to suffer, I also don't want others to suffer. If you completely realize this point, you can see why goodness is realized in Sangha, because it is mainly through our actions with other beings that we realize this goodness that we already have inside us, all the time. Other people become a mirror of my actions. Some religions talk about "original sin." It is true that we are all born with certain predispositions to cause suffering. However, this is only karma, and karma can be controlled or even taken away. If we *attain* our karma, and perceive that it is fundamentally empty, then we can *use* our particular karma to help other people. Because of this view, Buddhism does not claim anything like "original sin." Buddhist teaching points to the innate goodness that is our innate true nature and the true nature of everyone. That is a very important point. So, true goodness means correct direction—the road to experiencing this is precepts.

Some people still may not understand what this "goodness" means. One of my students once asked me, "Zen Master, you always talk about truth and goodness. But nowadays in competitive modern society, if you have a good nature, many people will take advantage of you, and you will always get a lot of suffering." That is a very interesting question. So it is important to understand that this goodness that we have been considering has no "I, my, me." It has no separate sense of self and other. If you have true goodness, then even your suffering is correct, because in this world all beings are always suffering a great deal—not just human beings, but all beings, every kind of being. So since all beings are suffering, the true bodhisattva is always sad, because the true bodhisattvas feel all beings' suffering, all the time, as if it were their own. It *is* their own. When the bodhisattva is sad, however, this suffering is not for himself or herself. It is not "my" sadness and "my" problem. This sadness leads directly to compassionate action that helps others because when you are sad for other beings, this goodness that we all have inside just wants to help take away the suffering that others experience.

Everybody knows about Ksitigarbha Bodhisattva, or Ji Jang Bosal (Jap. Jizo). This is the bodhisattva of our infinite vow. He is always represented holding a tall staff with six rings. Ji Jang Bosal is the bodhisattva who vows to save all beings from suffering, even if that means having to enter the torment of some hellish realm to liberate them. In most spiritual traditions, people who end up in some hell state are damned and forgotten: in Buddhism, we vow to help *all* beings, even those in hell. That is our vow. So the Chinese characters for Ji Jang Bosal's name are *Dae won bon jon* Ji Jang Bosal. *Dae won* means Great Vow. This means that when all beings are saved from suffering, then I will become Buddha. I *vow* that. If even one being cannot become Buddha, and is still in a suffering realm, I will not enter nirvana. I vow to return to this world life after life after life until the last being is saved. It is our Great Vow to have this kind of direction. And the second half of his name is *bon jon*, which means original face. This Great Vow to save all beings from suffering *is* our original face—it is our original nature, or substance.

Having a Great Vow is not something we *do*; it is something we already *are*, because this Great Vow *is* our original nature. Our vow to help others is just a reflection of our original nature that is the same as all beings' original nature—it is not something special. That is just another name for this goodness that we talked about earlier. Everybody already has it inside of them, all the time.

So the Three Treasures of Buddha, Dharma, and Sangha lead to "holiness, *moksha*, liberation." If you look at what is behind them, the Three Treasures are not special things. Buddha is not special. Dharma is not special. Sangha is also not special. What is his or her job? What is the ultimate *function* of these Three Treasures? Why does every Buddhist, regardless of their tradition, take refuge in them? As we said above, when you attain true beauty, you become Buddha: everything you see, hear, smell, taste, touch, and *think* is beauty, just as it is. When you attain truth and your correct Way, you attain Dharma. And when you attain your correct life, and can act with no hindrance to help all beings get out of this suffering realm, you attain Sangha. So that is why we say that the Three Treasures lead to holiness.

But this holiness is not holiness. Your mind is originally pure and clear: that *is* true holiness. It is your original nature. Holiness is only a name for something that has no name. Originally everything is completely empty and has no names or forms. Attaining that everything is empty is better than some special idea of holiness. There is a poem written by the German Christian mystic Angelus Silesius that says,

> The God who is pure emptiness
> Is created as form:
> Becoming substance, light and darkness,
> The stillness and the storm.

So "the God who is pure emptiness" is holiness. This holiness is not something special, OK? *Holiness* is only a temporary name pointing to a completely pure and clear emptiness that is our nature and the nature of the whole universe. If you attain that emptiness, you are free. In original Buddhism, they called that *moksha*, or "complete liberation." The correct function of the Three Treasures of Buddha, Dharma, and Sangha is to lead you to a direct attainment of emptiness. Then you can help all beings. This is true liberation.

2

Hinayana Buddhism

小乘佛教

1. Insight into impermanence

無常観

2. Insight into impurity

不淨観

3. Insight into nonself

無我観

THE BUDDHA ATTAINED enlightenment under the Bodhi tree in India. Then he got up and started teaching other people. He taught the Four Noble Truths, the Eightfold Path, and the Twelve Links in the Chain of Dependent Origination. He taught that life is suffering, and suffering is life, and how to get out of this. One name given to the Buddha's original teaching is Hinayana Buddhism.

"Insight into impermanence" is the Buddha's most basic teaching. He taught this first because impermanence is the basis of every kind of suffering that we experience. Look at this world: everything is always changing, changing, changing, changing. This is the basic nature of the whole universe. You go to a big river, and cross the bridge. It is eight o'clock. When you come back an hour later and cross the bridge again, you are not crossing the same river. The water is completely different. It is not the same river! The water you saw at eight o'clock is all gone, and the water which you see at nine o'clock is not the same water. The water is constantly flowing, on and on and on. You say to your friend, "Oh, there's the Hudson River." Then when you come back an hour later, you still call that the Hudson River. That is actually not correct. The Hudson River at eight o'clock is not the same river anymore. Yah, the outside form is the same; but inside, the water has already gone to the ocean. So this river is always changing, from moment to moment.

When you wake up in the morning, your body is somewhat different from the body you had the night before. In many respects you now have a new body. Extremely subtle changes have occurred in your health and appearance as you slept. The outside form of your body may look the same, but inside, the food you ate the day before has been digested, and gone to your face and teeth and skin. Then the waste all comes down, as the food turns to urine and excrement. Right now, in the morning, your face is already older than yesterday, even though you may not notice any visible difference. And every seven years you have an entirely new body, because every single one of your cells has been replaced. But nobody understands that. Nobody realizes that their body is constantly changing, from hour to hour. Someone may say, "Ten years ago I went to Paris." That is crazy speech! Ten years ago, some other body went to Paris, but it is not the same as the body which makes that statement right now. The name for that is impermanence.

And this does not only happen to human beings. A long, long time ago, this earth came from the sun, and the moon came from this earth. So the moon revolves around the earth, and the earth and moon revolve around the sun. Someday, many, many kalpas in the future, the sun's energy will run out and the sun will gradually become colder and colder. When the sun's energy stops coming in, the earth will also become colder and colder. Then all the animals will die. All the plants will die. Human beings will die too. Everything that we think is permanent now will completely disappear into empty space over time.

So in this world, everything is always changing, changing, changing, changing, because everyone is deluded by the name and form of things. We believe that name and form are permanent, so we suffer. Therefore the reason for suffering lies in our minds, where habitual attachment to name and form cover the real nature of this world. If you can perceive the actual nature of the phenomenal world, and you see that everything is constantly changing, then your desire-mind and the suffering that it causes also disappear. You can instantly perceive that anything that you acquire will soon pass. Everything you desire and get eventually disappears, because everything is always changing, changing, changing, nonstop. With this perception, your desire-mind and the suffering that comes from it will not control you so much. You will understand that suffering comes simply from attachment to impermanent things. Some people think: "Ahh, my life is no problem. I have everything. Perhaps I will live to be one hundred." Yes, perhaps this kind of person has no great difficulties now. But even if you manage to live past one hundred years, then what? You must still die. Everybody eventually dies. Then how will you feel? What will you do?

But most people don't understand this point. They don't understand this world's impermanence, so they hold on to many desires and anger. "I like this." "I don't like that!" People live their whole lives like this with a great deal of desire for impermanent things, always checking their minds and other people and this world. They hold their petty opinions about what they like and dislike, holding this up as the truth. We call this *attachment*. But if you correctly perceive this world's impermanence, you don't become so attached to things, so you don't suffer as much when things eventually change. Everything disappears so soon, so why be attached to anything? Even if you get some kind of happiness, how long can you keep it? Two people get married. In the beginning, they think, "Oh, now I will be happy. I have finally found the one I've been waiting for. This is wonderful!" And it is a very beautiful experience. But how long does this happiness mind really last? How long? One year? Two years? Three years? These days if you can keep it for more than three years, that is considered very unusual! [*Laughter from the assembly*] Many people can be like this for maybe three years. Then they start to think, "I don't like you!" "Oh, I don't like you!" They get separated and suffering appears in their lives. That is because human beings cannot get anything and cannot keep anything, since everything in this universe is constantly changing. So you must first understand this world's impermanence, and then you can put it down. In some Hinayana and Tibetan traditions the monks do meditation in cemeteries to help them have a deep experience of this body's impermanence. Then they can put down any kind of desire arising from this temporary body. This is insight into impermanence.

Hinayana Buddhism also teaches meditation practice based on "insight into impurity." But what is impurity? Let us say a beautiful woman appears, perhaps a very famous model or actress. She has very beautiful makeup on, and her hair is styled very fashionably. She is wearing beautiful clothes and has very expensive perfume on. She has a big diamond necklace, maybe ten carats. Everybody sees her and thinks, "Oh, she is wonderful! So beautiful!" Maybe some man will kill another man in order to sleep with her every day. But inside she has shit. On the outside, she is truly very beautiful; but inside, she is carrying two or three pounds of shit around with her wherever she goes. Even though she may have beautiful clothes, and sweet perfume, and a shiny diamond necklace, and wonderful makeup to cover this shit, everybody understands that that shit-thing inside is not beautiful, you know? Everybody sees these beautiful things on the outside, and they forget for some time about this shit. They are deluded by the temporary appearance of her body and makeup and clothes and diamonds. They don't see that what they crave is deeply marked with impurity. This is humans' basic delusion: our desire and attachment leads us to crave and covet things that cannot help our lives.

So if we truly realize this situation for a moment, we would say, "That's not straight, you know? That is not correct. Something is not in harmony there." We recoil somewhat because deep inside we all understand what impurity really is. And this is not just some way to view other people—you experience this with yourself all the time. Let us say you don't shower for one or two days. Yah, everybody here takes a shower every day, so ordinarily there is no problem with this. But if you don't shower for a few days, and you come into this meditation room, other people will quickly get insight into your impurity! Ha ha ha ha! You won't smell good. Your color will not look so good, and your skin will look bad. Then everyone around you immediately gets a bad feeling—even if you are a Zen master, nobody likes to experience this kind of impurity. If we are not careful about how we clean this body, all the time, a very bad smell appears. We must always pay a great deal of attention to this body just to avoid offending ourselves and others with its basic impurities. That is very interesting. So human beings' bodies are always very dirty, and this is something we all react to. It is not good and not bad; it is only our condition in this human form. The name for that is impurity.

But originally, "impurity" is not impure. Our ideas about pure and impure come from thinking and are determined by our thinking. Human beings don't like shit. But there are many kinds of animals that actually like to eat shit. Maggots eat shit. Ants eat shit. Flies eat shit. Also, many dogs like to eat cat shit. Horses will stay away from grass that has their own waste on it, but many sheep will happily eat grass that is smeared with their own waste. There is a special kind of pork you can buy in certain parts of Asia that is made from pigs raised on human excrement. The pigs are fed human shit every day. Later they are butchered, and this pork is a delicacy in parts of Asia. It is very expensive pork. That is very interesting. Some people will pay a lot of money to buy this pork in restaurants. So these animals and insects have some kind of consciousness, and this consciousness likes shit. Their sense of impurity is not the same as our own.

If this is so, then what actually is impurity? There is only this thought: "I don't like shit." "Such-and-such is impure." That thought makes "pure" and "impure." That is only some human beings' idea. But other animals like shit. Which one is correct? The answer to this is, Don't make "purity" and "impurity."

So by this we can see that thinking is the true source of impurity. The Buddha taught that the impurity which leads to suffering is the impurity we make in our own minds. If you have many desires, your mind becomes dirty. We sometimes hear about some famous person who wants money, wants sex, wants power: when you see that, you naturally say to yourself, "That's very dirty!" If you have many attachments and passions, your original nature gets covered and tainted with the thinking that comes from having too much desire. The name for that is impurity, because originally your true nature is perfectly pure and clear. When you are too attached to something, or you have too much desire for something, then your thinking becomes "dirty." However, when you practice meditation you can perceive the things that taint your mind, and then it is possible to take them away.

"Insight into nonself" means that originally we have no self. When you are thinking, you make "I." But the Buddha showed that this "I" does not exist: you cannot find it anywhere. This "I" appears only through thinking. Descartes wrote, "I think, therefore I am." When you completely cut off all thinking, where is this "I"? So the practice of "insight into nonself" means watching the mind very, very closely. It means seeing how every thought that appears in our mind is conditioned or formed by other thoughts. What we believe is "I" is just the coming together of various habit energies. There is no concrete, unmoving "I" behind it all. Thoughts are always appearing and disappearing through the constant interplay of the five skandhas. What we think is our self is just a collection of thoughts, feelings, perceptions, impulses, and consciousnesses that are constantly revolving around and around and around.

So, if you attain the three basic insights of Hinayana Buddhism, you perceive that human beings have no meaning, no reason, and no choice. This idea frightens most people. But why did you come into this world? Did you actually decide to do that? Do you really feel you have had a choice about the way you are and the things you have been given? Why do you do what you do in this world? For what? What do you *want*? What do you really understand? If you truly saw the nature of this suffering world, you would immediately drop everything, leave your good situation, cut your hair, and become a monk. But everybody is afraid, so they accept this suffering situation.

Most human beings truly have no idea why they came into this world. And most people don't really know what they truly want. Perhaps what they want most is money or some kind of fame, a social approval. But this is just an idea that they come up with in order to survive under conditions which seem to threaten them from all sides. I have one friend who is a very educated man. He is always very, very busy. He earned a Ph.D. from a great American university and founded many temples in America. Because he founded all these temples, he got some pride, so then he had to make an even bigger plan. "I want to build a very big and beautiful temple. Then I can start a Buddhist college. Naturally, I will be the president of the Buddhist college."

Everybody around him was saying, "Waah, you are very wonderful! This is a wonderful man!" He was becoming famous, and he was always very busy with his great big plans.

He was always so busy that he often had a struggle finding time to meditate. I used to say to him, "Sunim, you will soon found a big Buddhist college. That is very wonderful! But only meditation will help you find your true self. You must try that!"

"I know. I know," he would answer. "Soon I will finish this and that stage of the work, and then I can do a long retreat." But he would never actually get around to doing that. Then a month ago he was taken to the hospital with a stroke—*piitchhuu!* Now he cannot move half of his body. Then what? What do you *want?* Is a Ph.D. really necessary? Is it really necessary to spend all this time founding this Buddhist university? Is making another grand, beautiful temple the thing that will help you get out of the ocean of birth and death? What is truly necessary in this short life? When your body dies, what can you carry with you? What can you bring? One old Chinese Zen poem says, "Coming empty-handed, going empty-handed—that is human." And a Christian poem says, "The shroud has no pockets." That is the same point. So you come into this world with empty hands, and you also leave it with empty hands, no matter how much you achieve. You cannot even keep this body. So some other way is necessary.

This is why human beings have no meaning, no reason, and no choice. Actually, this means they have Big Meaning, Big Reason, and a Big Choice to help this world. But to attain this, first you must correctly understand what is a human being, through meditation. If you correctly understand human beings, then you gain the last insight: insight into nonself. Everybody says "I am." But where is this "I"? How big is it? What shape? What kind of color? Where do you keep it? If you completely perceive your mind, you perceive that, in reality, there is no "I." Nothing. Attaining that point is the goal of Hinayana Buddhism. The name for that goal is nirvana: entering a state of complete extinction and bliss. When you realize that originally your mind is completely empty, you get happiness. At that point, there is no coming, and no going; no life, and no death; no happiness or sadness. That point of nonself is already *beyond* everything. When you attain that point, you attain Hinayana Buddhism.

This kind of teaching is very interesting. Let us look more closely into these three insights of Hinayana Buddhism.

Insight into Impermanence
(The Eight Sufferings)
無常觀

（人生八苦）

Birth . . . Old age . . . Sickness . . . Death → The Four Sufferings

生　　老　　病　　死　　　四　苦

Being separated from those you love

愛別離苦

Being in the presence of those you dislike → The Four Sufferings

怨憎會苦　　　　　　四　苦

Not getting what you desire

求不得苦

The imbalance of the five skandhas

五陰盛苦

The Eight Sufferings

八苦

THE BUDDHA'S FIRST TEACHING after he got enlightenment was that all life is suffering. Everything is impermanent, and never stays in the same form, because everything is always changing, changing, changing, changing, nonstop. Because everything is impermanent, human beings constantly experience the Eight Sufferings.

Birth, old age, sickness, death

Birth, old age, sickness, and death are the basis of all suffering. Birth means everyday life: every living being experiences this, and it is the beginning of all the other sufferings. When human beings are born, they cry, "Waaaaa!" Consider this for a moment: we enter this world crying. That is a very important point. In Korea, we say that a newborn baby's cry sounds like "Ku ahhhh!" *Ku* means save, and *ah* means me. So everybody's first words in this world are, "Please save me! Aaaa, please save me!" Ha ha ha ha! "Oh, help me, please!" "Ku ahhhhh!" Ha ha ha ha! [*Laughter from the assembly*] Our own experience shows that life already begins with some kind of suffering. And this is not just Buddhism's idea. How many babies come into this world smiling or laughing, singing, "Oh, ha, ha, ha! It's very nice to be here"? Never! Babies enter the world crying, in some kind of pain, cold and wet. The doctor slaps the baby and cuts the cord to the mother. There is blood all over the place. We also give a great deal of physical pain to our mother in being born. All of this is not very wonderful. But that is the human way.

And this is just the beginning. There is much care and worry involved in raising children. To make a living in this world, with its highly competitive environment, is a continuous source of strife and suffering for all parents. But most people believe that their children are an extension of themselves, so they don't see this pain for what it is. They grow used to suffering. They want to help their children to be successful. This is a natural and very wonderful motivation. But deep inside their minds, most people only get involved in bringing children into the world and raising them so that their genes will continue forever. They think, "As much as I devote to them, my children will defend me when I am old, or they will be my cane." The constant supply of food, clothing, housing, pocket money, and huge education and medical expenses are earned with a great deal of pain and constant struggle, but it is not thought of as pain, however much they suffer their days to earn it. Korean and Japanese parents in particular endure extraordinary hardships to raise their children and get them admitted to good schools.

Because of the endless expectations they attach to their children, parents willingly submit to a great deal of pain and suffering. They accept this torment as their life.

So as we can see, living itself has some pleasure, but living is mostly an experience of various kinds of pain. We must constantly struggle to have enough to eat, maintain a place to sleep, get clothing, and provide medical care for this body. It is easy to talk about doing this, but is it actually that easy? Many Asians come to the United States and work so hard to live here. They put in long hours, repay huge loans, try to accumulate many material things so that they can prove to others that their hard work and virtue have paid off. But for years they don't eat much, don't wear the clothes they work so hard to obtain, and don't sleep much. Their health starts to deteriorate. When they lie in the hospital, they think, "What is this after all? What is it all about?"

I have met many people like this. I had one friend, a very successful, wealthy, and famous Korean businessman. He had achieved everything, and dealt with many prominent political and business leaders. His children had all attended the best American universities. They were all married off to successful partners and lived comfortably. He had healthy grandchildren. He had also traveled a great deal and had many enviable experiences. One day, as we were sitting having tea, I said to him, "Mr. Lee, you have done this and this and this. You have experienced this and that. Your children are successful and happy. What have you attained through all of this?"

Without the slightest hesitation, he replied, "Nothing." This is very strange! But this is the usual pain of living, and it is the sorrow of life. However much you struggle and suffer for things, you cannot get anything. It is actually so common that it is considered normal. This is why the Buddha showed that life is suffering. These are the first fruits of birth.

Then everybody ages. But why is aging painful? When you get old, you lose your strength. When you lose your strength, people begin to look down on you. We sometimes see old people working together with young people. The old person makes a mistake and the young person laughs. Young people will often treat old people as if they were children. When old people see this, they get angry. "What? You think I can't do this just because I am old?" It is so sad to be old. When you get old, try as you may, you can't do things the way you used to do. It is very frustrating. You don't have energy. But also, when you get old, you don't look nice. Your eyes sag. Your nose gets sharp and thin. Lips become thin and dark. Your ears don't work as well as they used to. There are many wrinkles on your forehead where there weren't any before. Perhaps you need a walker or a cane. Old age doesn't really look so good. So even little children poke fun at this state. You thought your youth would last forever. But very soon you realize your hair is all gray and white. When your teeth are gone, even chewing becomes a strange experience, and when you laugh it is even funnier to others. So you feel so sad and you get frustrated. This is why the Buddha taught that aging is a kind of suffering.

Some people think they can stop the aging process, but that is not possible. About thirty years ago, when I was teaching in Tokyo, one of my students, Mrs. Kim, brought her daughter to see me. Her daughter kept complaining about the fact that she was about to turn forty years old. She would say, "Oh, my face is getting old. I am so sad. I don't like my face!" She would come to the temple, but couldn't chant. Everybody would be strongly chanting "*Kwan Seum Bosal, Kwan Seum Bosal, Kwan Seum Bosal,*" even women who were much older than she was. But this young woman wouldn't chant. She couldn't bow. She would just sit in the corner, looking at herself in the mirror. "My face is not so good." She was nearly forty years old, so a few lines were starting to appear. "Oh, I don't like this style. I don't have a good face." [*Laughter.*]

Then for about one month she never came to the temple. Nobody had any idea what happened to her. After about six months, the elder Mrs. Kim visited me again, this time with an even younger daughter. I said, "Who is that?"

"Oh, that's my daughter."

"Your daughter? I never met this one."

"Yes you did. This is my only daughter. You met her a few months ago." But I could not recognize her—she looked like she was perhaps twenty-five or twenty-eight years old.

So I said, "Who are you?"

"I am Mrs. Kim's daughter."

"How did you become so young?"

"Oh, I had an operation."

"Operation? What kind of operation?" At that time, I didn't know about these new kinds of special operations.

Then she said, "Oh, it's called plastic surgery. The doctor cut here, then he cut here, and pulled the skin back like this—*piitchhuu*—then folded it—*tchick*—like this, and tucked it under—*tchick*—like that, and pulled this piece over—*tchick*—like this, and sewed it across here—*tchick, tchick, tchick.*" So at great pain and expense she had an operation that made all her lines disappear. Ha ha ha ha ha! But even if your face completely disappears, you cannot take away your age. Still you must grow old. While this young woman might again feel happy for a few more months or years, eventually the wrinkles will appear again. Perhaps she will experience even greater fear and frustration at the "return" of her old age! Getting old is another kind of suffering. When we grow old, our body suffers many kinds of pains. But also our mind suffers, because no one wants to grow old, and nobody wants to die. Everyone is very afraid of this, so they get a lot of suffering when it comes time to die. Old age is just the sign that this thing you fear is starting to happen to you, too: soon you will die, just like everybody else.

When we hear of someone reaching the age of one hundred, we envy them. One of my students once showed me a documentary about a man who had reached the age of one hundred and twenty. Everyone was saying, "Oh, he is so lucky! He is beating death!" But when this old man appeared on television, it was very, very sad. It was like seeing an old monkey. His eyes were constantly teary and his nose ran uncontrollably the whole time. His bottom jaw flapped almost up to the tip of his nose and made a strange clacking noise. All children cannot keep themselves from laughing when they see something like this. Meanwhile, those who have experienced something of life's joys and sorrows recoil in fear when they see such a thing. Everybody knows that our physical condition does not improve after a point, and only deteriorates further and further. So this is why the Buddha left his wonderful home, cut his good situation, and became a monk: to completely understand why this has to happen to every single being.

Regardless of age, we also experience sickness, and none of us like that, either. We may be able to say for a while, "OK, I can accept it." But why is there so much physical pain in every part of the body, especially as we get older? The leg hurts, back hurts, and you can't really hold urine as well as you used to. You are more prone to constipation. Indigestion is frequent. You are short of breath doing the simplest things. Going out or taking a walk is one thing, but many old people even have pain just lying down! This is what we call the suffering of being sick. Of course, not only old people get sick. Sometimes young children become crippled, or babies are born with some drug addiction or an incurable illness. Very strong, healthy young men are hospitalized and have serious operations that take years to pay off. Sometimes people get a contagious virus. We constantly have trouble with the ears, nose, eyes, and lungs. There is so much sickness in our lives.

There are occasions when we visit a hospital. You can see many, many suffering people in the hospitals—it looks like everybody is a patient, even those who are just visiting, because of the sorrow they feel at their loved one's sickness. Nearly everyone's face has a stricken look that says, "Why did this happen to me?" Or just walk down the street in a major city like New York. Everywhere you look, there is a great deal of physical suffering. And eventually, some kind of sickness usually leads right to death. Nowadays there are many new diseases in the world that cannot be cured. There are so many medications and so many techniques to support this temporary life. But no matter how wide you open your eyes, you cannot see one person who has yet been able to stretch their life beyond a certain point.

The Buddha left his good situation to practice hard to understand the origin of all this suffering. Yet what was the fruit of the Buddha's effort: did he live forever? No, his body also died. But he understood this body's aging and death. He got enlightenment, which means he perceived that the mind that leads this body never gets old or dies. The Buddha attained this truth. In this way he attained that there is actually no birth and no death; there is also no sickness or old age. These things are an illusion created entirely by our thinking minds. Our true nature is never born and never dies. What is so wonderful about the Buddha's life is that he attained this view in the midst of a temporary and impermanent life. Birth, old age, sickness, and death—these four sufferings nobody can physically overcome. Even the strongest man in the world cannot do that, as long as he has this impermanent body. But the Buddha very clearly showed how we can use this impermanent physical situation to gain deep insight into our true nature, which has no birth, old age, sickness, or death.

If you correctly understand the nature of your body, and if you perceive how impermanent it really is, then getting old is OK, and even dying is no hindrance. This body is just a rental car. Someday, you will have to trade in your rental car. My rental car was made in Korea, while some other people's rental cars are made in America or China or France. Perhaps my Korean rental car is not so good, and someday I'll have to trade it in: maybe next life I'll get a German rental car! Ha ha ha ha ha! [Laughter from the assembly] So changing this rental car should not be a problem. The rental car is not important. The most important thing is, Who is the *driver* of your rental car? Do you understand your driver, your original nature? Most people are only attached to their car, and never bother to understand who this driver is. Aging, sickness, and death are big problems for all people because no one makes an effort to meet this driver. Everyone is only afraid of losing their car.

But if you attain your driver, then even when it comes time to trade in your body, you do not suffer. You understand that this rental car—this temporary combination of the four elements of earth, air, fire, and water—has birth, sickness, old age, and death; but your driver is never born, never gets sick, never gets old, and never dies. That is a very important point. So you must understand your driver. This is the best medicine; it is the only medicine.

Being separated from those you love

These Four Sufferings that we have just considered explain primarily our constant experience of physical pain. They have to do mainly with attachment to our bodies. There are also four kinds of mind pain. Actually our physical pains—however great—are slight when compared to the suffering and anguish we cause with this thinking mind. On the most subtle level, all thinking is desire, and desire is suffering. Our thinking minds make such a horrible suffering for ourselves and others. Many years ago, I had a student in New York who had emigrated from Korea. He had an adoring fiancée in Korea whom he had left behind for a few years so that he could come to America and study. As they parted in their little village, vowing to marry when his work was finished in the West, there were many, many tears. "I will study very hard and get a good degree," he told her. "Then I will become a professor, and we can buy a house. Soon I'll come back to get you." So both of them were very, very hopeful. They loved each other very much and wrote several times every week. Their hearts would pound heavily whenever they opened the mailbox and found a letter.

The years slowly passed with both hopefully anticipating their plan. The man worked very hard every day preparing for their new life together. He earned a bachelor's degree and a master's degree and a doctorate. He started to work as a professor, all the while doing odd jobs here and there to save money for the down payment on a small house. But then he met a very rich woman who was also a professor at the same university. They fell madly in love. The new relationship got so deep that he couldn't stay away from his new lover for more than a day. Another year or two passed. And yet he continued to write letters to his beloved in Korea even while living with his new lover! Meanwhile his sweetheart in Korea was working hard, waiting for him to tell her that everything was prepared for her to come.

One day, a friend told the young woman that the Korean government had just announced a new plan for people to easily obtain certain immigration clearance for work abroad. "Why do you just sit around and wait?" her friend asked. "Just go!"

"You're right! I'll do all the paperwork without letting him know, and one day I'll surprise him. I'll just jump right out in front of him in America and give him a big shock! Oh, he'll be so happy!" So she immediately started working on her plan. Luckily, everything went so well that she was selected for the first immigration group. Her heart pounded with excitement as she replayed over and over in her head the sweet surprise that she would spring on her dear beloved. "Oh, boy! He will be *so* surprised to see me!" she would tell her friends. She bought new clothes with what little money she had. She had her hair cut and bought beautiful new shoes for their first meeting. Her hopes grew and grew with every passing day.

When she arrived at his house in the United States, it was six AM. With the help of a kind taxi driver, she found the apartment. Of course the door was locked, and she was just too excited to wait until he would go out for work. So she called her fiancé's name. "Open the door! Open the door!" Not recognizing the voice, he finally woke up and let her in. But something was very wrong here, she realized. Instead of showing joy, her fiancé's face had a panicked, stricken look. He would not let her go into the bedroom. "What is going on here?" She pushed her way into the room. In his bed, under the blankets, there was a naked woman.

Understandably, she flew into a tremendous rage. She ran to the kitchen and grabbed a huge kitchen knife. She held off her beloved and was fuelled by such a towering rage that he feared she would cut them both to pieces. The man and his new lover knelt down in front of her, sobbing uncontrollably and begging for mercy. But her sorrow was unforgiving. She kept them there for quite some time, naked and in this shameful position. Because of her loud screaming, a neighbor notified the police, and she was restrained. But not before this man and his lover were put through such shame and humiliation that it profoundly marked their lives forever.

We call this kind of suffering "being separated from those you love." It is a mental desire caused by our desire and attachment. This suffering is very common. Every human being has experienced it in some form many, many times. For many people, this kind of suffering is so much a part of their lives that it is considered a normal part of living. This suffering also applies to objects as well as to other people. Once I had a student who had some very expensive jewelry, including a very big, twelve-carat diamond. One day, she had to go to the hospital for an important operation. So she put her diamond in a box in her bedroom before she left. But the whole time she was in the hospital, she only thought about her diamond. "How is my diamond? Is it safe? Is anybody trying to steal it?" Even though her own body was terribly sick, she thought only about the safety of her precious diamond. That's already a kind of suffering, in addition to her body's suffering.

When she returned, she found that her house had been broken into, and the diamond was indeed gone! "Somebody took my diamond!" She was so sad that she started to go a little crazy. "Where's my diamond? I want to find my diamond! Where's my diamonnnnddddd?!" [Loud laughter from the assembly] She could not eat anything for several days. The day after she got home from the hospital, she felt so miserable that she started drinking lots of alcohol, even though her body was still sick. That is not correct. Diamonds are not important, especially when compared to the immeasurable value of gaining this precious human rebirth. Are diamonds and other possessions worth losing your reason and becoming crazy over? But most people are like this. Because of thinking, desire, and attachment even to impermanent objects, most people make suffering in their lives and in other beings' lives. They will kill others or themselves to gain or protect things that ultimately pass away.

And it is not only in such extreme cases. We all know the routine suffering that people get when they fall in love with someone else but cannot stay with the person. A man and woman meet and fall in love. They have a very strong feeling for one another, a very good feeling. "Oh, I love you, you love me! We were made for each other." But maybe one day the woman says, "I don't like you anymore." Then she breaks up with the man, so he is suffering terribly. "Oh, I want to have her back again. Life is not worth it anymore!" He cannot sleep so well after that. He sees food, but does not want it; eats it, but the food has no taste and only makes his stomach upset. Maybe he gets very sick.

Some people in this kind of situation will suffer so much that they will even kill themselves because of being prevented from experiencing this temporary love-feeling together. Passion actually means suffering, yet most people want passion in their lives! There was a famous story in Korea a few years ago. A young man and a woman met and fell deeply in love. But their parents said that they were blood relations—they shared some common relative around five hundred years ago. In any other country, this is not considered a problem at all. But Korea has very strong traditional rules about this. So their parents prohibited the marriage. The young man and woman were so sad that one day they just committed suicide together. They could not bear the thought of being without one another. If they could not be together, they would not stay in the world. But the law of impermanence means that everything eventually passes away, because nothing can stay in a fixed state forever, and all things soon disappear. If you don't completely understand this point, then when you cherish something too deeply and it eventually passes—when you cannot hold it—you experience a great deal of suffering. And if you cannot get what you desire, you also suffer. This is the human way.

Being in the presence of those you dislike

If you look at this world, you can probably say that more people dislike each other than love each other; there are more who are disliked than loved. In Korea there is a saying, "You will always meet your greatest enemy walking toward you on a narrow rope bridge." Imagine a rope bridge slung over a chasm. You walk down the sloping bridge, and out of the mist, coming from the opposite direction, is your greatest enemy. Neither one of you can edge around the other, the bridge is so narrow; and neither will turn back, but needs to continue on their way. This is an inevitable kind of human suffering for people who are attached to their like-and-dislike minds. They eventually find themselves in the presence of those they dislike, so they inevitably get a kind of suffering. It is a fairly common experience for nearly every person in this world.

Everybody has likes and dislikes. If you hold your opinion about other people, then you get suffering: cause and effect are always very clear. In America, resolving this kind of situation is very simple. Somebody may think, "I don't like you!" Then they take out a gun and kill the person—*piitchhuu!* Ha ha ha ha ha! In Korea, people don't do this very much. Inside they may think, "I don't like you," but on the outside they must keep a good face. So from that point on, they only think bad thoughts about that person. They hold this thinking very, very deeply. Sometimes they make very bad speech about the person to others, "Nya, nya, nya!" Any time there is a chance, they bicker and fight, nonstop. All this is suffering, and suffering appears because of a few opinions that people hold like a precious treasure. This whole great mass of suffering appears because of attachment to our like-and-dislike minds. But America is very simple. "I don't like you!" Then—*piitchhuu!*—kill. [*Laughter*] That is a very obvious kind of suffering.

Not getting what you desire

Most people who come to temple or church pray to get something. They come to have some wish granted rather than to find out what is the nature of themselves and this world. They want fame, money, children, or a better lover, house, or job. But in fact no one can get such things through any kind of prayer; the universe doesn't really work that way.

In Korea, there is a big election for the National Assembly. In one voting district, sometimes up to seven, eight, or even twelve people run for the same seat in the Assembly. But only one of them can be elected. Only one person will be happy after the election. Many, many others will be very sad and disappointed: they work very hard for several years, lose lots of money, spend time away from their families, make their minds all busy, and get nothing. Because they want this thing very much, when they cannot get it, they suffer. That's crazy! In a recent election, a rather good candidate who didn't have any money for his campaign went to his relatives for funds, borrowed money at exorbitant interest from other people, yet he still failed in the election. He was only five votes short of victory over his opponent. He went crazy, because not being elected was one thing; but soon all his relatives came screaming to be repaid for his failed efforts. He wanted to kill himself with some medicine overdose, but that would have cost additional money that he didn't have. So he thought, "Why spend more money than I have anymore?" He jumped from a tall building and got his wish: he died without spending an extra dime.

People who fail in entrance exams, in major sports events, in business—all of their pain is the same. Many people have this experience of not getting what they have staked their lives on, and only stay alive because they cannot kill themselves.

Suffering itself is neither good nor bad. There are different kinds of suffering. There is suffering that hurts us, and some kinds of suffering that can actually help us, if we have a strong try-mind. A student once asked me, "Zen Master, I can't get something. I am suffering so much."

"What can't you get?"

"I want to get a good girlfriend, but I cannot get one. This is the first thing. I also cannot earn much money: that's the next suffering. And I cannot get a nice job. That's the last suffering. When I am sitting in meditation, my mind is only thinking, 'girlfriend, money, job; girlfriend, money, job; girlfriend, money, job.' Always this thinking, thinking, thinking, thinking; coming, going, coming, going. I cannot sit, you know? When doing mantra, only my mouth is doing the mantra. But inside, my mind is saying 'girlfriend, money, job; girlfriend, money, job.' It never stops! Coming, going. I am suffering so much. This is making it impossible for me to practice meditation. I don't want to do sitting meditation, because then this thinking just seems to get louder and louder. That is why I am asking you for advice. What shall I do?"

Sometimes you cannot give usual Zen-style teaching to someone in this condition. Their mind is attached to some strong desire, but they haven't yet attained the nature of this desire and the suffering that it makes for them. They will hold their suffering like a treasure. So I answered, "More suffering is necessary."

"No, no!" he said. "Why should I have more suffering? I already have too much."

"If you have more suffering, you will get everything."

"If I suffer more, I will get everything? What does this mean? That's crazy!"

So I said to him, "You listen to me: if you have more suffering, then getting a girlfriend, getting much money, and finding a good job are possible."

"OK, OK. What kind of suffering?"

"Every day, you must do one thousand bows, and every day repeat Kwan Seum Bosal ten thousand times. You try that."

"But that's making more suffering. Why should I do that?"

So I said to him, "Yah, that's not just making suffering; that's using suffering to take away suffering. Chinese medicine teaches, 'For heat sickness, use hot medicine; cold sickness, cold medicine.' If you have suffering sickness, use suffering medicine. You're suffering, but this suffering is not clear. You must take it away with clear-suffering medicine. Then you can change your suffering."

"OK," he said. "I'll try that." So for one hundred days, this young man did a thousand bows a day and ten thousand Kwan Seum Bosal mantras—bowing, bowing, *Kwan Seum Bosal, Kwan Seum Bosal.* After one hundred days, he had a wonderful new girlfriend, a new job appeared, and he was earning enough money to be happy.

This kind of story may not be about high-class meditation practice. But the Buddha talked about having a different medicine for each of the eighty-four thousand sicknesses. We call the practice that this young man did a kind of dharma candy. He practices hard to get something that he wants. Along the way he also gets some taste of the nature of practice and the nature of his thinking, suffering mind. Then once he has started practicing, it is possible to give him true teaching about correct practicing. You use his sickness to take away his sickness. "Yah, now your practicing is not good and not bad," you can say to him. "But a more high-class practice is finding your true nature." This kind of speech is possible once he has had some experience of practice.

So if you just try something, and only do it, then you can get everything. But if you cannot get something, you just suffer pointlessly. "I want something, but I cannot get it. I am so sad." This is the usual kind of suffering that we see. In this world, all human beings want something. But they don't practice, and they don't make any effort: they only want, want, want, without any kind of direction. So there is always suffering in their lives, and this suffering is not directed anywhere or converted into some deeper under-standing of themselves and this world. However, meditation students can practice hard, attain their true nature, and completely connect with other beings. If you attain your true nature, you get everything. Which one do you like?

The imbalance of the five skandhas

The Buddha taught that human beings have no "I." What we normally call "I" or "mind" is only a fleeting combination of changing energies, divided into five aggregates: form, feelings, perceptions, impulses, and consciousness. In Sanskrit, these are called the five skandhas, or "heaps." Originally these five skandhas function in harmony, so your life is clear and you do not make so much suffering for yourself. But when they are not balanced, you get suffering, automatically.

Sometimes you see a very obese person. Their arms and legs and head are small, but their body is very big, so they have a hard time getting around and doing things. This means the aggregate of form is not in balance. Then also anytime they have food, maybe they eat too much, so their body always becomes bigger and bigger. Their tongue says, "I want chocolate, I want ice cream," but the body actually doesn't want it! The tongue and the body start fighting, and because of their strong karma, the tongue wins, so they continue eating! In this case the skandhas of form, feelings, perceptions, and impulses cannot act with harmony. This is an imbalance of the skandhas, and it makes suffering. "Your karma makes your body, and your body makes your karma." That is a very important point, because it points directly to the constant interplay of karma and the aggregate of form.

The aggregate of feeling is simply a composite of all our other sensations, both physical and mental. For example, a baby is born in this world. It begins its life with just feeling. Its first consciousness is merely experience received through the eyes, ears, nose, tongue, body and mind. Feeling means that when this baby wants to pee, it only pees. Then when the diapers get wet, this doesn't feel so good after a while, so the baby cries, "Waaaa!" Mother comes and changes the diapers, and the baby has a good feeling again. When the baby is hungry, this doesn't feel so good, so they cry, "Waaa!" Then mother gives it food. Babies only have this kind of feeling- and perception-consciousness. That is a very simple mind. But some people remain very strongly attached to this kind of mind their whole lives. When they feel like eating, they eat, and keep eating and eating for some time after their hunger is satisfied. This is done just to prolong the sensations of the mouth and tongue. When they feel like having sex, they go have sex, though there may be no love behind it. When they feel like sleeping, they sleep, all the time. When they feel like shopping, they go and shop, picking up things they may not need. But this feeling-consciousness is not clear, and nearly always creates some sort of suffering experience for them and for other people. Running on and on, from sensation to sensation, we make strong habit energies, or impulses, which then control our life.

Impulses are another name for karma. What do you like? That becomes your mind. So I often tell this story: During the Korean War, I was drafted into the army, just like all Korean men. While in the army, I had a very good friend, Mr. Song. We always did together-action. Anytime I had a little money, I would take him to a restaurant or we would visit a temple together. He didn't know that outside the army I was a monk. Every day I only tried to help him. He used to say, "Oh, thank you very much. You always help me, but I never have any money. I am sorry." One day, Mr. Song said, "Today it's my turn. I want to take you to a wonderful high-class restaurant in Taegu City for lunch!"

"But you don't have any money," I said to him. "How can you get enough money for that?"

"Oh, no problem, don't worry. I'll get some." So we went to the Taegu train station. It is a very big station, with many people coming and going. When we got inside, Mr. Song whistled three times very loudly. Suddenly three boys came running up to him.

They bowed deeply to him and said, "Hello, sir, where have you come from?"

He said, "We came from Pusan. Where are Mr. Lee and Mr. Kim? I want to talk with them."

The boys bowed and ran off, and within a few minutes two very well-dressed gentleman appeared. "Oh, brother, you've come today! How nice to see you!" They were very happy, and very polite to Mr. Song.

Pointing to me, he said to them, "This man is my very good friend. He's a captain. We've come to have lunch together. Can you get things ready for us?"

"Yes, brother," they said. So the two men brought a car around and drove us to this very wonderful high-class restaurant. Even though there was a war going on, this restaurant had plenty of delicious food. Meanwhile I couldn't understand what was happening. He had no money! But that didn't matter—we had very good food together, and Mr. Song was very, very happy.

After lunch I asked him, "What kind of happening is this? How is this possible?"

"Oh, it's a very long story," he said.

"Please tell me."

"OK. Before I went into the army, I was a top pickpocket. I was the boss, and those men were my assistants. One day I realized that this was all very bad action. So when the war started I repented, washed my hands of it forever, and went into the army. But all the time you have been helping me out, and I haven't been able to repay you—I have no money. Today I returned the favor: some repentance was necessary, so I called my old friends."

"Oh, thank you very much. It's very nice of you to do this for me," I said. "But that kind of action is not correct! If you really washed your hands of it, then that means *no more!*"

"OK, OK. I won't do this anymore," he said. "I promise." He had always been very correct in the army, and even became a captain at the same time as me. We worked together a lot, and I saw that his actions were always very meticulous and correct. So this pickpocketing was like an old habit, and he had worked very hard to change it. But impulses are very strong; karma cannot be changed with just some mental decision alone. Some kind of meditation practice is necessary.

One day, Mr. Song and I went sightseeing in the Sorak Mountains, a very beautiful and famous mountain range in Korea. The weather was very nice. Many people come from all over to see the mountains, so the bus station was very crowded when we arrived. There were many people waiting in long lines. We were waiting behind one elderly gentleman when all of a sudden, Mr. Song's hand shot into this man's back pocket and took out his wallet. It happened like lightning! Nobody around us noticed, not even the man in front of us.

But I was standing right behind Mr. Song and saw it all happen, so I hit him—*piitchhuu!* "Your hand is no good!" I said.

Mr. Song was also very surprised. "Oh, that's my old habit. I cannot help it. It just happens by itself!" He was very sorry, and very sincere. He didn't want to take this wallet, he didn't want to be a pickpocket and steal people's money anymore. But he saw a wallet and automatically his hand reached out and took it. It was a very strong habit. Another name for it is karma. He had very strong karma for this, so sometimes these actions just appeared by themselves, out of his habit-mind, whether he liked it or not.

I told him, "You must return that money!"

"Yes, yes." Then he tapped the shoulder of the man standing in front of him. "Excuse me, sir. Is this your wallet? I found it on the ground."

The old man turned and saw Mr. Song holding his wallet. "Oh, goodness, my money! Thank you, thank you very much! I was on my way to the market to buy a cow with this money. If I had lost it, I wouldn't have been able to buy the cow for my farm. Oh, thank you very much!" He took out some money to give to Mr. Song as a reward.

But Mr. Song only waved his hands humbly. "Oh, no, no. I couldn't!"

Still the old man persisted. "No, you are so honest. I must thank you."

"No, no, no . . ."

Then I elbowed Mr. Song in the side. "It's OK to take a little. Right now that's your job!" So Mr. Song took a little money. Then everyone was very happy. [*Loud laughter from the assembly*]

So as we see, for Mr. Song this kind of impulse was very strong. Even though his thinking-consciousness had learned that stealing was a bad action, that this impulse was not correct, and he stopped doing it, sometimes the same kind of impulse would appear, and he instantly followed it. If we do some kind of action many, many times, it becomes an impulse. Another name for that is karma. It is simply the spontaneous action of our habit-mind. When we cannot control this impulse, then sometimes it is not balanced with what our consciousness understands to be correct or not correct behavior, and so it makes suffering for ourselves and for others. This is just another kind of suffering that comes when the five skandhas are not in harmony with each other, and one of them is too strong or cannot function correctly with the others.

Then the last skandha is consciousness. Buddhism teaches that what we call consciousness is actually made of nine separate consciousnesses. We will talk about this in greater detail later when we talk about Mahayana Buddhism. When we are born, we have the six consciousnesses: seeing, hearing, smelling, tasting, touch, and thinking. These are the basic six consciousnesses. After some time, when a baby is about two years old, a very simple kind of discrimination appears. The child remembers all the impressions it has received through its six consciousnesses: it likes some, and it dislikes others. This is the appearance of the seventh consciousness, which is like-and-dislike mind. We often call it the discriminating consciousness, because it is the mind which separates this from that, good from bad, up from down. "I like this, I don't like that." "Noooo!" Maybe American children develop a very strong discriminating consciousness that learns only "No." "You should do this." "Nooo!" "Please come here." "Nooo!" Ha ha ha ha! American babies learn this very early. They understand only "No, I don't like that." That is the appearance of the seventh consciousness, or like-and-dislike mind.

The mind that remembers all our actions and experiences is the eighth consciousness. It is also called the storehouse consciousness because this consciousness stores everything we have ever done, thought, or experienced. It is also known as memory: not only actions from this life, but all our actions committed since beginningless time are kept in this consciousness. This consciousness is like a very meticulous computer, because it records everything we have ever done and seen and heard and smelled and tasted and touched and thought, both in this life and in all our previous lives. At night, when we have dreams, that is the working of the eighth consciousness.

Another way to look at this is that the sixth consciousness is our will consciousness. The seventh consciousness is our emotional consciousness, because this is what discriminates and makes likes and dislikes. The eighth consciousness is our intellectual consciousness. The last consciousness that Buddhism teaches is our ninth consciousness. This is our Buddha-consciousness, our Dharma-consciousness. Another name for it is *dharmakaya*. We also call it true self, or original nature, or true nature, or Buddha-nature. There are many names for this, but originally it has no name and no form.

So we have the six consciousnesses connected to our eyes, ears, nose, tongue, body, and mind. There is the seventh consciousness, which discriminates good from bad. And the eighth consciousness stores all our experiences and thoughts. Imbalance means these consciousnesses separate, and do not do together-action with one another. They do not function harmoniously. So some people with strong mental problems actually have imbalances among these eight consciousnesses. When it's time to eat, they may sit there, thinking, "Eat? Not eat? Eat? Not eat?" This kind of sickness appears. Maybe you see someone in the street, talking aloud, but there is nobody else there. He is having a conversation with himself. "Oh, I like that. You are good boy. La la-la la, li li-li li. Why do you say that? Pss pss pss pss pss . . ." He is waving his hands and looking around, sometimes getting angry and then suddenly breaking out into laughter. But no one else is there. Such people do this because although their body is there, their consciousnesses have separated and are communicating with each other. The name for that is imbalance.

And everybody experiences this kind of imbalance, in one form or another. During chanting, your mouth is chanting "*Kwan Seum Bosal, Kwan Seum Bosal, Kwan Seum Bosal*," but your thinking goes to New York, to Poland, to 1989, or to some problem, then back to the Dharma Room, then to yesterday, to your mother, and your college, your last boyfriend. Around and around and around and around. That is a simple kind of imbalance. Then at one point, one of your consciousnesses says, "Come back, OK? This is chanting time. Why go around and around?" So that wandering mind that everyone experiences is merely the three different consciousnesses working, each one doing a separate action. Your chanting-mouth and ear that hears the chanting are the sixth consciousness, the mind that flies around and around is the eighth consciousness of memory, and the mind that says "Come back to practice!" is your seventh consciousness. They are fighting each other inside. Every day, every minute, your consciousnesses are fighting each other inside, sometimes a little and sometimes a lot. When your consciousnesses are fighting inside, that is called imbalance of the five skandhas. It means you cannot decide anything. Sometimes we are stuck: "Oh, what should I do? Should I do this, or should I do that? I don't knowww!" We experience confusion inside. If this struggle becomes stronger, then people say you are crazy. All of us have heard of the term *mentally imbalanced*. That is the same point. But if your consciousnesses becomes balanced—*boom!*—you become Buddha, and then from moment to moment you can just *do* it. However, having an imbalance means you cannot decide something, so you cannot do anything.

Taken together, all these many kinds of suffering add up to the Eight Sufferings. This is the narrow world that most people create for themselves. Their whole life is like a fly buzzing around in a small, narrow bottle. It has followed some sweet smell into the bottle, but now it cannot escape. It is trying to find a way to get out, buzzing and buzzing against the clear glass, which tells it that freedom and empty space are not far away. Most people are like this. Something they have made in their minds over and over again strongly prevents them from having a complete life. They are desperately trying to get out of a suffering realm that they have made themselves by becoming blindly attached to sensations. But it doesn't work that easily. The simple reason for their difficulties is that they don't understand impermanence. This is the path of human beings' suffering. Everything in this world happens by natural process. You make everything, so you get everything, which means you get some kind of suffering. "I don't like getting old." "Oh, my relationship with him ended. I feel so miserable." "I hate being sick like this." "I don't like him." "I can't believe my grandmother died." We all suffer. But if you correctly attain this insight into impermanence, then you can take away these Eight Sufferings. If you don't understand that all things are impermanent, however, then you become easily attached to things that must eventually pass. As a result, you cannot take away your suffering, and you only continue to make more suffering for yourself and for this whole world.

Insight into Impurity
(The Five Human Desires)

不 淨 觀

（ 人 生 五 欲 ）

Desire for material wealth

財 欲

Desire for sex

色 欲

Desire for fame

名 欲

Desire for food

食 欲

Desire for sleep

睡 欲

L ET US LOOK AT "insight into impurity" more closely. Some people claim that the body is impure. Others claim that the desires of mind are impure. Hinayana practice is to examine closely this body's many impurities, and then from this point to view the impurities created by our thinking minds. Under your skin there is blood flowing. If you could look deeper, you would see organs, bile, excrement, and urine. Everything is held up by snow-white bones. And every day, through these nine holes, we constantly throw out many impure things. When you think of this, how could you possibly say that we are clean? People think they are pretty. They put on powder and cream and blush and makeup and perfume. They cover themslves with silk and hang around with their head high up, holding some attractive pose so that others will be attracted to them. But when you really look at the inside, we are just a sack of blood and excrement and pus. Being aware of this is an important practice in many Hinayana traditions.

Originally there is no impurity. People become attached to the desires of their mind, and it is this attachment that makes the mind impure. Hinayana Buddhism and any Buddhist tradition emphasize the impurities in our mind. But these impurities are caused by our attachment to bodily sensations. As I said before, Buddhism teaches, "Your karma makes your body, and your body makes your karma." So the desires of this body that craves for sensations make the mind impure, because these desires make karma, which hinders our ability to perceive this world clearly, just as it is. An animal cannot control its desires: if it wants to have sex, it just has sex. If it feels like eating, it will eat whatever it finds, whenever it wants. Most human beings often act like this. Even though human beings understand differently, if they only follow their desires, they get suffering. This is a kind of impurity.

Not only while you are alive, but even after you die you are impure. When you die, friends who loved you dearly in life will throw away your corpse as fast as possible, and even dogs won't want to be near your body because your corpse is so unclean. This is why so many Hinayana sutras talk about impurity so often. They talk about nine impure aspects or "marks" of a corpse: the body swells; because of wind and sun, it becomes grossly discolored; it collapses and deflates when rotting; at this point, blood and pus swell out of their natural channels; it becomes rotten and gradually disintegrates; birds, animals, and insects will swarm over it to eat it; bones, flesh, head, hands, and other appendanges will be dispersed; only white bones will remain; and after cremation there is only about one handful of ashes, which are thrown to the wind.

Many Hinayana Buddhist practices emphasize this meditation on impurity. Such practices show how our birth is simply the result of karma from previous lives. This view teaches a basic awareness of the impurities present at every stage of our lives. Our beginning inside a mother's womb is impure, because this place is full of blood and pus and waste and urine. After birth, filthy substances are constantly being emitted by the nine holes of our body. Meanwhile, the thirty-six kinds of wastes are continuously circulating throughout our body. This body eventually dies, rots, and decays. Yet while alive, we take great care of this impure, impermanent body. We put expensive things on it. We clean it. We perfume it. We powder it. We must spend a lot of effort to keep it healthy and in good working order. If we don't, we aren't any different from dogs and pigs at all.

Hinayana Buddhism particularly emphasizes five kinds of impurity. Let us look at them in more detail.

Desire for material wealth, desire for sex, desire for fame, desire for food, desire for sleep

There are five kinds of impurities, called the Five Poisons, or the Five Human Desires. If you look at this world, you will see that most of the suffering human beings create is caused by their pursuit of these five desires. And everyone understands this, inside. That's why, when someone has too many desires, people think, "What a dirty man! He's attached to his money! Attached to sex! Attached to fame! Attached to food! Attached to sleep!" If there is too much of any kind of desire, the mind becomes dirty: it only follows its karmic habits. Everybody says, "That's no good! This man is dirty." This style of mind appears.

Money is important for living our lives. It is not good or bad. But if you become attached to money, your mind becomes clouded by this desire. Nowadays many people want to become millionaires. Then sometimes they will perform actions that cause themselves and other beings to suffer, just for the sake of money. One of my students was a Korean professor who studied at Yale University. His father had gotten married at eighteen. After he had one child, he told his wife he didn't want to have any more children, because he thought he would not be able to save much money if he did. Whenever he was paid, he only gave money very grudgingly to his wife and son. He saved all his money in a locked cabinet, and he counted it once a day. Counting and arranging this money was his only real pleasure in life. He never ate in any restaurants. He never had even a cup of coffee outside the house. He did all this just to save money. In moderation, such a mind is called virtuous; in excess, it is greedy. One day, his wife said to him, "I can't live with you anymore. I can't eat in a restaurant even once if I live with you." But this didn't seem to bother him in the least. He just said, "If that's the way you think, we must get a divorce." So they divorced—in their sixties! That is crazy. Because his wife was paid out of some kind of pension, she could live without his help.

One day, the son, my student, asked his father: "Father, you are living for the pleasure of counting your money every day. Why do you do this? What will you do after you die?"

"I don't know what I will do after I die. I just live with this pleasure. It is not useful for me to have a son or a wife." Soon after this, his father died. When the son opened his father's locked cabinet, there was several hundred thousand dollars inside. The money was neatly counted and organized and stacked as if it were a bank. As he looked at this money, stored so neatly in the cabinet, the son broke down and cried. He realized that his father had sacrificed everything in his life for something he could never take with him.

Money itself is not good or bad. Saving money is not good or bad. Yet when it is truly time to die, money is unable to extend our life by even one moment. Actually, the real pleasure of money lies in using it properly. But if we pursue it simply to satisfy our passing desires, then eventually the karmic effects of this kind of thinking will poison our minds. We lose our direction and cause suffering for this world. That is a very important point. So that's why we call the desire for money an impurity.

Sex, in itself, is also not good or bad. Everything owes its birth and life to the coming together of the natural energy of male and female. But some people make this attraction the precious treasure of their deluded minds. One day a woman came to see me while I was staying at the Providence Zen Center. She was a graduate student at some college in New York. She explained that she was dating her seventy-seventh boyfriend. She asked me, "What would you say if I want to marry my one hundredth boyfriend?" In the West, many people have these sorts of intimate relationships before committing to marriage. It is not like in the East, where men and women may date for several years without much or any intimate contact. When I learned that this was her seventy-seventh partner, I told her about the great bodhisattva Pass-a-Million.

There is a very famous story about a woman who actually used sex only to save other people. The Avatamsaka-sutra teaches about fifty-three great masters of skillful means. The thirty-sixth master was called Pass-a-Million. She was a prostitute who lived during the Buddha's lifetime. She was very, very beautiful, and many people believed that she had gotten enlightenment. Every day, many men came to her for sex. Sometimes she asked for money, and sometimes she didn't. But every man who had sex with her didn't have any desire for sex when he left. Many, many of her lovers eventually became monks, got enlightenment, and became great teachers of others.

Pass-a-Million never used sex for her own pleasure. Rather, she only used this body to serve other people. She kept a clear mind, and was simply using sex to take away these men's desire for sex, so she helped them get enlightenment. This famous story shows that even sex can sometimes be used to help other people, if the direction is clear. There are many other stories about the use of such skillful means. In itself, sex is not good or bad: the most important thing is, why do you do something? Is it only for yourself or for all beings? Pass-a-Million was a great bodhisattva who acted without hindrance, so her sex was not for her, for her pleasure alone. Her sex was save-all-beings sex. This story can be found in the Avatamsaka-sutra.

After telling this story to my student from New York, I asked her, "Why do you have sex? For whom?"

"I have it for him and for me."

"You still have 'I,' so that is no good. You must completely take away 'I,' then your sex is bodhisattva sex." Then I said, "Your life is already half over. From now on, you should not live for yourself alone. Only help this world, and help all beings." About a year later we received a letter from her. She had married, after the seventy-seventh partner, and eventually became a good wife and mother.

Men and women should be partners in life, not merely instruments of each other's physical enjoyment. They should be good dharma friends. If they are helping each other understand their true selves, and are deeply committed to this in every way, having no thought for themselves, then having sex is no problem. It can also be a Dharma. The name for this is do ban, a "companion on the Path." But this is extremely difficult practice for most people, who just have sex with others for their own enjoyment: this is dirty. This is why we call someone "filthy" if they only have sex mindlessly, like an animal. The most important thing is, how do you consider sexual relations? The way you think about sex makes it either pure or impure.

"Desire for fame" is very interesting. Even more than the desire for sex, it represents the greatest potential to make the mind impure. Most people are attached to name and form. Everybody also believes "I am." This is a basic delusion. Name and form have no self-nature, and this "I" does not exist. They are both created entirely by thinking. But human beings are not just content with that. They also want this illusion of "I am" to get bigger and bigger and bigger, all the time. "I am this." "I am that." "I am a brilliant professor." "I am a famous actor." "I am friends with so-and-so." And they are not happy until other people recognize this "I am" and are somehow controlled by it. In North Korea, one man's strong belief in "I am" completely controls the minds of many millions of people—even several years after his death! If you don't believe in his "I am," maybe you will go to prison or die. That's crazy. Every single day, people in this world kill other people simply to protect their names and their reputations. And the suffering that is created from this impulse is not limited to dictators and criminals alone: in most cases, we all ruthlessly compete with one another in our everyday lives just to promote our "I am" over someone else. We lie and deceive. We argue and make bad speech about one another not just to become famous, but to show one another that my "I am" is somehow better than yours and hers. And all this suffering and pain comes from just one delusive thought that everyone is attached to: "I am."

People put themselves through horrible hardships to get and maintain high social position. They will do shameful things because of their attachment to this completely empty thought. There was once a Korean woman of high social rank who had a vary famous romantic affair. Her husband was a high-class government minister. She had an affair with a man who had a reputation as a kind of Don Juan. In the beginning, she was interested only in spending time with this man. Eventually, the man began to request her money and cars and jewels. He threatened that if she didn't hand this over, he would go public with their affair. Because she was so afraid of losing her high social standing, she gave in to him. She let him completely control her because he controlled her greatest fear. Eventually, she went bankrupt, and the scandalous behavior came out as a result. Her reputation was ruined, and because of this, she felt as if her life was completely finished. She thought of suicide many times. All this was the result of her attachment to the temporary and completely empty pleasure gained from having others' approval.

When we say "desire for fame," we are not only talking about the desire to become well known by many people. Most people, when they hear about the "desire for fame," think it is just an impurity of "famous" people's minds. But actually this also means the desire for some kind of social approval, some respectability or popularity with people. This desire causes constant suffering in our everyday lives. We suffer when others don't think well of us. We are jealous when people approve of someone we don't like. Maybe we make some bad speech about this person in order to bring them down. We conform and lie to gain the approval of others. We don't want to be "left out." In Asia, many people dress well and try to show others their high material well-being, even if they are poor. It is like an "I" competition. I knew a man once who drove a very nice car and wore very expensive clothing in public, even though he worked in a small office and did not earn much money. He wanted others to believe he was a success. At home, he had to deny his family certain basic things to pay for this approval, and his children suffered for his false social standing. Also many people in Japan and Korea push their children extremely hard, from the moment they are born, to get into a good university just because of what this will say about the parents. Every year or so, several Japanese or Korean students kill themselves because they did not get into the top-ranked university and felt they had shamed their parents. All this comes from mind's basic delusion that "I am," a delusion that people force on themselves and others.

If you meditate correctly, however, you can perceive that this "I" actually does not exist. Since this "I" does not exist, then what thing could become famous or earn others' approval? If people realized that this "I" does not exist, they would not suffer so much—and cause others to suffer—in order to attach some reputation or good name to this "I." Also they would not care when other people seemed better liked than them: jealousy of others would not appear. This "I" simply does not exist anywhere. That is why if you meditate, you attain that the desire for fame is an impurity.

We all understand the desire for food. This is very powerful, because it means your tongue karma completely controls you. In Buddhist temples in the Orient, when someone dies there is an important annual memorial ceremony. After the ceremony, there is always good food at the family's house or in the temple. The dates and locations of these ceremonies are often published in the neighborhood where the deceased has lived. I have a student in Korea whose father had a very strange habit. He used to carry around two books in his pocket: in one book he had written the dates of all the memorial ceremonies at some of the temples in his area; and in the other book were different people's birthdays. So every couple of days, he would check his books. Whose father died, whose mother died? Then he would go there, and join the ceremony, or arrive at the end. There would always be very good food to eat. The same thing with birthdays: "Ah, this is Mr. Kim's birthday, Mr. Park's birthday, then Mr. Song's birthday . . ." He would go over there, join the ceremony, and then eat like a pig! There was always lots of very good food, and best of all, it was free. So this was his job: first check his books, then follow the food. "Today, what? Today, what? What kind of ceremony this weekend?" Ha ha ha ha ha ha! [*Laughter from the assembly*] His tongue completely controlled him. "I want good food, every day." So he always kept these two books. That is not a very good way to keep your mind, you know? And he was not satisfied with just this strange habit. Every day he would go to a different restaurant to eat, even though his wife was a very good cook. One day was a Chinese restaurant, another day was an American restaurant. If he ate with others, he would always crave the food on other people's plates, not his own! Sometimes he would ignore his own plate entirely while reaching around the table to sample everyone else's. The name for this, in Buddhism, is "hungry ghost."

That all comes from having too much desire. It is worse than being an animal. Actually, in some respects an animal has a very simple mind: when it is hungry, it eats, and when it is full, it stops. It is not attached to the desire for food, or to the taste. But human beings are too attached to their tongue, so even after we are full, if we like the taste of this food, we will continue eating. Many people get up from a meal in some kind of pain or discomfort, having eaten too much. But the real point of food is to keep our body alive so that we can use this rare human rebirth to gain enlightenment. If we serve this body just for itself, for its fleeting desires, however, we become slaves to it. That is a basic impurity.

The same is true of sleep. For most people, from six to eight hours of sleep a day is more than enough. But we always see people snoozing in the meditation room, in class, or in the office. They may get eight hours of sleep the night before, but the moment the meditation period starts with the sound of the *chugpi*, they start snoozing on their cushion. Why is this so? The desire for sleep is also a kind of karma, just like any other. The more sleep you get, the more you crave it. In a temple or Zen center, we wake up early every day to do meditation. This is because *Buddha* means "wake up." Many people come to the Zen center, but they don't want to wake up early with everyone else. "No, no. I want to sleep. I must get eight hours of sleep!" Then the Head Monk says, "Buddha means 'wake up.' So you must get up!" But many people, when they move out of the Zen center, still want to get up at five in the morning to practice. They want to keep a temple schedule at home. That is wonderful! "Every day I will wake up at five o'clock." Then they set the alarm clock. At five o'clock, the clock goes off—*brrrrring, brrrrrng, brrrrrrr-rng!* It is very noisy. "Oh, more sleep is necessary!" They hit the snooze button and go back to sleep. If you want to wake up at five o'clock to practice, then when the clock rings you must get up. Why hit this snooze button? "That's too noisy, OK? Today I am tired, so more sleep is necessary." That kind of attitude is not so good. Everybody wants sleep, and more and more sleep. The more you sleep, the more you crave sleep. That's a very important point. But the Buddha taught that this whole life is a dream—when will you ever wake up?

Many people think that because they are often sleepy in the Dharma Room they will never be able to practice hard. But this is not so. A long time ago in Korea, there was a monk who got enlightenment because of his very strong sleep karma. He was later known as Millstone Master. Before he got enlightenment, he could not control his sleep. Whether sitting in meditation, or working, or walking, or eating, he would always fall asleep. As soon as the head monk hit the *chugpi,* beginning a meditation period, he would fall asleep. Eventually he could not stay in the meditation hall anymore. One day, while walking in the street, he fell asleep, and bumped his head on a big tree that was overhanging the road. Some women standing nearby saw this monk and giggled at his misfortune. He was very ashamed of himself! So he decided to fix this problem, once and for all. Taking a rope, he tied a heavy millstone around his waist. Whether walking or studying or working, he always wore this millstone around his waist. If he started to sleep, he would fall down. He made a strong effort, every day. Because of this effort, he eventually conquered his strong sleep habit. One day, after much hard training, he got enlightenment, and became a great Zen master. This is the story of the Millstone Master who conquered his sleep demons.

Most people are restricted by these Five Human Desires. But if you get enlightenment, and become a Great Man or Great Woman, these need not bind you. You do not use these desires for your own enjoyment. You can act with no hindrance just to help all beings. The most important thing to remember is, how do you use these desires to help others?

Insight into Nonself

無我觀

The characteristics of all external phenomena		Aspects of the mind
萬 相		心 相
Arising		Arising
成		生
Stability		Stability
住		住
Decline		Differentiation
壞		異
Dissolution		Extinction
空		滅

Cause	Effect	Samsara
因	果	輪迴

Primary cause

原 因

Dependent origination

緣 起

Result

結 果

A good cause leads to a good result. A bad cause leads to a bad result.

善因　　善果　　　惡因　　　惡果

The characteristics of all external phenomena: arising,
  stability, decline, dissolution

EVERYTHING IN THIS universe that we experience arises, remains for
some period, decays, and disappears again. That is the nature of all
things. You look at the rain or snow: it appears one moment in some form,
stays, and then begins to melt or evaporate, and finally it is gone. A human
being appears in this world, is alive for some time, grows old, and dies. The
same is true of mountains, rocks, trees, animals, the sun, the moon, the
stars—everything. We have already talked about how the earth and moon
appeared out of the sun many hundreds of millions of years ago, and now
they revolve in space. Many more kalpas from now, when the sun also begins
to disappear, the earth will grow cold, and both moon and earth will crumble
and disappear. This whole world comes out of emptiness and eventually
returns to emptiness. It can happen in a single moment, it may last only as
long as dew, or it may take many hundreds of kalpas. But ultimately everything is the same. Everything arises, remains for some time, declines, and
passes away. This is not just Buddhism's idea: you can see it everywhere you
look.

But there is one thing that never appears and never disappears. Can you
find it? One of my students once said, "Space is like this." But space is already
always emptiness, yah? Space comes from where? Ha ha ha ha! So we must
find that not-broken thing. That is a very important point.

Aspects of the mind: arising, stability,
  differentiation, extinction

This teaches that our minds are also the same as all the things in this universe. Our minds function according to the same laws that govern the rocks
and trees and moon and stars. Our thoughts constantly come and go. One
thought may last one minute or two minutes. Our minds are always changing. Everything that has name and form will arise, remain for a period, become differentiated, and return to emptiness. Since our minds are the same
substance as this whole universe—the sun, the moon, the stars, mountains,
rivers, trees, everything—they follow the same laws. Mind arises, stays for a
period, then changes, and returns to emptiness. This usually happens very,
very quickly. There is an old Asian saying that a woman's mind changes

twelve times between the kitchen and the dining room. In olden times, when she would serve dinner to her parents or husband, a woman would have to carry this low table of food from the kitchen to the room where they eat. "Maybe my parents won't like this food. Maybe they'll like it. Maybe this preparation is correct. Maybe it's not correct. Maybe I cooked it too much. Maybe I cooked it too little. Maybe there's too much food. Maybe there is not enough. . . ." Changing, changing, changing, changing, changing, checking, checking, checking, checking, checking, thinking, thinking, thinking, thinking, thinking. [*Laughter*] Ha ha ha ha! That is an old Asian saying about a wife's mind, but actually it applies to all our minds. If your mind changes, then the color of your face changes. Sometimes your face is red, sometimes it is yellowish, sometimes dark, sometimes pale—the color is always changing as your thinking changes. As your mind changes, the color of your face changes, because mind and this universe follow the same law. You get "energy up," and your face becomes red; "energy down," and it becomes pale. If you experience too much thinking, or attachment to some strong feeling, your face becomes dark. This color is always changing. So our mind always appears, remains for a period, changes, and disappears. It can happen very, very quickly.

Everything that has name and form changes because name and form have no self-nature. If you completely attain that point, you attain that mind also has no self-nature: this is the insight into nonself. You attain nonself. So, insight into nonself is a very important practice, because then you attain nirvana. "Ah, my body appears, and disappears. This is my hand, that's my foot, that's my head—that's my body. But this body is not 'I.' " This body is merely a rental car. One person's rental car is made in the U.S.A., another's is made in Korea, another person's car is made in Japan. If you correctly attain that this body is just your rental car, then attaining nirvana is no problem, because you attain this body's impermanence: My rental car is impermanent, and it is always changing, changing, changing. My true self *is* nonself.

Cause, effect, samsara;
  primary cause, dependent origination, result

This entire world is made by cause and effect. Every single thing we ever experience is the effect of some cause, and this effect causes some other effect, which in turn becomes a cause. One day the Buddha was walking along a dusty road with his faithful attendant, Ananda. Suddenly the Buddha told Ananda to pick up a piece of straw that lay across their path. Holding it in his hand, Ananda smelled a very strong odor of fish. He realized that this piece of straw had once been used to tie fish for the market, so he threw it away.

The Buddha saw this. "Do you smell something, Ananda?"

"Yes, Teacher. It smells very strongly of fish, so I threw it away."

"Well, do you think that this straw originally smelled like fish?"

"No, because it tied fish at one time, that is why it smells like fish now." The two continued walking for a little while. After some time they passed a piece of clean, white paper in the street.

"Ananda, pick it up and see what it is," the Buddha said. So Ananda bent over and picked it up. "Do you smell anything?"

"I smell a good fragrance like an expensive incense," Ananda said.

"Do you think that that paper originally smelled that way?"

"No, sir. It smells that way because at one time it must have been used to wrap incense. That is why it smells that way."

"That is so," the Buddha said. "Now you know that everything in this world, no matter how small, occurs because of the constant operation of cause and effect." Ananda understood and thanked the Buddha.

But what did Ananda attain? He understood that the law of cause and effect does not come from some remote place. It is not special. Cause and effect comes from the nearest event, the nearest relationship to us in every moment and every situation. So it is very important that you completely understand the true nature of this cause and effect. You were born in the U.S.A.; I was born in Korea. Why is one person reborn in the United States, while another person has their rebirth in Korea? A woman is born with no liver, a man is born blind, and another man is born into a rich family; someone is born black or white, Catholic or Jewish, or very intelligent, or artistic. There must be some reason for this. Understanding that is very important for your life.

How do a man and woman become husband and wife? Among so many millions of people, some become husband and wife through matchmakers, while others just happen to meet, fall in love, and get married. Regardless of the conditions of their relationship, their meeting occurs as a result of cause and effect. Already, at that time and in that place, this man and woman were supposed to meet. They made some cause together through actions in a previous life, and when certain conditions come together, this cause produces the effect of their meeting today. It is very simple! In this world nothing happens by chance. Everything is already decided because of actions we have done in our previous lives. The Buddha taught that if you merely brush past a person on the street, it is the result of many thousands of lives that you have done together-action with that person. Now think of how many more lifetimes of action together cause you to fall in love with someone or marry!

All things appear in this realm of sentient beings because of some primary cause acting under certain conditions to produce a result. We often call this karma. Karma is just our habit-mind. If you think or do something many, many times, you create a mental habit, which means that there is a very good possibility you will do that same thing again, and again, and again, given the same conditions. So our thinking and our actions make our karma. Through our thinking, through the choices we have made over and over again, we have made ourselves the way we are: this is Buddhism's basic teaching.

In previous lives I was Korean, so I made certain karma with Korea and its people. Therefore it is no accident that in this life I am reborn in Korea. All things happen by natural process. Buddhism's name for natural process is cause and effect, or karma. You have made American karma before, or Polish karma, or German karma. When your body disappears, you carry this karma with you. Then when you are reborn, this karma finds conditions that will again make a German body, or an American body, or a Polish body. It all depends on how strong this karma is, and what conditions it meets. Sometimes a child appears in this world, and when very young can play the violin very, very well. Everybody is familiar with the story of Mozart. He could perform and write beautiful music at a very early age. How is that possible? In a previous life, this person played some instrument many, many times, and played very well. That creates a strong kind of mental habit, or karma. When the person's body dies, this consciousness goes around, around, around. Then perhaps some woman gets pregnant. Maybe her husband likes music very much, or perhaps she herself is a music teacher. They have a strong affinity for the activities that this person engaged in before they died. This wandering consciousness meets these conditions and a result naturally appears. The child is born, and this talent for playing the violin or piano becomes ripe very quickly. The child already has very strong music karma, and when it meets these similar conditions in a new body, this mental habit-force produces the same result all over again.

We say that you can control your karma. Some people would say that you can control your destiny. Are they the same or different? There is a way to show this: you can sit under an apple tree and wait for an apple to fall. If you just sit there, one apple will eventually fall right into your lap. And in another way, you can shake the tree or branch and cause an apple to fall into your hands. Either way, you get an apple. The first way is merely a kind of destiny. By sitting under this tree, you were "destined" to have an apple eventually fall into your lap. This kind of destiny is commonly understood by most people. You wait for the effect of some actions to produce an action or event. But when you shake the tree, this is controlling your cause-and-effect relationship to this world. Your action is a cause that creates an effect, and this effect becomes the cause of other actions or thoughts. So when you were born, everything was already decided for you by the habit-mind that you have created over countless lives. According to your effort in this life, you can either control your cause and effect or be controlled *by* it. If you want to change karma, you must study your mind with great determination. Every day you must do sitting meditation and bowing and chanting. Mantra is also important. Then you can return to your original nature, and you can control the results of your karma. You can also prevent bad karma from happening as much. Don't blame your bad karma for things: just practice hard. Cut your lazy mind, and only go straight, don't know.

The Buddha's teaching about primary cause, dependent origination, and result point to the same thing. Here is a match. This match represents some primary cause that each person has inside. Under certain conditions, it can become a flame, and under most other conditions, it cannot. This matchbox represents some condition. When this primary cause meets this condition, you get a certain result: fire. The match is pushed by my hand against the matchbox, and goes up in flame. If these kinds of conditions do not appear, the match will not produce this result. Let's say a piece of paper appears. Then this match meets this paper, but fire does not result. Or the match and the matchbox may be present together, but my hand does not bring them together.

In the same way, Buddhism teaches that everyone has some primary cause in their consciousness. Our thinking makes this primary cause. If this primary cause keeps meeting certain conditions, it produces certain results, time after time, no matter what the person thinks or decides they can do to change it. The primary cause gets deeper and stronger as a result. But if these conditions are not met, then taking away our primary cause is possible. Slowly, over time, the primary cause goes down by itself through natural process.

Let's say one person is an alcoholic. The *desire* for alcohol is a primary cause. The alcohol—or the opportunity to obtain it—is a condition. Anytime they can have alcohol, they make suffering for themselves, and their habit becomes stronger. But if they strongly decide something and actually avoid this alcohol—this *condition*—then the primary cause can slowly go down, down, down. Alcohol itself is not good or bad. As long as this primary cause of desire meets these conditions, however, suffering always results. It is very important to realize this.

A good cause leads to a good result; a bad cause leads to a bad result

If you put seeds for yellow beans into the ground, you will get yellow beans. When you plant green beans, you get green beans. You never get yellow beans by planting green beans' seeds. Green beans never come from yellow seeds. Buddhism's teaching is very simple, and not very special: Everything happens by natural process. If you have a good cause, you get a good result; a bad cause, a bad result. Everything comes from our mind alone.

So if you want to understand your karma and your life, just look inside: how do you keep your mind, right now? Your just-now mind makes your whole life, as a ray extends out from a single point. When you do some good action, you get happiness. When your action comes from a bad cause, you always get suffering. That is all. Many people look at their lives and say, "Why do I always have to suffer?" But in this world cause and effect are very clear. We have created some mind-habit—a primary cause—so we keep getting the same result over and over again because we do not change or let go of the condition that inflames this primary cause. Not only from this life, but from many previous lives we experience the fruits of our thoughts, our speech and our actions. The habit that drives us now has been created over countless rebirths. Our consciousness cannot move it, so it is often very difficult to change this habit. One person always makes lots of money, has a nice car, a nice house, and a nice job. But someone else may be more intelligent, and work just as hard as this person, but cannot be nearly as successful. Why? In a previous life this successful person did many good actions that now have some result in this life. Perhaps he created this habit for success in many, many lifetimes of effort, so in this life, that habit just appears and functions naturally, almost effortlessly. It is the natural result of many previous actions and thoughts. At the same time, the second person, while certainly trying hard, perhaps created certain hindrances and difficulties through karma made in past lives. While he works diligently in this life, those karmic hindrances appear and ripen in this rebirth, making it difficult for his good efforts to bear fruit.

Only keep a good mind: that is Hinayana Buddhism's teaching. If you are always suffering, however, you must first perceive that you have made this yourself. "Oh, that is not an accident. That is my fault. I have made some kind of suffering, either in this life or in some previous life. So now I am getting some suffering." When you truly perceive this point, you can begin to take away your primary cause and get happiness. If your center is not moving, and you just practice very hard, then it is possible to change anything. In this world, everything you experience is from your previous life. Everybody's karma has already been determined by their thoughts and actions, the mind-habits they have made over many kalpas. So in this life, from moment to moment this habit appears and disappears, appears and disappears. That is all merely natural process. When you practice meditation, however, you can take away this primary cause, and then the condition changes, and therefore the result must change. Most people who experience suffering blame the outside conditions for creating this suffering for them. "That person is bad. They're not good to me." "He is always bad to me, so I am suffering." Nearly everybody believes that their parents, their spouse, even the government or society are the reason why they are suffering now. Yes, in some way these may be the visible sources of our suffering. Yet it is not the complete view. Nobody realizes that it is actually this primary cause inside us, which we have made over countless rebirths, that makes suffering. When we practice hard and take away our primary cause, then even if we meet some bad condition, we don't produce the same result. Suffering disappears as our primary cause goes down through natural process.

Dependent Origination

緣 起

To arise from conditions.

從 緣 生

To be extinct from conditions.

從 緣 滅

If I exist, that exists.

我 有 他 有

If I cease to exist, that ceases to exist.

我 滅 他 滅

W E CAN LOOK at this whole world in terms of two dimensions: time and space. When did mind appear? How does it change over time? And when does mind disappear? We already talked about how everything appears, and changes, and disappears. But when does mind begin? Then how long is it changing, changing, changing before it disappears? This view considers the dimension of time. And when we consider space, we ask, Does this cup exist, or does it not exist? Does this stick exist or not exist? If it exists, then what? If it doesn't exist, then what? That is a way of considering the dimension of space. The name for that is *dependent origination*.

We can say that Mahayana Buddhism is concerned with questions of space. Does this world exist or not? Do human beings exist or not? [*Tapping his cup with a stick*] Does this cup exist, or not exist? Is this cup true or not? But Hinayana Buddhism means having some insight into when this cup ap-

85

peared, and how. When does suffering appear? When does mind appear, and how? What happens to it over time?

So I ask you, when does this world begin? When does our mind begin? How does it change, and how does it disappear? We already talked about how everything appears out of the coming together of conditions. When a certain condition appears, then everything appears. When that condition disappears, then everything disappears. So if I am here, then something is over there. If I am not here, that thing disappears. Another way of saying this is, You make your world. God made God's world. The Buddha made the Buddha's world. A dog makes a dog's world. A cat makes a cat's world. A woman sees a mouse and shrieks, but when a cat sees this same mouse he is happy. "Ah, food!" So I make my entire world. If I make a "good" world, I have a "good" world; if I make a "bad" world, I have a "bad" world. If I am here, then I have my world. If I disappear, my world disappears.

But even if you disappear, there is still something there. Somebody may say, "You disappear. Then the sun in the sky also disappears?" No, if I disappear there is still a sun in the sky. But that is not "my" sun, the sun I saw. That is somebody else's sun. Ha ha ha ha! Because originally the sun does not exist. We make "sun," so if I disappear, my sun also disappears. If I am here, then something is there. If I disappear, then that thing disappears. That is Buddhism's first course.

This story will explain it better: One day, while I was sitting in my room at the Dharma Zen Center in Los Angeles, there was a knock at the door, and in walked an elderly Korean gentleman. He was a very distinguished-looking man, well dressed, with white hair and a long, white Confucian-style beard. He said, "I want to see Seung Sahn Sunim."

"Oh, wonderful. That's me!" He handed me a large fruit basket, filled with all kinds of beautiful food. "Thank you very much," I said as he sat down. "I must first put this on the altar and offer it to Buddha. Then we can talk."

But he waved his hands politely: "No, no, no. I am not offering these to Buddha. They are not for an offering. I only give them to you." Ha ha ha ha!

Then I thought, "That's strange. If he's a Buddhist, he understands that I must first put this kind of gift on the altar and offer it to the Buddha. But he's only saying, 'No, no, no.'" I had to check his mind a little. "Maybe he's not Buddhist. That's OK. No problem." So I just said, "Oh, thank you very much, then. I will just keep them in my room." We sat down. We had tea and cookies and fruit.

Then he started to talk. Once he started, he didn't stop. It was like I wasn't even there. He completely understood Confucianism, Taoism, and Buddhism. He also understood Western philosophy very well. He talked very easily about Socrates, Plato, and Aristotle. He knew German philosophy, French philosophy, and American philosophy. He understood modern physics, science, psychology, and literature. Talking, talking, talking, talking. His mouth was like a waterfall, you know? I could not say a thing. [*Laughter.*] He understood everything! He just kept going on and on and on about all these different philosophies. All the while, I could only say, "Yah. Yes, sir. Yes, sir. Yah, correct. Yes, sir. Correct. How true. Correct. Correct. Correct." Finally, after a great deal of talking at me, he pointed to my teacup and said, "Zen Master, where does this cup come from?" Suddenly it was like Zen-style talking! [*Laughter.*]

Then I was a little surprised: "Hmmm, maybe this man is a Zen master, you know? Maybe I have a little problem. . . ." [*Loud laughter.*] So first I checked him by saying, "You already understand. . . ."

"Yes," he said. "Somebody bought this in a store and brought it here!" So that is not a Zen-style answer! [*Loud, sustained laughter.*] He doesn't understand Zen. So I got a little rest-mind! [*Loud, sustained laughter from the assembly.*]

This man understood many, many things. But his understanding was not complete. He did not have very clear insight into the true nature of this cup. All he understood were words and concepts, things he had read in books. It was all just conceptual understanding. We call that "dead words." So it was necessary to hit his mind. "Yes, you are right," I said to him. "Somebody bought this in a store and brought it here. But where did the cups in the store come from?"

He replied, "Maybe from a cup factory."

"And before it leaves the factory, where does it come from?"

"Well, there is a president of the factory. He controls everything. So he made this cup."

"Yah, correct, correct . . ."

"So this factory president is a very important man. He makes everything, and sells it to all the stores. Then many people buy these things from the stores."

"Yah, correct, correct . . ." You could not interrupt him. He was on a roll again.

"In the same way, somebody also made the sun, the moon, the stars, mountains, rivers, and human beings."

"Yes," I said. "Somebody *made* all of this."

It was clear then that he wanted to hit my mind with a certain idea, not with the truth of the way things are. So then I understood that he was Christian. He asked me, "Who made all this?"

"*You* did!"

"Me? How can you say that?" He was very shocked. His back straightened up and his face went pale.

"I already understand your mind. You only think that I can answer that God made all this. But I am a Buddhist monk: how can I possibly say that God made this?"

"How can you say that I made the sun, moon, and stars?" he shouted. "Are you *crazy*?"

Then I said to him, "You listen to me. Let's say that here is a rainbow. Who made this rainbow? God? Buddha?"

The man was visibly shocked for a moment longer, and slowly relaxed. He blinked back into conversation. "Well, um, well, maybe sunlight hits the water spray, and then the rainbow appears before my eyes."

"Yes, but I am asking you *who* made this rainbow?"

He was stuck for a long time. He could not answer, so he bowed and said, "Please teach me."

"The sunlight, the water, and your eyes come together to make this rainbow. That is true. Therefore, if I am here, my rainbow is there. If I am not here, my rainbow is not there. Do you understand that? So if there are five people right here, there will be five rainbows over there. Each person sees a rainbow. That's very simple. Let's say I am here, and there is someone standing ten feet away. Then my rainbow is here [*pointing in one direction*], but their rainbow is over there [*pointing in another direction*]. Our rainbows are different! To me, the rainbow is 'here,' but to him, the rainbow is 'over there.' " I put a cup on the floor right in front of me, about six inches away from my leg. Then I continued, "To me, it's right 'here,' but from where you are sitting, you say it's 'over there.' " The man was stuck and could not say anything. Eventually he left, shaking his head. His face was very sad.

So ten people have ten rainbows. If there are twenty people, then twenty rainbows appear. "My" rainbow means I made my rainbow. If I don't look at the sky, my rainbow is not there. Or if I look in another direction, my rainbow also disappears. The Buddhist teaching of dependent origination explains that point. If I sit and look out the window while talking on the phone, maybe I will say to my friend, "Wonderful, there's a rainbow!" But he has no rainbow! If you are at my friend's house while I am telling him this on the phone, and you ask him, "Is there a rainbow over there?" or, "Does the rainbow exist or not?" he cannot answer you the way I can. Neither of you can say that the rainbow exists, as I do. The reason for this is because I make my rainbow. A rainbow is just the coming together of certain conditions at a certain place and time: water vapor, light, my eyes and consciousness. But the "rainbow" itself does not really exist. It does not have any existence independent of these conditions. Everyone sees an object and thinks, "Ah, there is a thing. That thing exists, so therefore I exist." This kind of view is complete delusion, and can be disproven through experience, as we have shown above. Buddhism teaches, rather, that if I "exist" then that thing "exists."

All things are like this. Everything is always changing, changing, changing, changing, nonstop. So if I am here, something is there. If I am not here, then that thing is not there. If I disappear, my world disappears. Yes, you still have "your" world; but "my" world disappears. We make our world: this is Buddhism's basic teaching. That is because I make my time, I make my space, and I make my cause and effect. And then all these things control us.

There is another way to consider this: A human being looks down on an ant hill. He sees many, many tiny ants running to and fro. They spend great effort carrying crumbs and sticks and pieces of leaves. So he thinks, "What a small world they have. They are very low-class." But they do not view it this way as they lumber under huge crumbs and leaves. They may believe that their ant-world is very big, and filled with large, heavy objects. Sometime you look at a drop of water. Inside this drop of water there are thousands and thousands of bacteria living and eating and growing and dying. That is a small world! But to a single bacterium, this same droplet-world that you look at is a very big world. That is *its* world. To a human being, it's a very small world. Then someone flies on a rocket around the earth. He looks down on the earth, and thinks, "How small it all is!" If you look out the window of an airplane you have the same thought. Standing on the ground, the world seems one size, and the skyscrapers tower above you. But when you go up very high, your world changes. The things which were so big to you while on the ground—mountains, trees, big rivers, buildings—suddenly seem insignificant from this vantage point. They do not have the same daunting effect on your mind from this point of view.

So you make your world. You make your time and your space. You also make the cause and effect that controls your life. All these things come from our minds. First, what is time? Past, present, and future do not exist. Where is the past? Where is the future? You cannot find them anywhere. Everybody knows this, and contents themselves with the belief that at least the present exists and is real. Yet if you even say that the present exists, it is just as great a delusion. Where is the present? Saying "present," it's already past. The moment you say that word—"Present!"—it has already become "past." Your thinking makes past, present, and future, so you have time.

You make time. And the time that you make is your time, not my time or anybody else's time. Let us say someone is waiting for his wife. They are supposed to meet at five PM, but it's already six-thirty and she hasn't arrived yet. If she is late, he will be at least a little angry with her. This is the view of "my" mind, "my" time. It may be that she is late because she is working on something in the office, and she is getting something done. "Her" time may be passing quickly, and she's not going to get angry. But while I am waiting in the car, "my" time is passing slowly, and "my" time is being wasted. "My" time is suffering-time, passing slowly. But "hers" may not be the same; she may be working hard, meeting a deadline, and that same period of time is actually passing *too* quickly for her to get it done. This is "my" mind. We make our time either good or bad, happy or sad. We make time with our thinking minds.

We make time either long or short. We make it good or bad. Here is another example: At eight o'clock, you go to a disco, and you are dancing with all your favorite friends. It's a wonderful party. Everybody is having a very good time. Then at one point you look at your watch: "Oh, it's already eleven-thirty! Almost time to go home! That's too bad!" Three or four hours pass like maybe one hour. But then on another occasion you go to the airport to pick up your girlfriend. You have not seen her for one month, and you are very, very excited. But this plane is one hour late. The minutes pass so slowly. It seems like a very, very long time. "Why is this plane not coming? I want to see her soon. But the airplane is not coming!" This one hour waiting for your girlfriend is a very, very long time, and it feels like one month or one year! Ah, suffering! [*Loud laughter*] But at the disco, dancing with your friends, the same exact measurement of time feels like it passes in five minutes. "Only one hour. That's too bad!" Ha ha ha ha! So your mind makes one hour either long or short. It all comes from your thinking: How do you keep your mind, right now? What kind of mind do you have?

Our thinking also makes space because originally space, too, simply does not exist. America is here, and Korea is over there. America has north, south, east, and west; Korea also has north, south, east and west. But America's north, south, east, and west are different from Korea's north, south, east, and west. "I am here. I have north, south, east, and west. When I disappear, where is my north, south, east, and west?" Does a dead man have north and south? There is nothing, yah? Ha ha ha ha! Also two men stand facing each other. One man lifts his right arm and points it straight at the wall to his side. "That's the right wall." But to the man facing him, that is the left wall! Which one is correct? If there are one hundred people in a big room, each facing a uniquely different direction, and each one does this, maybe you will have a problem. [*Laughter*] This is where all war and conflict come from. The reason for this is because everybody makes their "left" and "right," and everybody believes that their "left" is the correct one.

So as we see, we make our time and space, and we make our cause and effect, and all these then control our lives. But how does this connect with dependent origination? Time controls primary cause, while space controls condition and the inevitable result. Since time passes, our primary cause is always capable of changing, changing, changing. You can look at it like a cross: time is represented by a horizontal line that always intersects with space, represented by a vertical line. So our primary cause always intersects some condition, and we get some result. That is very easy to grasp. If you have some situation, that is also space. Your situation may mean your location, your room, your relationship, your house, your experience, your life. The primary cause in your mind intersects some condition or situation and produces a result: suffering.

This is why we say that you should not be attached to your situation or condition. If you hold your situation, and hold your condition, then primary cause cannot disappear: it is always inflamed by the appearance of some condition that you hold, and produces the same suffering nearly every single time. This suffering then makes the primary cause stronger. Time and space, primary cause and condition come together. That is something you make, and you cannot get out of it if you do not let go of your thinking. If someone is very attached to alcohol, for example, and if they are attached to some condition that lets them have alcohol, then they always get suffering. Whatever their conscious intentions might be, if this primary cause meets this condition, some kind of suffering will be produced, either now or later. Let us say that some woman has been hurt by men. That experience makes some cause in her mind. Then if she also strongly holds this experience, it becomes a kind of primary cause. Then she always thinks, "I am a woman. I was hurt. I don't like men." That is a condition. By holding this primary cause, and holding the condition or situation, many kinds of suffering will always appear in her life. Her primary cause always crosses this condition. Anywhere she goes, she will find this kind of suffering near at hand, in this life as well as the next. Reading even one hundred books won't make it disappear. Therapy won't take it away.

If you truly want to make your suffering disappear, you must not make time and space. Don't make cause and effect, and don't hold cause and effect. Put down your opinion, your condition, and your situation, and slowly, slowly, over time, primary cause goes down by itself. You make your world. But if you keep a don't-know mind—always and everywhere—then that is already beyond time and space. [*Hits the table.*] In this point, time and space cannot control you. Primary cause disappears, and you can use any condition or situation in your life only to help other beings. The name for that is freedom. Do you like that?

So Buddhism teaches that we must understand this whole world, just as it is. We must not be attached to our world, to our way of looking at things, which is limited by our ideas and opinions, condition and situation. The earth and moon revolve around the sun. That is a small world. In Sino-Korean, we call that *sok chon*, or "small heaven." But Buddhism teaches a very wide perspective. The name for that is *dae un gae*. One solar system is very large. But three thousand solar systems together are only considered a middle-sized galaxy. Then take three million galaxies, and what do you have? The universe seems so infinitely vast. So our human world is a very small world. There are millions and millions of galaxies in the universe. Buddhism teaches us to keep this kind of wide view. Then we will not be so tempted to hold on to the narrow view of this world that we create with our thinking. In that way, we will consider the ant worlds and bacteria worlds and animal worlds and plant worlds. Many people only live in a very, very small world, created by their petty opinions, their likes and dislikes. But the Buddha taught that we should keep our mind large and open and clear like space. Then we can always function compassionately for others. That is a very important point.

It is very easy to see how you make your world and whatever you experience in it. Yet some people say that God made this world. But who made God? Remember, everything comes from some primary cause—this is understood by enlightened wisdom. Then what is God's primary cause? Who made primary cause? Some people say that God understands everything. They say that God made Paradise and Eden and human beings. God also made the

Tree of the Knowledge of Good and Evil. Then he said, "If you eat these fruits, you will get sin and death." But if this is so, then God is certainly attached to something. "Maybe I will make this tree. Then when they eat the fruits, they will understand everything. But if they do that, I will have to give them death." If God truly loved human beings, he would have taken away the tree. That is God's big mistake. Why wouldn't he take it away? If you make some poison, put it in front of your child, and then tell your child not to eat it, who do you blame when your child eats it? Whose mistake is it? He made this tree. So the teachings of primary cause and dependent origination are very interesting. They simply and clearly point to, Who made this? Who made that? God made this tree, and whatever came from it, not Adam and Eve. So who made God who made the tree and all the suffering that came from it? If you want to understand who made God, here is a hint: Saying "God" is already a big mistake. If you open your mouth, primary cause appears. If you keep it shut, then primary cause disappears. It is very easy to see. Don't make God. Don't make Buddha. From moment to moment, don't make anything.

The Twelve Links in the Chain of Dependent Origination

十 二 緣 起 說

1. Ignorance

   無 明

2. Mental formations (karma)

   行

3. Consciousness

   識

4. Name and form

   名 色

5. The six senses

   六 入

6. Contact

   觸

7. Sensation

   受

8. Desire

   愛

9. Clinging

   取

10. Existence

    有

11. Life

    生

12. Old age, suffering, death

    老 死 憂 悲 苦 惱

THE BUDDHA SHOWED that there is a very clear chain of extremely subtle mental activities that always result in suffering. Each link is the effect of the previous link, and in turn conditions or creates the next link. When you practice meditation very strongly, you can perceive this chain appearing and disappearing in your mind from moment to moment. If you completely keep don't-know mind, however, the Chain of Dependent Origination never appears or disappears.

The chain begins with the appearance of a single thought in our minds: ignorance. *Ignorance* means not perceiving that this world is impermanent, believing that it is real or existent. It is a very simple point. When we don't realize this world's impermanence, we believe that our thinking and everything else is real and has some abiding, independent existence. Ignorance causes us to become attached to our thoughts, our desires, and the sensory life of our bodies, because ignorance is the subtle belief that all these "things" are real. This arising of ignorance leads to some idea, some *mental formation.* Another name for mental formations is karma, the habitual force that we have brought into this life from another. Through the habit-force of our mental formations, *consciousness* appears. It can be likened to a seed, the beginning of some aggregate thought that "I am." From this point, thinking and consciousness begin to create the realm of *name and form.* Once you have fostered this sense of "I am," you create ideas about the things that are not part of this "I." The *six senses* (eyes, ears, nose, tongue, body, and mind) begin here, and so then humans enter the realm of touch, or *contact* with things in the world of name and form. We experience these *sensations* made on the six sense organs through contact. From this point on, human consciousness is completely controlled by our habitual experience of the six senses. Because from sensation comes a desire for more sensation, and more sensation, there naturally arise *desire* and *clinging* to these sensations. "I liked that. I want more. I need more." This kind of mind appears. Now "I" has made name and form, and through the six senses has become attached to this world and its many sensations. Therefore the belief in some kind of *existence* follows. "I think, therefore I am." "I see, therefore I am." "I hear, therefore I am." If something exists, then something else must not exist. This means the creation of *life.* "I am alive. I am thirty years old." When our thinking makes life, it also makes *old age, suffering,* and, ultimately, *death.* That is our suffering world.

That is the Chain of Dependent Origination. The Buddha showed that to take away suffering means making each of these links disappear. It is very clear.

The Chain of Dependent Origination shows that I make my world. It all happens in an extremely short span of time. If ignorance appears in my mind, then life and death appear. I make my suffering. But where does ignorance come from? How do you not make ignorance? So, a long time ago a very famous Sri Lankan monk came to the Providence Zen Center to give a big lecture on Hinayana Buddhism. He spoke for two days about many subjects, and talked at length about the Twelve Links in the Chain of Dependent Origination. After he finished speaking, one student asked him, "You have just said that ignorance causes everything, including birth, old age, sickness, and death. My question to you is, when did ignorance appear? And why does it appear?"

The monk replied, "The Buddha taught that ignorance appears by itself."

But this did not satisfy the student, so he asked again, "But *how* does it appear 'by itself,' and why does it just appear by itself? If everything causes everything else, what causes ignorance?" Then the monk was stuck. He was thinking, thinking, thinking, but could not remember what the sutras said about this. He was completely stuck and could not answer. Ha ha ha ha ha! So that's a very important point: When does ignorance appear, and why? If you practice meditation with great determination, you will eventually understand that point.

So, when does ignorance appear? Do you understand? [*No response*] Don't know? Ha ha ha ha! The answer is very, very clear. I'll give you a hint: if you open your mouth, ignorance appears. If you ask, "Why does ignorance appear?" it also appears. You have a question, so ignorance appears. If you have no question, it never appears and never disappears. So you must understand this question. More practicing is necessary! [*Laughter*] Ha ha ha ha!

The Four Noble Truths

四 聖 諦

Suffering	→	All things are suffering
苦		一 切 皆 苦

Origination	→	The twelve links of dependent origination, in order
集		十 二 緣 起 順 觀

Stopping	→	The twelve links of dependent origination, in reverse order
滅		十 二 緣 起 逆 觀

The Path	→	The Eightfold Path
道		八 正 道

THE BUDDHA TAUGHT that this life is an ocean of suffering. In Sino-Korean, the term is *go hae*. Everything is impermanent, so everything is always changing, changing, changing. Because we attach to things, we constantly suffer, since despite however much we love things they must always change and disappear and return to emptiness. But human beings are very, very stupid. We don't understand this, so we don't understand why our lives are filled with so much suffering. This is why the Buddha taught the First Noble Truth, "All things are suffering."

Of course, many religions teach that this life has some suffering. But only the Buddha attained that this suffering is made entirely by our minds and it can be taken away the moment we gain true insight into the nature of our mind. We even make "mind." Yet where is your mind? Do you have one? What is this "I"? Nobody understands that point, so there is suffering. Human beings also make a great deal of suffering for other beings because humans do not understand their mind. The Buddha showed how this suffering appears out of ignorance. When ignorance appears in our minds, "I" appears, and then everything appears: life, death, good, bad, happiness, sadness, you, it, the sun, the moon, the stars. Everything is made entirely by our minds alone. This is the teaching of the Twelve Links in the Chain of Dependent Origination, which is the Second Noble Truth.

But how do we get out of this ocean of suffering? This was the Buddha's big question. As a young prince living in a beautiful palace, surrounded by wealth and luxury, he was filled with disgust at human suffering, and he vowed to answer this great question on his own. He gave up his wealth and power and practiced very hard for six years. "What is life? What is death? What is a human being? *What am I?* Don't know . . ." He finally attained enlightenment under the Bodhi tree. This means that the Buddha woke up to his true, original nature. We say he attained his mind. When the Buddha got enlightenment, he perceived that all beings were suffering very much. He saw that all this suffering comes from our minds. We *make* that. If we make this suffering, we can also take it away. When ignorance disappears, mental formations disappear. When mental formations disappear, consciousness disappears. When consciousness disappears, then name and form disappear. Eventually, life and death, old age and sickness also disappear, because these things, too, come from our mind. Seeing this is already attaining how to stop suffering: the Third Noble Truth. When he saw how these things appear, the Buddha also saw the path that leads to freedom from all this suffering. He saw how we can take it all away with some simple practices that apply to every aspect of our lives. That path is called the Eightfold Path. It is the Fourth Noble Truth. Let us look at it more closely.

The Eightfold Path
八 正 道

1. Right View
正見

2. Right Thought
正思惟

3. Right Speech
正語

4. Right Action
正業

5. Right Livelihood
正命

6. Right Effort
正精進

7. Right Mindfulness
正念

8. Right Meditation
正定

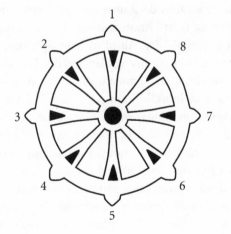

THE BUDDHA TAUGHT the Eightfold Path for taking away desire, anger, and ignorance and returning to our true nature. Our human consciousnes is very complicated, and it has many kinds of delusions. This Eightfold Path is like having eight different medicines for our mind's fundamental sicknesses. One medicine is Right View, sometimes called right understanding. Right View actually means holding no view. It means having no idea. Put down all your thinking and opinions and see this world exactly as it is. When we correctly perceive the nature of this world, we see that many billions of beings are going around and around and around the wheel of suffering. They cannot get out. We perceive that all beings suffer because they only follow their anger, ignorance, and desire. When we see that, we only want to help them. Everybody has lingering attachments, or karma. Having a Right View means understanding that actions based on desire, anger, or ignorance will always lead to suffering, both for us and for others. Everything is impermanent: why should we pursue the temporary feelings and desires that flit across our mind? So if we understand this, then when we are tempted to do something out of desire, anger, or ignorance, immediately we become aware of where this action will lead. "Why do I do something? Only for me, or for all beings?" This question makes our direction. When our direction is clear, our whole life is clear, and then any kind of action can benefit other beings. But whenever you do something for yourself alone—because of your own desire, anger, or ignorance—you cannot help yourself and you cannot help this world. When we want to do something, we should always be guided by this question: "Why do that?" Another name for that is Right View.

Right Thought is very similar. All of us have opinions, and we are often very attached to them. We have strong likes and dislikes. We are also attached to our condition and situation. "I am a woman." "I am a man." "I am a Zen Buddhist." "I believe in Jesus." "I am American." "I am Japanese." When we hold on to these conditions, we cannot completely connect with this world and all beings. We only see this small "I, my, me" world we have made, and we cannot help others. Right Thought means not becoming attached to any views, not holding our opinion and condition and situation, and only keeping a before-thinking mind that spontaneously wants to help all beings. Our Temple Rules have this point in mind when they say: "Do not cling to your opinions. Do not discuss your private views with others. To cling to and defend your opinions is to destroy your practice. Put away all your opinions. This is true Buddhism." These are very interesting words.

So I always say that if you are thinking, your mind and my mind are different. If you cut off all attachment to thinking, your mind and my mind are the same. Your before-thinking mind is your substance; my before-thinking mind is my substance. Then your substance, my substance, and this whole universe's substance are the same substance. But that point is before thinking. If you attain that before-thinking mind, your mind is clear like space. Then you perceive that you are the same as all beings, and true thinking can appear by itself. You no longer harbor thoughts of selfish desire, ill will or hatred. The name for this is wisdom. Another name is Right Thought.

Many people are attached to their tongue. This tongue is very interesting. We have two eyes, two ears, and two nostrils: Why do we only have one mouth and one tongue? This mouth has a very big job! It is always eating and talking, nonstop. It always desires some good feeling—from food or drink or from the pleasure of making lots and lots of speech. Most of our strongest attachments come from the desires of this tongue. Not so many attachments come from our ears or nostrils or eyes. Perhaps if we had another mouth and tongue, our life would be much easier, because then this one mouth and tongue wouldn't feel they always have to do so many things all the time. But this one tongue already causes many, many problems for this world, so actually we are lucky not to have another one. In fact, you could say that, of our five primary senses (eyes, ears, nose, tongue, and sense of touch), when we are not careful this tongue causes the most suffering for ourselves and for this world. That is why all religions teach that we must control this tongue and all its desires.

In Zen we sometimes say, "The tongue has no bone." This is because the tongue can say one thing in one sentence, and in the next breath say an entirely different thing. The tongue can make anything. This is the source of all lies and gossip. By itself, the tongue has no direction, so it has no bone. An eminent teacher said, "Your evil tongue will lead you to ruin. You must keep the stopper in the bottle. Only open it when necessary." This is our temple rule. And in the Bible, Jesus taught that it is actually not the things that go into our mouth that cause impurity and suffering. Rather, what comes out of our mouths brings suffering to this whole world. Right Speech means from moment to moment being careful about what this tongue does. It means using your tongue to help people with clear, compassionate speech. If you put down your opinions and condition, and don't make anything in your mind, then Right Speech appears by itself.

Action comes from our mind and returns to our mind. Whatever we do in the world is a reflection of our thinking. The Buddha had very clear teachings for how we could help this world with Right Action. This is sometimes called the path of precepts. He taught that we should not take any life, or lie, or steal, or have illegitimate sexual relations, or take intoxicants to produce heedlessness. Whenever we do something, if we are thinking, that action becomes karma. We create a kind of mental habit for that action. If we don't do good things, we naturally make bad karma. But if we only try to do good things for other people, then we make bodhisattva karma. This is action that only tries to serve other people. Right Action means always being aware of how our actions affect other beings, because that also affects our mind. This is why Right Action is sometimes translated as "right karma."

Right Livelihood is very interesting. We say that everyone has two jobs. Our inside work is keeping clear mind. Our outside work is cutting off selfish desires and helping others. Saying this is one thing, yet how do we actually do it? We all have some job. Some person's job is to go and work in an office to make money; another person's job is to live in a temple and teach other people. But how does this outside job help other beings? Is this work done only for me, only for my family, or for all beings? It is certainly true that in this world, everyone has to make money. But many people's work entails killing many animals, or polluting the air and water. This is not so good. Selling alcohol, drugs, explosives, or guns to other people only makes more and more bad karma for you. It cannot help this world at all. Even if you are doing this to make money to help your family, in the end you will only add suffering to this world, just in order to get money. How can you ever become a buddha that way? Be careful: In this world cause and effect are always very, very clear! So the Buddha taught that we must have jobs that don't hurt this world. As I said before, the most important thing is, "Why do that?" If you ask this question, then your Right Livelihood becomes very clear.

Right Effort means always trying hard in your meditation practice. Sick or healthy, busy or free, tired or rested—it does not matter. Only try, try, try, for ten thousand years, nonstop. Only do it. That is all!

Then how do you keep your mind, right now? Just as a ray continues out from one point to another to make a straight line, how you keep your mind in this very moment makes your whole life. Many people only follow their thinking, their desire, anger, and ignorance. So they get suffering in situation after situation. But if you wake up, right now, you get happiness. Which one do you like? The name for this "wakeup" is sometimes called paying attention. The Buddha called it Right Mindfulness.

Finally, the Buddha taught that correct meditation is the most important thing you can do to wake up. Right Meditation means from moment to moment keeping a not-moving mind. In any situation and any condition, keep a mind that is clear like space, yet that functions as meticulously as the tip of a needle. Some people think the point of meditation is just to experience some kind of "peace mind." They only like stillness and quiet. Our first Zen center in America was located in Providence, Rhode Island. After some time, a rock-and-roll band moved into the apartment directly beneath the meditation room. They were very, very loud! Their daily practice upset many Zen students. "Zen Master, their music is so loud. It's disturbing my meditation! Can't we ask them to stop?" But these rock-and-roll musicians were great bodhisattvas. I said to my students, "You don't worry about them, OK? Finding quiet in the quiet is not true quiet. Quiet in the noisy is true quiet." Yes, having a quiet place to meditate is desirable. But we shouldn't become attached to a quiet experience alone, because life is not always like this. If your mind is not moving, then even Forty-second Street in New York City could be a wonderful Zen center.

There are also people who think that correct meditation just has to do with doing very hard sitting meditation practice. But doing this alone is not complete meditation practice. This kind of thinking is attachment to body-sitting. True meditation means correct mind-sitting: regardless of condition or situation, how do you keep your *mind*, right now? That makes your life. If your mind is clear, the whole universe is clear. If your mind is not clear, the whole universe is not clear. That is a very important point. So doing strong meditation is important. Having a good sitting practice is very, very important. But the most important point of all this is cutting off all attachment to thinking and returning to your before-thinking mind. "What am I? Only don't *know* . . ." Can you do that in every condition and situation, off the cushion as well as on it? If you can do this while driving, that is driving meditation. If you do it while eating, that is eating meditation. If you can do it while cleaning your house, that is working meditation.

Of course, to train your mind to do this, some kind of formal practice is necessary. When you are sitting, you cross your legs and straighten your back. If you cannot maintain this sitting posture, that should not prevent you from practicing. We had one student several years ago who did a whole ninety-day meditation retreat at the Providence Zen Center lying on his back because of chronic back and leg problems. While everyone else was facing the wall, he was facing the ceiling! He was able to sit up long enough to do formal meals and a few chants. He was also able to sit up for the length of an interview with the teacher. But for the rest of the day, he only lay down. An eminent teacher said, "When walking, standing, sitting, lying down, speaking, being silent, moving, being still—at all times, in all places, without interruption, what is this?" These are very important words. True meditation practice is certainly not dependent on being able to maintain some formal sitting posture for great lengths of time. It means just keeping a great question: only "What am I?"

It is also good to control your breathing. Breathe in slowly, and breathe out slowly. Your exhalation should be a little more than twice as long as the inhalation. If you breathe in and out very slowly, you can more easily cut off all thinking and not be attached to the coming and going of your mind. Over time your energy comes down, down, down into your center, and you can better control your feelings and your emotions. Through all of this, however, it is important to emphasize that true meditation is not some bodily posture. It is how you keep your mind, from moment to moment, in the midst of any daily activity.

The Three Seals of Existence

三　法　印　法

All compounded things are impermanent.

諸　行　無　常　印

All Dharmas are without self-nature.

諸　法　無　我　印

Nirvana is perfect stillness.

涅　槃　寂　靜　印

FOR HUNDREDS OF CENTURIES, people in China, Korea, and Japan have marked all their official documents with a red-ink seal. A carved stamper is pressed on a lump of red ink and stamped on the document. This declares the document to be genuine, an original. If you practice the teachings of Hinayana Buddhism, your consciousness is "marked" with three fundamental experiences. In Sino-Korean, these are called the *sam boep in do*. This can be translated as "the teaching of the three dharma seals."

We have already spoken about this first seal: "All compounded things are impermanent." Everything in this universe is always changing. Everything arises from conditions, remains for some period, and returns to emptiness. If you attain this point, you will not be so easily attached to things, so you will not suffer. Then you can find the one thing that never changes, the thing that never comes or goes. This "not-changing thing" is your true nature; it is not even a "thing." To truly experience this you must first attain that all things, all experiences, and all aspects of mind arise from conditions and are impermanent. When you attain this point, then—*BOOM!*—this realization indelibly marks your consciousness like a seal. If you have this experience even once, very deeply, you never forget it.

When you attain this world's impermanence, you attain that "All Dharmas are without self-nature." All Dharmas, all laws, principles, ideas, beliefs, human beings, dogs, cats, trees, mountains, and everything in the universe have no self-nature. The name and form of all things are constantly changing, changing, changing. Everything appears out of emptiness and eventually returns to emptiness. Nothing stays forever, because nothing has any kind of "thing" that we can call a self, a lasting nature. The attainment of this view is another seal that marks your consciousness.

Attaining that everything is impermanent, you don't hold on to anything, because you understand very deeply that everything eventually disappears. Realizing that all things are without self-nature, you are not taken in by names and forms. You do not follow the mistaken view that things and their myriad appearances actually exist. You realize that names and forms are just temporary appearances. That leads you to the last seal: "Nirvana is perfect stillness." If you attain these first two points, you can then realize that this world is already completely empty and still. Nothing ever comes or goes. God, Buddha, nature, substance, mind—where do they all come from? Do you understand that point? Buddhism shows how all Dharmas, all laws and principles come from complete stillness. Nirvana is simply a name for this state of perfect stillness. Everything appears out of complete stillness and extinction and everything eventually returns to emptiness and extinction. To realize this is to be marked with the last seal: "Nirvana is perfect stillness." The nature of all things is perfect stillness.

So if you attain these seals, you attain complete stillness. The Bible says, "Be still and know that I am God." Buddhism teaches, "All Dharmas come from complete stillness." If you want to find God, if you want to find Buddha, if you want to find mind, or consciousness, or true self, or the Absolute, you must attain this point of complete stillness and extinction. This stillness is true emptiness: it is the nature of our minds and this whole universe. A poem by the seventeenth-century Catholic mystic Angelus Silesius says:

> The God who is pure emptiness
> Is created as form.
> Becoming substance, light and darkness,
> The stillness and the storm.

That is the same point; only the names are different. Originally this point has no name and no form. Name and form are opposites thinking. But in true emptiness there are no opposites. There is no coming or going. That is our true self, our nature, universal nature. Another name for it is nirvana. So Hinayana Buddhism means practicing hard to attain this nirvana point, the place of complete stillness and extinction that has no birth or death. Attaining that is the purpose of Hinayana Buddhist teaching.

Three Kinds of Practice

三　學

1. *Sila*—Precepts

戒

2. *Samadhi*—Meditation

定

3. *Prajna*—Wisdom

慧

I F YOU WANT TO BE marked with these three seals of Hinayana Bud-dhism, it is important to do three kinds of practice. These three kinds of practice function together to help you attain your originally pure mind. Each of these three practices comprises a corresponding group of practices from the Eightfold Path.

Hinayana practice stresses the importance of keeping the Buddha's precepts. We keep the precepts because our backseat driver is always trying to control us. We think, "I want only to go straight and find my true self. I want to follow the Buddha's teaching and help all beings." But though we may make some effort, there is a backseat driver in our mind, and he is always saying, "You do this, and this, and this. Go that way, then turn there." Even though you don't want to go in that direction, the backseat driver is very strong. It is very hard not to listen to him! So keeping the precepts means turning around and shouting, "You shut up, OK? I must go *this* way!" Precepts help you cut off your backseat driver so that you can get to a good place. If you only follow your backseat driver, you cannot find your way, and you cannot find your true direction.

Precepts are very important for your practice. They are like having these very clear signs on the road. Let us say that you want to drive from New York to Los Angeles. Along the way, there are many, many road signs indicating which highway to take and where to turn. But you are not checking the signs. You are only following your own idea. "I am free! I don't care about these signs. I already understand how to get there." So you ignore the signs. Then finally one day you arrive, and get out of your car. "Ah, palm trees! Los Angeles!" Then someone says, "No, this is Miami, OK?" Ha ha ha ha! [*Loud, sustained laughter from the assembly*] This is why precepts are so important. Precepts mean clear directions for leading a correct, compassionate life. Precepts mean Dharma, and Dharma means the correct way of this universe. And having a correct way means living a clear life. So precepts are very important. The precepts represent the practices of Right Speech, Right Action, and Right Livelihood.

When you keep the precepts, you can control your condition and feelings, and then you can control your understanding. If you cannot control your feelings, then you cannot control your understanding, and suffering always appears. It is very, very clear. But why is it necessary to control your understanding? To some people that sounds a little too strong, so I will explain. Our desire comes from our intellectual minds. All thinking is desire, and desire leads directly to suffering. Our emotional mind makes strong likes and dislikes. Your understanding is always checking this world, and holding its opinions. Also, if your understanding is too great, you will have too many desires because you will have too much complicated thinking. Then your emotions attach strong likes and dislikes to the things your understanding makes. As a result your mind is always moving, moving, moving. It is constantly being pulled hither and thither by the strong feelings you have and what you like and dislike about other people and this whole world. It is very, very difficult to keep your center strong while having all these strong desires and feelings and likes and dislikes constantly pulling you around. So that is why we have precepts: these are natural rules for controlling your desire-mind. When you practice the precepts, your center becomes stronger by natural process. You can perceive this world, just as it is, and then it is possible to help other beings.

Correct meditation means keeping a not-moving mind, always and everywhere. If your mind is not moving, then when you see, when you hear, when you smell, when you taste, when you touch, and when you think, everything—just like this—is the truth. The word *samadhi* just means deep meditation. But we shouldn't become attached to any ideas about meditation. Many people think that true meditation means some intense absorption in sitting meditation. That kind of meditation is not good, not bad. But many people only want to hold this good feeling that meditation brings. There are many, many people who believe that meditation is only about having some kind of stillness and bliss all the time. "Oh, now everything is peaceful and still. Wonderful!" This kind of thinking is a very bad sickness. It is not true meditation, because it becomes attached to some kind of situation. If you become attached to this kind of practice, your wisdom cannot grow up. Your meditation cannot function clearly in many different situations to help other beings. Meditation represents the practices of Right Effort, Right Mindfulness, and Right Meditation in the Eightfold Path.

So, experiencing some kind of deep meditation practice is good. But a much more important training is keeping this mind when driving, eating, talking, working, and being with your family. I had one student who only wanted to do deep, quiet meditation. We call this having peace mind. If a car drove by the meditation room, he did not like it. If some children were playing outside, he would get angry and shut the window, because it disturbed his peaceful experience. "Be quiet or go away! I am meditating, can't you see?" His family had to keep very quiet during his special meditation periods at home. After a while, they came to resent meditation practice and Buddhism. This man's practice was not true meditation. This is making meditation "special." But if you can keep a not-moving mind while engaged in everyday activities, that is true meditation. That is true samadhi. It is the true nature of this practice.

Lastly, what is the correct function of meditation? Many people understand many different things. This understanding is only somebody else's idea. The sky never said, "I am blue." But yet you say, "The sky is blue." Somebody once taught you that the sky is blue, so ever since then, you have said, "The sky is blue." "The sky is blue." "The sky is blue." This is just understanding. It is somebody else's idea, not yours. Korean people never say, "The sky is blue." They say, "*Hannulun purumnida.*" Japanese people say, "*Sora wa aoidesu.*" Polish people have a Polish idea, and Russian people have a Russian idea. But none of these ideas is the true idea, because the sky never said any of these things. It never once said, "I am the sky and I am blue." The most important thing is that you must find this universe's original way. That way has no speech or idea.

So if you want to understand yourself, you must perceive this world just as it is. If your mind is not moving, then you can perceive this world's true nature. When you see, when you hear, when you smell, when you taste, when you touch, when you think, everything is the truth. Then when you see the tree, only green. When you hear a dog barking, only "Woof! Woof!" When you taste sugar, there is only sweetness. Everything is already truth. The universe is always teaching us truth at every moment. It is always giving us a wonderful Dharma speech. Simply keep a not-moving mind, and this truth instantly becomes yours. This is Right Understanding and Right Thoughts. The name for that is "wisdom." In Sanskrit, the term is *prajna*.

The goal of Hinayana practice is, as we said before, to attain nirvana. You attain that everything is completely empty, and this emptiness is itself the true nature of this world, the universe, and all of our minds. But what is the correct *function* of truth? How do we *use* truth to help this suffering world? That is the teaching of Mahayana Buddhism and Zen.

Let us now turn to consider the view of Mahayana Buddhism.

3
Mahayana Buddhism

大亲 佛教

1. Insight into the existence and nonexistence of the Dharmas

法体 有 空 観

2. Insight into the fact that there are no external tangible characteristics and that all is emptiness

無 相 皆 空 観

3. Insight into existence, emptiness, and the Middle Way

有 空 中 道 観

4. Insight into the true aspect of all phenomena

諸 法 實 相 観

5. Insight into the mutual interpenetration of all phenomena

事 々 無 礙 観

6. Insight which sees that phenomena themselves are the Absolute

即 事 而 真 観

MAHAYANA BUDDHISM's teaching is a little different from Hinayana Buddhism. We talked about this before. Some people say that Hinayana Buddhism was the Buddha's first teaching to sentient beings in this world. For six years he did hard training, and got enlightenment under the Bodhi tree. Then the sutras say that the Buddha doubted if others would understand this teaching. He thought about not teaching, because this was a very high-class realization that he had attained. Perhaps it would be too hard for people to grasp. Also at that time in India there were many different kinds of religions: there were many forms of Hinduism and yoga. There were many teachers, and many, many kinds of teaching, and all of them claimed to be the correct teaching. "My teaching is correct! Your teaching is not correct!" Many people taught like this. Who would believe this deep insight he had, which does not depend on a god or guru or anything else outside our own minds? One legend says that Brahma appeared to the Buddha and said, "Some people only have a little ignorance. They will understand you. You must teach for them." So the Buddha got up from the Bodhi tree and started to teach.

However, it is said by many that the Buddha began his teaching with what is recorded in the *Avatamsaka-sutra,* one of the main sutras of the Mahayana tradition. But no one could fathom this extremely wide view. Because this insight was so deep, and so different from anything that had ever been taught before, the Buddha had to give very, very simple teaching instead. He had to prepare his students' minds for this great view. He talked about ignorance, and desire, and suffering, and how to get out of them. "First you must perceive that this is a suffering world. Where does this suffering come from? You must attain this world's impermanence, and attain insight into impurity and nonself." He taught the path to these basic insights. He taught about attaining nirvana. "If you do good actions and avoid bad actions, you can get happiness. You must also attain these basic insights. You must only keep these precepts, all the time. Then you can attain your pure mind. You can take away your own suffering and find a good way to a place of complete stillness and bliss." This was the Buddha's first complete teaching. The name for it is Hinayana Buddhism. According to the Mahayana view, the Hinayana teaching was given because few could yet grasp the insight we find in the *Avatamsaka-sutra.*

Then what is Mahayana Buddhist teaching? As we said, Hinayana Buddhism teaches first that this whole world is a suffering realm. The way to get out of this suffering realm is to attain complete emptiness, or nirvana. This is the end point of the teaching. But even during his life, as his students' practice matured under this basic teaching, the Buddha started to teach Mahayana Buddhism. This kind of teaching does not place such great emphasis on suffering. It does not concern itself so much with whether things are pure or impure, or good or bad. Rather, the Mahayana view shows what we can do with this suffering to take away all beings' suffering. What is our correct *function* in this world? Mahayana Buddhism begins by showing that this world is completely empty. Human beings have no meaning but what they make. Everything is created by the mind alone. It also demonstrates how name and form are always changing, changing, changing, but behind it all, originally everything is fundamentally empty. If you attain this emptiness, then your suffering will disappear, because suffering is also empty. This is a way of showing that originally there is no suffering! That is very interesting teaching, yah? So, Mahayana Buddhist teaching *begins* at this point of complete emptiness; Hinayana Buddhist teaching culminates in it. Only teaching that this world is a suffering realm is not complete teaching, according to the Mahayana view.

Most importantly, Mahayana teaching declares that this whole practice is not only for me, to save myself. "How can I save all sentient beings from suffering?" To practice the Mahayana means vowing not to enter the infinite stillness, extinction, and bliss of nirvana until the last sentient being is saved from suffering. The name for this path is the Great Bodhisattva Way. My life is not for me, but only for all beings. So we sometimes say that Hinayana Buddhist teaching is like a bicycle: if you ride it correctly, only one person arrives in nirvana. But Mahayana Buddhism is like taking a bus or train. Not only me, but all beings arrive together at a good place. The Buddha started to give this teaching at first, but then he saw that everyone could not understand it. This teaching was far too advanced a view for their consciousnesses at the time. So that is why he had to step back and first teach a simpler path, or Hinayana Buddhism. That is also a very important point.

As their practice matured, and their minds ripened, the Buddha taught his students the Big View. It has six main teaching points.

Insight into the existence and nonexistence of the Dharmas

Mahayana Buddhist teaching has a very clear path. It begins with the insight that originally everything is fundamentally empty. When you truly perceive this, you can perceive your true nature. Then helping all beings is possible. The first step toward this attainment is perceiving that all Dharmas do not exist. What does this mean? You must perceive that all substance is empty. Your substance and universal substance are the same substance, and this substance is without self-nature. It has nothing. But everybody is attached to their bodies more than anything else, so we cannot see this point. In China, they used to teach a kind of practice called "insight into your body as a corpse." When you practice in this way, you can see the true nature of all the desire and attachment that this body inspires in our minds. One Zen master used to always ask his students, "Why are you dragging this corpse around?" That is because this body is not "I." It is not your real self. This body is completely empty. It is always changing and eventually disappears. So you must keep this kind of mind: "I am a corpse. I am a corpse. I am a corpse." Ha ha ha ha! If you keep this kind of mind, then you can attain that your body is empty and everything is empty. You cannot even keep this body—sometime it will disappear. It has no fundamental existence. How can you hold your body? So we sometimes say, "You are already dead!" If you are a corpse, then everything is no problem! Nothing can hinder you, because everyone knows that a corpse is empty. "A dead man has no desires." That saying teaches the same point.

All substance is also like this: everything in the whole universe is the same substance, and this substance is empty. It cannot *do* anything. If you attain that, you attain that substance can actually do everything. This is insight into the existence and nonexistence of the Dharmas. You begin to attain the correct function of substance. This is a very important insight to attain.

Insight into the fact that there are no external tangible characteristics, and that all is emptiness

This may seem like a very complicated statement, but its teaching point is very clear: it means having insight into the true nature of all names and forms. You must perceive that all names and forms are also fundamentally empty. Name and form do not exist—they are created entirely by mind alone, so they are empty. Human beings make names and forms for everything, and they believe that these things exist. So they inevitably have suffering when these names and forms change. The sun, the moon, the stars, mountains, rivers, and trees—all these are just temporary names and forms that we give to things. In the previous insight, we are shown the view that all substance is empty. That is Mahayana Buddhism's first course. But this insight is our second course. It shows that you must perceive that the names and forms of this universal substance are also completely empty.

Insight into existence, emptiness, and the Middle Way

If you perceive that everything is empty, that view is already the Middle Way. The Middle Way means there is no good and no bad. There is no high and no low, no coming or going, no birth or death. The Middle Way is simply another name for the path of emptiness. This emptiness is the complete way, because it points to the fact that everything is empty, and this emptiness is itself the Absolute. The Absolute is always complete. Our thinking makes good and bad, and high and low, and coming and going, and birth and death. Our conceptual thinking makes "I am." This is our fundamental delusion. Thinking makes "I," so it also makes "I am not." If we have these things, we believe that we are not complete. When we are not complete, we get suffering, and we make suffering for all other beings. But originally these things do not exist. They cannot hinder you at all. Everything is not moving! Nothing is ever born or dies. Nothing ever comes or goes. Everything is completely empty, which means that everything is already complete. If you attain emptiness, you attain the complete way, the Middle Way.

Insight into the true aspect of all phenomena

When you attain that everything is empty, you can perceive that this emptiness is itself the Absolute. Emptiness is the fundamental truth of this whole universe. This is "the true aspect of all phenomena." It is the complete way. There are no opposites, because opposites come only from thinking. When our deluded clinging to opposites disappears, then the Absolute appears clearly right in front of us. That is another word for "complete world." As we said before, everything is empty, so everything is the Absolute, therefore everything is complete. If you attain this completeness, then when you see, when you hear, when you smell, when you taste, when you touch, and when you think, everything is the truth. The Sino-Korean characters we use are *shil sang*, or "truth." The true aspect of all things is emptiness. Then everything is truth. The sun, the moon, the stars, the mountains, rivers, and trees are all the truth, just as they are. With this view, name and form are also truth. What is not truth? Hinayana Buddhism teaches that everything is impermanent, so it cannot be true because it is always changing, changing, changing. Everything always deceives you. This is an important point.

But this fourth insight of Mahayana Buddhism teaches that if you completely attain the emptiness of this whole universe, then you can take one more step. You perceive that everything is already the truth just as it is. This is the true aspect of all phenomena. The wall is white: that is truth. The tree is green: that is truth. A dog is barking outside: that is truth. One man hits another man on the street: that is truth. It is now seven-fifteen PM: that is truth. But few people can perceive that these ordinary, everyday views are truth, because they make good and bad, and they believe that this thinking about good and bad actually exists. This is why the Buddha had to teach something simple at first before he could teach the Great Bodhisattva Way of Mahayana. Hinayana Buddhism's main teaching is that everything is impermanent. That is correct. Everything is suffering. That is correct. Everything is nonself. That is also correct. But everything is empty. Everything is the Absolute. Everything is complete. So everything, just as it is, is truth. Someone is suffering right now. That is the truth. How is that *not* truth? This point is like a Ph.D.-level course: substance and name and form and everything are completely empty—that is the Absolute, which means that everything is already the truth. It is very simple, but no one can see that. Ha ha ha ha! But how do we make this truth *function* correctly to help all beings? That is a little more difficult. Maybe finding that is Zen's job. Ha ha ha!

Insight into the mutual interpenetration of all phenomena

Everything is already truth, so everything coexists with no hindrance. For example, here is space. Clouds are constantly coming and going. Rain comes, and rain goes. Lightning comes and goes. Wind comes and goes, back and forth, back and forth, back and forth. Storms appear and disappear all the time. But though these things ceaselessly come and go in space, space is not hindered by them in the least, because space is complete emptiness. Clouds and rain and wind and sun and night and day are not hindered by one another. Your mind is exactly the same. If you practice meditation with great determination, you can completely attain the fundamental emptiness of this universe. Then when feelings come and go, and thinking comes and goes, and good situations come and go, and bad situations appear and disappear, nothing can hinder you at all. Everything is empty! When happiness appears, you can use that for other beings. When suffering appears, you can use suffering to help other beings. You can use good situations and bad situations, good experiences and bad experiences, only to help all beings get out of suffering, because all these "things" are completely empty, and this emptiness is our originally compassionate nature.

You know from your experience that if you hold something in your mind, you always have suffering. But if you don't hold any empty thing that appears and disappears in your mind, then any feeling, any thinking, any situation, any problem cannot touch you. Your thinking is truth. Your happiness is truth; your sadness is truth. A bad situation is truth. A good situation in your life is also truth. Everything is the same emptiness, and so everything is truth, just as it is. What is not truth? Can you find that thing? Please show it to me! That is very interesting, yah?

Insight which sees that phenomena themselves are the Absolute

We are already living in a truth-world. All things are empty, and this emptiness is all things, so everything is already the complete way. If you just understand this point, intellectually or academically, it cannot help you. Some attainment is necessary. You must actually *attain* that all things are the Absolute, just as they are. You must *attain* that everything is no hindrance, and then your action, from moment to moment, is Great Love and Great Compassion for all beings. It is possible to live this way for others because there is no "I." So there is also no thinking, since thinking is no-thinking. Suffering is no-suffering. Everything is empty, so helping other people is possible. Nothing can hinder you. At that point, your moment-to-moment job becomes clear: every one of your actions is the truth, and it completely connects with the suffering of all beings. "How can I help? How can I help?" This is our human job. That is the truth. That is the complete way, the true way, the big way. Compassionate action is not some idea or action: it is universal substance itself. Another name for that is bodhisattva: these actions are not for me, because I have perceived that there is no I or even any actions. All beings and I are not separate. Their suffering is my suffering: the same substance. Their happiness is my happiness. So I can only function for all beings. In Sino-Korean, this is called *dae ja, dae bi shim,* Great Love and Great Compassion mind. This is the way of the Absolute.

So Mahayana Buddhism has six kinds of insight. First, you must attain that everything is the same universal substance, and this substance is fundamentally empty, at its origin. Then you must attain that the myriad names and forms for this universal substance are also completely empty, and have no self-nature, and no true meaning. Next, if you truly attain this, you attain that this emptiness of all things *is* the Middle Way, the true way, and the correct way. From this point, you can perceive that any Dharma and any name and form is therefore the truth, so then you can see that nothing can hinder you. When you attain this no-hindrance mind, all your actions are bodhisattva actions, because all your actions are truth. All your actions function to connect with this universal substance that you share with all beings and all things. Once you attain this no-hindrance mind, there is no longer any "I" that is separate from "you," so all your actions are already Great Love and Great Compassion.

Once a student asked me, "The first two of Mahayana Buddhism's Six Insights say that everything is emptiness. But the fourth one says that everything is truth. How can everything be truth if everything is emptiness?" This is a very good question because it goes right to the heart of the most important teaching point in Buddhism. The answer to this question is very easy. Go home and check the mirror in your bathroom. The mirror has nothing in it. It is completely empty. But if you hold a red ball in front of it, a red ball appears. If you hold a white one before it, a white one appears. When a mountain comes, it reflects mountain. In that moment it does not reflect water, or a tree, or a human face. It simply reflects the mountain, exactly as it is. If you take the red ball away from the mirror, the mirror no longer reflects the red ball. It does not hold something after you have taken it away from the front of the mirror. The images only stay in the mirror while you hold them. Otherwise the clear mirror is always completely empty, and it does not hold anything. Then anything is reflected with no hindrance. Everything can come and go, come and go, come and go in front of this empty space and is reflected, just as it is, with no hindrance. Nothing is added or left out. The sky is blue. The tree is green. The wall is white. That is truth. The mirror and everything it reflects are completely empty, and yet they are also truth. Everybody can understand this quite easily.

But our human minds are usually not like this mirror: If we hold red in front of our mind, we may reflect red. But then if we take it away, and hold white there, this mind-mirror is usually still thinking about "red." It is thinking how much it likes white better than red, or wondering when will be the next time it will have to look at red again, or thinking about what red reminds it of. All these other mind-objects appear in our mind-mirror at the same time as this red ball is being held in front of it. Only sometimes do we simply see the red ball, just as it is. If you take away the red and put white there, our mind-mirror reflects things like, "Oh, maybe I like red better. This white is not so good. I want more red. Oh, maybe white is also OK. I don't know . . ." Our mind-mirror starts to remember other red things it has seen. You are standing there, holding something white, but usually the mind won't reflect it as it is, because it is still holding something about this red thing. This is why we cannot function compassionately for this world: because we do not always reflect this world, just as it is. We have incredibly strong desires. We hold our likes and dislikes instead of just perceiving this world's truth and using that truth to function compassionately for all beings, from moment to moment. That is a very important point.

The teaching of Mahayana Buddhism is that you are a bodhisattva. A bodhisattva is a being whose life is only for all beings because the bodhisattva has attained this view: everything is completely empty, so everything is the same. With this view, compassion appears by itself. "All beings are not different from me." In the morning, we vow, "Sentient beings are numberless; we vow to save them all." This vow is very important, because it means that my life is not for me. These words show that you can just *do* it. "I will not enter nirvana until every sentient being is saved from suffering." When "I" appears, then a human being appears, and he believes himself separate from all other beings. But if "I" disappears, then "I" never exists at all. Hinayana Buddhism teaches that this "I" is nonself. Mahayana Buddhism teaches the same point, but from a different perspective, so it has a slightly different function in the end: the Mahayana way begins with the point of emptiness where Hinayana teaching leaves off.

Instead of stopping here, Mahayana Buddhist teaching takes this experience of emptiness and reveals the ultimate truth of the world, just as it is. This world is completely empty, so "I" is also empty. Substance, name, and form are empty. Because everything is empty, this emptiness is truth itself. That is the teaching of the Middle Way. Everything is already truth; everything is already complete. When you attain this fundamental truth of all things through meditation, nothing can ever hinder your effort to save all beings from suffering. With no hindrance in your mind, compassionate bodhisattva action appears by itself, which means that you are already a bodhisattva. There is nothing to "get to." As the *Heart Sutra* says, "There is no attainment, with nothing to attain." From moment to moment your actions only help all beings.

The Diamond Sutra

金剛経

All appearance is delusion.

凡所有相　皆是虛妄

If you view all appearance as nonappearance,

若見諸相　非相

Then that view is your true nature.

即見如來

Do not become attached to any thoughts that arise in the mind.

應無所住　而生其心

If you see form as the Absolute, if you search out the Absolute with your voice,

若人色見我　以音声求我

You are practicing the wrong path, and you cannot see your true self.

是人行邪道　不能見如來

All compounded things are like a dream, a phantom, a bubble, or a reflection.

一切有為法　如夢幻泡影

They are like dew or lightning. Thus should you view them.

如露亦如電　應作如是觀

THE *DIAMOND SUTRA* is one of the most important teachings ever given. Though it can be read in less than an hour, it represents the core of the Buddha's teaching. Its most important teaching point is that everything is impermanent and completely empty. Name and form are also completely empty. It talks about matters that both Hinayana Buddhism and Mahayana Buddhism address, so reading the *Diamond Sutra* is like walking across a bridge from Hinayana teaching to the view of the Mahayana. It contains the view of both traditions, yet it emphasizes the direction of the bodhisattva way.

All appearance is delusion. If you view all appearance as nonappearance, then that view is your true nature.

This is a very important line. It is one of the most important lines in the *Diamond Sutra* and one of the most well-known Buddhist teachings. All appearance is constantly appearing and disappearing. So, everything that you see is impermanent. Everything that you hear, smell, taste, and touch is also impermanent. Finally, you, too, are impermanent! This is teaching that is central to Hinayana Buddhism.

But this teaching is also somewhat curious. Nearly every translation of this sutra says that if you view all appearance as nonappearance, then you will see your true nature, your true self, the Tathagata. There is the sense here that some "subject" views an "object." But if everything that you can see, hear, smell, taste, and touch is impermanent, and you are also impermanent, how can impermanence see impermanence? You are impermanent: then how can this impermanence *see* impermanence? *What* sees *what*? More importantly, if you are impermanent, and you perceive impermanence, how can you possibly see your true nature? Our true nature is never moving, and it never comes or goes. But if impermanence sees impermanence, how can that see our true nature, this not-moving "thing" that is beyond impermanence? This statement in the sutra is not very clear. If you are impermanent, you do not exist. What you are composed of is always changing and moving, nonstop—there is no thing that permanently "exists." So how can that moving thing "see" your not-moving true nature? What is there that perceives our true self? If you read any translation of the *Diamond Sutra*, it has words to this effect. The teaching in these words is not very clear, and not correct teaching. It is very confusing.

It is important to retranslate this sutra, otherwise its point is not clear because of the technical language. If you correct the way this sutra is always translated, then its point becomes clear: So we say, "All appearance is delusion. If you view all appearance as nonappearance, this view is your true self." That is a little different. On the one hand, "If you view all appearance as nonappearance, then you will see your true nature." Some impermanent "thing" sees some not-moving "thing." This has the distinct sense of there being some subject and object. On the other hand, it would be much clearer if we said, "If you view all appearance as nonappearance, this view is your true nature." That view. That *view*—the perception itself, the *perceiving*—is your true nature. What kind of view are we talking about? Seeing all appearance as nonappearance is itself your true nature. Perceiving *is* your true nature. You can *see* this world. You can hear this world. You can smell this world. Just seeing, just hearing, just smelling, just tasting, just touching is your true nature. *That* view *is* your true self. We sometimes call this "just seeing," or "just perceiving." It has no subject or object. This is a very important point.

So, when you hear, that is the Absolute, your true nature. [*Hits the table.*] That view means you can see that this world is empty. The act of merely perceiving that sound is already your true self. There is no longer any subject or object. [*Hits the table.*] The sutra says that "Then you will see your true nature." True nature means, Who is seeing? Who sees what is seen? Who? But first we must be clear that these lines in the *Diamond Sutra* are nearly always not translated correctly, because impermanence cannot see impermanence. It would be clearer to say that the perceiving is itself our true nature.

Do not become attached to any thoughts
  that arise in the mind.

Before he received transmission, the Sixth Patriarch was known as Layman No. He was a very simple, uneducated man who only worked hard to support his mother. Every day, he went to the mountains to gather firewood to sell in the markets and towns near his home. One day, before he entered the monastery, he was finishing the delivery of some firewood to a customer. As he walked through the bustling marketplace, he passed a monk who was chanting a sutra. Layman No heard the line, "Do not become attached to any thoughts that arise in the mind." Hearing this, he was suddenly enlightened. He realized something about the nature of his mind. Before that moment, he never knew anything about Buddhism. He never studied sutras. He didn't know Dharma. He didn't even know how to write Chinese characters! He never understood anything. Layman No was completely stupid. He heard only this line, "Don't become attached to any thoughts which arise in the mind" and—*BOOM!*—he got enlightenment! When you see, hear, smell, taste, touch, and *think*, everything—just like this—is the truth. So thinking is also truth if you do not let yourself become attached to thinking as it comes and goes in your mind. But very few people can do this. They believe that their thinking is real, and follow it everywhere. This is desire, and all desire is suffering. If you simply let your thinking go, then that same thinking is the truth. When you see a red light, stop; when you see a green light, go.

This line in the *Diamond Sutra* makes a very simple point, but it is very deep teaching. It shows us a very clear way to experience nonattached thinking. Just think. "Just think" means there is no "I." "Just think" means there is no subject and no object. Inside and outside always become one. It means just do it. When you see the sky, there is only blue. That is "just think." When you see the tree, there is only green. Just think. The wall is white. Just think. It is now seven fifty-six PM. Right now we hear the wind blowing outside. Just think. It means just perceive. This is nonattachment thinking: thoughts come and go in your mind with no hindrance. This is very, very important teaching.

If you see form as the Absolute, if you search out the Absolute
with your voice,
You are practicing the wrong path, and you cannot see your
true self.

Many people are attached to seeing God or Buddha. They see things superficially and look for God and Buddha in outside things, expecting miraculous events. Also people try to pray to God or Buddha for things. But this kind of view can never see the true Buddha. *Form* means outside things that you can perceive. It also means inside things, like thoughts that arise in the mind. It means feelings, perceptions, impulses, and consciousness, in addition to outside objects. It means any kind of form. So if you believe that any forms actually exist, you are practicing the wrong path. Originally, there are no forms, feelings, perceptions, impulses, or consciousness. Outside things are also impermanent, without names and forms. They are completely empty. If you are attached to these things, you cannot see your true nature: attachment comes from the deluded view that things exist. Because of this basic delusion, you believe that there is some outside world of objects and things. You believe, too, that there is something inside. You make inside and outside. You believe that these things exist, because you have now made self and other, this and that. This is still only thinking and attachment. Deeply perceiving your true nature is a view that has no inside or outside. You attain the Absolute which has no subject or object whatsoever. There is no name and no form. This view is your true self.

So, seeing your true self and seeing truth are a little different. Seeing your true self means perceiving the Absolute. [Hits the table.] Just that point. You can perceive primary point. [Hits the table.] Everything returns to this point. [Hits the table.] Everything is universal substance, the same substance. It is realizing your true self. This is a first step. But perceiving truth means first attaining your true self [hits the table], and then, once you attain this, realizing that everything is already the truth. When you see, when you hear, when you smell, when you taste, when you touch, everything, just as it is, is the truth. Attaining the Absolute [hits the table] is the teaching of the Diamond Sutra. But this point takes us only midway into Mahayana's teaching; that is why we say that this sutra is a midpoint between Hinayana and Mahayana Buddhist teaching. Showing us the complete view of truth is the job of the Heart Sutra, the Avatamsaka-sutra, and the Lotus Sutra.

The most important point of the Diamond Sutra is that everything is impermanent. Everything is completely empty. The Diamond Sutra explains the fundamental importance of the attainment of emptiness as an experience of our true nature. If you want to attain your true nature, you must become completely empty. You must attain emptiness: understanding emptiness conceptually cannot help your life. You are already empty, but you don't realize it. You believe in inside and outside. This is delusion. You believe that things exist and don't exist. This is also delusion. But if you attain your original emptiness, you attain your true nature. You attain that you and this whole universe are completely empty. Then when you see, when you hear, when you smell, when you taste, when you touch, and when you think, everything is this emptiness. Everything is the Absolute. You are also the Absolute. From this point it is possible to perceive truth.

All compounded things are like a dream, a phantom, a
bubble, or a reflection. They are like dew or lightning.
Thus should you view them.

These lines are very important teaching. If you are attached to your thinking, then everything has name and form. This is the world of opposites. But name and form are always changing, changing, changing. Because of this, everything is impermanent. Everything is like a dream, is like dew, is like a bubble or a flash of lightning. Nothing stays but is always in a process of change. Rather than being some constant, fixed reality, this whole universe constantly appears and disappears. But there is a way to experience the true nature of this constantly changing universe. Simply do not become attached to the opposites world. Don't become attached to any outside world. Don't become attached to names and forms. If you keep that point, then your mind is not moving. You attain that names and forms are fundamentally empty. This whole universe is completely empty. You are completely empty. Nothing ever comes or goes. Nothing ever appears or disappears. When you keep this mind, you soon attain your true self.

That is the *Diamond Sutra*'s teaching: attain emptiness, and you attain your true nature. Though it is a Mahayana text, the *Diamond Sutra* does not concern itself with whether this world is truth or not. More importantly, what kind of thinking do you have in your mind? What is your mind's orientation? How do you keep your mind, right now? That makes this whole world. The Buddha says, in the *Avatamsaka-sutra*, "Everything is created by mind alone." This is more high-class teaching. The *Diamond Sutra* begins by showing the impermanence of everything, and how we must attain emptiness in order to cut through this thinking dream.

But reading this sutra is not enough. If you want to cut your suffering dream, you need to use a diamond sword. Only keep a don't-know mind: this is your true diamond sword. As I said before, if anyone really looked closely at this world, they would cut their hair and become a monk, and let go of this suffering dream. Only practice. Only practice. Only *do* it.

The Maha Prajna Paramita Heart Sutra

般若心経

Perceiving that all five skandhas are empty saves all beings from suffering.

照見 五薀皆空 度一切苦厄

Form does not differ from emptiness, emptiness does not differ from form.

色不異空 空不異色

Form is emptiness, emptiness is form.

色即是空 空即是色

No appearing, no disapppearing.

不生不滅

No taint, no purity.

不垢不淨

No increase, no decrease.

不增不減

All Dharmas are marked with emptiness.

諸法空相

No cognition—no attainment.

無智 無得

Nirvana.

涅槃

Unexcelled perfect enlightenment—*anuttara samyak sambodhi*.

正等正覺

Gate, gate, paragate, parasamgate, bodhi svaha!

THE *HEART SUTRA* has only two hundred seventy Chinese characters, yet it contains all of Mahayana Buddhism's teaching. Inside this sutra is the essence of the *Diamond Sutra,* the *Avatamsaka-sutra,* and the *Lotus Sutra.* It contains the meaning of all the eighty-four thousand sutras. It is chanted in every Mahayana and Zen temple in the world. In Korean temples and in our Zen centers in the West, the *Heart Sutra* is chanted at least twice every day, in the morning and at night, and during retreats it is chanted more. Sometimes if you find that your mind is not clear, and meditation does not help so much, you must read this sutra. Then your mind will become clear.

Maha means big, great. *Prajna* means wisdom, and *paramita* means "going beyond," or perfecting. *Hridya* means heart. And the Chinese characters for *Heart Sutra* are *shim gyong,* or "mind road." So this sutra is the "great path for the perfection of wisdom."

The word *maha* in the title of this sutra points to something of very great size. What is truly numberless in time and space? Someone may say that the ground is the biggest thing. When you really stop to think about it, the oceans seem to be the biggest thing—there is more water than land. Or is the sky the biggest thing? Maybe space is the greatest thing we know of. Perhaps sky and space together are the number one biggest thing! The universe is infinite in time and space, and contains infinite worlds—is that the biggest thing? Everybody probably thinks that this is so. But an eminent teacher said, "This whole universe covers my body, yet my mind can cover the whole universe." This is a very important point. The universe covers and surrounds our world and everything inside it, so it must be truly big. But in the instant that you think of the universe—"universe"—you have already covered the whole universe with your mind. Therefore our mind is bigger than the infinite time and infinite space of this universe. How wonderful! The *Heart Sutra* points to this biggest thing: mind. It shows how we can discover and cultivate the proper use of the biggest thing, so that is why this little sutra is called *maha.*

Perceiving that all five skandhas are empty saves all beings
  from suffering and distress.

There is suffering everywhere we look in the world. All beings are in pain and distress. But where does suffering come from? People are struck with a hopeless love for somebody, or they pursue the desire to obtain some material things. People have ambition to become things that they feel will complete their life, or to be recognized and approved by others. But no matter how hard we struggle for these things, even when we get them, we cannot keep them. And this causes all our suffering. But originally this suffering does not exist. It all comes from our mind, as a mirage rises up from a hot road and appears real. If I am suffering over some matter, and then I die, my suffering also disappears. When we realize this—that suffering is merely the product of our minds, and does not have some independent existence—then there is no longer any suffering and distress.

So, what is this mind that is so great? If you are thinking, you cannot find your mind anywhere. If you cut off all thinking—which means if you cut off all attachment to your thinking—then your true nature appears everywhere. We already considered some important points in Hinayana Buddhism's teaching. The Buddha first taught that what we call mind or "I" is only the five skandhas of form, feelings, perceptions, impulses, and consciousness. These skandhas, or aggregates, are constantly changing; they are only heaps of mental energy. Since human beings are attached to form, feelings, perceptions, impulses, and consciousness, then when they inevitably change, we get suffering. We never get out of the suffering world. This is because we believe that these things are real, and that they are the real "I." This is a central teaching of Hinayana Buddhism.

However, the *Heart Sutra*'s opening line shows that these skandhas are originally empty. Since that is so, where is suffering? What can possibly suffer? Here is a cup of orange juice. If you have "cup," then you can keep this orange juice here. But if this cup breaks, how can the orange juice remain? You cannot keep the juice there, yah? Suffering is the same as that. Where does suffering abide? If you are attached to the five skandhas of form, feelings, perceptions, impulses, or consciousness, then suffering has a place to stay. But the *Heart Sutra* shows the view that these five skandhas are empty. Mind is completely empty: where can suffering possibly stay? So this teaching about emptiness is very, very important to attain. When you practice the way of the perfection of wisdom, you attain that all five skandhas are actually empty. Attaining this view saves us from all suffering and distress. Merely understanding these views cannot help you—you must *attain* something.

Form does not differ from emptiness, emptiness does not
differ from form. Form is emptiness, emptiness is form.

The *Heart Sutra* teaches that "form is emptiness, and emptiness is form."
Many people don't know what this means—even some long-time students
of meditation. But there is a very easy way to see this in our everyday lives.
For example, here is a wooden chair. It is brown. It is solid and heavy. It
looks like it could last a long time. You sit in the chair, and it holds up your
weight. You can place things on it. But then you light the chair on fire, and
leave. When you come back later, the chair is no longer there! This thing
that seemed so solid and strong and real is now just a pile of cinder and ash
which the wind blows around. This example shows how the chair is empty:
it is not a permanent, abiding thing. It is always changing. It has no independent existence. Over a long or short time, the chair will eventually change
and become something other than what it appears. So this brown chair is
complete emptiness. But though it always has the quality of emptiness, this
emptiness is form: you can sit in the chair, and it will still hold you up.
"Form is emptiness, and emptiness is form."

But why is it necessary to understand this? The reason for this is that many
human beings are attached to name and form, and this attachment to name
and form is the cause of nearly all suffering. If we want to cure human beings
of this attachment, then we must apply name-and-form medicine. We must
begin by showing that names and forms are not real and permanent: they
are always changing, changing, changing. If you are rich, you must see that
the riches you covet are empty. If you are attached to fame and other people's
approval, you must see that these things that you struggle and suffer for are
empty. Most people treasure their bodies; they use a lot of money to make
their bodies strong or beautiful. But someday, soon, when you die, this body
will disappear. You cannot take this empty body with you, however much
you treasure it. You cannot carry fame with you. You cannot carry money.
You cannot carry sex. You cannot carry anything! Nowadays, many people
are very attached to these things. They treasure names and empty appearances above nearly all else, harming themselves and others just to protect
them. They want to get money, or a good reputation, or a good relationship.
They struggle desperately to get high positions. People always subject their
minds to the worst kind of abuse and suffering just to try to get and then

keep these empty, impermanent things. Nowadays many humans are very attached to sex. But none of that is necessary. All form is empty, so thinking that you can get anything or keep anything is a fundamental delusion. This line teaches that point.

The most important thing is, what do you want in your life, right now? What you want in this very moment makes your mind, and that mind makes your life. It determines this life and your next life. By perceiving that all things are originally empty, you can put it all down and just live, without suffering over these impermanent things.

If you are not attached to name and form, you are completely free. There is a famous story about this. A long time ago in Athens, there lived a very great philosopher named Diogenes. Even though he was the most high-class philosopher in ancient Greece, he lived just like a mangy dog. He always slept outside, didn't worry about whether he'd be able to eat that day, and usually didn't wear any clothing. Diogenes' teaching was all about natural-style living. Then early one morning while sleeping in the street, he suddenly felt a little chilly, and woke up. Standing over him was Alexander the Great, who was at that time the most powerful man in the world. He had conquered many, many countries, and because of his extraordinary military power and intelligence, he was feared and admired by everyone. Today Alexander the Great wanted to visit Diogenes for some teaching. He stood there, in full military regalia, the grand figure of his muscular body casting a dark shadow over the still-reclining Diogenes.

Diogenes squinted up at him, "Oh, Alexander the Great! How are you?"

"I am fine. But I want to help *you*, Diogenes. I have already conquered this whole world. I have palaces and gold and wealth beyond measure. If you want something, I can give it to you. Anything—land, money, a high position—I will give to you. Only mention it, and it is yours. What do you want?"

"Oh, you want to help me?"

"Yes," Alexander the Great said. "I want to help *you*."

"Oh, thank you!"

"So, do you want anything?"

"Yes," Diogenes said. "I want something."

"Just name it, and it's yours. Anything."

"Alexander the Great, please move out of my sunlight."

"Oh, OK, OK! I am sorry. I am sorry." Alexander moved to the side.

Then Diogenes said, "Thank you, thank you! That's enough." Ha ha ha ha ha! [*Long, sustained laughter from the assembly*] This is a very simple story. But it teaches us a lot about form and emptiness. Alexander the Great was just blocking the sunlight, so it could not come in. That is all. Ha ha ha ha ha! So when he was offered anything in the whole world, Diogenes only said, "Please move out of my sunlight." Only that! That point has no desire. Diogenes already attained the whole truth: he attained that substance is empty. He attained that name and form are also empty, so therefore he was not interested in having wealth or fame or a lover or family or a high position. Everything is empty—why crave these empty things? They cannot truly help my life. But, just now, I want some sunlight. That is all. Diogenes was completely free because he completely attained "form is emptiness, emptiness is form." If you attain that point, there is no desire worth clinging to because you realize that you are already complete. Right now you lack nothing. That's a very important point. Then meditation is not necessary. Sitting retreats is not necessary. Dharma speeches are also not necessary. But if you are attached to your thinking, then meditation is very necessary. If you do not attain that "form is emptiness, and emptiness is form," then sitting many long retreats is very important for your life, and you must do lots of hard training. When you stop and look at it for a moment, the need for practice is also very stupid. Ha ha ha ha!

No appearing, no disappearing. No taint, no purity.
No increase, no decrease.

The *Heart Sutra* is known for its very interesting way of describing our true nature. It uses "no" many times. When you attain true emptiness, there is no speech or words. Opening your mouth is already a big mistake. So words and speech cannot describe our original nature. But to teach people still caught in words-and-speech delusion, sometimes words-and-speech medicines are necessary. The *Heart Sutra* recognizes both these points. So it describes our true nature by completely describing what our true nature is *not*. You cannot say what it is, but you can give a sense of what our true nature is not like. "It's not this or this or this or this or this. It's not like that or that or that. Understand?" Ha ha ha ha!! This is a very interesting technique. The *Heart Sutra* only says "no," because this is perhaps the best that words and speech can do.

This line points right to the fact that, in our original nature, nothing ever appears or disappears. There is no such thing as taint or purity, because these are merely qualities created by the thinking-mind. And in original nature there is neither increase nor decrease. Our true nature is completely still and empty. It is the universal substance of which everything else is composed. How, then, could it ever appear or disappear, or be tainted or pure? More importantly, since our true nature is the same as the universe, how could it ever increase or decrease? Infinite in time and space, it has none of the characteristics that apply to things we can describe with speech and words.

All Dharmas are marked with emptiness.

No cognition, no attainment. Nirvana.

The *Heart Sutra* says, "All Dharmas are marked with emptiness." But all Dharmas are already empty and nonexistent even before you say this. Name and form are already empty. How can you even mention Dharma, and then say it's empty? That is a big mistake! In the true experience of emptiness, there are no words and no speech, so there is also no Dharma. When you open your mouth to say "All Dharmas are marked with emptiness," that is already no longer emptiness. So be careful. The point of this is that if you just understand words and speech, and keep only an intellectual understanding, this sutra and any other sutra cannot help your life. Some actual attainment of what these words point to is necessary.

So when we say that everything is empty, we are saying that therefore there is also no cognition and no attainment. This point of emptiness is the Absolute. [*Hits the table loudly.*] There *is* nothing, so what could you possibly attain? These words in the *Heart Sutra* are only wonderful speech and words. But however interesting or wonderful the speech and words are, if you just understand them conceptually, they cannot help your life. Again, you must truly *attain* something. You must *attain* that there is actually *nothing* to attain. Everything is already truth, exactly as it is. You are already complete. But be careful! Merely understanding these beautiful words is one thing, and attaining them is quite another.

The *Heart Sutra* begins with the Hinayana experience of emptiness and takes it one more step. If you attain true emptiness, there is no speech and no mouth. In attaining "no mouth," you attain the Absolute, or nirvana. We already talked about the Four Noble Truths and the Eightfold Path of Hinayana teaching: a path which perceives that everything is suffering, and which then leads to stopping suffering, stopping birth and death. This is nirvana. There are no opposites: no coming or going, no high or low, good or bad, birth or death. So in the true experience of emptiness, you perceive that there is *already* no birth or death, no coming or going. How can you stop something that doesn't even exist? There is already no suffering: how can it have an origin, and how can it possibly be extinguished? That is why the *Heart Sutra* talks about "no suffering, no origination, no stopping, no path." It completely "hits" the opposites-thinking of the Four Noble Truths that there is suffering, and an origination of it, and a stopping of it, and a path. So Mahayana Buddhism teaches that there is one more step from Hinayana teaching. If you only stop at this point, at complete emptiness, you only attain nirvana. Mahayana Buddhism's view means taking another step.

Unexcelled perfect enlightenment— anuttara samyak sambodhi

Anuttara samyak sambodhi is a Sanskrit phrase meaning "unexcelled perfect enlightenment." It is simply another way of saying "truth." When you see, when you hear, when you smell, when you taste, when you touch, when you think—everything, just-like-this, is the truth. Before, just at the point of nirvana, there is no cognition, and no attainment with nothing to attain. So the bodhisattva depends on *Prajna Paramita,* and attains nirvana. But then these three words appear: *anuttara samyak sambodhi.* Before, there is no attainment; now, all buddhas *attain anuttara samyak sambodhi.* What does this mean?

If you just attain true emptiness, this is only nirvana. It is an experience of complete stillness and bliss: there is no subject or object, no good or bad, no coming or going, no life or death. There is nothing to attain. But Mahayana means your practice continues "beyond" this point, so that you *attain* no-attainment. You must find nirvana's function in the world. The name for that is unexcelled perfect enlightenment. If you attain no-attainment, then you attain truth. Your mind is empty, and clear like space. This means your mind is clear like a mirror: If a mountain appears before the mirror, there is only mountain; water appears, and there is only water; red comes, red; white comes, white. The sky is blue. The tree is green. A dog is barking, "Woof! Woof!" Sugar is sweet. Everything that you see, hear, smell, taste, touch, and think is the truth, just as it is. Nirvana means attaining emptiness, which has nothing to attain. *Anuttara samyak sambodhi* means *using* the experience of emptiness to attain truth. With an empty mind, reflect this world, just as it is. That is Mahayana Buddhism and the Great Bodhisattva Way.

Gate, gate, paragate, parasamgate, bodhi svaha!

So there is yet one more step. If you attain emptiness, and then attain truth, how does this world's truth *function* to help other beings? All buddhas attain *anuttara samyak sambodhi,* or unexcelled perfect enlightenment. This means that they attain truth. They can see that the sky is blue, and the tree is green. At the end of the sutra we are told that there is a great transcendant mantra, a great bright mantra, an utmost mantra, a supreme mantra: *Gate, gate, paragate, parasamgate, bodhi svaha.* It can be translated as "Gone, gone, gone to the other shore beyond." So this mantra at the end of the *Heart Sutra* means only action. Up until this point, everything is just speech and words about attaining emptiness and truth. It is all a lot of very interesting description. But this mantra means you must just do it. Some kind of action is necessary if you want to help this world. For the bodhisattva, there is only bodhisattva action. When you attain unexcelled perfect enlightenment, you must attain the *function* of this enlightenment in the world. That is what we call moment world. From moment to moment, perceive suffering in this world and only help all beings. That is a very important point.

The *Heart Sutra* is very, very interesting. It begins by showing the opposites world, and then shows the Absolute world, and finally leads to complete world, or what we call moment world. Opposites world is "form is emptiness, emptiness is form." The Absolute world is emptiness, or nirvana: "no form, no emptiness." The complete world is *anuttara samyak sambodhi*—truth, just as it is: "form is form, emptiness is emptiness." Attaining truth alone is not enough. Because our experience of truth must function for other beings from moment to moment, the sutra closes with some exhortation to action: *Gate, gate, paragate, parasamgate, bodhi svaha.* This mantra means keeping moment world, which is Great Love and Great Compassion. It is the path of the bodhisattva. When you do together-action with all beings, then Great Love appears by itself. Together-action only means acting together harmoniously, from moment to moment. That is world peace. Only *do* it. Only *do* it. If someone is thirsty, give them something to drink. If someone is hungry, give them food. When a suffering person appears before you, you only help, with no thinking or checking. The early part of this sutra has no "do-it," just good speech about attainment and no-attainment. But if you attain something, you must do it. That is the meaning behind *Gate, gate, paragate, parasamgate, bodhi svaha.* Step by step, we attain how to function compassionately for others, to use truth for others, spontaneously, from moment to moment. This is the whole point of the *Heart Sutra.* From moment to moment, when you are doing something, just do it.

The Mahaparinirvana-sutra

涅槃經

All formations are impermanent.

諸行無常

This is the law of appearing and disappearing.

是生滅法

When both appearing and disappearing disappear,

生滅滅已

Then this stillness is bliss.

寂滅為樂

WE ALREADY TALKED about the view of dependent origination in Hinayana Buddhism. This view reveals how all things in the universe are merely the coming together of certain conditions, so therefore everything is impermanent. Appearing and disappearing are this world's fundamental rules. Everything in the universe appears out of emptiness, stays for some period—long or short—and eventually returns to emptiness. This law is not merely some Buddhist idea: it governs everything in the entire universe. If you make this rule, then everything follows this rule. However, if you don't make this universe, and don't make this world, then you don't have this rule. So even appearing and disappearing can disappear, because if you truly experience emptiness you attain the more profound view that originally everything is already beyond appearing and disappearing. Nothing ever appears or disappears. The *Mahaparinirvana-sutra* addresses that point.

So we have substance, and name and form. Name and form constantly appear and disappear because they are created entirely by thinking. But substance never appears or disappears. So we must perceive both: substance, and the appearing and disappearing of name and form. When he started teaching, the Buddha first gave this very simple teaching that everything appears and disappears. That is the teaching of dependent origination. It is a kind of dharma candy, a teaching expedient. The Buddha used it to open his students' minds. But when his students' minds matured, the Buddha grabbed the candy away from them. That is the teaching that there is actually no appearing and no disappearing. Then next, he taught that appearing is just appearing, and disappearing is just disappearing. His last teaching is how you find the correct *function* of appearing and disappearing to help other beings.

Everything appears and disappears. You can *see* that in this world. You can *smell* that. You can *taste* that. But where does everything in the universe appear and disappear? By looking closely at the true nature of this world, and practicing meditation, you can see that all appearance and disappearance occurs only in your own mind. Mind makes everything. So in the *Avatamsaka-sutra*, as we will see, the Buddha says, "Everything is created by mind alone." When you have mind, then there is appearing and disappearing. If you have no mind, then you perceive that nothing ever appears or disappears. Nothing ever comes or goes.

Then what is the correct function of appearing and disappearing? This is a very important point. Only help other people. First you see that everything in this world appears and disappears, around and around nonstop. But then you inevitably want to understand where this world comes from that appears and disappears so much: Who made this world which appears and disappears? Where does everything appear from, and where does everything go when it disappears? If you practice hard, you can see that your own mind has made this whole world, and everything in it. Then who made this mind? "I" did. If "I" disappears, mind disappears, and this whole universe disappears. When "I" disappears, appearing is only appearing, and disappearing is only disappearing. That is because when there is no "I," your mind is clear like space, which means it is clear like a mirror. When a red ball is held in front of the mirror, red appears. When a white ball is held there, white appears. But this clear mirror itself never appears or disappears. It only reflects mountains and rivers and trees and dogs and cats and people just as they are. The clear mirror reflects this whole world's appearing and disappearing, yet the clear mirror itself never appears or disappears. So there is no appearing or disappearing, and yet appearing is just appearing and disappearing is just disappearing.

If you attain this clear mirror, which means attaining your true self, then what is the correct *function* of appearing and disappearing? How can you use appearing and disappearing to help other beings? That is the sole job of our meditation practice.

A long time ago in Korea, the great Zen Master Hyo Bong gave a very interesting dharma speech that points to how we can find this function. Sitting on the high rostrum in the Main Buddha Hall at the great Haein Sah Temple, he hit his Zen stick on the stand three times and said to the assembly of monks, "All things and all Dharmas are constantly appearing and disappearing, appearing and disappearing. But originally, everything comes from complete stillness. This stillness is universal substance itself. If you attain substance, you attain truth and correct function. Then appearing and disappearing are truth, and it is possible to attain the correct function of appearing and disappearing.

"Then my question for all of you monks today is, where do substance, truth, and function come from? If you open your mouth to answer, this already makes opposites. By keeping your mouth closed, you show an attachment to emptiness. So how do you, with your mouth neither open nor closed, attain substance, truth, and function?" Nobody in the vast assembly of monks could answer.

"I'll give you all a hint," he said. "*Katz!* Everybody return to your rooms and have some tea." Then Zen Master Hyo Bong descended from the high rostrum.

It is not difficult to attain the function of "when appearing and disappearing disappear." Appearing and disappearing disappear, then this stillness is bliss. Everything is already complete. Nothing is lacking anywhere. Nothing is not truth. When you see, when you hear, when you smell, when you taste, when you touch, and when you think, everything is already complete. We use this word *complete* to point to moment-mind. In moment-mind, appearing is just appearing, and disappearing is just disappearing. This is because moment-mind is already beyond time and space. It means having just this moment [*hits the table*]. Moment is a very short time. In this short time, appearing is just appearing, and disappearing is just disappearing. But when our eyes, ears, nose, tongue, body, and mind don't keep this moment-mind, then everything is illusion. That means that everything is not complete, and not truth. When you live in that illusion, you actually believe that everything in this world appears and disappears. You believe that things come and go, that they are born and die. This is where human suffering comes from.

Everyone thinks that this is extremely difficult teaching, something beyond their reach or experience. How can things appear and disappear, and yet there is, originally, even in this constantly moving world, no appearing and disappearing? A student once said to me, "The *Mahaparinirvana-sutra* seems very confusing. Everything is always moving. And yet everything is not moving? I don't understand this Buddhism . . ." But there is a very easy way to understand this: Sometime you go to a movie. You see an action movie about a good man and a bad man—lots of fighting, cars moving very fast, and explosions all over the place. Everything is always moving very quickly. Our daily lives have this quality: everything is constantly moving, coming and going, nonstop. It seems like there is no stillness-place. But this movie is really only a very long strip of film. In one second, there are something like fourteen frames. Each frame is a separate piece of action. But in each frame, nothing is moving. Everything is completely still. Each frame, one by one, is a complete picture. In each frame, nothing ever comes or goes, or appears or disappears. Each frame is complete stillness. The film projector moves the frames very quickly, and all of these frames run past the lens very fast, so the action on-screen seems to happen nonstop. There is no break in the movement of things. But actually when you take this strip of film and hold it up to the light with your hands, there is nothing moving at all. Each frame is complete. Every moment is completely not-moving action.

Our minds and this whole universe are just like that. This world is impermanent. Everything is always changing, changing, changing, moving, moving, moving, nonstop. Even one second of our lives seems full of so much movement and change in this world that we see. But your mind—right *now*—is like a lens whose shutter speed is one divided by infinite time. We call that moment-mind. If you attain that mind, then this whole world's movement stops. From moment to moment you can see this world completely stop. Stop. Stop. Stop. Stop. Stop. Like the film, you perceive every frame—*this* moment—which is infinitely still and complete. In the frame, nothing is moving. There is no time, and nothing appears or disappears in that box. But this movie projector—your *thinking* mind—is always moving, around and around and around, so you experience this world as constantly moving and you constantly experience change, which is impermanence. You lose moment-mind by following your conceptual thinking, believing that it is real.

When you practice meditation for a long time, however, you can stop your mind-lens, and then you can actually experience that each moment of your life is truly infinite in time and space. This is why we call it moment-mind. It is not moving, and it is always complete. It is mind that is actually beyond time and space. Then when you see, when you hear, when you smell, when you taste, when you touch, when you think—everything, just as it is, is already complete. It is very important to attain this point: only then can you attain this sutra's meaning. The sutra becomes yours. You attain the bliss of "when appearing and disappearing disappear." But just understanding these words is not enough if you do not actually attain the very real experience to which they point.

A long time ago, in China, there was a famous sutra master named Ji Do. He read many, many sutras. He studied the sutras for thirty years. Thirty years! Not only three years. He was studying them every day for three-zero years. Ten years, ten years, ten years he read the sutras intensively. [*Laughter from the audience.*] He understood all of the sutras with no hindrance. It is said that you could read him a line from any of the eighty-four thousand sutras, and he could recite back, by page and line number, the text that it was from. He was very high class. No sutra ever presented him with a problem, except for the *Mahaparinirvana-sutra*. Try as he could, over and over again, he could not understand the *Mahaparinirvana-sutra*'s true meaning.

One day, he visited the Sixth Patriarch, Hui Neng. "Zen Master, I have read the *Diamond Sutra*. I understand what the *Diamond Sutra* means. I also understand the *Heart Sutra* and the *Lotus Sutra*. I understand nearly all the sutras. But I cannot understand this *Nirvana Sutra*. Please help me with some question I have. . . ."

"What is your question?"

"The *Nirvana Sutra* says, 'All formations are impermanent. This is the law of appearing and disappearing. . . .' "

"Yes. . . ."

"I understand this point. But it also says, 'When appearing and disappearing disappear, then this stillness is bliss.' I don't understand what that means."

"What exactly don't you understand?" the patriarch asked.

"Master, when appearing and disappearing disappear, there is nothing. So then who can possibly get bliss? In complete stillness, there is nobody, and no 'I, my, me.' All of us have two kinds of bodies: our physical form-body and a dharma-body. Our form-body is composed of the four elements (earth, air, fire, and water), so it is always appearing and disappearing. It is always getting sick, getting old, dying, and being reborn again, over and over again. Because of this, it is always suffering. It cannot get bliss. Yet the dharma-body has no form, no feelings, no perceptions, no impulses, no consciousness, no thinking. Because it has no feeling or consciousness, it is like a rock or a tree, so it, too, cannot possibly get bliss. Yet the *Mahaparinirvana-sutra* says that 'When appearing and disappearing disappear, this stillness is bliss.' Please teach me."

The Sixth Patriarch looked at Ji Do and said, "That is a wonderful question. When appearing and disappearing disappear, that is stillness. So I ask you, are form-body and dharma-body the same or different?"

"Different!"

"If that is so, then is the thing that is asking me your form-body or dharma-body?"

"It is both."

"Both? *Who* said 'both?' "

"I did."

"Oh, 'I' made that. Is this 'I' form-body or dharma-body?" Ji Do was completely stuck and could not answer. So the Sixth Patriarch said, "Put it down; let go of your conceptual thinking. Don't make 'form-body' or 'dharma-body.' You *make* these things, so you have a problem. Your form-body never said, 'I am form-body.' The dharma-body never said, 'I am dharma-body.' You make form-body and dharma-body, so you have lots of thinking and intellectual desire and suffering. Completely let go of your thinking! There is no form-body and no dharma-body. Do you understand now?"

Ji Do heard that, and got enlightenment. "Oh, yes, sir! Yes, sir!" he said, bowing deeply. "Now I understand!"

So that is a very interesting story. If you want to understand this teaching of the *Mahaparinirvana-sutra*, from moment to moment don't make anything. This important sutra's teaching is already very, very clear in front of you. If you open your mouth, you can never understand this point. [*Hits the table.*] That point cannot be explained. [*Hits the table.*] It has no speech or words. [*Hits the table.*] If you attain that, you attain "not appearing and not disappearing." It's very simple, and not a special experience. If you're thinking, you will never understand this point.

The Lotus Sutra
法 華 經

All phenomena, from their very origin,

諸法從本來

Always have the aspect of stillness and extinction.

常自寂滅相

When the disciple of the Buddha walks this path,

佛子行道已

He will become a buddha in future lives.

來世得作佛

THE *LOTUS SUTRA* teaches us about truth. In Chinese characters, this sutra is called *shil sang myo boep kyong*. *Shil sang* means "true," *myo boep* means "mystic Dharma," and *kyong* means sutra. So this is the "true mystic Dharma sutra." It shows how to attain One Mind. It also shows how we can attain infinite time and infinite space.

The *Lotus Sutra* teaches us about attaining a mind of complete stillness. We sometimes call this One Mind. All these are just names for our original mind. It is not something to "get" to, but something we already are. When a single thought appears, however, we lose this original mind of stillness and extinction. While you hear my words, and you follow some thought that flits across your mind, you and I become vastly separate. But by just cutting off all thinking and returning to simply listening, you return to being completely in this act. When you cut your attachment to thinking, then my speaking and your listening are completely the same. The speaking and listening are not two things. That is already the true Buddha, the true Jesus, the true God. This experience has no Korean or American or German or Chinese. There is no male or female. [*Hits the table.*] I sometimes call it primary point.

Several years ago, while I was teaching in Paris, a group of French priests came to see me at the Zen Center. We had tea, and they asked me questions about Buddhism and Christianity. Finally, one of them said that he had attended the public Dharma talk the night before, and something that I had said bothered him all night. "At the talk, you said that this 'primary point' is infinite in time and space. Then what is the relationship between primary point and the creation of God?"

I hit the table with my hand like this [*hits the table*]. That's all. There were several seconds of silence, during which the priest got a strange, confused look on his face. So I explained, "Talking about the creation of God is just thinking. But this point [*hits the table*] is before thinking. It is before Jesus and the Buddha. [*Hits.*] It is before the universe. [*Hits.*] It is before the creation of God. If you truly attain that point, you can see God."

Then another priest smiled and asked, "Well, then, Zen master, can *you* see God?"

"Your shirts are black."

The *Lotus Sutra* shows us how this point [*hits the table*] is our nature and the nature of all phenomena. It also teaches that one who can completely perceive this point "will become a buddha in future lives." This is a very interesting line. It does not mean that you get enlightenment in some "other" life; our next life is actually not the next life. This is only a distinction that comes from using words to describe something which has no words. There is actually nowhere else for us to become a buddha but right now, in this place. It does not "happen" anywhere else or at any other time. A disciple of the Buddha simply practices. By just practicing, right now, then "next life" means this moment. [*Hits the table hard.*] You only have this moment— "next life" does not exist. Your "do-it" mind in *this* moment is already Buddha. This truth is invaluable. Attaining Buddha-mind is not difficult. It does not occur at some point in the future. It simply means that right now there is no inside or outside, no subject or object. In this moment, subject and object—*BOOM!*—become one. Only do it, and you are already Buddha. But be careful!

Everybody knows that many people use the title of this sutra to attain an experience of One Mind. Followers of the Japanese Nichiren sect chant

Namu myoho renge-kyo to get things that they want. *"Namu myoho renge-kyo, Namu myoho renge-kyo, Namu myoho renge-kyo."* That is this sutra's title in Japanese. If they do that, they believe that they can get happiness, a beautiful house, or a wonderful wife. Maybe they can make a successful business by chanting this all the time. They believe that anything is possible if you just repeat this title over and over again. The title of this sutra is like a mantra for getting something. That kind of practice is not good and not bad. It is only about keeping One Mind. This is good if you want to get something.

But the correct practice of meditation means attaining one-pointed mind without wanting anything. This is the goal of any mantra practice, not only *Namu myoho renge-kyo.* Any kind of mantra is the same. Even repeating "Coca Cola, Coca Cola, Coca Cola," if done with complete determination, will have the same result. The most important point is, How do you take away your thinking? How do you keep your mind? How do you keep your mind empty? If you keep empty mind, that is the Absolute. We sometimes call that primary point. When you keep primary point for a long time, you can take away your primary cause. All your happiness and suffering come from primary cause. Then as you take away primary cause, your condition changes and you get a different result. You will change your suffering so that compassion and happiness can appear. This is the teaching of dependent origination.

So how do you take away primary cause? Only keep One Mind. When you are doing something, just *do* it. Just do it. In just-do-it mind, there is no subject and no object. Inside and outside become one. As a result, you can connect with universal energy. The name we sometimes use for that is primary point. When you keep primary point for a long time, then slowly, slowly, slowly primary cause disappears. Thinking *makes* your primary cause. So taking away your opposites-mind takes away opposites energy, and primary cause disappears, like water when left out for a long time in the sun. It evaporates by itself. When you practice hard it is very easy to do this! But your thinking makes karma, and karma blocks the sun, so this primary cause water cannot evaporate as quickly.

Chanting *Namu myoho renge-kyo* is not good or bad practice. It is possible to have insight into your true nature by repeating *Om mani padme hum* or the Great Dharani. Even using "Coca-Cola" as a mantra could help your life, if you practiced correctly. Whatever your practice is, keep a Great Question and only do it. If you have try-mind and a Great Question, then any kind of practice can help you attain your true self. A long time ago in Korea, there was a monk named Sok Du, which means "Rockhead." He was a very, very stupid monk, but he had a strong try-mind. One day, Sok Du asked a Zen master, "What is Buddha?"

The Zen master replied, "*Juk shim shi bul*," which means "Buddha is mind." But Sok Du misheard him. He thought his teacher said, "*Jip shin shi bul*," which means "Buddha is grass shoes." So for three years, he only kept this question: " 'Buddha is grass shoes.' What does this mean? I don't *know*..." He never checked his practice. He never checked the question. He never checked his teacher. He did not think good or bad. Sok Du only kept this question with one-pointed determination in the midst of all his daily activities, whether sitting, standing, eating, or working.

Then one day, while carrying firewood down a hill, Sok Du's foot hit a rock. The wood spilled out of his hands, and his straw sandals flew in the air as he tumbled on the ground. When the sandals landed, they were all torn up. Seeing this, in that moment Sok Du attained enlightenment. His torn sandals and his mind and the whole universe completely became one. In that point, he saw his true nature. "Waaaahhh! Buddha is grass shoes!" He rushed back to his teacher, shouting, "Zen Master! Zen Master! Now I understand Buddha!"

"Oh? Then bring me your understanding."

Sok Du hit the Zen master on the head with his grass shoes.

"Only that?" the Zen master asked.

"My grass shoes are all broken!"

The Zen master threw his head back and laughed. "Ah, wonderful! Now you truly understand Buddha!"

This is a very interesting story about how to practice and keep One Mind. Only do this practice, and keep a Great Question, and soon everything will become clear to you. It is very easy! But the most important thing is, you must try. When you are doing something, only do it. Only *do* it. This is the bone of the *Lotus Sutra*.

The Hua-yen (Avatamsaka) Sutra

華 嚴 経

If you wish to thoroughly understand

若人欲了知

All the buddhas of the past, present, and future,

三世一切佛

Then you should view the nature of the whole universe

應觀法界性

As being created by mind alone.

一切唯心造

THIS SUTRA REPRESENTS Mahayana Buddhism's best-known teaching. The *Avatamsaka-sutra* teaches the view that everything is truth. In Hinayana Buddhist teaching, for example, getting angry and then acting on that anger is not such a good state. But the *Avatamsaka-sutra* displays Mahayana Buddhism's extremely wide view: like everything else in this universe, anger is also truth. For example, a child misbehaves and plays in a dangerous street. The parent sees this and becomes very angry. The parent scolds or even spanks the child. "How many times have I told you not to do that?" The child's misbehavior is the truth: it is not good or bad. The parent's anger is the truth: it is not good or bad. The scolding and the spanking are also neither good nor bad, and they are also the truth. Whereas the Hinayana view is to try not to act on anger, in this view—the view of the *Avatamsaka*—the anger and the scolding and the spanking are meant to prevent the child from causing harm to himself and others. They are simply truth.

There is a story that illustrates this view. A long time ago in China there lived a very greedy monk. Whenever there was some temple donation, or a distribution of money from a rich layman, this monk was always the first in line. He officiated at many ceremonies, accumulating enough money to buy even the nicest house in town! He was so greedy for money, it seemed he took pleasure only in the joy of collecting it, and never spent any of it. He never even bothered to spend it on himself. His clothes were still quite shabby despite the fact that everyone knew he had a lot of money. "There's the greedy monk in his ragged clothes," the laypeople would say. "He's so cheap he won't even buy something for himself."

Then one day, it started to rain, and the rain did not stop for several weeks. The little town below the temple was washed out. Houses were destroyed, farms were submerged weeks before the big harvest, and cattle perished. The whole town faced a terrible winter without food or housing. The villagers were very sad and frightened.

Then one day, the villagers woke up to find a great number of carts filling the village square. The carts were loaded with many bags of rice and beans, blankets, clothing, and medicine. There were several new ploughs, and four sturdy oxen to pull them! Standing in the middle was the "greedy monk," in his shabby, patched clothes. He used half his money to buy these supplies, and he gave the rest to the mayor of the town. "I am a meditation monk," he told the mayor. "Many years ago I perceived that in the future this town would experience a terrible disaster. So ever since then I have been getting money for this day." When the villagers saw this, they were ashamed of their checking minds. "Waaah, what a great bodhisattva he is!" This is the story of the greedy monk.

This monk's greedy mind was the truth. It was not good or bad. It was not pure or impure. All along, this monk was clearly violating precepts against monks accumulating wealth. For many years he was called a "bad" monk. This shows one of the main differences between Hinayana Buddhism and Mahayana Buddhism. In Mahayana Buddhism, all our actions are not meant for ourselves alone, but are for all beings. Anger for all beings. Greed for all beings. If you are following the path of the Mahayana and do any kind of action for yourself alone, however, this is following the wrong way.

According to the *Avatamsaka-sutra*, your mind makes everything. It is very simple. We already talked about how your mind makes time and space. We talked about how your mind makes the same length of time either longer or shorter. Your thinking makes here and there, up and down, good and bad.

Originally these things do not exist. They come from thinking. When mind appears, everything appears. When mind disappears, everything disappears. Our mind makes this whole universe. There is a famous story that explains this point.

A long time ago in Korea, there was a great Zen master named Won Hyo. When he was a young man, he had to fight in a terrible civil war. He saw many, many men killed. He watched helplessly while innocent women and children were also ruthlessly slain in the pointless give-and-take of battle. Lands were overrun and livestock slaughtered. This hit his mind. "Human beings have no meaning in this life," he thought. "Why must we make so much suffering for ourselves and all beings?" So he decided that society was no good. In disgust, and yearning to find some answer to his deep question about the nature of existence, he shaved his head, became a monk, and headed for the mountains, vowing never to return until he had understood the absolute truth about the nature of existence. In a very short time, he fathomed the teachings of the great sutras. But this did not satisfy him. Even the Buddha's own speech could not lift the heavy burden that lay on his heart like a boulder as he looked at the misery of everyday life. Seeing his condition, several of his friends told Won Hyo about a great Zen master in China who, it was reputed, had been completely enlightened as to the matter of life and death. Perhaps this master could help him. Together with another monk, Won Hyo packed away his sutras and, with backpack and straw hat, headed north across the mountains for China.

Won Hyo traveled on foot for many, many months. Although he was very tired and weak, his determination to find a teacher was unbending. One day, he ran out of water, and as night came he collapsed on the ground, very exhausted. He awoke in the middle of the night, gripped with thirst. As he groped around for something to drink, his fingers felt the edge of a cup, filled to the brim with water. Taking it with both hands, he gratefully drank the water, which Buddha himself must have sent to help him! The water felt cool and refreshing as it ran down his throat. Because he was so thirsty, it seemed like the most delicious water he ever tasted. Happy with his great fortune, Won Hyo settled back into sleep.

In the morning, Won Hyo woke and found beside him what he had taken for a cup the night before. It was a human skullcap in which some rainwater had collected. There were maggots and larvae moving around the sides. The skull wasn't so old, too, so there were still bits of flesh clinging here and there. When he saw that, his stomach convulsed in nausea. Falling on all fours, Won Hyo's mouth opened wide, and as the vomit poured out, his mind suddenly opened and he attained enlightenment. In that moment, he completely attained the true nature of his mind: Last night, since he hadn't seen or thought anything of the water, it was delicious. But now, seeing the skull and thinking about it, the water suddenly became very bad and made him sick to his stomach. "Ah ha," he realized. "Everything is created by mind alone!" Won Hyo realized that his thinking made the water good or bad, delicious or disgusting. Thinking makes things pleasant or unpleasant. Thinking makes the whole universe! Won Hyo attained this point and realized that finding a teacher in China was no longer necessary. He returned to Korea and eventually became the National Teacher. He is known as one of the greatest Zen masters in the history of Korean Buddhism.

Everything is created by mind alone. You made this whole universe. You made dog, and cat, and tree, and God, and mountain. You made the sun, the moon, and the stars. You constantly make life and death, coming and going, past, present, and future. All these things come from your mind. A dog never says, "I am a dog." *You* make that. But don't believe my speech. And don't believe the sutras. Sometime you should go ask a dog, "Are you a dog?" Then he will have a good answer for you. He will show you that *you* make "dog."

So everything in this universe comes from your mind. But where does this mind come from? This is a very important question. Simply talking about mind cannot answer this. Reading books and hearing Dharma talks will not truly solve it. About eighty years ago in Korea, there was a great gathering of monks at Haein Sah Temple. This is the temple in Korea where they keep a collection of many thousands of woodblocks containing the world-famous Tripitaka, for many years the only complete collection of sutras and their commentaries in the world. Several thousand monks came from all over the country to Kaya Mountain to hear the teaching of two great sutra masters, Han Yong Sunim and Kwang Sang No, a famous university professor who had written many important books. The masters lectured for over a week on various subjects. There was lots of discussion. There were seminars on the various sutras. They talked about Hinayana Buddhism and Mahayana Buddhism. From morning to night the sutra masters talked, and talked, and talked. Then finally, at the end of the lectures, the most famous sutra master in the land, Han Yong Sunim, said, "The Buddha taught for forty years, but he only said one thing: 'Everything is created by mind alone.' Therefore, you don't need to seek the Way outside your own minds." All the monks were very impressed with his closing talk. Then he asked if there were any questions.

At that moment, a young monk stood up. He was perhaps eighteen or nineteen years old. He was a hippie monk, wearing tattered, patched robes and with an unshaven face. But though his appearance was shabby, the young monk's eyes sparkled like little jewels. "Master, I have a question," he said.

"Yes?"

"You said that everything is created by mind alone . . ."

"Yes . . ."

"Then who made mind?" The great master was stuck and could not answer. His mind flipped through all the pages of all the sutras piled in his memory, but could not find the answer anywhere. In the building behind him were stacked the eighty-four thousand woodblocks of the Korean Tripitaka, which he had spent his whole life studying. But none of this could help him either. He was completely speechless and stared at the young monk as if he were suddenly paralyzed.

"You don't understand this point!" the young Zen monk said to him. "You can spend one whole week talking on and on about mind, and yet you don't know where it comes from? That's rotten speech!"

So the teaching of the *Avatamsaka-sutra* is very clear: our mind makes everything. Perhaps many people can grasp this point. But where does this mind actually come from? Whether mind appears or disappears doesn't matter. Where does mind come from? What is mind? Sutras can only talk about this matter, but they cannot answer it for your own life. For this kind of teaching ever to help you, you must experience what the sutras and the words of the eminent teachers point to. This is why meditation practice is so important. If you have this kind of question, only understanding sutras cannot help you. Hinayana teaching was not enough, so Mahayana teaching appeared. Mahayana teaching was not enough, so Zen appeared. But don't attach to any way as being more "correct" than any other. Zen people feel that their way to attain mind is correct. Mahayana believes that its way is correct. And maybe some Hinayana Buddhists feel that their way is correct. If you say that any one of these is correct, you don't understand the Buddha's true teaching. The Buddha said that all things have Buddha-nature. But Master Joju said a dog has no Buddha-nature. Which one is correct? Attaining that is a very important point. If you open your mouth, it is already a big mistake! So, Hinayana Buddhism is correct teaching. Mahayana Buddhism is correct teaching. Also Zen Buddhism is correct teaching. The most important point is how you use their teaching to attain your own mind.

There is a very good story that illustrates this. A long time ago in Korea, there was a famous Zen master named Hak Un. He lived alone on a high, craggy mountain. In the valley below his hermitage were two nuns' temples. One day, there was a disagreement between the nuns of the Eastern temple and the nuns of the Western temple. The Eastern temple nuns said, "When you chant to Kwan Seum Bosal, you must pronounce it 'Kwan Se-*um* Bosal.' " But the Western temple nuns countered, "No, that's not correct. It's 'Kwan Se-*oom* Bosal!' " So this sound is a little different for each temple. One group of nuns said, "Kwan Se-*um* Bosal" is correct, the other claimed, "Kwan Se-*oom* Bosal" is correct. In each temple, there were more than two hundred and fifty nuns. So they were always fighting, fighting, fighting. "Ours is correct!" "You're no good! *Oom* is correct!" Ha ha ha ha! [*Laughter from the audience*] So they could not decide which one was correct.

One morning the head nun for the Eastern temple stood up in front of her dharma sisters. "We cannot decide anything. So maybe we should ask the great Zen master up the mountain." All the nuns thought this was a good idea. "So tomorrow night at nine o'clock we'll talk to the Zen master and get his opinion on the matter." Ha ha ha ha!

But the abbot had been a nun for more than thirty years. This problem really worried her a lot. "We say '*um*,' they say '*oom*.' Maybe '*oom*' is really correct after all? If we are wrong, we will all lose face. How can we be sure we are right?" Then she spoke with some other nuns. They talked back and forth all night. "Maybe we should speak with the Zen master before our meeting. Only how can we ask him the right way? This is a very important matter!"

Suddenly one young nun said, "Last year I was Zen Master Hak Un's attendant. I know he really likes rice cakes. You make some special rice cakes, give them to him, and then ask him. If we do this, maybe a good answer will appear!"

Then all the nuns said, "Waah, that's a good idea! You are wonderful!"

Now, making rice cakes is very easy. You take the rice dough, and roll it around, and slice off rice cakes with a sharp knife. So the nuns quickly prepared a wonderful plate of rice cakes. And they didn't want the Western temple nuns to see them. In Korean temples, a bell is rung at nine o'clock, and all the lights go out and the nuns must go to sleep. So they rang the bell as usual, and worked on the rice cakes in very dim candlelight. After finishing the rice cakes, two of the most senior nuns were selected to make the trip up the mountain to see the Zen master, carrying the heaping plate of rice cakes.

After lots of climbing, the nuns finally reached his tiny hermitage. This old Zen master doesn't sleep so much, you know?

KNOCK, KNOCK, KNOCK. From the other side of the door, the Zen master's voice could be heard. "Who's there?"

"Oh, sir, we are from the Eastern nuns' temple."

"It's already past nine o'clock. What's wrong?"

"Oh, we have some—well, um, there was a big birthday party for one of the older nuns. So we made these rice cakes. And now we think about *you*, alone on this mountain with nothing to eat! You like rice cakes?"

"Oh! Rice cakes! Wonderful!" He was very happy, you know? So he let them in. The monk was laughing happily as they entered. Mountain monks don't have so many cookies, not so much of anything, so rice cakes are a very wonderful treat. Monks love rice cakes! Ha ha ha ha! "Oh, I like rice cakes!" Then the nuns gave him all the special cakes. "Very good! Very good taste! Wonderful! Delicious!"

The nuns were also very happy. "Oh, sir, do you like them?"

"Oh, yes! Wonderful! Wonderful! Delicious! Thank you! Thank you!"

"Zen Master, we have to ask you something . . ."

"Oh, any kind of question is no problem!"

"Our question is . . ." And they proceeded to tell him of the day's events. They told him about the argument with the nuns of the Western temple. "They say 'Kwan Se-*oom* Bosal. We are Eastern temple nuns. We say 'Kwan Se-*um* Bosal.' Are we right? Is Kwan Se-*um* Bosal correct?"

"Of course! You are correct! Kwan Se-*um* Bosal is the correct way."

The nuns were very, very happy. "Oh, sir, tomorrow we will have to decide together with them. We want you to come and decide. So you will say Kwan Se-*um* Bosal is correct, right?"

"No problem!" [*Laughter from the audience*] Then the nuns hurried back down the mountain, and went to sleep. Their plan worked, so they were very happy! Now they wouldn't lose face in front of the nuns of the Western temple.

Meanwhile, the nuns of the Western temple had a problem. All day they talked about the meeting that they would soon have with the nuns of the Eastern temple. "What can we do?" One nun thought they should approach the Zen master before the meeting to get his opinion. "But how can we ask him?" They were thinking, thinking, trying to come up with a good idea. Then one nun spoke up. "I understand this Zen master's mind."

"Oh, what kind of mind does he have?"

"Our Zen master's good friend is Zen Master Such-and-Such. He is also my friend. So I know they both like noodles!"

"Noodles?"

"Yah, noodles. We can make some special noodles, and carry them up to him tonight. Then we can ask him whether Kwan Se-*oom* Bosal is correct!"

"Oh, that's a good idea!" the nuns said. "We must ask him before the other nuns do." So the nuns of the Western temple started to make very special noodles for the Zen master. Now, making noodles is not easy. It takes a long time. Making rice cakes is simple, but noodles are very difficult to prepare. You must first prepare rice powder, and roll it out, and then carefully slice the noodles, one by one. Then you can only throw the noodles in the broth right before they are served, or else they'll get too soggy, and there's not such a good taste. It was very late by the time they finished. Then two senior nuns were selected to bring the noodles up the mountain to the Zen master. He is an old monk, so he doesn't sleep so much. Old monks sleep a little in the daytime, but at night they don't sleep so much, you know? [*Laughter.*]

KNOCK, KNOCK, KNOCK!

"Who is it?" came a voice from the other side of the door.

"Sir, we are from the Western nuns' temple."

"Oh, it's almost midnight! What is wrong? Come in, come in."

"Yes, um—sir, there was a very big memorial ceremony at our temple tonight." In Korea, when someone dies, the family will have a memorial ceremony. These ceremonies sometimes take place at night. "We had this big ceremony, and made lots of noodles. Now we think about *you*, up here on the mountain with nothing to eat. Zen Master, you like noodles?"

"Oh, yes! I *like* noodles!" [*Loud laughter from the audience.*] Ha ha ha ha! In Korea, there is a saying: "Rice stomach, cake stomach, noodle stomach, and wine stomach are all different." Different people like different things better than others. But this Zen master wasn't like that. It seemed like he could eat anything. "Oh, I like noodles! That's wonderful!" He slurped them down in a delicious frenzy. Very good taste! "Oh, wonderful noodles. Thank you very much for your hard work! You think about me, so I am very lucky!"

"Oh, no problem, no problem, sir. You are welcome." The nuns were beside themselves with glee that soon they would certainly win the argument.

Also this Zen Master was very happy. The nuns waited a few more minutes and then one of them said, "Zen Master, we have a question . . ."

"Oh, what kind of question? Ask me anything. No problem."

"Sir, our nuns say 'Kwan Se-*oom* Bosal,' but the nuns of the Eastern temple say 'Kwan Se-*um* Bosal.' Zen Master, '*oom*' is correct?"

"Of course! '*oom*' is correct."

"Oh, thank you very much! Now we understand why you are such a great Zen master. Tomorrow morning at eleven o'clock, we all want to meet with you so you can decide. So at that time you will say that Kwan Se-*oom* Bosal is correct?"

"Of course! Kwan Se-*oom* Bosal is correct."

"Oh, thank you! Thank you!" They were very happy and relieved. They bowed at the door and left. They practically ran down the steep mountain to bring the news to the others. When they got back to the Western temple and told their dharma sisters what the Zen master had said, everyone shouted, "Waah, we win! We win! We win! The Zen Master said we are correct!" Everybody was very happy. Then they all went to sleep.

The next morning at eleven o'clock, the great temple bells were struck in each temple. Five hundred nuns gathered in the Main Buddha Hall to bring the matter to the great Zen Master Hak Un. He climbed onto the high rostrum and adjusted his long ceremonial robes. All together, the five hundred nuns did three full prostrations to the Zen master. Then two senior nuns appeared, one from each temple. One nun said, "Zen Master, yesterday we all had an argument. We believe that Kwan Se-*um* Bosal is correct!"

"No, no! Kwan Se-*oom* Bosal is correct," insisted the other.

"Kwan Se-*um* Bosal!"

"Kwan Se-*oom* Bosal!"

"Sir, we cannot decide anything. So we all want to ask you. Which one is correct: Kwan Se-*um* Bosal or Kwan Se-*oom* Bosal?"

The Zen master closed his eyes for a few moments. His body bobbed back and forth ever so slightly in his seat on the high rostrum, pondering their profound question. Many of the nuns leaned forward, anxious to hear what he would say about this great matter. After a long time, he slowly said to the assembly, "This is a *very* difficult question!" [*Laughter from the audience.*]

"What do you mean, difficult? Yesterday we talked about Kwan Se-*um* Bosal being correct . . ."

Other nuns said, "But, sir, you said—"

The Zen master remained silent for a moment, his eyes still closed. "But it is very easy . . ."

Each group of nuns heaved a sigh of relief. "Oh, it's very easy!" Each group thought to themselves, "We will be correct after all!"

He said, "A long time ago, when I was a young monk, I studied the most profound sutras of our tradition. The Rice Cake Sutra says Kwan Se-*um* Bosal is correct. But the Great Noodle Sutra says Kwan Se-*oom* Bosal is correct!" [*Loud, sustained laughter from the audience.*]

The nuns started arguing with each other. "You made rice cakes for the Zen master! You're no good!"

"You gave him noodles! That's low class!"

"You're no good!"

"You're no good!!" Back and forth, back and forth. Thinking, thinking, thinking, thinking, thinking. Checking, checking, checking, checking.

Suddenly the Zen master shouted, "KAAAAAATZ!! Put it all *down*! Kwan Se-*um* Bosal is Kwan Se-*um* Bosal. Kwan Se-*oom* Bosal is Kwan Se-*oom* Bosal. When you're chanting, only *do* it!"

The nuns were very shocked. Instantly their minds became clear. "Oh, thank you very much!"

"Thank you very much for your teaching!"

"Don't attach to speech and words," the Zen master continued. "Only *do* it!" Then he got down off the high rostrum and went back up the mountain.

So, practicing Hinayana Buddhism is very good. Practicing Mahayana Buddhism is very good. And practicing Zen Buddhism is also very good. *Namu myoho renge-kyo* is not a bad practice. *Om mani padme hum* is very good. *Shin myo jang gu dae dharani* is also very, very good. Even repeating "Coca-Cola, Coca-Cola, Coca-Cola" as a mantra can help you if you do it with complete determination, always letting go of your opinion, your situation, and your condition. The most important thing is, when you do something, just do it, one hundred percent. The words themselves are not important. If you want to get enlightenment, then what you need most of all are a Great Question and try-mind. Complete determination. Only try. Only try. Only *do* it. That is the best way to practice.

The Song of Dharma Nature

The nature of the Dharmas is perfect. It does not have two different aspects.

法性圓融無二相

All the various Dharmas are unmoving and fundamentally still.

諸法不動本來寂

They are without name and form, cut off from all things.

無名無相絕一切

This is understood by enlightened wisdom, and not by any other sphere.

證智所知非餘境

The One is in the many, the many are within the One.

一中一切多中一

The One is many, the many are One.

一即一切多即一

Numberless kalpas are the same as one moment.

無量遠劫即一念

One moment is the same as numberless kalpas.

一念即是無量劫

THIS IS AN EXCERPT from a long teaching-poem based on the *Avatam-saka-sutra*. It was written by a very famous master, Ui-Sang, during the golden age of the Shilla Dynasty in Korea. These verses are chanted every day in most temples in Korea. They point directly to the nature of Dharma. Many people say, "Dharma is this. Dharma is that." But what is Dharma exactly? Originally, true Dharma has no name. Dharma has no form. Even calling it "Dharma" is already a big mistake. Dharma is not Dharma, OK? You must understand that. So, Dharma or Dharma-nature are just names for your universal substance. This substance, of which everything in the universe is composed, does not have two different aspects. It does not even have two different forms. It also does not have one aspect or form. It is not one and not two. It is also not a "thing." It takes every form of every thing in the universe, and yet it takes no form, because form is completely empty. It is like electricity. Sometimes electricity appears to us by making fans move and radios emit sound. It produces air-conditioning. It can freeze water and heat a room. It can move a long, heavy train, and yet you walk around with it in your body. It can completely disappear into space. So if you say that electricity is just one thing, you are wrong. If you say that it is all these things that it does, all these actions that it performs, you are also completely wrong. Electricity is none of these things, and yet it is all of them. Similarly, rain, snow, fog, vapor, river, sea, sleet, and ice are all different forms of the same substance. They are different things. But H_2O is unchanging, and composes all of them according to their situation. They are all water. The same is true of Dharma-nature. It is not one and not two. That is a very important point.

So Dharma-nature is universal nature, and it takes many, many different forms. Sometimes it is a mountain, or the rivers, or the sun, the moon, the stars, this cup, this sound, and your mind. They are all the same, because they are all the same universal substance. When any kind of condition appears, Dharma-nature follows that condition, and then some form appears. But when condition disappears, then name and form disappear. That is the meaning of "everything is complete" in these lines. "Complete" is this Dharma-nature, this universal substance that goes around and around and around with no hindrance. It never lacks anything, anywhere. Sometimes it is a mountain, and sometimes it is a river, or trees, or rocks, clouds, humans, air, animals. But originally it is complete stillness. Even while taking form as everything in this universe, it is completely not moving. It takes these forms, but it is none of these forms and is not touched by these forms. Dharma-nature is the same as your true self. It cannot be understood with conceptual thinking. Books and learning cannot give you this point. One hundred Ph.D.'s will not help you attain it.

The One is in the many, the many are within the One.
The One is many, the many are One.
Numberless kalpas are the same as one moment.
One moment is the same as numberless kalpas.

Everyone believes that time and space exist. Ha ha ha ha! That's very funny! Your thinking makes time, and your thinking makes space. But no one really understands this. So these lines state that time and space are the same, and they are one. They are also not one. This One is completely empty. "The One is in the many, the many are within the One. The One is many, the many are One." That is talking about space. Everything is one point, and that one point is everything. There are not two separate things. We can think of it this way: Empty space is only one, indivisible, but in space there are many individual things—mountains, rivers, human beings, trees, dogs, cats, the sun, the moon, the stars. All of these "things" comprise space. Everything is part of space, but that space is not two, because everything is contained within it. There is nothing "outside" space.

This poem has very interesting teaching about the true nature of time, too. "Numberless kalpas are the same as one moment. One moment is the same as numberless kalpas." Time is not long or short. As we saw earlier, since our thinking minds make time, we also make it either long or short. If you practice meditation, however, you can actually perceive that in one moment, there is infinite time. In one moment, there is infinite space. In one moment there is everything! One moment is endless time and space. To most people such a statement must be describing some special realm or experience. So how big is one moment? If we want to imagine this, we can illustrate one moment as being one second divided by infinite time. That is a very short time! A camera can teach you this. There are some special cameras with very high shutter speeds. This kind of camera can photograph a speeding bullet. A moving bullet is invisible to the naked eye. When this camera shutter opens, very quickly, it "catches" the bullet on film. You can see the bullet stopped in midair, not moving. But if you look closely at the photograph, you can tell that this bullet is still moving, though it seems stopped in space. The same is true of our minds, just as they are. If you take your don't-know camera—your mind *before* thinking arises—and perceive just one moment, very deeply, very clearly, you see this bullet not moving. You see everything not moving. This whole world is not moving. That's very interesting! Your mind and this whole universe have the same nature. Originally everything is completely still and not moving. This sutra says, "All the various Dharmas are unmoving and fundamentally still." This is the same point. Stillness simply means our moment mind: one second divided by infinite time. We sometimes call that moment world. It is infinite in time and space, which actually means that it has no time or space.

So this *gatha* has very interesting poetic speech about Dharma-nature and universal substance. But this is only beautiful speech, and even the Buddha's speech cannot help your life if it does not completely become *yours*. Then where does universal substance come from? Where does universal energy appear? It comes from complete stillness. "The One is in the many, the many are within the One. The One is many, the many are One." So everything has it. [*Hits the table.*] Everything comes from complete stillness. [*Hits the table.*] Everything comes from this one point. Sometimes this point is called universal substance, or energy, or Buddha, or God, or consciousness, or holiness, or mind, or the Absolute. [*Hits the table.*] These are all names, and names come from thinking. But originally, this complete stillness point has no name and no form whatsoever, because it is *before* thinking. Yet it is present in all things, and all things have it. In Zen there is a famous kong-an, "The ten thousand things return to One. Where does the One return?" If you attain that point [*hits the table*], you attain One, and you attain everything. That means you attain moment. You attain complete stillness and extinction. But mere intellectual understanding of this cannot help you. Only meditation practice can give you this experience directly. [*Hits the table.*] When this experience completely becomes *yours*, you attain your wisdom. That is the teaching of the Song of Dharma Nature.

The View of Mind-Only and Karma

唯識論과 六途輪廻 因果說

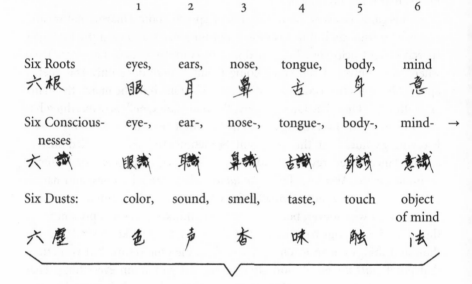

	1	2	3	4	5	6
Six Roots 六根	eyes, 眼	ears, 耳	nose, 鼻	tongue, 舌	body, 身	mind 意
Six Conscious- nesses 六識	eye-, 眼識	ear-, 耳識	nose-, 鼻識	tongue-, 舌識	body-, 身識	mind- 意識 →
Six Dusts: 六塵	color, 色	sound, 声	smell, 香	taste, 味	touch 触	object of mind 法

Eighteen Realms

十八界

Results received in this life

現報

Results received in the next life

順報

Results received in the life after next

順後報

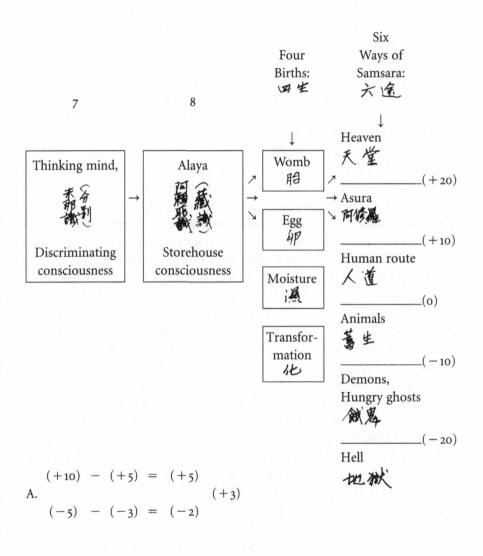

A.
$$(+10) - (+5) = (+5)$$
$$(+3)$$
$$(-5) - (-3) = (-2)$$

B.
$$(+15) - (+5) = (+10)$$
$$(-15)$$
$$(-30) - (-5) = (-25)$$

HUMAN BEINGS APPEAR in this world in physical form. Yet our body is not "I." Something inside controls our body. Its name is soul or mind. Some people call it spirit, ego, or self. Others call it consciousness, soul, or being. But originally it has no name and no form. It is not even a "thing." In this section, for the sake of discussion, we will simply call it "consciousness."

Human consciousness is very, very meticulous. It is like a very high-class computer. But this consciousness is always revolving around and around and around. It can take us from heaven to hell in one instant of thinking. The reason for this is that everybody has some primary cause which meets a condition and produces a result. Then we get some kind of suffering or happiness. But even this resulting emotion or state of mind is always changing and does not stay. It simply becomes the cause of something else. So while our consciousness can be so meticulous, and makes humans the very highest of all animals, it is always wandering around and around the six realms (heavenly realm, *asura* realm, human realm, animal realm, hungry ghost realm, hell realm). It makes suffering for us and for others and for all beings. What is the nature and structure of this consciousness?

Every kind of tree has roots. If there are no roots, this tree cannot stand up and will soon die. Human beings also have roots, what the Buddha called the six roots of eyes, ears, nose, tongue, body, and mind. Eyes see. Ears hear. The nose smells. The tongue tastes. The body senses. And mind perceives. By merely talking about these roots, we already make something, so inside- and outside-thinking appear. So "outside" these six roots are what we call the six dusts. The six dusts are the six corresponding "objects" of perception of the six roots: color, sound, smell, taste, sensation, and objects of mind.

So each one of these six roots (eyes, ears, nose, tongue, body, and mind) has some kind of consciousness. Otherwise, it cannot function by itself. Let's say you have eyes, but you cannot distinguish colors. The name for this is color-blindness. This is another way of saying that one's eye-consciousness is not functioning properly. Having eyes or ears or a nose alone is not enough: each root needs its corresponding consciousness to be present in order to do its job. Moreover, each consciousness must function harmoniously with its corresponding root to make a complete sensation. So I often tell this story: One autumn a long time ago, at Su Dok Sah Temple in Korea, the monks were all harvesting hot red peppers for the annual preparation of food for the winter retreat season. Everyone had a big burlap bag. The monks bent over the rows of red and green peppers, filling their burlap bags. We were supposed to gather only the red peppers and leave the green ones for later.

There were not so many red peppers, but one monk was very, very good at getting them. Everyone else could only get less than half a bag. But his bag was quickly filled nearly to the top, so much so that he could hardly close it. Everybody said, "That's wonderful! How did you get so many?"

"Oh, it's no problem," he said. "There are many, many red peppers over where I was working." The abbot was standing there, and he was also really impressed with this diligent monk's hard work. Then the monk carried his bag over near the kitchen area and emptied it out. But very few red peppers came out—they were mostly just green peppers. The abbot hit him with his walking stick. "You're no good! We only need red peppers. Those green ones aren't ripe yet!"

But instead of realizing his mistake, the monk said, "Sir, those are red peppers!"

Then everybody understood—"Ahh, this monk is not stupid. He's just color-blind!" Ha ha ha ha! [*Laughter from the audience.*]

This is a very interesting story. Having eyes alone is not enough. Perhaps you have two eyes, but these eyes are blind. Having ears is not enough. Some people have ears, just like everybody else, but their ear-consciousness is not working, and so they are deaf. Sometimes you catch a cold, and your nose cannot smell anything, and even your tongue cannot taste things very well. Yah, you still have a nose and tongue on your body. But the sickness has caused some imbalance, so your nose-consciousness and tongue-consciousness have disappeared. These roots have some kind of consciousness that functions with them to produce a result. If this consciousness is not working, or does not function harmoniously with its root, then there is some imbalance in perception.

I have a friend in Osaka, Japan. He is a Korean man named Mr. Lee. Mr. Lee is very, very smart, and he is blind. He understands many, many things. One time, when I was at his house, he was "reading" a copy of the *Diamond Sutra*. Actually, he was just slowly turning the pages of a printing of the *Diamond Sutra* that had been given to him as a gift many years before. The printing was a rare Chinese antique, and Mr. Lee often liked to feel the old parchment and, where possible, "read" the extremely faint impressions imprinted by the woodblocks. So at first, I could not understand: is he reading this, or not? How is that possible? But he was sitting there, turning the pages and holding the book as if he were reading! So it was necessary to test my old friend.

"Mr. Lee, you are reading the *Diamond Sutra*! That is wonderful. But your book is upside down!"

"Oh! I am sorry," he said, and turned the book around. But he had a strange look on his face. Originally, he was holding this book correctly, so I thought then that he really didn't know what was the right side up.

So after a few more moments I said to him, "Oh, no, I am sorry. You were holding it right before. I made a mistake."

"Yes, I was correct the whole time. You are a naughty Zen master!" The strange look disappeared from his face. Then I knew: originally, he could understand what was correct or not, even though he could not see. He could "feel" the right way to hold the book. His understanding and memory are very, very sharp. He has a very clever mind.

One day, we were talking together about some mutual friends, about how they were getting on in life. Sometimes I could not remember certain details about the person, or things we had done together. But Mr. Lee's mind-computer never missed anything. He hears something just one time, and never forgets anything! "Such-and-such was born in that city. His mother's name was Such-and-such, he went to this and that school. He graduated in such-and-such year. His sister married So-and-so from Such-and-such city." I forgot all this long ago, but Mr. Lee remembered everything as if he had heard it that very morning! So I said to him, "Mr. Lee, how can you remember all of that so well?"

"I hear things one time and never lose them." This is very interesting. I used to see him more often when he lived in Seoul many years ago. Friends would drop by the house unexpectedly and ring the bell. Mr. Lee would open the door, and before they could say hello, he would greet them all by name. "Oh, Mr. Park! How are you?" "Mr. Kim, how are you?" "Mr. Chang, how are you?" Even if several people came together, he would turn and address each of them by their family and given names. He could do this even when guests came without notice. How could he do this? He may have just met Mr. Park once, several weeks ago, and had a very short talk with him, perhaps just a hello. But when the door opened, Mr. Lee would instantly recognize him, and remember all his names. That is very strange, you know? He is blind. Not only that: Those of us who have eyesight often meet many people and see their faces and learn their names. But if even one week passes and we meet them again, we often have a hard time remembering their names. Outside we are smiling, and saying "Oh, hello! How are you? Glad to see you again!" Inside we are thinking, "Is this Mr. Park or Mr. Kim or Mr. Song? I don't remember . . ." We already forget. But my friend, Mr. Lee, never forgot anything.

One time I asked him, "How do you do this? We only met that Mr. Park once, several months ago. And we only spoke with him for a few minutes. But you can open the door and immediately you recognize him, even before he has a chance to open his mouth. How is that possible?"

Then Mr. Lee didn't say anything. He just pointed to his nose. His nose was keener than a dog's nose. "I open the door, and it pulls the smell in. Then I understand, 'Oh, that's Mr. Park Such-and-such, and there's Mr. Kim Such-and-such.'" His nose is very meticulous. That is why I often teach that if you use your eyes to understand this world, you always lose a lot of energy. These eyes use maybe eighty percent of your energy. If you close your eyes, if you are blind or you control what you look at, then your eyes' energy all comes to your nose or ears. So Mr. Lee's eye-consciousness wasn't working, but this made his ear-consciousness and his nose-consciousness very strong.

Some of you may have seen these famous Japanese movies about the blind monk, Sato-Ichi. He is called the Blind Samurai. Sato-Ichi is a very great bodhisattva. Though usually very quiet and humble by nature, he uses his samurai sword skills only to help other people. He does not like to fight at all, but if somebody needs help, Sato-Ichi instantly becomes involved in a fierce and exciting battle. Perhaps some bad men come to the temple to make trouble, or he comes across bandits stealing money from people along the road. Then his sword comes out. Many, many people are trying to attack him. They are coming from the front, from the sides, and even from behind him. There are swords slicing at him from many directions. But no one can lay a blade on him! Sato-Ichi cannot see anything with his eyes, but his sword is very, very meticulous. Even though he is completely blind, and even though he is sometimes fighting shoulder-to-shoulder with other people who are helping him, his sword never misses the bad man. He never hits the wrong person. And Sato-Ichi always strikes the most important point with just one blow. He doesn't waste a shot. He does not kill someone unless he has to, preferring instead to land a careful blow that will just hurt his opponent for a short time and not kill him. How can he do this? Sound and smell and his sense of the wind created by the movement of people's bodies tell him everything. So his nose-consciousness and ear-consciousness and body-consciousness are better than anyone's open eyes!

This teaches us that if you concentrate your energy, you can do anything. Sometimes you cannot see or hear or talk. But this energy goes to some place, and you become very sharp and very meticulous. If you have no eyes, no ears, no nose, no tongue, no body, and no mind, then your mind-light is shining everywhere.

So human beings have six roots (eyes, ears, nose, tongue, body, and mind), six dusts (color, sound, smell, taste, touch, and object of mind), and six consciousnesses (eye-consciousness, ear-consciousness, nose-consciousness, tongue-consciousness, body-consciousness, and mind-consciousness). Taken together, these roots, dusts, and consciousnesses constitute the eighteen worlds. We spend our whole lives wandering around in these eighteen worlds, and this makes happiness and sadness, coming and going, here and there. These eighteen worlds make the whole universe in which we live. Human beings cannot get out of the eighteen worlds made by these six senses, allowing themselves instead to be trapped and controlled by attachment to them. Everything is always appearing and disappearing in the eighteen worlds. Then sometimes at night we have dreams. But the eighteen worlds have no dream world: they come from our senses alone, which function while we are awake. Where do dreams come from? Having a dream world means that some other kind of consciousness is also functioning in our minds.

A baby is born in this world. The six consciousnesses appear in a human form. A baby is only eyes, ears, nose, tongue, body, and mind. But the mind hasn't started to function very meticulously yet. The baby's whole life at that point is mostly just centered on feeling and sensation. Up until about one year of age, when this baby senses hunger, he cries "Waaah!" Give him milk, and then he goes "Ahhh . . ." When he feels like peeing, the sensation of a full bladder doesn't feel so good, so he just pees. "Aaahhhhh!" Then he feels better again. He is merely a bundle of raw sensations. He has no clear consciousness. For the first two years, the baby is only absorbing all these sensations and spontaneously acting on them.

But all along, he notices the difference between sensations that he likes and those he doesn't like. "This feels good." "That feels bad!" His mind-consciousness is starting to form. When mother comes, he is happy. If other people appear, he is not as happy. "No, no, no!" He only thinks, "I like Mother. I like Father." If Mother plays with him, he will just do it. If some stranger tries to play with the baby, the baby will often have a mind of "No, no, no. I don't want to. I don't want to. Waaaaaa!" Then Mother appears, and again the baby is very happy. This is the beginning of the seventh consciousness, the mind that discriminates good from bad, like from dislike.

This seventh consciousness is a slightly more developed feeling consciousness and comes from our emotions. "I like this," "I don't like that." Before, what we described as the original six consciousnesses is just raw will, action. But all our ability to discriminate comes from this emotional response we learn to make to the world. Yet still there is nothing we can truly call real memory. The baby only recalls simple sensations and what it likes or doesn't like about them.

As the seventh consciousness becomes more developed, our minds begin to organize these impressions into some kind of order. We become more meticulous about what we have seen and heard, about what we like and dislike. This is the beginning of the eighth consciousness, or memory. This is sometimes referred to as the "storehouse consciousness," because in this consciousness is stored everything that we have ever thought, seen, or done. It is like a computer. Every single thing we experience is "written down." This human computer is very, very meticulous—it does not forget a single thing, strong impressions, feelings, experiences, and perceptions from lifetime to lifetime. Something appears to us through one or more of our six consciousnesses. Perhaps it is compared to something else we have done, through the seventh consciousness. Then we can say, "Ah, this is this. That is that." Everything is being written down here, even when we are not aware of it. Good actions and bad actions, good thoughts and bad thoughts—your eighth consciousness stores them all. This is our intellectual center. It is the realm of pure memory.

Then at night, you no longer see or taste or feel or hear. You don't engage in conscious thinking. Eyes, ears, nose, tongue, body, and thinking mind are not active, except if some sharp sensation appears. We say your six consciousnesses stop working. But this seventh consciousness and eighth consciousness never stop working. Your will-mind of pure sensation is not functioning, but your emotions and your intellectual mind are still engaged. While you are sleeping, the seventh and eighth consciousnesses are still active, so you experience all these images and sensations and emotions that have been built up through experience and habit-force. Maybe you fly in the sky, or talk with your grandmother, who died several years ago. You fight with monsters and bad men, meet many people, and go to interesting places. And you experience this all the time, even in the meditation room. All of you have experienced sleepiness during meditation. You doze for just a second, but in that very, very short time, you go to New York, meet an old friend, change your body, go to San Francisco or Warsaw. Maybe you fight with a bad man, or visit your family. In that moment, your eighteen realms are not functioning for a split second when you fall asleep. But your seventh and eighth consciousnesses remain engaged, and they do together-action with each other. What you get is some strong memory- or feeling-image that appears in your mind through the cause-and-effect interplay of the seventh and eighth consciousnesses. This feeling-image seems completely real for as long as you are engaged with it. This is the nature of dream.

So it is important to understand that the substance of dreams is simply the things we have already experienced, which are "written down" in our storehouse consciousness. I already spoke about my very good friend, Mr. Lee. One day I asked him, "Mr. Lee, you have been blind since birth. So you have never seen objects and things. When you sleep, do you have dreams?"

"I am a human being," he said. "Of course I have dreams!"

But this was still a little confusing to me. "Oh, then you can see images of people and mountains and buildings, different colors and places? You have a sky in your dreams?"

"No, I don't understand that. I can't see things like the sky."

"But you said you have dreams. Why then can't you see the sky?"

"Because I have never actually seen the real sky, so it does not appear in my dreams as I imagine it must appear to you."

"Oh. Then what do you dream about?"

"Well, I dream about walking, eating, talking, sitting, dressing, showering. Things like that."

So this is very interesting. Mr. Lee is teaching us about the nature of dreams: where they come from and how they function. Our dreams are just the things that we have experienced through our eyes, ears, nose, tongue, body, and mind, which are "written down" in our memory. When we have no eye-consciousness, we also don't "see" objects in our dreams.

We have all seen crazy people in our lives. This just means that someone's mind-energy is unbalanced. When your mind is unbalanced, it means that your consciousnesses are imbalanced. They have only followed some strong desire, and so their consciousnesses cannot function harmoniously together. The consciousnesses "peel away" or separate from each other. The sixth consciousness, seventh consciousness, and eighth consciousness are not balanced and cannot connect. You will often see someone on the street talking with himself or herself. There is nobody else there, but this person is laughing and gesturing as if talking to a real person! They may believe that their body can fly in the sky. Sometimes you will see someone take off their clothes in public, or not care about their body, or fight with imaginary demons. The consciousnesses have become separated because these people have followed some strong desire to the exclusion of all else. But these consciousnesses always want to connect with each other. So their sixth consciousness will "talk" to their seventh consciousness, and the eighth consciousness (which contains dream images from actions previously experienced) will "talk" with the other consciousnesses. The eighth consciousness is not balanced by the other consciousnesses. It is not balanced by the sixth consciousness, which is actually seeing and hearing and smelling and tasting the world exactly as it is. The eighth consciousness dominates everything, and so all these dream images appear and the person believes they are real, because they no longer believe their eyes, ears, nose, tongue, body, and mind, which are from the sixth consciousness. Most people are at least a little crazy, because nearly everyone's consciousnesses are a little imbalanced. But truly crazy people are people who have experienced this imbalance for so long, and so strongly, that the consciousnesses no longer do together-action with each other.

So it is very important to balance your mind-energy. It is one benefit of meditation practice. If you practice hard, you can get absolutes energy. It is like trying to put two magnets together. If someone is strongly attached to their desire for some particular things, then they create this strong energy for that thing. Like trying to make the two "plus" poles on a magnet stay together, this is not possible without creating some strong force that pushes the magnets away. So the consciousnesses become separated in the same way. But if you practice, your "plus" energy can connect with this universe, which is like the "minus" pole. You can attain this balance in your mind and in your life. So practicing is very, very important. How do we practice? When you are doing something, only do it. Don't make anything in your mind. Just do it. Whenever you check your feelings, your condition, or your situation, and then hold that, some imbalance appears. You generate opposites energy. The longer and deeper you hold something, the greater the imbalance and disharmony in your mind. But if you keep a clear mind, and don't check anything, then everything in this world is no problem for you.

There is a famous Zen kong-an about this. Every day, Zen Master Soeng Am used to stand out in front of the meditation hall, face the blue mountains in the distance, and say to himself, "Master!"

Then he would answer, "Yes?"

"Keep a clear mind!"

"Yes!"

"Don't be deceived by others, anytime, anyplace!"

"Yes! Yes!" These are two minds, yah? Perhaps that kind of behavior seems a little crazy. "Master?" "Yes!" "Keep a clear mind!" "Yes!" "Don't be deceived by others, anytime, anyplace!" "Yes! Yes!" What is the calling master? What is the answering master? Are there two masters, or one? Maybe someone will say that this calling master is the eighth consciousness, and the answering master is the seventh consciousness? Do you know which master is which? Be careful! Ha ha ha ha! [*Laughter from the audience.*] We have many consciousnesses—the sixth consciousness, the seventh consciousness, and the eighth consciousness. Which one is our true master? If you completely attain this kong-an, you will understand the correct function of your consciousnesses. One Zen master told his student to begin asking himself every day upon waking and all throughout the day: "Who is the master of this body, and where does he reside?" The monk practiced very hard with this question, and one day he got enlightenment. And another great master once asked his student: "When you are sleeping very deeply, a sleep so deep there aren't even any dreams, where is your true master then?" Finding that is very important work. Can you find it? So you must find your true master, your original master. Then you can cut this suffering dream.

But sometimes we experience things in dreams that we don't remember ever experiencing while awake. If our dreams all come from our storehouse consciousness, how do these unfamiliar things appear in our dreams? Where do they come from? Sometimes you read things in a book, or see some piece of a movie or television show, or notice some stranger's face on the street. People tell us many stories about people and places and events, which we then forget. Every day we see many, many faces on the subway, in stores, and in school. You may have seen some cartoon in your childhood, or some pictures in a magazine, and the images from them are still in your storehouse consciousness, though you are not aware of them. But when you sleep, these images can be just as strong as the ones you received today. Not only that—everything you have ever done or experienced in all your past lives is also recorded here, because this storehouse consciousness is not bound by time and space. This is a very important point. This high-class computer never loses anything, ever.

One time, while I was teaching in Kyoto, I had to go to the Korean temple in Osaka. But none of the people knew exactly how to get to the Osaka temple. Then one of them said, "Zen Master, Mr. Lee is staying at a friend's house here in town. Maybe he can tell you how to get to the Osaka temple."

This was a very good idea. So I went to the house where Mr. Lee was staying and knocked on the door.

Mr. Lee opened the door. Before I could open my mouth, he said, "Oh, Zen Master! How are you?"

"I am fine. How are you, Mr. Lee?"

"I am fine. Come in, come in." We talked for a little while, and then I said, "I need to get to our temple in Osaka. Can you tell someone how to drive me there?"

"Oh, no problem, no problem," he said. "I will just take you there myself. Follow me." Then here was a person with eyesight following a blind man. That is a very interesting situation. Ha ha ha! [*Laughter from the audience*] Many people have eyes, but they don't understand even the simplest things. But this Mr. Lee's eyes were completely no-hindrance eyes.

Mr. Lee decided we should go by taxi. We left the apartment building and went out on the street. "I know a good taxi stand," he said. So we walked down the street, made a left, and a right, and another left, walked up a few buildings, and crossed the street at this foot bridge some distance down near the middle of the block. He knew exactly where the foot bridge was, even though it wasn't at an intersection. His body just turned and stepped up onto it without any hesitation. I could not believe this! "Mr. Lee, how did you know where this foot bridge was?"

"Oh, we walk past the fish store, and then there is usually a little breeze coming down the alley between those two buildings after it, and then the bridge is right here, halfway to the gas station. Smell it?" I looked down the road, but this gas station was still very far away. Try as I did, I could not smell anything, but Mr. Lee had already smelled a little gas!

After crossing a few more streets, and navigating an underground walkway with many exits, we reached the taxi stand. In Japan, the taxis are very interesting. If you stand on the right-hand side of the road, when the taxi comes, you don't have to open the door. The driver opens the door mechanically from inside. We stood on the side of the street, and when the taxi appeared and the door opened, Mr. Lee's hand went right for the handle. *Puunk!* He grabbed the handle exactly, without having to move his hand along the door. Then we got inside. The whole time, Mr. Lee was wearing dark sunglasses, so the driver did not know he was blind. Also he never carried this long white pointing stick that blind people use. He didn't need it. He gave very meticulous directions to the driver in fluent Japanese. "Go to such-and-such highway, get off here, then go through this intersection. Make a right at the bakery, and two blocks later make a sharp right, and then after two lights, make two lefts and a right at the park." The whole time the driver nodded at Mr. Lee's good directions. In no time we had arrived at the temple.

Then I said to him in Korean, "Mr. Lee, you are blind. You have never driven in Japan, OK? How do you know these roads so well?"

"Oh, I came here for Buddha's Birthday a few years ago!"

This is a good story. Our storehouse consciousness never loses anything. If you even see or hear or experience something one time, it stays in there forever, even after you die. Though your body disappears, your storehouse consciousness does not stop working, and it takes you someplace. Many people often ask me, "Oh, can you tell me what I was in my previous life?" If you want to understand your past lives, just look very closely at your present life. What do you like to do? All of this comes from our karma, our actions and thinking that are stored in our storehouse consciousness. In the same way, every single thing which you think and do now in this life will determine your next life. So be very careful! Ha ha ha! That is very interesting.

Several years ago, one of my students gave birth to a baby boy. When I was teaching at the New Haven Zen Center, she brought the infant over. The baby was at that time only four or five days old. He was very small, and his eyes were still closed. But the baby would not stop smiling. He couldn't see his mother or anyone else around, so he wasn't just reacting to the people he liked. Whether asleep or awake, the baby's face always bore a big smile. Whatever was going on around him, he never seemed disturbed, and most of all, it never changed this smile. Where does this come from? This baby had just been born, and his karma from the previous life was producing this happy smile. Perhaps he was very happy in his previous life, was a very funny person, or was loved very much.

Then when we die, what happens? Our body is not "I." It is merely a temporary coming-together of earth, air, fire, and water. We have already talked about that before. Time is always passing, and your body gets sick and dies. This body returns to emptiness. But the seventh and eighth consciousnesses never die. They wander around and around and around the six realms, looking for a new home. Eventually they get some new body according to the karma they have made, the habit-mind they have chosen to follow. What kinds of things have you done in your life? This makes your new body. "Your karma makes your body, and your body makes your karma." This is the Buddha's teaching. One person has only done good actions for other people, so their accumulated actions bring them a body in the heavenly realm where everything is stillness and bliss. Some people will again be reborn as human beings.

Nowadays many people in this world only follow their desires and spend their whole lives just satisfying their body's craving for things. This is an animal's mind: only me, only me. "I don't care about other people." A dog doesn't care about a cat's situation, and a snake doesn't care about a bird's condition. Most human beings also live like this. Because of the karma that this kind of life creates, maybe they will be reborn in the animal realm. You can already see how that takes place: whenever you walk down the street, you see many, many examples of this. All people have human faces, but if your intuition is clear, you can see that inside, most people have some animal conscious dominating them. They may have a human form on the outside, but inside there is only a snake's mind, or a dog's mind, or a cat's mind. Perhaps they are eighty percent snake and only twenty percent human consciousness. That is a result of their karma, a mind habit that was created by their actions and even subtle mental attachments made in previous lives and in this life. They only follow their karma, so their karma always controls them, and they cannot get out. "I want this," "I want that." "I like this person," "I hate that person." These habit-forces are stored in their eighth consciousness. If they do not practice, they cannot return to their original human nature—which means having love and compassion for all other beings. Then when they die, their karma will pull them into a rebirth in the lower realms of animals, hungry ghosts, or hell.

If you make something, you get something. That is only the law of cause and effect in this world. It is not special. The Buddha did not invent this view of cause and effect, but he taught it based on his perception of the world as it already is. When the Buddha got enlightenment, he clearly perceived the ways in which sentient beings wander from one kind of birth to another—sometimes human, sometimes animal, sometimes as hungry ghosts— always attached to their desires for things. So how you keep your mind right now makes your whole life. It also makes your next life. Controlling your karma is very, very important practice.

The Four Kinds of Birth
Womb, egg, moisture, and transformation

Everything is born and lives according to the karma it makes. Men and cows and pigs have mammal karma, so they are born through wombs. Birds, reptiles, and fish enter this world through eggs, while bacteria and amoeba appear through moisture births. Spirits appear through transformation, moving from one realm to another as fire is transferred from one lit candle to another. Sentient beings make birth and death, so we all enter this world through four doors. The Buddha teaches that being born is already a big mistake. How do we make this mistake correct? What is the correct *function* of this mistake? How do we *use* this mistake to help other beings? This is our practice. Which door do you like? Ha ha ha!

So our storehouse consciousness can be called a kind of energy. When our body dies, this energy is transferred to another form through a womb, egg, moisture birth, or transformation. What physical form results depends on the nature of the activities that one has done in this life. You must be clear about what kind of energy is in your storehouse consciousness when you die. Do you have plus karma or minus karma? Is there sports karma, music karma, art karma, fighting karma, anger karma, sex karma, or bodhisattva karma? This karma is like the seeds of your next rebirth, the seeds that you are making in your consciousness right now. These seeds are a primary cause, and in this world, cause and effect are always very, very clear. A green-bean seed always makes green beans; a yellow-bean seed only produces yellow beans.

The Six Ways of Samsara
Heaven, asura, the human route, animals, demons/hungry ghosts, and hell

We have already talked a little bit about these Six Ways of Samsara in other contexts. The Buddha taught that all sentient beings constantly wander around and around and around the circle of life and death. The name for this is samsara, the Wheel of Suffering. Sentient beings cannot get off of this wheel if they do not attain their own original nature. These six ways or realms are not places "somewhere else." Heavenly and hellish states are not realms that one "gets to" at a later time. The Buddha taught that everything is created by mind alone. So these places are also created by thinking, and exist entirely in our minds right now whenever we are following our thinking minds. You experience every one of them in your life. The most important thing is, where do you stay? If you cannot control your karma, then when you die, your karma pulls you and you are reborn in one of these states. The six ways are made by your karma, and your karma is made entirely by your thinking. If you are attached to your thinking, you have heaven and hell, life and death, happiness and sadness. If you keep a complete don't-know mind, and don't make anything, then you are already complete, and the six ways of samsara disappear. Then you are free from the Wheel of Suffering.

The heavenly realm is a place of stillness and bliss. In this state, there is only complete happiness. Sentient beings can get to this state by doing only good actions and making the good karma that comes from it. This is not like the biblical heaven. In this realm, the beings do not follow some god. It is a realm or state of mind created by those who have made bliss karma. And eventually, having enjoyed the blissful fruit of doing good actions, their good karma is exhausted—you could say that the balance account is used up. When this occurs, they must fall back to some lower realm after a period of time. The heavenly realm is like a vacation land, a very good situation, so you cannot practice there. Everything is always changing, changing, changing. So if you make karma, you have karma. If you have karma, then even if this is good karma, the karma must eventually change. You must leave heaven! You experience the suffering that comes from then having to endure the relative pain of a less-blissful state. The most important thing you can do is not make anything in your mind: then every place is heaven. Even hell can be heaven if you keep a don't-know mind. All human beings want to go to a good place. But when your karma changes and you have to leave, it is not a pleasant experience. If you attach to heaven, then you cannot function everywhere to help all beings. So don't make anything, not even heaven: then you are free.

The *asura* realm is the condition of fighting mind. We sometimes call this the god army. If you have some anger, or jealousy, and strong dharma energy, you become an *asura*. These are the fighting spirits. This place is not so good, and not bad.

The level under that is the human realm. The Buddha taught that this is the most precious and difficult birth to obtain because only human beings can hear the Dharma and practice. Only human beings can get the enlightenment that cuts off birth and death and transmigration among these realms. Getting a human body is very difficult, so we should not waste this opportunity. It is very, very precious. If you fall from the human realm, it takes many, many kalpas to return to your human state.

The lower realms are next. The following three states of existence are often called the lower or hellish realms because they represent states of complete agony. The animal realm is called a lower realm because animal mind cannot hear the Dharma. They cannot practice, and they cannot get enlightenment as animals. They must become human beings in order to hear the teachings of a Buddha. Being an animal is not so good because people catch you and eat you. Something is always hunting you. You are constantly worrying about food, a safe place to sleep, and the threat of predators. So you have no time for practice. What is worse is that an animal can only follow its animal karma: it cannot change its karma except over many countless eons of existence. So it will stay in this state for a very long time and suffer unimaginable things.

The hungry-ghost realm is the mind that only follows its strong desires. The Buddha taught that these beings are like creatures with very, very large mouths, but their throats are very thin. Although they are always hungry, even one grain of rice or a single tiny crumb cannot pass down their throats, so they are never satiated. If you only stay attached to your desire-mind, we call that having a hungry-ghost mind. You want many, many things in this life, but you cannot get anything. So you are always suffering a great deal. We can see this kind of mind functioning in many people nowadays. Be careful!

The lowest realm is the hell realm. This is the realm of complete suffering. If you make very bad karma, this karma pulls you into some kind of hell mind. When you die, this condition of extreme suffering continues for many kalpas of existence.

Of all the realms, the human realm is the most important. When you are enjoying the bliss of a heavenly state, you have a very good situation and don't arouse the aspiration to get enlightenment. So you cannot practice there, and eventually you fall to a lower state. That is not very wonderful. Animals, hungry ghosts, and hell beings cannot hear the Dharma and practice. This is why all of the sutras say that a human birth is so rare and precious. Only here can you change your karma. Only here can you cut the karma that causes you to wander in samsara. Other realms are only results of good or bad karma. But a human birth is a chance to change primary cause and condition. In other realms you cannot change these things, so you always get a lot of suffering.

Taken as a whole, the Six Ways of Samsara are very interesting teaching, because they are not separate from your own mind. They are not conditions that only befall "other people." You can always experience them, passing through different suffering realms from one minute to the next. Sometimes during one period of sitting, you get a wonderful feeling of stillness and bliss.

But even later during the same period of meditation, you may suddenly experience extreme anger, or some very strong desire-mind or bad feeling that appears out of a memory. "I don't like this meditation. I want to eat some food now." But you are sitting, and you cannot eat for another half hour, so you suffer. The minutes pass by like hours and days! That is suffering. Maybe you remember someone you don't like, and you fight with them in your mind. Coming and going, coming and going, coming and going, nonstop. Happiness, anger, jealousy, desire, boredom, fear—all these are the Six Ways of Samsara. If you are attached to your thinking, then you are always coming and going among these realms. Perhaps you mostly stay in the desire realm of the hungry ghosts, or the anger realm of the *asura*. Many people attach to their animal-minds of desire and hatred. If you keep this mind, this mind controls you. Then when you die, when your physical body falls away, this mind just continues, and you get an animal rebirth, or you are reborn in some hellish state. That is not very wonderful.

So if you want to get out of the six realms of samsara, only keep a don't-know mind, one hundred percent. Don't touch your mind, and don't make anything in your mind. Then these six realms disappear, because originally they do not exist. We make the six realms just through attachment to our thinking-mind. So this is why we suffer in them.

Results received in this life. Results received in the next life.
  Results received in the life after next.

In this world, cause and effect are always very, very clear. It is not only Buddhism's idea. If you look at this world, you can see this operating everywhere. The name Buddhism gives to that is karma. This is a Sanskrit word for "action." Karma is not a special idea. If you make something, you get something, and so something hinders you. That is all.

The effect of karma is felt in this life and in many lifetimes hereafter. Perhaps you do some bad action to somebody. Then this person doesn't like you. Maybe their friends also don't like you because they hear about this bad thing which you did to their friend, and they are not friendly toward you. You suffer. Whenever you suffer, you are reaping the fruit of some karma-seed you have planted through some thought, speech, or action. Sometimes you cannot remember having done anything bad to anybody, but you are suffering, and you don't know why. You may meet someone for the first time, and already they don't like you. Or you have a collision with another car, and your leg is broken. These are not accidents. They are just the result of some previous karma between you and that person. It may have been planted in this life. But it may also come from some previous life.

There is another way of looking at this. Let us say that there are two people, A and B. Person A does ten units of good action. Maybe he gives some food to poor people, always helps sick people, or he supports some monks. Actions like these make very good karma. We say he receives some karmic result of those actions in this life, and he will receive some results in his next lives. But let's say that he only receives five units of happiness for those good actions in this life. He gets some kind of good situation, or some kind of happiness that somehow results from these good things he has done. Then meanwhile he does five units of bad action, and while he is still alive, he experiences three units of bad result. The result may be manifested as his contracting a bad disease, or becoming very poor, or having some other difficult experiences. So some of that bad karma manifests itself now, and some of it isn't ripe yet, and will not appear until his next lives. Therefore he has five units of good karma to experience later, and only two units of bad karma. The net result is three units of good karma. Then when he dies, this amount of good karma causes him to get a certain kind of rebirth. If we look at the column under Six Ways of Samsara, it would mean that he gets a human rebirth. The way we have explained it here, three plus-units, in a human rebirth, is a "low" rebirth, because the human realm is from zero to plus-ten. He is reborn in the lower part. Maybe he will be born with some kind of suffering situation. Maybe he will be reborn in some difficult part of the world, or have some problem with his body to struggle with. He could be poor or hungry. This is a way of showing how the karmic force of his previous good actions combines with the force of his previous bad actions to produce some kind of a result, not only in this life, but also in his following lives. This continues for as long as he makes karma.

Now let us look at person B. This woman does many, many good things, say, fifteen units of good action in her life. But because of the way her life is, from the effect of karma made in previous lives that may only ripen in this life, she only experiences five units of some good result. So there is still a leftover of ten units of some good result that she will experience in subsequent lives. In the meantime, she does many, many bad actions. Let us say that, while she does some good things in her life, she cannot control the bad karma that she has previously made. She wants to do good things, but her bad karma is always pulling her around very strongly. So she is always angry and fighting with people. Maybe she hurts many people. So she does thirty units of bad action. In the world you can always see this: some man does many bad things, but he always has a nice car, a nice job, good money, and a nice house. He has some kind of good situation for the time being. This is because he is now reaping good karma from before, while the bad karma that he is making now has not yet ripened.

This is what we mean when we say that person B only experiences five units of this in her life. So what is left for her to experience is twenty-five units of the result of this bad action. She has ten units of good karma left over, but so many bad actions leaves her with twenty-five units of bad karma. When her body disappears, there are fifteen units of bad karma. She has made much more bad karma than good karma, so maybe she will not even get an animal body when she dies. She used her present human rebirth to do many bad things, and the effect of these things pulls her down into a rebirth in the realm of the hungry ghosts. These are desire beings that crave everything but cannot get anything.

This is just a very simple way of explaining karma. We use it to show how our good karma combines with our bad karma to make some clear result in our present and future rebirths. It also shows how good karma made in this life may or may not seem to have good results in this life, since it must be affected by the appearance or ripening in this life of karma made in previous rebirths. Originally, this scheme does not exist. It is just a teaching device. Also karma does not exist, and the Six Ways of Samsara do not exist. They only come from our thinking and desire. If you are thinking, you make karma, and karma controls you. If you completely cut off all attachment to your thinking, then you do not make any karma. An eminent teacher said, "Our karma comes from our minds. If our minds are extinguished, our karma is also extinguished, like fire burning dry grass." So the most important way to avoid falling into this samsara is by not making anything in your mind in this moment.

A student once asked me, "One meditation teacher told me that if you do only good actions all the time, this can change your karma. Is that true?" This is a very important question. You must understand that good actions cannot change your karma. Good actions may make some kind of happiness, but this happiness is also karma. People sometimes call this good karma. But good karma is still karma, and karma is created by thinking. Everything that is created by thinking always changes. So good karma eventually runs out and becomes bad karma. If you truly want to change your karma, do not make good or bad. That is correct practicing. How do you use your karma to help all beings? If you only want to change your karma, that is already a big mistake. If you have karma, you must find the correct function of your particular karma: this is how you take away your karma. But don't become attached to these words. *Function karma, change karma,* and *take away karma* are the same point: only the speech is different.

So it is very important to practice correctly. We already talked about the eighth consciousness, the storehouse consciousness. Behind the storehouse consciousness is your ninth consciousness. The Sino-Korean term for it is *baek jong shik,* which means "pure white nature." This is our true self, our pure original nature. It is always functioning, all the time. If you attain this original nature, then it is possible to change your karma. But the only way to do this is through having a strong practice. This cannot be emphasized enough. You must perceive that karma is thinking: it is completely empty. It has no self-nature. You can perceive this yourself as your practice becomes stronger and clearer. In the meantime, simply don't make good or bad, and this will soon become clear to you. At that point, what is your original face, your original substance? Nobody can give this to you, this is something you can attain only through the practice of meditation.

Karma
業

Bodhisattva karma—complete compassion
菩薩業　　大慈大悲

Good karma—happiness
善業　　福

Primary Cause
原因

Bad karma—suffering
惡業　　苦

Dependent Origination
緣起

Accumulated karma—predispositions
積業　　素質

Result
結果

Same karma—same action
同業　　同行

Everything appears through karma, and disappears through karma.
萬相　　從緣生　　　從緣滅

Mind appears, then Dharma appears; Dharma appears, then form appears;
form appears, then suffering appears.
心生即法生　　法生即相生　　相生即苦生

Mind disappears, then Dharma disappears; Dharma disappears, then form
disappears; form disappears, then suffering disappears.
心滅即法滅　　法滅即相滅　　相滅即苦滅

All things are created by the mind alone.
一切唯心造

ALL ACTIONS THAT we do now—actions of body, speech, and mind— bear fruit in this life and in future lives. The name for this is karma. If you look at the situation in most parts of the world—especially in Africa or India—you see that there are many, many suffering people. They cannot get food, many die early from disease or starvation, and there is often lots of fighting. Whole groups of people fight each other and kill many, many people. Even babies and small children, who haven't lived long enough to make bad karma with others, are killed, or they are born poor or with some terrible disease. Why does this happen? In this world, cause and effect are always very clear. Everything that we are or do is not an accident but comes from the habit-mind we have made in previous lives. All this comes from their previous lives. Your thinking makes your actions, and this makes karma, so you get a result.

So the most important point is, from moment to moment, how do you keep your mind? Perhaps you get a lot of happiness or money in this life. Maybe you have some sort of good situation. That is not good and not bad. But if you are only attached to your good situation, and only attached to your happiness, then you will have a big problem when this inevitably changes. In this life, happiness or sadness do not really matter. Your particular situation also does not matter. Everything is always changing, so from moment to moment, how do you keep your mind? The state of your mind in this very moment determines the next moment, which conditions the next moment, and so on, as a line begins with one single point. This makes your next hour, your next two hours, and tomorrow. It makes your next life. Everything you are and have and do now is the result of the way you have kept your mind up until this moment. It is very easy to see this!

If you want to make your karma clear, then from moment to moment keep a correct situation, correct relationship to your situation, and correct function. In that way you can change your karma. When your center is not strong, outside conditions and outside situations will always control you. That is simply your karma controlling you. Then finally, when you die, when your body disappears, the force of your karma takes you someplace. Maybe you go to some kind of hell, or you are taken by some demon. If you do many bad things, or steal money, or do bad things to this world, or become attached to your fame, then maybe you will wander as a demon or hungry ghost. If you make bad karma by taking somebody else's money or house or food, you can be reborn as an animal. But then there is some man who only does good things for this world and keeps a correct human mind. He again becomes a human being and can practice and attain enlightenment. If you always do good actions for other people, and help all beings, then maybe you will attain some heaven realm.

This world is always very, very clear. From moment to moment, what are you *doing* now: a good action, or a bad action? Is your mind clear, or is it filled with desire and anger? The way you keep your mind—right now—makes your next life. If you do not make good and bad, you can escape this samsara that you make. You can get enlightenment and become Buddha. Then you can come and go everywhere with complete freedom—sometimes to a heavenly realm and sometimes to a hell realm, only functioning compassionately with a mind that wants to save other beings. You can come and go with no hindrance. Yet if you are attached to your thinking, then good actions can bring you to heaven, and bad actions can bring you to hell. But originally there is no good and no bad. Don't make good and bad. If your life and your actions are always clear and correct, then you get complete freedom in every situation. Coming and going between heaven and hell, nothing can hinder your original job of saving all beings from suffering.

Bodhisattva karma—complete compassion
Good karma—happiness
Bad karma—suffering
Accumulated karma—predispositions
Same karma—same actions

Primary cause, dependent origination, result

We have already said a lot about how everything comes from karma and makes more karma. Nothing happens to you by accident. Your life has already been determined to a very large extent by the force of karmic habits made in previous rebirths. Because we follow what we have previously made, we wander around and around and around in samsara. Can you use your karma to help other beings, or does your karma use you?

The Buddha showed us that all karma comes from our minds. If mind disappears, karma also disappears. Karma is only thinking; it is not special. Only keep a don't-know mind, from moment to moment, and then you keep an empty mind that does not make karma. The reason for this is that when your eighth consciousness is empty, all "plus" and "minus" karma disappears. Empty mind has no karma. You return to your original nature. When you return to your original nature, you control your direction. You can decide what kind of form you will take in the next lifetime, how you want to help people again.

Having bodhisattva karma means living a life only for all beings. My life and my actions are not for me. Every day in the temple, we recite the Four Great Vows together. The first vow is, "Sentient beings are numberless. We vow to save them all." Also, the Temple Rules begin by saying, "You must first make a firm decision to attain enlightenment and help others." These vows talk about our main job in this world: How can I help other beings? They do not just mean how we live this life. Lifetime after lifetime after lifetime, my life is not for me. This is the meaning of having bodhisattva karma.

We already spoke about good karma and bad karma. If you do good things every day, you make good karma, and you get happiness. If you do bad things, you make bad karma and get suffering. My primary-school teacher in Korea always used to say to us, "Every day do one good action." Saying and hearing that are very easy, but accomplishing it is very difficult. Just look at what you do every day. Even in one day, we do many bad things to other people and to this whole world, in thought, word, and deed. But in this world, cause and effect are always very clear. When your body disappears, your bad karma may bring you to some animal rebirth or a hell. So doing good actions is very important. But more important than that is not making good and bad in your mind, and only focusing all your energy on finding your true self and helping others. Just keep the question, "What am I?" and soon everything will become clear.

Accumulated karma in some activity makes strong disposition for those actions. If you make the same kind of karma every day, then in this life and the next, that habit appears again. This is why we sometimes say that karma is a mind habit. Some children can play the violin or piano very well at a very young age. Or they play a certain sport well, or can do very good drawings. Everybody knows about Mozart, who could write and perform very good orchestral music as a young boy. The karma for those actions comes from a strong habit that he made doing those things in some previous life. Then when people like him appear in this world again, that particular karma naturally appears again and can manifest itself very quickly. Accumulated karma applies to the working of karma in individuals.

Many years ago in Korea, a certain old monk died in his temple. According to custom, his body would have to be cremated within one week. So the monk's body was dressed in his best robes and placed in a coffin. The temple faithful gathered around the coffin in the Main Buddha Hall and performed a long chanting ceremony.

After five days of chanting, a knocking sound came from the inside of the coffin! "Open up! Let me out! Let me out!" All the people jumped back. A few women screamed. After a great deal of nervous hesitation, they finally pried open the coffin. The old monk sat up, squinting. Several people fainted.

"Waaahhhh, Sunim!" they shouted. "You are alive! You are alive!"

The monk looked very shocked at these words. "What do you mean alive? Was I dead?"

"Yes, you have been dead for four days. Now we are doing your funeral ceremony."

But the monk could not believe this. "That is not possible. I was just having a dream . . ."

"Dream? What kind of dream?"

"I went to many interesting places," the monk said. "But then I had a strange experience." He recounted that in his dream he found himself under a big, knotty tree. There was a tall house on a high hill near the tree, with a long set of stairs leading up to the front door. He walked up the steps and was greeted with the sight of people singing and dancing and calling his name. It was a very strong force that pulled him up the stairs, and he could not resist being there—it was as if he flew there. He stayed for some time and felt very happy to be there. Suddenly a great big giant appeared and shouted, "You! Why did you come here? Go back—you are not wanted here!" The giant picked up the monk and threw him on the ground. His head hit the ground with a heavy thud, and he woke up. He found that he had hit his head against the lid of the coffin. That is when he started knocking from inside.

Everyone was amazed at his dream. "What could it possibly mean?" "What is happening? Did this monk die, or was he just dreaming?"

Just then the Zen master came by. He had heard the people's surprise and commotion from his room. So the old monk told him about his experience.

"This is a very easy question," the Zen master said. "Go outside and look at the tree in the front courtyard." The old monk went out and saw that it was the same tree he had seen in his dream! When he looked up, he saw a birdhouse nailed to the highest bough. The shape of the birdhouse was very similar to the house he had approached in his dream. The Zen master told him to climb the tree and look inside the birdhouse. He found a newborn bird in the house, dead.

"Zen Master, what does all of this mean? I still don't understand!" Everybody was very confused.

"This situation is very clear, but no one understands karma, so I will explain: You died. But you made a little bad karma in your life, so you became this bird. The music and chanting you heard was all your students and friends chanting for you to get a good rebirth. Their faith-mind is very strong, so their clear-mind energy pulled you. Then you could not become this bird, so the bird died—it was only a baby, and you still had strong human karma."

The old monk bowed. "*Aigo*, everybody, thank you for your hard practice! Everybody is helping me."

"Now you must pay them back," the Zen master said. "Only go straight, don't know. Find your true self, and that will help your students."

"Thank you very much for your teaching," the old monk said, and bowed.

When people do things together, they make some of the same karma together. The Buddha taught that when you walk down the street and just brush shoulders with some person, that is because you have made karma with that person for more than five hundred lifetimes. That is very interesting! Imagine how much karma you have made with your parents and brothers and sisters to be born in the same family with them! A man and woman meet and fall in love, or two people meet and become best friends. This is not an accident. It is the result of many, many thousands of lifetimes spent together, doing similar things with one another. Then in this life, their karma with one another connects. They feel like they have always known each other. And this also happens with practicing people. You go to some dharma talk and sit in the room with many people you don't know. You probably wouldn't have anything to do with each other, and no reason to be friends. But all of you have the same interest in hearing the Dharma. This is because in previous lives we have all gathered together to hear this teaching. Chinese people have the same general karma together, so in this life some people are reborn Chinese. Korean people shared the same general karma together in Korea, so that is why they are reborn Korean. The same is true for Americans, Japanese, Germans—any country or group.

Animals also have different karma; each has a different kind of consciousness. One dog seems sad all the time, while one dog is very smart—he can find anything! And yet another is known as being a very stupid dog. In many temples you see stray dogs and cats. Sometimes a dog will always stay outside a certain Buddha Hall during chanting, while a certain cat will always stay inside a Buddha Hall during ceremonies. Even though they cannot get good food in the temple, and there is no meat for these animals to eat, try as you may, you cannot get them out of the temple. This is very interesting. These animals were practicing students in a previous life but because of making some bad karma, they were reborn as animals. This habit mind created by being around Buddhist teaching continues, even in this rebirth. Now they are being helped by the practice of other people. So these animals are always teaching us to be careful!

I have already spoken about one of my students who was very attached to her pet snakes. She always spent a lot of time with them and always took them wherever she went. She loved her snakes more than she loved her own family members! Once, when her mother was very sick, this woman would not leave a meditation retreat to visit her mother in the hospital because there was no one to take care of her snakes while she was traveling. She was afraid that if she left the snakes for a long time, they would die. So she didn't visit her mother right before her mother died. This is very interesting karma. We can see that human beings do together-action with one another and make karma with one another through this. But human beings make karma with other beings, too, and this karma can be just as strong as the karma they make with other human beings.

So with regard to karma between a human and his pet, there are two kinds of karma at work: On the one hand, some human beings and animals lived together as master and pet in some previous life. Then in this life, the animal is again this human being's pet. This is a very simple kind of karma. But another form of karma has to do with particularly strong actions performed between human beings. For example, let's say some human being, in his previous life, perhaps stole some money from someone, or kidnapped someone, or captured someone and kept them prisoner. Maybe some human being kept servants, or slaves, and tightly controlled their lives. Perhaps also some man was chased by the police, was caught and thrown into jail for his actions. He has only followed his animal desires and did not perform correct human actions, so the negative force of the karma that this makes has caused him to lose his human stature when he dies. In this life, this bad man gets an animal body. So the animal-mind that he makes is the same as in the previous life where he did all those bad actions, only now it gets an animal form on the outside too. And it also still has this karma that it made with another human being, or another group of humans. So now this animal body is controlled by another human being and must stay in this house. This animal becomes this one man's possession. The pet cannot leave, and the human controls it: how much food it can have, and when and where it goes to the bathroom. Maybe the human being will force the animal to do hard work or live in a cage, just as in the previous life when the animal-mind human controlled this other human being.

Everything appears through karma, and disappears through karma.

Mind appears, then Dharma appears; Dharma appears, then form appears; form appears, then suffering appears.

Mind disappears, then Dharma disappears; Dharma disappears, then form disappears; form disappears, then suffering disappears.

All things are created by the mind alone.

Any kind of bodily form that we have comes from our karma, and our karma comes from thinking. As we said earlier, "Your karma makes your body, and your body makes your karma." Human form, dog form, cat form, heavenly form, hungry-ghost form—all these states come from karma. The karma made in your previous lives determines what kind of body or "form" you receive in this life. This is the meaning of "Your karma makes your body." Now, most people cannot see their karma, and because of the attractive power of karmic habits, they are attached to their particular karma. This means they are attached to their thinking, their bodies, and the conditions and situations that mind and body make. Because they are attached to this form, they continue to repeat the karma that comes from their body's desires and even make it deeper and stronger. That is the meaning of "Your body makes your karma." The cycle goes around and around and around, making more suffering for themselves and for this whole world. The name for that is samsara, or the endless cycle of birth, sickness, old age, and death. Another name for that is ignorance. We sometimes call it suffering.

So if mind appears, then Dharma appears. When Dharma appears, then any kind of form appears. Whenever any kind of form appears, this form always remains for some period, changes, and then returns to emptiness. We make form and become attached to it. Then when it inevitably changes and disappears, because we are attached to it, we get suffering. But when mind disappears, all Dharmas disappear; when Dharma disappears, all forms disappear. This means that all karma disappears, and so suffering also disappears. The Buddha taught that everything is created by mind alone. This is an explanation of that point. If you have mind, you always have karma, and this karma controls you. It always makes suffering for yourself and for this world. But if you don't make mind, none of this ever appears. When you return to your true nature, there is no longer any name or form. There is no karma, and no suffering.

So karma is very simple: Right now, what do you like? That mind makes your next moment, next moment, next moment. All of this makes your next life, like pearls strung together on a necklace. In this world, cause and effect are always very clear—not only in the human realm, but in everything you see. If rain comes, flowers appear everywhere. If there is no rain, the flowers do not grow. When the sun comes out, it is warm; when the sun is hidden by clouds, it is cool outside. The same is true of human beings' life. If you want to take away your karma, strong practicing is very important. Then you can control your karma and use your karma to help all beings. That is a very important point.

Since you share similar karma with certain other people, you can use this karmic affinity either to hurt or help them. Nearly everyone is deeply attached to their thinking, so they are attached to their karma. They are completely asleep, and cannot help other people. If you cut off all thinking and all desires, you will wake up. If you keep a thinking mind, however, then your daily life is a dream. Waking up from this dream is more difficult than waking up from an ordinary dream, so you must try very hard. When you wake up, then you can control your karma. With no special effort, this helps those around you. So you must wake up!

Long ago in Korea there was a very rich and famous sutra master. At that time, five hundred years ago, rich monks had many students and poor monks had very few. The rich ones paid their students so they could afford to go to sutra school. After sponsoring ninety-nine students over the years, the sutra master decided he would take on just one more student, and then retire. The hundredth monk was named Dol Um. He was given plenty of food, clothing, and money to learn the sutras, and he studied hard for three years. One day he realized, "These sutras are not necessary. All sutras only save your mind. If your mind is empty, of what use are the sutras?" He understood then that he had to practice at a Zen temple. So the young monk said to his teacher, "Master, this sutra style is no good. We must go to a Zen temple. You are old and will soon die. When your body disappears, where will you stay?"

I don't know," answered the sutra master. "You are right. We will go. But who will take care of my land, my barns, my books and possessions?"

"You have many capable students. Leave everything with them."

"OK, then. It is decided. We will leave tomorrow."

None of the other monks were like Dol Um. They only thought, "I want to be rich; I want to be a famous sutra master." But this hundredth monk was very clever. As the old sutra master watched Dol Um pack a few belongings in his sack, he thought, "Ah, I decided to stop at one hundred students, and Buddha has helped me by sending this especially clever boy. It is good to follow his direction."

There was a meeting of the whole monastery at which the teacher announced that he would be going to the Zen temple with his youngest, newest student. Then he told everyone to take care of his rice fields and large barns, assigning each monk some responsibility. Early the next day, they packed provisions, said good-bye, and left for the Zen temple. After walking about three miles up the mountainside they stopped to rest and drink some tea. Looking down at the monastery in the valley, the student noticed a fire. "Master, look! A fire! What is burning?"

"Oh no! It is my barn!" the old monk shouted. "You go on alone. I must return to the temple!"

"But Master, soon you will die. Where are you going?"

"No, no, no. I must go back!"

So the sutra master returned to his monastery. Dol Um realized that his teacher had many attachments and that even in ten thousand years he could not change his teacher's mind. He continued straight on to the Zen temple.

Three years passed. The famous sutra master died, and the news of his death spread across Korea. The traditional forty-nine-day ceremony was planned, with a thousand guests expected. Many monks came to share the food, the drink, and the master's money. Dol Um, too, came to the funeral ceremony. He was met by a Dharma brother, the head monk, who said, "You're no good. When the master was dying, you did not visit him. You're coming now just to get a share of the property."

"No, I am not interested in land," Dol Um replied. "I want no money. But I would like two pots of rice soup, please, if this is possible."

"Only this?"

"Yes."

"OK."

It was the custom to make an offering of food to the local demons so that they would be afraid to trespass on the ceremonial grounds. So Dol Um took the soup to a large field outside the funeral area. He left the soup out near a group of large rocks that were used for milling rice. Then he returned to the Main Buddha Hall and struck a column three times. Immediately a large snake appeared, slithered outside to the rocks, and drank all the rice soup. Dol Um approached the snake as it finished its meal. His eyes were sad as he looked down on it.

"Teacher," said Dol Um, "why did you get this body?"

The snake replied, "I am sorry. I should have listened to you. Now I have a snake's body." For years, the sutra master had pursued fame and wealth. He made bad karma, even though he was a monk. His consciousness had become competitive, desirous, and spiteful. So in this life he received a snake's body.

Dol Um said, "Teacher, you have many desires. You have eaten all this soup, and still it is not enough. This snake's body is not good for you. It is only a desire body. You must hit your head against the rocks and get rid of this body."

The snake replied, "Oh, this body is not so bad; I cannot!"

"You must try!" But the snake only lay there crying. "You must try!" Then Dol Um hit the snake three times and killed it.

A cloud of blue smoke appeared and floated away. Dol Um followed it. A bird flew nearby, and the cloud began to assume its form. "No good!" shouted Dol Um. Again it floated on and began to enter the form of a cow. "No good!" he shouted again. Then the cloud floated further and further into the mountains, deep into the mountains to a little house where a middle-aged couple lived. The cloud entered the house. Dol Um waited for an hour, and then knocked on the front door.

"Hello, how are you?"

"Fine, thank you, Venerable Sunim. Why have you come here?"

"I am here to tell you that soon you will have a baby."

"What? We built this house twenty years ago, and we have not been able to have children all this time. You must be mistaken. My wife is now more than forty-five years old. It is not possible."

"OK, but if you have a baby, you must give it to me."

"Alright, if we have a baby, we will give it to you."

"Wonderful. I will be back in one year."

As time passed, the woman's belly began to swell, and the couple realized that the monk had, in fact, been right. They were very happy. After nine months passed, they had a fine boy. On the day of the birth, Dol Um appeared.

"Sunim, you were right! We have a child."

"Wonderful! Now, as we agreed, you must give me the boy."

"Oh, no!"

"But you told me before that you would give him to me."

"No! He is our boy. After living here for twenty years, praying for children, we finally have a son!"

"Alright. But this boy will not live more than three years. You must understand this."

The boy grew for another year, then two years, and there was no problem. His parents thought the monk must have been wrong. Then one day the boy became sickly. He had no appetite, and in a few days he was near death. His parents were sick with worry.

Exactly three years after the boy was born, Dol Um again appeared.

"How is your boy?"

"He will die soon," he said, and fell silent.

"This is just what I told you."

"What shall we do?"

"You must give him to me."

"You will take good care of him?"

"Of course."

As soon as the boy was in Dol Um's hands, the sickness disappeared. He was laughing and happy, and the color returned to his cheeks. The parents finally saw that he had very strong karma with this monk, so they were happy to let him go. Dol Um took good care of him every day, and the boy was never sick again.

Several years passed. One day, while Dol Um was sitting in meditation, the boy went to the kitchen and picked up a knife. "I will kill my teacher," he thought. Just as he was about to strike, Dol Um turned and said, "Put down the knife and come here. You know who I am; why do you want to kill me?"

"I don't understand. I just don't like you, so I want to kill you."

"Why?"

"I don't know." The boy was bewildered by his strong feelings.

"In the future you will understand, but not until you understand yourself."

"Yes, sir. But how?"

Dol Um led him to a rice paper window and poked a tiny hole. "You must sit here and look through this hole until a great big cow comes into the hole. Only this. Don't think about anything else. Only watch for this big cow. When it comes, you will understand your true self."

So the child only ate, slept, and looked through the hole in the rice paper. "When will the cow come?" His very clear child's mind held only this one question. One day passed, two days, almost one hundred days, when one day the hole grew bigger and bigger, and a huge cow appeared—"*Mooooo!*"

"Waaaaaahhhh!" the boy cried out. "Master! Master! The cow has come!"

Dol Um rushed over and slapped his face. "Where is the cow now?"

"Oh!" The child understood himself completely, and attained enlightenment. Then he looked at his teacher and said, "Hey, you were my student before!"

"Yes, sir," said Dol Um, bowing.

So this story's teaching is, wake up! This child woke up early. In his previous life he had many desires, so he could not wake up. His student liked him and cared for him. Dol Um understood his teacher's mind, so when his teacher was getting a new body, Dol Um followed the blue smoke of his teacher's consciousness.

The hundredth student and his teacher had very good karma together, so in the next life they were again teacher and student. This is interesting. Having the same karma is very important. But having a strong direction is most important. Before Dol Um studied at the Zen temple he could not use his karma with his teacher; after he understood himself, he understood his teacher's mind as well. So first you must find your True Way, then understand your karma, and then you can use the strong karma you have with other people to help them. Only in this way can you save all beings from suffering.

The Six Paramitas

六婆羅蜜行

Generosity

布施

Precepts (Conduct)

持戒

Perseverance (Patience)

忍辱

Effort (Energy)

精進

Samadhi (Meditation)

禪定

Wisdom

智慧

THESE SIX PARAMITAS are practical guides for the view of Mahayana Buddhism. We have already talked about some of the main teachings of Hinayana Buddhism. The three main insights of Hinayana Buddhism are Insight into Impermanence, Insight into Impurity, and Insight into Nonself. In Mahayana Buddhism, these are the Six Paramitas. They are the essential practices of the Mahayana view. They also point to our direction, which is our vow, lifetime after lifetime, to practice hard and attain enlightenment so that we can save all beings from suffering.

The meaning of *generosity* is very clear. All human beings have possessions. But why do you obtain and keep these things? Are they only for your own pleasure, or do they help you to help others? This is a very important point. Many people keep their things only for themselves, or for their family. This causes attachment, and attachment always leads to suffering. When you die, what can you carry with you? "Coming empty-handed, going empty-handed—that is human." A famous Christian proverb says, "The shroud has no pockets." And you cannot even take your body with you when you go! So human beings cannot carry anything with them: why should we be attached to our things in this life? However much you value your possessions, they cannot help your true self. We must all remember this. So Mahayana Buddhism teaches generosity to help us keep our direction clear. My life is only for all beings, so my possessions are also only for all beings. If money comes, that is OK. If money goes, that is also OK. How do my money and my things function to help other beings? And this generosity does not apply just to physical objects: everything I have and everything I am is only for all beings.

We already talked about the *precepts*. This is a very important part of the Buddha's teaching. In Hinayana Buddhist practice, you follow the precepts in order to keep a pure mind. If your mind is pure, maybe someday you can attain nirvana and get out of this suffering realm. The precepts are like a fence that protects you from evil. They keep the thieves from stealing your treasure. Mahayana precepts are the same precepts, but we practice with them a little differently. In Mahayana practice, my precepts and my practice are not for me: they are only for all beings. So I keep these precepts not for myself, but to help other beings. This means that sometimes, in some situations, breaking the precepts can help others much better than holding the precepts. If your mind is clear, then keeping the precepts is correct practice, and breaking the precepts is also correct practice. The most important point is, why do you do it? Is it only for you, or for all beings?

If you keep these precepts just for yourself, to keep yourself pure, sometimes that is not very clear practice. Let's say that one day you are gathering firewood in the mountains. A rabbit runs down the path next to where you are. It reaches a fork in the road and runs down the right fork. A few moments later, a hunter comes running after it. He is carrying a high-powered rifle. The hunter sees you standing there and asks, "Which way did the rabbit go?" You have just taken the Five Precepts. One of the most important of the precepts that the Buddha himself taught is to refrain from telling lies. On many occasions during his life, the Buddha emphasized the need to keep this precept. Now, if you think, "I just took these Five Precepts. I am a correct Buddhist. I must keep a pure mind, so I must keep the precepts—I cannot tell a lie!" then you will tell the hunter which way the rabbit ran. You will tell the truth. Then this hunter will find the rabbit and kill it. The rabbit dies, and the hunter makes bad karma with the rabbit. That is called keeping the precepts only for yourself. It is a very narrow practice of the precepts.

But there is another way. It is a very wide way on which you travel to liberation with all other beings. This wide way is the function of your moment-to-moment clear mind to help others. So when this hunter comes down the road, you are filled with sadness for the rabbit, who may die if you tell the truth. Also you look at this hunter and you know that, by killing the rabbit, he will only make more bad karma for himself. This bad karma will cause him a great deal of suffering in the future. So you point down the left fork in the road, and you say, "The rabbit went that way! He went that way! Hurry up!" You send him down the wrong path. By saying this, you have broken one of the most important precepts given to us by the Buddha. But this precept is not for you, to help your own situation and condition at that moment. We must realize what the precepts are for: they give our practice its basic direction. The precepts exist so that we may help all beings. So, by breaking this precept, in this situation, you have spared the rabbit's life. You have also saved this hunter from making more bad karma. In the Mahayana tradition, the precepts are not for me—to keep my mind pure—but for all beings. We sometimes call this a clear-mind precept. How do the precepts function, from moment to moment, to help all beings? So in our precepts ceremonies we say, "Know when the precepts are open, and when they are closed; know when to keep them and when to break them." This is a very important kind of practice.

A famous sutra says, "The Buddha taught all Dharmas in order to save all minds. When you do not keep all these minds, what use is there for the Dharmas?" So, if you have mind, then having precepts and keeping precepts are very important practices. But if you have truly cut off all thinking and truly do not keep any mind, then precepts are not necessary. Freely using good and bad to help others, your life is already bodhisattva action.

Another important part of our practice is our *effort*. In most Mahayana Buddhist traditions, every morning is begun by vowing aloud together, "Sentient beings are numberless; we vow to save them all." This means that, from moment to moment, my life is only for all beings. The name for this is *perseverance*. It means that whether good feelings or bad feelings appear, in a good situation or a bad situation, whatever condition appears, whether suffering or well, I only try to help all beings. We sometimes call this try-mind. Try, try, try for ten thousand years, nonstop. Not only in this life, but I vow that in life after life after life I will attain enlightenment and help others get out of suffering. That is our practice. Our practice never ends, because our job of saving all beings never ends. Another name for that is the Great Bodhisattva Way.

Practice is not only what we do in the meditation room. Rather, from moment to moment, what are you *doing* now? That is correct practice. It is often called *effort*; we sometimes call it try-mind. It is very simple, yah? There is no need to make it complicated.

If you practice with this kind of direction and determination, you attain a not-moving mind. In any condition or situation, your mind is clear like space. This means it is clear like a mirror: when red comes before the mirror, there is red; when white comes, white. The clear mirror never holds anything, and it is never moved by what appears in its infinitely empty face. Then when you see, when you hear, when you smell, when you taste, when you touch, and when you think—everything, just-like-this, is the truth. The name for this is *samadhi*, or deep meditation.

But samadhi is not special. Many people think that meditation ultimately means only keeping a kind of strong, deep, and uninterrupted meditative state of samadhi during sitting. "I must do hard practice, only sitting. Then I will get samadhi!" This kind of effort is not good and not bad. But true meditation is not just what you do on the cushion. True meditation is how you keep your mind from moment to moment. Many people can practice samurai-style meditation: on the cushion, they have very deep meditative states. "Oh, this is samadhi! Two hours, not moving. How wonderful!" But they cannot make this meditation connect with their everyday lives. This kind of samadhi-mind makes meditation special. For these kinds of people, meditation and everyday life are separate and do not function together. But true samadhi means keeping a not-moving mind from moment to moment, whether sitting, standing, walking, lying down, driving a car, or washing the dishes. This is correct meditation and true samadhi. It is not special.

In the sixteenth century, the Japanese army invaded Korea. The invaders were ruthless in their destruction of the countryside, looting cities and temples, carting off priceless treasures, and burning to the ground whatever else was left. Everyone was very afraid of the foreign troops. One day, a division of soldiers entered the precincts of Pae Yop Sah temple on Gu Wol Mountain, in what is now North Korea. They chased out all the monks and entered the main hall to claim the large gold statue of the Buddha.

As they tore off the front doors, the soldiers came upon an old monk, sitting quietly in the darkness. The monk did not move or flinch as they poured in and surrounded him, brandishing swords, spears, and clubs over his head. "Get out, old man!" they shouted into his ears. "Beat it now, or we kill you on the spot!" But the old monk simply did not move—it was as good as shouting at an old stump! Some of the soldiers shoved him, pulling his ears up in an attempt to force him up from the cushion. Others jabbed him in the back with the blunt ends of their staffs. Yet the old monk wouldn't move. One soldier had evidently had enough and fired a warning shot directly into the finely painted ceiling over the old monk's head. Other soldiers jumped at the sudden report, but the monk was completely unmoved.

A senior officer leaned into the monk's face and said, "Old man, aren't you afraid of dying anymore?" Many of the other soldiers laughed heartily at this.

Suddenly, the monk looked up at the officer and shouted, "*Katz!*"

Meanwhile, a general had been watching all this from outside. Admiring the old monk's fearless mind, which did not move at all in the midst of the threats and abuse poured out on him, the general strode in and apologized to the monk. Then he led his troops out of the temple, leaving the old monk and even Buddha behind.

This is true samadhi. Your mind is not moving in any situation or condition.

If you practice in these ways, true *wisdom* appears. We can say that wisdom is the medicine that cures ignorance. When you keep a pure and clear mind, wisdom appears naturally, by itself, as you continue practicing and digesting your experience. But pure mind and clear mind are different roads to wisdom. In many traditions of Buddhism, the emphasis is on trying to keep your mind pure and free of any kind of taint. So these Buddhist traditions always teach about having insights into impurity: you must see that everything is impure, and then you can take away impurity. You can attain a pure mind. But Mahayana Buddhism and Zen teach that if you do not make mind, there is no mind. Then your mind is clear like space, which means that your mind is already beyond pure and impure. Originally pure and impure do not exist.

So the experience and function of pure mind and clear mind are different. Let's say you have a baby. This baby's mind is very pure. It does not have strong ideas about the world. It does not have so many attachments and desires. Its mind is very simple: when I'm hungry, I eat; when I'm tired, I sleep. This is a very simple mind. It is very pure and not tainted. Some of the original Buddhist traditions emphasize this point: we must remove all impurity from our minds and return to our original purity.

This kind of teaching is not good and not bad. It is important to experience your originally pure mind. But one more step is necessary. If you just keep a pure mind, your wisdom cannot grow up. Let's look again at this child. His mind is very, very pure. It does not have so many attachments. It is not tainted by so many desires. But having a pure mind alone is not enough. How does this pure mind *function* to help others? If this child's mother gets very sick, or if she has some problem, or gets injured, this child cannot respond to that situation. In the same way, when suffering people appear, or there are situations that do not have such clear-cut solutions, or there is perhaps a need to break a precept to truly help someone, a mind that only wants to be pure cannot always function so well. Practice that emphasizes attaining a pure mind does not show the student how to cultivate a spontaneous wisdom that functions clearly in any situation. A pure mind cannot always respond meticulously when different situations appear. But having wisdom means your clear mind is able to function spontaneously in any situation. It uses good situations to help people. It also uses bad situations to help people. This is because true wisdom is beyond good and bad, purity and impurity. That is a very important point.

So you must always keep a clear mind, from moment to moment, and then your mind functions clearly to help all beings. Through this, you can digest your actions and your understanding and make wisdom. Then when you see, when you hear, when you smell, when you taste, when you touch, when you think, everything, just-like-this, is the truth. The sky is blue. The tree is green. A dog is barking, "Woof! Woof!" Sugar is sweet. When you are hungry, what? When you are tired, what? A suffering person comes to you: what can you do? The name for that is wisdom. It is not complicated.

4

Zen Buddhism (Cham Soen)

參 禪 佛敎

1. To pass through this gate, do not attach to any thinking that arises in the mind.

入 此 門 內　　莫 存 知 解

2. Not depending on words, a special transmission outside the Sutras.

不 立 文 字　　敎 外 別 傳

Pointing directly to Mind: see your true nature, become Buddha.

直 指 人 心　　見 性 成 佛

3. The Buddha taught all the Dharmas in order to save all minds.

佛 說 一 切 法　　爲 度 一 切 心

When you do not keep all these minds, what use is there for the Dharmas?

若 無 一 切 心　　何 用 一 切 法

ZEN MEANS UNDERSTANDING my true self. "What am I?" Everybody says, "I am." Descartes said, "I think, therefore I am." We always say "I." But what is this "I"? Where does this "I" come from? When you die, where does it go? These are the most important questions you can ever ask. If you attain this "I," you attain everything. That is because this "I" is part of universal substance. Your substance, this desk's substance, this stick's substance, the sun, the moon, the stars—everything's substance is the same substance. So if you want to understand your true nature, first you must attain your original substance. This means attaining universal substance and the substance of everything.

But speaking like this is also a problem. Substance means the Absolute. In the Absolute there are no opposites. Our words and speech are all opposites-thinking. So the moment you even say "Absolute," it is no longer the Absolute. The moment you say "substance," it is no longer just substance. You have already created the world of opposites. An eminent Zen master said, "Even mentioning Buddha is like dumping dung on your head." This is the same point. True substance, your true nature, and truth are already beyond speech and words. So, a long time ago, an eminent teacher said, "The true form has no words. Truth is unmoving." If you open your mouth, you rely on speech and words and language, and so you have already lost the truth. Words and speech cannot describe this point. Speech and words cannot show your true nature. So we often say, "Silence is better than holiness." That is a very important point.

Everything in this world—the sun, the moon, the stars, mountains, rivers, and trees—everything is constantly moving. But there is one thing that never moves. It never comes or goes. It is never born and it never dies. What is this not-moving thing? Can you tell me? If you find that, you will find your true self and attain universal substance. But understanding cannot help you find that point. Even one hundred Ph.D.'s will not show you your true nature. If you were to read all eighty-four thousand sutras, learn all the Buddha's speech, and earnestly study all the teachings of all the eminent Zen masters, you would never attain your true self through understanding. None of the struggle and toil that gets you this knowledge can help you as much as one moment of insight into your true nature. Our true nature cannot be found in books and academic studies because our true nature is before speech and words. It is *before* thinking. If you find that before-thinking point, then it is possible to attain your true self. So, a long time ago, Descartes said, "I think, therefore I am." This is where philosophy begins. But if you are *not* thinking, what? This is where Zen practice begins.

Zen teaching simply shows how to reach this point that has no speech and words. We have already looked at Hinayana Buddhism and Mahayana Buddhism. Both of these traditions have very clear roads. Each of them has a map and a kind of vehicle in which you travel. Hinayana Buddhism is like taking a bicycle from New York to Boston. Through my own efforts, I eventually arrive at some destination. Hinayana Buddhism does this by teaching us about this suffering world. We live in a realm of name and form, a world of opposites that create suffering. If I can take away this opposites world, I can arrive in nirvana, or the world of Absolutes. In nirvana, there is no coming and no going, no life or death, or happiness or sadness. Everything is complete stillness and extinction. And I can get there all by myself: I don't need a god or some kind of belief that is outside my own mind. This is a very rare and wonderful teaching that appeared in the world!

Mahayana Buddhist practice is like taking a bus from New York to Boston: not only I, but all beings get to some good place together. "All beings on the same day get enlightenment." The Mahayana accomplishes this by first teaching that originally there is nothing. Originally there *is* no suffering, and no nirvana. If you *make* suffering, there is suffering. But suffering is originally void and empty. Your body is also originally empty and has no self-nature. By completely attaining Nothing, you attain that there is no time and no space. Everything is already complete, just as it is: When you see, when you hear, when you smell, when you taste, when you touch, when you think, everything is complete, just as it is. There is no suffering to get *out* of, and no nirvana to *get* to. That means that everything is already truth. The wall is white: that is truth. The sky is blue: that is truth. Right now, a car is passing by outside: that is also complete truth. When you attain this point, and attain that everything is already truth, then from moment to moment you can live clearly for other beings. Your life is only for all beings, because you attain that you and all beings are not separate things. You always do together-action with other beings. So Mahayana Buddhism is like taking a bus or a train, because your practice is about taking all beings together to liberation.

So as we see, Hinayana practice and Mahayana practice both have very, very clear roads that you can follow. Hinayana Buddhism and Mahayana Buddhism use these roads to explain our true nature. If you do Hinayana Buddhist practice, maybe someday you will attain your true self, nirvana. If you do Mahayana Buddhist practice, then maybe you will understand your true self. But if somebody asks you, "What is your true self?" "Where is your mind?" "What is nirvana?" then even if you have attained it, and even if you understand your true nature, you cannot say anything. We say it is like a mute who has had a very wonderful dream: inside, he understands something very, very deeply and clearly. But he cannot say anything. He cannot even open his mouth, because our true self is before thinking. This point is beyond the grasp of speech and words, so how could it ever be described? If you want to show this true nature, if you want to teach it to others, only some kind of demonstration is possible. [*Hits the table.*] At that point, a different kind of teaching style is necessary. [*Hits the table again.*] We call this teaching style Zen meditation.

Zen has no road. It has no map. Practicing Zen is like taking an airplane to Los Angeles. You get in this plane, and—BOOM!—you and all beings arrive together in Los Angeles. An airplane has no road! There is no path or way to come or go on. You attain your true self directly, completely, but you do it without any kind of map. It is not dependent on the sutras. It is not dependent on Buddha. It is not dependent on time or space, name or form, or speech or words. It does not even depend on Zen. If you want to ride this plane, then from moment to moment just don't make anything, and then you will realize that you are already complete. That is Zen mind. It is very simple.

To pass through this gate, do not attach to any thinking that arises in the mind.

Entering the gate of Zen practice simply means returning to your mind as it naturally is before thinking arises. This point is universal substance and your true nature. People sometimes call it true self, or nature, or Buddha, or God, or energy, or mind, or consciousness, or holiness, or the Absolute. People call it many, many things, but originally this point has no name and no form. [*Hits the table.*] That is because this point is already *before* thinking. It cannot be grasped with conceptual thought. If you call it anything, or give it any kind of name, this is only thinking and understanding, and none of that can help you. The great Chinese Zen master Nam Cheon said that attaining our true self is "not dependent on understanding, and not dependent on not-understanding. Understanding is illusion; not-understanding is just blankness." Your relationship to this world and your relationship to yourself are not based on thinking. Your correct relationship to this life does not come out of any kind of understanding. You cannot reason life or death. So if you want to pass the gate of Zen, first you must completely cut off all attachment to thinking, and return to your mind *before* thinking arises. For teaching purposes, we sometimes call this point don't-know mind. Attaining it is very simple, and not far away. Simply ask yourself, very deeply, "What am I?" What appears is only *"Don't know . . ."* This is already your true nature.

Not depending on words, a special transmission outside the
  Sutras. Pointing directly to Mind: see your true nature,
  become Buddha.

So, finding your true nature is not dependent on any kind of explanation. It is not dependent on the Sutras or academic knowledge. No concept can ever express it. Speech and words cannot touch it. Zen teaching points directly at your own mind so that you can wake up and become Buddha. But if you want to become Buddha, even understanding the Buddha's own speech cannot help you. That is what is meant by "a special transmission outside the Sutras." The Sutras cannot give you this point: they only explain it, and even one hundred explanations of your true self will not help you when your body disappears. This is a very important point. Using intellectual understanding to find your true nature is like expecting a hungry man to satisfy his gnawing hunger with a picture of a banana. Zen teaching is not like this. Zen teaching says, "Open your mouth. Here's a banana. Now eat!"

Even being the most learned master of the Buddhist Sutras cannot amount to much if you don't understand your own true nature. A long time ago in China there lived a famous sutra master named Dok Sahn. He was renowned for his extremely profound knowledge of the *Diamond Sutra*. He would travel from temple to temple, testing the monks in their knowledge of this important and subtle teaching. Dok Sahn always won every debate in which he took part. Nobody could match him! He also wrote many commentaries on the *Diamond Sutra*, and carried them with him wherever he went.

One day, Dok Sahn heard about a Zen temple in the south of China where the monks just ate, slept, and sat in meditation all day, facing the wall. He heard that many of the monks became Buddha through this kind of practice. This is another way of saying that they got enlightenment. "That's crazy," he thought. "They don't read sutras, they don't understand the Buddha's teaching. How can they become Buddha?" But many people said that these monks got enlightenment. So Dok Sahn packed his commentaries on the *Diamond Sutra* into a backpack and headed south. "I will hit them with the *Diamond Sutra* and wake them up to the Buddha's teaching."

He traveled for many days, over mountains and through deep valleys. One day, while walking down an old country road, Dok Sahn passed a small tea house. As it was lunchtime, he decided to stop for a meal and some rest. The owner of the tea house was an old Buddhist laywoman who practiced very hard, every day. She greeted Dok Sahn at the door. "Oh, great Sutra Master Dok Sahn, how are you?"

"I am fine. How are you?"

"Fine. Where are you going?"

Dok Sahn replied, "There is a temple in the south where the monks only eat, sleep, and then sit all day, facing the wall. People say that many of them have become Buddha. That is crazy! I will go hit them and wake them up with the *Diamond Sutra!*"

"Oh, that is wonderful," she said. "You are such a famous sutra master. You understand all the Buddha's speech. You understand the Buddha's teaching. May I ask you a question?"

This surprised Dok Sahn. "Of course, ask me anything!"

"OK, if you answer this question correctly, then lunch is free. If you cannot answer correctly, you must pay."

At these words, Dok Sahn grew very angry! "How dare you speak to me like that! Do you know who you are talking to? I am the greatest sutra master in the land!" But the woman's center did not move at his words, and she was not afraid. "Go ahead, ask me anything," he said.

"In the *Diamond Sutra* it says, 'It is impossible to keep past mind, impossible to hold on to present mind, and impossible to grasp future mind.' So, Master Dok Sahn, with what mind will you eat lunch?"

Dok Sahn was completely stuck and could not answer. In his mind, he ran back and forth through the *Diamond Sutra* and all the commentaries written on it by all the eminent teachers. His mind went around and around and around this question, thinking, thinking, thinking, thinking, thinking, but no answer appeared. He was very shocked! His face turned pink, then red, then white, then yellow—his mouth was completely stuck, and could not say anything.

The woman laughed. "You don't understand the *Diamond Sutra*'s true meaning. You don't understand anything! You only understand the Buddha's speech, but you don't understand its true meaning. If you cannot answer this question, how will you hit the Zen monks in the south?"

Master Dok Sahn was very ashamed and in that moment lost his high position. "Where did you get this understanding?" he asked her.

"I didn't get this understanding from anybody. Everyone already has it inside them, if they only look."

"Yes, yes. . . . But has anyone guided you to it?"

The woman replied, "There is a great Zen master named Yong Dam who lives on a high mountain in the next province. If you ask him, maybe he will help you."

Dok Sahn was completely ashamed of himself. So he gave up his plan to hit the Zen monks in the south and instead headed east to find Zen Master Yong Dam. After several more weeks of travel, he arrived at the Zen master's temple and was granted a meeting with Zen Master Yong Dam very soon after arriving. While having tea with the Zen master, Dok Sahn tried to explain his understanding of the *Diamond Sutra* and Buddhism. He explained emptiness and nonappearance. He expounded the nature of the Tathagata and wisdom. Dok Sahn talked for hours and hours and hours. The Zen master could not get a word in, because Dok Sahn's speech and understanding were like a mighty, unstoppable torrent.

Finally, it was getting late, and it was time to retire for the night. As he was leaving Zen Master Yong Dam's room, Dok Sahn saw that it had gotten dark out—so dark that he couldn't see even one foot in front of him. "Master," he said, "there's no light. I can't see anything." Zen Master Yong Dam handed him a lit candle taper. As Dok Sahn stepped into the thick darkness, the Zen master leaned over and blew out the taper, plunging Dok Sahn back into complete darkness. At that moment, Dok Sahn's mind opened, and he got enlightenment. He completely attained his true nature.

Zen Master Yong Dam asked him, "What did you understand from this?"

"From now on I will believe the teachings of all the Zen masters in the world," he replied. The next day, before an assembly of monks, Zen Master Yong Dam mounted the high rostrum and said, "Among you there is a great man whose fangs are like swords, and whose mouth is like a big blood pot.

You may strike him with a stick, but he will not turn his head. One day in the future, he will make his way to the top of a very high mountain."

Dok Sahn instantly took out his notes and commentaries on the *Diamond Sutra*. He held up a flaming torch and said, "Even though one may completely master various profound philosophies, it is like placing a single strand of hair in the vast sky. Even if one gains all the essential knowledge in the world, it is like casting a drop of water into a deep canyon." Then, taking up his notes and commentaries, he burned them all, and bowed gratefully. Dok Sahn was now a free man.

So this story shows us that even if you understand all the Buddha's speech, if you cannot demonstrate this understanding when called upon, it is worth nothing. Dry cognition cannot help your life. Even if you read all the eighty-four thousand sutras and attend dharma talks regularly, it will not help you as much as experiencing one moment of clear mind. At the moment of your death, what will your intellectual understanding do for you? In the future, you will eventually lose this body: at that time, how will your academic knowledge help you get a new one? All of our understanding is only somebody else's idea. No matter how great this understanding is, if it hasn't been digested and become yours through the practice of meditation, it cannot help you.

There is another story about this. A long time ago in China, there was a famous sutra master named Guji. He was known all over China because he had completely mastered all eighty-four thousand sutras of the Buddha's teaching. By his mid-twenties he was already recognized as a great teacher. At any one time, as many as seven hundred monks lived and studied at his temple. Monks and academics came from all over China, just to have the benefit of hearing even one of Guji's lectures on the Buddhist sutras. No one could defeat him in debate. It is said that Guji could cite from memory, by line and page and fascicle, even the most obscure passages in the sutras. He was a very high-class scholar!

One day, Guji was a bit tired, so he went out into the small backyard behind his simple hermitage for a little rest. He sat under a tree, where it was shady and cool. He had been reading a sutra for several minutes when suddenly, the gate to his yard was flung open. In walked a tall nun wearing a broad-brimmed straw hat. She held in her right hand a tall staff, from the top of which hung six little rings. This kind of stick was only used by high-class Zen masters and patriarchs of Zen lineages, so Guji was very surprised to see it in the hands of this strange visitor.

The nun marched through the gate and walked straight up to Guji. Her tall figure cast a shadow across the pages of the sutra he was reading. Now, in Buddhist tradition, a student or visitor must always bow when greeting a monk, especially when the teacher is a high-class master like Guji. Also, at that time in China, the rule was that a nun must always bow to a monk. Even if the nun was ordained for fifty years, she must still bow even to a monk who received *bikkhu* precepts the day before. But this tall nun did not bow to the great Master Guji! Also she did not remove her hat, but stood over him while he sat. This was very arrogant behavior. After a few moments, the nun began to circle Guji three times. Every other step, she banged the staff on the ground loudly. It was very, very noisy!

So Guji was the greatest sutra master in China. There were hundreds of monks studying under him at any one time. He completely understood everything about Buddhism. He understood what were the correct rules and what was the correct tradition. So he knew that this nun was definitely not acting right. "She doesn't understand her correct situation!" he thought. "She doesn't understand her correct relationship and the correct temple rules! Who is her teacher?" Inside, he was very angry! All his energy went up into his face. He put down his sutra and, with a disbelieving look, only watched this nun's arrogant action as she circled his chair, banging the patriarchal staff on the ground at every other step. Then Guji's angry mind exploded: "You! Come over here!"

But the nun did not move. She stood in front of Master Guji, towering over him and looking down on his face. After a few moments, she started to speak. "You are the greatest sutra master in China." Her tone was very arrogant. This made Guji even angrier.

"So, what?" he shouted.

The nun continued looking down on him, and then burst out: "I hear you teach the sutras. But I don't like sutras! I don't like any of the Buddha's teaching. I want to hear your own true speech. Right now, give me just one word!"

Guji was stuck and could not answer. His mind went around and around, searching for some answer. But there was none. "What is my true speech?" he thought. Meanwhile, all the eighty-four thousand sutras of the Buddhist canon revolved around and around and around in his head, looking for an answer. But nothing appeared! "What is my true speech? I don't know . . ." Thinking, thinking, thinking, thinking, thinking. His academic mind was all jammed up, trying to find his own true speech somewhere in all the books he had read. So in that moment, the great master Guji lost all his understanding—he was completely stuck!

A dog understands a dog's speech, and a cat understands a cat's speech. All animals understand their true speech. But what is a human being's true speech? What is *your* true speech? Can you find it? That's a very important point. The great master Guji also didn't understand, and all the Buddhist Sutras could not give it to him. As he sat there, his face became red, then became white, then became dark. Then it got tight. He was completely stuck! So Shil Che Bikkhuni said, "You, the great Master Guji, don't even understand your own true speech! How can you possibly teach the Buddha's speech?" Then she snorted, "Hunnhh!" and marched out through the gate of Guji's backyard.

So this incident hit Guji's mind like a lightning bolt. Everything he had been working for was lost in one instant. In the East we would say that he completely lost his face. He realized he had just spent his entire life repeating the Buddha's speech without having the slightest clue about what it truly pointed to. Guji returned to his room and put on his great long robes. Then he ordered his attendant to ring the great temple bell five times, a signal for some great event or emergency. Unexpectedly for the monks in the temple that day, a deep, solemn sound suddenly filled the woods and valleys. *B-bong-bong! Bong! Bong! Bong! B-bong-B-bong!* Out in the fields, in the hills surrounding the monastery, in the study halls and rooms, all seven hundred monks heard this sound. They looked up from their work, confused: "What's happening? Has someone died? Is our teacher unwell?" They all stopped what they were doing and headed for the Great Hall.

When the monks had assembled, Guji ascended the high rostrum, and after a few long moments, he began to speak. "Today a strange nun appeared and asked me for my own true speech. I could not say anything. I don't understand my own true speech—how can I possibly teach the Buddha's speech to all of you? That has hit my mind. I have been a monk for thirty years now. I understand all about Buddhism. I understand all the sutras. But still that cannot help me. So today this nun strongly taught me my correct direction. I must answer her question now, before ever opening my mouth again."

The seven hundred monks in attendance were confused. "Our teacher not teach? That's not possible!" But when they looked at their teacher, they saw that his noble face was truly sad and broken.

Guji understood their thinking, and this made him even sadder. "I am sorry," he said. "Today I have failed all of you. So now I must close this school forever. You must all find another teacher. Better yet, go and find a meditation hall where you can sit and look deeply into this great matter. Some day soon each of us must eventually die. Do not fool yourselves any longer: you must all solve this question for yourselves. You must all find your correct direction, and then you can find your own, true original speech." With this, Guji descended from the high rostrum and returned to his room.

So now these monks were all very surprised. Some cried. Some shouted for Master Guji to reconsider. Others argued about whether or not their teacher was doing the right thing. The whole temple was very, very disturbed by their teacher's speech. But Guji paid no attention to the commotion in the temple that day. He had strongly decided to do something, so there was no turning back. From that day on, he ate only once a day. He never lay down to sleep. And he only sat in meditation, strongly keeping the question, "What is my true speech? *What am I?*" And all that appeared out of this was a deep "Don't know . . ." All thinking was completely cut off. In time, when they saw that their teacher would not reconsider, the students packed their belongings and drifted away, out of the valley, to other mountains and temples. The great temple doors were closed—*boom!*—and locked. And with unshakable determination, Guji remained seated in his room, facing the wall. "What am I? Don't *knowww . . .*"

Then late one night, several years later, someone banged on the great temple gate. It was midnight, and as usual, Guji was sitting in his room, facing the wall, very deeply keeping don't-know mind. His attendant rushed to the gate and said, "I am sorry. My teacher is not seeing anyone anymore. Please go away."

But the stranger persisted. "Let me in! Let me in! I want to see Master Guji. I want to see Master Guji."

"No! No! You cannot!"

The stranger would not leave and kept banging loudly on the gate. "Please, I must see your master!" He continued to argue with the attendant to let him in. They argued back and forth for almost one hour!

While all this was going on, Guji continued sitting, only keeping a strong don't know. In China, a temple's gate is located very far from the master's house. Even so, Guji could still hear the commotion and shouting. Ordinarily it would not disturb him—he had a Great Question that held his mind like a giant vise. Yet the stranger would not leave, and persistently argued on with the attendant. People will usually go away immediately when a great master's attendant tells them that he is not seeing any visitors. But this man stubbornly refused, and only argued back and forth with the attendant. So as Guji heard this, a very angry mind appeared in him. "Maybe they are bad men. What if they are beating my attendant?" He stood up, grabbed a big stick, and marched out to the great temple gate. "You must go away," he shouted through the gate. "Nobody can come in!"

"Oh, are you the great Master Guji?" came a voice through the gate. "Pleased to meet you."

"Are you crazy?" Guji shouted. "Who are you? How dare you cause such a problem at this hour?"

But the stranger was unmoved. In fact, his face was kind and compassionate, his eyes full of light even in the midnight darkness. "I am sorry to disturb you, Master Guji," he said. "I am Cholyong, from the southern mountain."

When Guji heard this name, the big stick fell from his hands. His jaw dropped open. This was none other than the great Zen Master Cholyong, the most famous Zen master in all of China! Guji had wanted to get enlightenment and make the long trip to Cholyong's mountain, to be tested once in dharma combat. And now this Zen Master Cholyong had appeared at his gate. So Guji was very surprised. He immediately opened the gate. "Zen Master, I am sorry! I am sorry! My bad speech to *you*—"

But Zen Master Cholyong only waved his hands with a smile as he entered the gate. "That's no problem. In fact, it is I who must apologize. I have just learned that my student, Shil Che Bikkhuni, came here and made some bad speech to you some time ago. So I have come here to apologize."

"Apologize? To me?" Guji said. "Oh, sir, that's not necessary. Your student only came and woke up my mind. Her question has pointed me in the correct direction. So I am very grateful to her."

Cholyong smiled. "Oh, that's very wonderful! She didn't make some bad speech to you?"

"No, sir! No, sir! Her bad speech has cleared my mind. But please, sir, do come to my room. I have a question for you, if I may . . ." When they entered the master's quarters, Guji put on his formal robes and asked Cholyong to sit on the high rostrum. Then Guji proceeded to give Zen Master Cholyong three full prostrations and humbly knelt before him.

"So, you have some kind of question?" Cholyong asked.

"Yes, sir, I do."

"So, then ask me any kind of question about your life, your problem, or your practicing."

Guji said, "Zen Master, I don't like any of the Buddha's speech. I don't like the Sutras. Sir, what is your own true speech? Please give me one word."

Cholyong did not say a thing. Looking directly into Guji's eyes, he slowly raised one finger. When he saw this one finger, Guji's mind suddenly shot open, as if by a bolt of lightning. *Piitchhuu!*—he got enlightenment! Now Guji understood Dharma. Now he understood truth. Now he understood Buddha's mind and the teachings of all the eminent teachers. One finger! The language of the eighty-four thousand sutras was revealed by that one finger, and Guji felt as if the meaning of the entire universe had just been opened up to him and a weight had been lifted off his neck. Now he attained the correct way, and truth, and his correct life. Guji had found his own true speech, at last!

With tears filling his eyes, Guji slowly stood up. He bowed deeply and said, "Oh, thank you very much for your teaching."

Cholyong smiled and said, "You are welcome. But now I ask you, Guji, what did you get?"

Without the slightest hesitation, Guji lifted one finger. Cholyong was very happy and laughed out loud, clapping his hands. That is Guji's correct speech! That is Cholyong's correct speech! That is also all beings' correct speech! Zen Master Cholyong descended from the high rostrum and gave Guji *inka*. He later gave Guji full Transmission of the Dharma. The great sutra master Guji cut his thinking-mind and completely attained his true nature. So in this one finger, this high-class sutra master attained his true nature and the nature of all things. This is how Guji became a great Zen master.

From then on, Guji no longer stayed in the temple. He moved to a little hermitage high in the mountains. And he continued to practice very, very strongly, even after his great enlightenment. The Sino-Korean term for that is *bo in*. When you boil a pot of rice, even after the rice is finished cooking, you leave the lid on the rice for about ten minutes before serving. It is very important to keep this steam in for a little while longer. Otherwise, even though the rice is cooked, it is not completely finished and won't have a good texture or taste. The same is true for people who have some kind of enlightenment. A keen-eyed teacher will urge them to deepen their realization with further practice for a certain period. The name for that is *bo in*.

So Guji stayed in his mountain hermitage all day, only practicing. But word about him quickly spread, and many people braved the steep mountain paths to ask him questions. "What is Buddha?" Guji would raise one finger.

"What is Dharma?" Guji would raise one finger. "What is truth?" Guji would raise one finger. "What is Buddhism's highest and holiest teaching?" Guji would raise just one finger. "What is nature?" Guji would raise one finger. Zen Master Guji could answer any kind of difficult question with just this one finger. His one-finger Zen opened many, many minds and earned Guji the name Il Che Soen Sa, or One-Finger Zen Master. So this is the story of Guji's one-finger Zen. It is very famous teaching.

One day, Zen Master Guji had to go down to the village to visit the head temple. It was a whole day's journey. So he left right after breakfast, and wouldn't be back, he told his thirteen-year-old attendant, until evening. The attendant was left alone at the hermitage all day. Some time after Guji had left, a monk entered the temple and knocked on the door. He was very tall and wore a big straw hat. "I want to see Zen Master Guji," he said to the attendant.

"I am sorry," said the attendant. "The master is gone for the day."

"When will he be back?"

"Oh, I don't expect him until after dinner."

"Oh, that's my bad karma," the monk said. "I want to see him now, but I am very busy. I can't stay long. That's a big problem . . ."

"Why is that a problem?" the boy asked.

"I have some question, but your master is not here. Now I have come all this way, and I cannot ask him anything. What a shame . . ."

"You have some question?"

"Yes, I have a question."

Then the attendant said, "Oh, that's no problem!"

"What do you mean, 'That's no problem?' "

"I can answer for you!" the attendant said, folding his arms and smiling brightly. This young attendant had a big mouth!

"How can you answer me?" the monk asked. "Do you understand Zen Master Guji's teaching?"

"Of course! I've lived at this hermitage for three years. I understand all of my teacher's Dharma!"

"Oh, that's wonderful. Please teach me!"

Then the boy said, "OK, OK. Follow me." He led the monk to Guji's receiving room. While the monk waited nervously, the attendant donned his teacher's long ceremonial robes and ascended the high rostrum. He held Guji's big Zen stick across his lap. After taking several moments to adjust his posture, the boy said, "OK, we must follow the correct form. First, bow three times, as you would to my venerable teacher, whose rare and ineffable teaching you are about to receive."

Eager to have the great Master Guji's teaching given to him, the monk was only too happy to oblige. "Yes, yes." He did three full prostrations to the attendant and remained kneeling humbly before him.

"So," the boy continued. "You have some kind of question? You can ask me anything: your life, your problem, your practicing. Any kind of question . . ."

The monk bowed his head. "Sir, I want to understand: What is Dharma? Dharma comes from where?" The attendant closed his eyes until they were just two very narrow slits. He bobbed back and forth slowly on the high seat, as if deeply pondering the old monk's question. Then suddenly the boy raised one finger right in front of the old monk's face—*piitchhuu!*

At this, the old monk's eyes grew as big as saucers. "Oh, thank you very much for your teaching!" he exclaimed, and bowed deeply to the boy.

"You are welcome, you are welcome," the attendant replied, and waved him out the door. Overjoyed at his good fortune to receive this rare and profound teaching, the monk left the temple and made his way back down the mountain in high spirits. He had been walking for about two hours when he met an older monk who was on his way up the mountain. "Are you Zen Master Guji?" the monk asked.

"Yes, I am," Guji replied.

"Oh, Zen Master, thank you very much for your teaching! Now I understand what is Dharma." The monk looked very happy and smiled as he bowed deeply to Zen Master Guji and continued on his way.

"What does he mean, 'Thank you for your teaching'?" Guji thought to himself. When he arrived back at the temple, Guji cried out, "Attendant!"

"Yes, sir?"

"Did you teach this monk?"

"Yes, sir. I was teaching him."

"So, then, I have a question for you: Do you understand Dharma?"

"Yes, of course, sir. I understand your Dharma!"

"Then I ask you, What is Dharma?"

The attendant, not thinking anything, quickly picked up one finger—*piitchhuu!* Now, every Zen master has a special knife, called a precepts knife. This knife is used to cut a monk's hair off on the appropriate day of the month when monks shave their heads. When cutting the hair, we say we are cutting the monk's "ignorance grass," his attachment to the normal world of name and form. So this knife is very, very sharp and also has great meaning for monks. When the attendant raised his finger, Zen Master Guji pulled out the knife and cut the boy's finger in one stroke—*piitchhuu!*

The attendant screamed out in pain, "Waaahhh!!" and ran out the door. He ran down the path away from the building, holding his bloody hand and crying. Suddenly Guji shouted, "Attendant!"

He instantly forgot everything and turned his head. "Yes, sir?" Zen Master Guji simply raised his finger. The boy saw that and got true enlightenment—*piitchhuu!* He attained his own true speech. Guji's one finger finally became his own true wisdom. That is a very famous story.

So the stories of Zen Master Dok Sahn and Zen Master Guji are very interesting. They tell us about the purpose of Zen practice and Zen teaching. Both of these monks were great sutra masters. Both of them completely understood all the Buddha's speech. They understood the whole Buddhist tradition, they understood various profound philosophies, and they understood all the eminent teachers. But when someone asked them for their own true speech, they could not say anything. They could not show their true nature to anybody. Understanding is not good and not bad. But what are *you*? This is very important. That point is beyond the reach of understanding. That point cannot be read in some book. Even Buddha himself cannot give you that point. The reason for this is because our true nature is *before* thinking. If you do Zen meditation, that point becomes clear, and is shining everywhere. It can do *anything*.

In Florida they have dog races. It is a very popular betting sport. People go to the dog track and bet money on the greyhounds, and if their dog wins, they win a lot of money. It is very simple. Everybody understands how the greyhounds race, yah? The dogs come out of a starting gate, and start heading around the track. Meanwhile, there is an electric rabbit that is carried along the inside rail of the track. Actually this is not a real rabbit. It is a fake rabbit with real rabbit fur on it. Dogs have very keen noses, and they follow a good smell. So this rabbit fur leads them around the track. All the dogs think they can catch the rabbit if they just run a little faster. Meanwhile, some man is watching the dogs and controlling the speed of the rabbit. If the dogs are very fast that day, he speeds the rabbit up; if they are slow, he slows it down. He always keeps this rabbit just within range of the dogs so that they think they can catch it. Every single day, the dogs go around and around and around this track. Race after race after race, the dogs just follow this rabbit.

One day, a very interesting thing happened at the races in Florida. There was a certain dog named Clear Mary. She was a very fast greyhound, and usually always won her races. But Clear Mary was also a very clever dog. One afternoon, she ran out of the starting gate with the other dogs, as usual. The rabbit hummed around the track, and the dogs sped after it. Running, running, running, running—around, around, around, around. Every day, sometimes several times a day, these dogs did the same thing, over and over and over again. And today they were doing it again, as usual. Chasing the electric rabbit.

But in the middle of the race, Clear Mary suddenly stopped. Many of the people in the grandstand stood up, fixing their binoculars on this dog. "What is happening?" they said. "What's wrong with that dumb dog?" Some people had placed lots of bets on Clear Mary, so they were very angry. "Run! Run! You dumb dog! What's wrong with you?"

But Clear Mary did not move for a few moments. She looked up at the grandstand. She looked at the tail ends of the other dogs scampering around the bend. And she looked at the rabbit, whirring around the bend and over to the other side of the oval track. Everything was completely still and silent for that moment at the races that day.

Suddenly, Clear Mary leapt over the guard rail that kept the dogs on the track. She sped straight across the big center infield like a flash. Leaping at just the right moment over the other guard rail, she caught the rabbit! *Boom!* Ha ha ha ha ha!

So that is a Zen mind. Everybody wants something in life. Everyone only follows their karma. They follow their ideas and their opinions, and believe that this is a true life. But Clear Mary is like a high-class Zen student. She was trained very strongly for many years only to follow the rabbit. Every day, she was taught to go around the track—around and around and around. But one day she stops and takes a close look. That is just like Zen practice: stopping and taking a close look at what is happening in life. Then she perceives something clearly, and just does it, one hundred percent. She doesn't check inside or outside. Inside and outside—*boom!*—become one. That is a Zen mind. It's very simple, yah?

The Buddha taught all the Dharmas in order to save all
minds. When you do not keep all these minds, what use
is there for the Dharmas?

The Buddha taught about mind. For forty years, he talked about Dharma. His whole teaching was concerned with how you can use Dharma to attain your mind. Attaining your mind actually means losing mind. The Buddha's teaching is that when you have mind, you get suffering, and you have a problem. If you have no mind, then everything is no problem. So if you want to take away suffering, you must take away mind, which means cutting your attachment to thinking. When you practice hard and keep a great don't-know, you see that you already have no mind. Already having no mind, why would you possibly need sutras? Why would you need dharma speeches and explanation? If you are not sick, why eat medicine? If you have no mind, then sutras are not necessary, dharma speeches are not necessary, Buddha's teachings are not necessary, everything is not necessary. But human beings constantly delude themselves. Everybody *thinks* they have mind, and then they hold their mind, and get suffering. So then sutras are necessary, dharma speeches are necessary, Buddha's teachings are necessary, and everything is necessary. This is already a big mistake!

Zen points directly at our no-mind mind. So that is why, in Zen, sutras are not necessary. Sutras only talk about mind and explain mind: "Everything is created by mind alone." "The Buddha taught all Dharmas in order to save all minds." "All Dharmas come from complete stillness." These words are very wonderful medicine for our thinking-minds. All sutras and Dharmas are wonderful pictures for showing a hungry man what a banana actually looks like. If he is not attached to these pictures, he will learn from them what a banana looks like, go buy one himself, and eat it. Only eating the actual banana will take away his suffering; the pictures cannot do this.

So if you have mind, you need sutras. But if you have no mind, then what? An eminent teacher said, "When mind appears, Dharma appears; when Dharma appears, name and form appear; when name and form appear, like and dislike, coming and going, happiness and sadness all appear. But when mind disappears, Dharma disappears; when Dharma disappears, name and form disappear; when name and form disappear, then like and dislike, happiness and sadness, and coming and going all disappear." When you have no mind, everything disappears. Then Buddha and sutras and Dharma are not necessary. These are only medicines for our thinking-minds. That is Zen teaching.

The Classifications of Meditation

禅　分類

Outer Path Meditation

外道禅

Common People's Meditation

凡夫禅

Hinayana Meditation

小乘禅

Mahayana Meditation

大乘禅

Utmost Vehicle Zen

最上乘禅

IN THIS WORLD there are many, many different kinds of meditation. Most religions have some kind of meditation practice hidden somewhere in their teaching. Also, even within Buddhism there are many, many different kinds of meditation. On the outside, all these kinds of meditation seem different. They are just techniques. They are not good and not bad. Someone once asked, "How is Insight Meditation different from Zen meditation or some kinds of Tibetan meditation?" In Japan, when people want to eat, they just use two chopsticks. In Korea everyone uses chopsticks and a spoon at meals. In the West, people use a knife and fork. And in India, many people

just pick up the food with their fingers and put it directly in their mouth—
puung! The techniques are all different. The tools are not the same. But the
most important point of all these techniques is: Did you get a full stomach?

So if you want to choose a kind of meditation, first you must understand
its basic direction. People use meditation for many, many different things.
Most people use meditation to get something. Maybe they want to get a good
feeling. Many people want stillness and peace. Others do meditation in order
to get material things. There is one tradition of practice where you chant
something over and over and over again in order to get a nice car or house
or relationship. But correct meditation means looking very deeply inside in
order to attain your true nature and help all beings. True practice actually
means not wanting anything to come out of your practice. When you practice with a wanting mind, your practice is already heading in the wrong
direction, and will drag you straight to some kind of hell. Such practice
cannot help you find your true self.

Outer Path Meditation

Nowadays many Christian people like meditation. There is also Sufi meditation and some kinds of New Age meditation. There is yoga meditation, holis-
tic meditation for health, and Divine Light meditation. In Asia we have
Confucian, Taoist, and Hindu forms of meditation. All these kinds of practices are Outer Path Meditation. This is any type of practice that is attached
to some object, or that aims at creating a good state of mind or feeling.
I went to a very popular meditation center several years ago. All the
students just breathed in and breathed out very slowly. Breathe in,
breathe out, breathe in, breathe out. They were nearly all sleeping—
"*Zzzzzzzz* . . ." Yet still everyone said, "Ah, this is wonderful! Such stillness!"
Their teacher said that if they only did this, they would soon feel very peaceful and happy. And it was true: almost everybody was smiling and happy. In
itself, that is not good or bad.

But everyone was just trying to get a good feeling and make some kind of
peaceful love-mind for the group to feel. At the end of the day, everybody
was holding hands or rubbing each other's shoulders—very happy. Yah, that
kind of thing is not wrong. But this is only about creating some feeling, a
good feeling. People talked about how they were doing this meditation to
make some happiness in their lives. Others were trying to "create a sacred
space." But eventually, even a very good feeling changes and becomes its

opposite. Then the person who practices this meditation may become sadder than before, because their meditation is attached to this good feeling. It can be like a kind of drug: when the pleasant feeling changes, the person gets some suffering. The meditation makes some happiness, but when you make happiness, you also make its opposite. You create an opposites-world. That always happens if your practice has some object, something that it is attached to. We call this good-feeling meditation, or peace mind. Its direction is not clear, and it attaches to some outside object or feeling or thing. So this kind of meditation is always dependent on some feeling or object. When it does not get this object, or cannot keep it, the person will lose their happy feeling. "Where is God? I want to see God!" Meditation that is attached to some object or feeling or idea is called Outer Path Meditation.

Common People's Meditation

Common People's Meditation means any kind of meditation practice that is used to improve your performance in some activity. This kind of meditation is very popular nowadays. It has some particular function or performance in mind, so many people like it. They believe that if they do this meditation they will get something. It is sometimes called concentration meditation. There are people who do meditation as part of their martial arts practice. "Ah, I do karate meditation. If I meditate, my mind will become clear and my karate will become better." It is very popular today to teach creative writing, drawing, and painting as meditation. Many people also like this ancient Japanese tea ceremony or doing calligraphy as meditation. Some people try to use meditation to help solve emotional or psychological problems that they are working on together with a therapist. And some use it to relieve mental and physical stress. Again, this kind of meditation is not bad and not good. It is better to do this than not doing any meditation at all. If you do meditation, it can help your karate, and it can help your artwork. It can help you play the piano better, or do a more careful tea ceremony. Perhaps it will also help your therapy.

But this kind of meditation cannot help you completely attain your true nature. It will not cut you free from the wheel of birth and death. True, its techniques may benefit you for a time, but its teaching is not complete. The direction of this kind of meditation is not always clear: it does not vow to serve all beings, but rather can often make your "I, my, me" mind grow and become stronger. "I want to solve my emotional problems." "I want to make my body healthier." "I want to be number one in judo, or tea ceremony." But what is this "I"? Such meditation never asks that question in a complete way. Whenever meditation has some object, then it means "I want something." If you want something, as we said before, that is already a big mistake. You fall back into the deep pit of "subject" and "object." This is not the way to completely cut off the root of suffering. That is because, by its very nature, want-something meditation always makes subject and object, this and that, good and bad. This kind of meditation does not completely show you what is this thing we call "I." Also, it does not help you take away your karma, and its direction is not clear. Practicing any kind of meditation that has some object in mind or some level of performance, while giving a good feeling, can often make your "I, my, me" even stronger. If you practice with this kind of mind, you are practicing Common People's Meditation.

Hinayana Meditation

We have already spoken about the meditation practice of Hinayana Buddhism. In the West nowadays, Hinayana Meditation is very popular. It is sometimes called Vipassana meditation, or Insight Meditation. This meditation helps the student have insight into impurity, insight into impermanence, and insight into nonself. This practice also emphasizes the path of precepts (*sila*), keeping a not-moving mind (*samadhi*), and wisdom (*prajna*). The goal of this form of meditation is to attain complete stillness and extinction, or nirvana.

Mahayana Meditation

We also spoke earlier about Mahayana practice. This kind of meditation is based on the six fundamental insights of Mahayana teaching: insight into the existence and nonexistence of the Dharmas; insight into the nature of form and emptiness; insight into existence and the Middle Way; insight into the nature of phenomena; insight into the interpenetration of all phenomena; and insight which sees that phenomena themselves are the Absolute. The practice of these six insights can be expressed by the teaching of the *Avatamsaka-sutra*: "If you wish to thoroughly understand all the buddhas of the past, present, and future, then you should view the nature of the whole universe as being created by the mind alone."

Utmost Vehicle Zen

If everything is created by mind alone, what makes mind? Directly attaining the true nature of mind is the aim of Utmost Vehicle Zen. This kind of meditation is further divided into three types. Conceptual, academic, or intellectual understanding of Zen is Theoretical Zen. Attaining an experience of emptiness and perceiving the oneness of mind and the universe is Tathagata Zen. Patriarchal Zen means attaining that everything, just like this, is already truth. This means a relaxed mind, the attainment of Big I. Big I is infinite time and infinite space. Actually, the three kinds of Zen are only one, not three. We sometimes separate them to simplify the teaching and to test a student's understanding.

Utmost Vehicle Zen

最 上 乘 禪

Theoretical Zen	Form is emptiness. Emptiness is form.
義理禪	色即是空、空即是色
Tathagata Zen	No form, no emptiness.
如來禪	無色．無空
Patriarchal Zen	Form is form. Emptiness is emptiness.
祖師禪	色即是色．空即是空

Theoretical Zen: Form is emptiness. Emptiness is form.

THEORETICAL ZEN is all based on thinking. It is only dry intellectual theory about the nature of form and emptiness. "Form is emptiness, and emptiness is form." Many high-class scholars and artists already understand this point conceptually. Also some people will take drugs and, for a short time, realize that everything is the same and that everything comes from the same point. If you ask any of these people, "Here is a pencil. Are you and this pencil the same or different?" they will usually answer, "The same!" They understand this point: everything in the universe is the same. All things are the same substance. So "Form is emptiness, emptiness is form." I am you and you are me. Understanding this is correct, but this is still only thinking. It is not complete attainment.

One day a student came to my room at Hwa Gye Sah Temple outside Seoul and banged on the door. "Zen Master! Zen Master! I think I got enlightenment!"

"Oh, that's wonderful," I said. "So, what did you attain?"

The student said, "I attained Nothing!"

"You attained Nothing? That's *very* wonderful. But *who* has attained Nothing?"

"Well, *I* attained Nothing."

Then I hit him with my stick—*boom!* "Who attained *that?*" The student was stuck and could not answer. Ha ha ha ha ha! Yah, perhaps this student understood something, but this is not a complete attainment. It is *understanding* something about attainment, yet still, it is not true attainment. We call this Theoretical Zen.

There are many people who have a strong conceptual experience that "form is emptiness, and emptiness is form." But when this just remains as dry cognition, it cannot help their life. On another occasion, a man came to me at Hwa Gye Sah and said, "Zen Master, am I standing right-side up or upside down?"

This seemed like a very strange question. "Are you asking because you truly don't know for yourself?"

"Well," he said, "I am not sure anymore . . ."

"Why is that?"

"The earth is round. So I stand this way, but right now, the Western people on the other side of the earth must be standing upside down. Or else they're standing correctly, and I'm standing upside down. What do you think?"

So I said, "What do *you* think?"

His face brightened. "I understand which one is true . . ."

"So, what do you understand?" I asked him.

He said, " 'Form is emptiness, and emptiness is form.' Right-side up is upside down and upside down is right-side up."

"And how do you understand that?"

"My mind figured it out," he said.

"Where is your mind? Please show me."

The man was completely stuck and could not answer. And in that moment I remembered the old Korean proverb which says, "To understand things like this is no better than having a cancer." As we spoke further, I learned that this man was about to board a bus one day when he saw a farmer propping his A-frame backpack on a stick so that it would stand up. The farmer's friend walked by and accidentally kicked out the stick, and the pack fell. It gave him a big question: How can this happen? He thought about the earth, and the fact that Westerners on the other side of the globe had the same situation. It just did not make any sense to him anymore. The real problem began, however, when a friend suggested he go to a lecture series on the *Heart Sutra* being given by a famous professor. When the man heard the words, "Form is emptiness, emptiness is form," these ideas went very deeply into his consciousness. He got the point of these words, conceptually, but he became too attached to them to see what they were pointing at. This kind of thinking is like a bad disease.

Tathagata Zen: No form, no emptiness

The *Mahaparinirvana-sutra* says, "All formations are impermanent; this is the law of appearing and disappearing. When appearing and disappearing disappear, then this stillness is bliss." This means that when there is no appearance or disappearance in your mind, that mind is complete stillness and bliss. It is a mind utterly devoid of thinking. This is your mind before thinking arises.

Here is a pencil. Are you and this pencil the same or different? If you say "the same," I will hit you thirty times. If you say "different," I will also hit you thirty times. What can you do? [*Pauses for a few moments, then hits the table loudly.*] This is Tathagata Zen. [*Hits the table again.*] *This* mind, only this point. You cannot open your mouth to express it. This point has no Buddha, no Dharma, no good, no bad, no light, no dark, no sky, no ground, no same, no different, no emptiness, no form, no *anything* in it. This is a truly empty mind. [*Hits the table.*] Empty mind is the mind that does not appear or disappear. Keeping this mind at all times is Tathagata Zen.

It is not possible to explain this point using words and speech. Whenever someone asked Zen Master Lin Chi any question, he would answer by shouting, "*Katz!*" If someone asked Zen Master Dok Sahn a question, he would only hit them. And Zen Master Guji answered every kind of question just by lifting one finger. These actions are all very high-class teaching, because they do not rely on speech and words to demonstrate our true nature or the Absolute. There is just this action that delivers the experience directly. This kind of style teaches that everything is originally the same substance, and this substance has no name and no form. But this point cannot be explained or described to you. No words could ever convey it. Instead it is only demonstrated through direct action. [*Hits the table loudly.*] Before, someone said that he and the pencil are the same. This "same" is only thinking. It is only dry understanding. But if you ask me if the pencil and I are the same or different, this is how I answer [*hits the table loudly*]. This is Tathagata Zen.

Patriarchal Zen: Form is form. Emptiness is emptiness.

So everything in the universe is the same universal substance, and this substance has no name and no form. [*Hits the table loudly.*] But all things also have a specific job and function. From moment to moment, what is the correct *function* of substance? This is a very important point. Attaining the correct function of substance from moment to moment is the teaching of Patriarchal Zen, sometimes called enlightenment Zen. Attaining this point means being able to use all situations and all things to help other people.

Patriarchal Zen cultivates insight into the correct function of our mind and this universe. To describe this function more clearly, we can look at Patriarchal Zen by further dividing it into two views of expedient means. We say that there are two ways of describing function. Metaphysical-style function is, we say, "like-this truth." But a more meticulous and complete function is concrete-style function, or "just-like-this truth." For example, someone asks, "What is Buddha?" There are many, many possible ways to answer this, because everything is truth. The sky is blue. The tree is green. Sugar is sweet. Salt is salty. Buddha, Dharma, mind, nature, God, self, true self, absolutes, energy, consciousness, substance—everything is Buddha, yah? What is *not* Buddha? This is a very wide question; it does not stand on one point. We call this a metaphysical-style question, because what it is asking for points at some general expression of truth. Everything is truth, so everything is Buddha. Everything is God or nature or mind or truth. This kind of answer shows metaphysical-style function.

However, we encounter many kinds of situations every day that require us to respond more meticulously and clearly. They require some action that works more completely than a mere reflection or explanation of truth. Most situations in our life demand a complete function, some complete action. To take a very simple example, here is a white cup. Someone asks you, "What is the nature of this thing?" If you answer by saying, "It is a cup," this shows that you are attached to name and form. If you say it is not a cup, then you are attached to emptiness. So, is this a cup or not? How can you answer?

Maybe you will say, "Oh, the sky is blue," but that is also not correct. "The tree is green." "When I am hungry, I eat." Yah, the sky is blue: that is truth. The tree is green: that is also truth. "When I'm hungry, I eat." That answer may also be an expression of some universal truth, but in this case, all these answers are not correct. They do not express your connection or *relationship* to this situation in this moment—the situation created by the question. So again I ask, what is this? [*Lifts the cup and drinks from it.*] Only that! A one-point question requires a one-point answer. It is very easy.

Let us look at another example. Here's a watch. If you say this is a watch, you are attached to the realm of name and form. If you say it is not a watch, you are attached to emptiness. So is this a watch or not? At that time, some people will say "The watch is the tree, and the tree is the watch." This is a Theoretical Zen style answer, because "form is emptiness and emptiness is form." It is only intellectual explanation. Other people will usually answer with something like "Your robe is gray" or "Your eyes are brown." This way of answering is not bad; it expresses some general truth. But in this particular situation, these answers are also not correct. While true, they are not the specific, concrete truth of this particular situation with which you are presented.

A one-pointed question demands a one-pointed answer. So, is this a watch or not? [*After a few moments, looks at the watch face.*] "Ohh, now it's two-fifteen." That is, we say, Patriarchal Zen. It is very easy. Substance, truth, and function come together in one point. That is your true way and correct life, from moment to moment.

So Patriarchal Zen has two forms of expression: metaphysical function and concrete function. Both metaphysical function and concrete function express the highest teaching of the *Heart Sutra*: "Form is form, emptiness is emptiness." But metaphysical function means that we simply reflect this truth, as it is. The sky is blue. The trees are green. This wall is white. Outside, a dog is barking, "Woof! Woof!" Our mind is like a great, round mirror. Only reflect, reflect, reflect, reflect. Everything is truth "like-this."

However, sometimes just reflecting truth as it is cannot help this world very much. Nowadays our society is very, very complicated. Everything is moving very quickly and changing very rapidly. There is a great deal of suffering. How do we help this world? Of course, when keeping a mind that is clear like space, we reflect this world as it is. When a red ball comes before our clear-mirror mind, red is reflected; when white comes, white. But when a hungry person comes before our clear mirror, do we become hungry? When a sad person comes, do we become sad? Does simply reflecting back truth completely help these people? Some more meticulous and complete response is necessary, yah? This is how "truth just-like-this" teaching appears.

Simply reflecting this world as it is may sometimes not be enough when we are called upon to help suffering beings: from moment to moment, what is our correct *relationship* to truth as it is? Yah, the sky is blue. The trees are green. This is truth. How do we make realization of these truths *function* correctly in our everyday lives to help all beings? To attain that is what we mean by concrete function. Merely attaining truth as it is means attaining metaphysical function. But spontaneously attaining the correct moment-to-moment *function* of truth means attaining your correct life. It means attaining your correct situation, attaining your correct relationship to your situation, and attaining your correct function. Universal substance, truth, and function come together in one spontaneous action that benefits other beings.

There is another way to express this. We sometimes say, "Keep a mind that is clear like space, but let your mind function like the tip of a needle." Patriarchal Zen is very, very meticulous practice. From moment to moment, perceive your correct situation, correct relationship to that situation, and correct function. We have already spoken a great deal about keeping a clear mind. When you see, when you hear, when you smell, when you taste, when you touch, and when you think—everything, just like this, is truth. This is keeping a mind that is clear like space. It means always keeping a very wide view. But our practice means meticulously honing how this truth functions as new situations constantly appear. Everyone has seen a monk's large *kasa*. This robe is sewn together very carefully in many different places. It is very difficult to make one of these. If the person who makes this does not use the needle meticulously, there will be some mistake. Then the whole *kasa* must be unthreaded and sewn all over again.

Simply having love mind is keeping a mind that is clear like space. This is very wonderful. But this is a very wide mind experience. It does not always perceive how to function appropriately in a given situation for others. However, Buddhist teaching is about expedient means. This is another name for compassion. The compassion that the utmost vehicle teaches is love conditioned by wisdom. If you have no wisdom, and only experience some kind of love mind, then this love mind cannot always respond to people's different needs in different situations. But if you attain truth and digest your understanding, then wisdom appears. Love plus wisdom equals compassion. One action for each situation. A different function for every being's need automatically appears in every situation. "Keep a mind that is clear like space, but let your mind function like the tip of a needle." This is very high-class teaching.

To function for others, however, and to perceive our correct function, we must first attain truth. A long time ago in China, a man once asked Zen Master Dong Sahn, "What is Buddha?"

He said, "Three pounds of flax."

The man didn't understand, so he went to another Zen master, reported his encounter with Dong Sahn, and asked, "What does 'three pounds of flax' mean?"

The Zen Master replied, "In the north there is pine; in the south, bamboo."

The man still didn't understand, so he went to one of his friends who had been practicing Zen for some time and asked what these two Zen masters meant. His friend said, "When you open your mouth, your teeth are yellow. Do you understand?"

"I don't know," the man replied.

Then his friend said, "First you must understand your mind, then all of this will be clear."

So Patriarchal Zen means attaining that everything, just-like-this, is the truth. The sky is blue. The tree is green. A dog is barking, "Woof! Woof!" Salt is salty; sugar is sweet. When you see, when you hear, when you smell, when you taste, when you touch, and when you think, everything is truth, just as it is.

A monk once asked Zen Master Joju, "What is Buddha?"

"Go drink tea!"

Another monk asked, "What is Dharma?"

"Go drink tea!"

"What is life?"

"Go drink tea!"

"What is Buddhism?"

"Go drink tea!" The name for this is concrete function.

There is a famous story that demonstrates these three kinds of Zen. My grand-teacher, the great Zen Master Man Gong, became a monk when he was only thirteen years old. He was the attendant to a busy sutra master at Tong Hak Sah Temple, which at the time was the most famous sutra temple in Korea. The best sutra monks from all over the country traveled to Tong Hak Sah to study the Buddha's teaching.

One day, there was a big graduation ceremony for the monks' college. According to tradition, the senior monk ascended the high rostrum to deliver the formal farewell address. After sitting down and adjusting his ceremonial robes, the monk said, "You must all continue to study correctly and become like great trees, from which temples are built, and like large bowls, able to hold many good things. An ancient poet once wrote, 'Water takes the shape of its vessel. Human beings conform to the company they keep.' So today you are all graduating. That is very wonderful. If from now on you make friends with good and virtuous people, you will naturally become good and virtuous and fulfill your greatest obligation to heaven. But if you associate with bad people who follow a bad way, you will eventually become bad. Always keep the Buddha in mind and only keep good company. Then you will become great trees and containers of Dharma. This is my parting advice to you." Everyone liked this speech. Sitting far in the back of the hall, the young attendant Man Gong Sunim thought, "Oh, that's wonderful teaching!" All the monks were very happy.

As he returned to his seat, the senior monk turned to a strange-looking figure sitting off to the side. Clothed in rags, with long hair and a long, thin beard, this monk was an imposing figure among the neat, shaven-headed monks. But though his appearance was unkempt, this big monk's eyes shone like diamonds. It was none other than Zen Master Kyong Ho, who just happened to be visiting the temple. He was already known all over the country as one of the greatest Zen masters in the history of Korean Buddhism.

The sutra master asked, "Please, Zen Master give us one word."

Without looking up, Kyong Ho Sunim only shook his head. "No, no. I am only a wanderer, passing through. I have nothing to say." Then Kyong Ho Sunim fell silent.

"Please, Sunim. Today is such an important day." The younger monks also implored him to speak, so after several more moments of silence, Kyong Ho Sunim ascended the high rostrum.

He said, "All of you are monks. Monks are free of petty personal attachments and live only to serve all beings. Wanting to become a great tree or container of Dharma will prevent you from being a true teacher. Great trees have great uses; small trees have small uses. Good and bad bowls can all be used in their own way. None are to be discarded. Rather, you must become great carpenters. If you are a good carpenter, you never throw away big trees, or small trees, or good trees, or bad trees. A skillful carpenter can use any tree in his work. He never discards a single thing. Good and bad do not matter. If good things come, you must know their proper use; if bad things come, you must also know how to use them correctly. Don't attach to the good or push away the bad. You must use good and bad and make them correct. So keep both good and bad friends, and never reject anything. This is true Buddhism. My only wish for you is that you free yourselves from all conceptual thinking."

The child-monk Man Gong Sunim heard this, and immediately his mind became clear. "This is my teacher! This is my teacher!" he thought. As Kyong Ho Sunim left the dharma hall, Man Gong Sunim jumped up and followed him. Kyong Ho Sunim sensed someone behind him and turned to the boy.

"Why are you following me?"

"Zen Master, I like your speech," Man Gong Sunim said. "I want to become your student. Please let me go with you!"

"Who are you?"

"I have no name and no form."

"If you have no name and no form, then what is following me?"

"Oh, your speech was very wonderful!"

"You're attached to my speech!"

"No, sir, I never attach to your speech. I only follow your mind!"

Kyong Ho Sunim smiled and tested Man Gong Sunim again. "You are a very bad boy. But children are incapable of learning Buddhism."

"Human beings may age, but in original nature is there young or old?"

The Zen Master laughed hard. "Oh, you naughty boy! You've killed and eaten the Buddha. Someone must take care of you. Come with me!" Then Kyong Ho Sunim took Man Gong Sunim to Chung Jung Sah temple and left him in the care of the abbot.

Man Gong Sunim practiced diligently and worked very hard around the temple. Five years passed since his meeting with Zen Master Kyong Ho. In a short time he mastered all of the ceremonial chants. It is said about Man Gong Sunim that when he opened his mouth to chant, the very sound of heaven itself came out. Many Buddhist faithful would ask him to chant ceremonies for them, so he was always very, very busy. From morning to night, Man Gong Sunim chanted, often missing meals in order to satisfy the many requests that were made on him. One spring evening, the day before Buddha's Birthday, Man Gong Sunim was walking out of the Main Buddha Hall. He had just finished a big ceremony and was heading over to the temple office with the day's donations. Man Gong Sunim had not eaten since early morning and longed for a short rest before beginning his evening sitting meditation. He was very, very tired.

As he was crossing the temple courtyard, a young boy from the nearby village approached him and bowed. "Happy Buddha's Birthday, Sunim!"

"Yes, and to you also."

His hands folded respectfully before him, the boy said, "Sunim, I have a question for you . . ."

"Oh, what kind of question?"

"Well, the ten thousand Dharmas return to the One . . ."

"Of course," Man Gong Sunim said, "the ten thousand Dharmas return to the One. I understand this point."

"So my question for you is, Where does the One return?"

Man Gong Sunim was completely stuck and could not answer. His mouth opened, but no words would come out. The little boy looked up at him smilingly, while Man Gong Sunim groped for something to say. Several seconds passed. But Man Gong Sunim's mouth remained silent. His face turned red, then white, then dark!

"Huh!" the boy said. "You don't understand that! You don't understand anything. What kind of a monk are you?" Then the boy turned on his heel and, just as suddenly as he had come, he was gone.

Now Man Gong Sunim was not happy! "Where does the One return? Why can't I answer this question? I don't *know* . . ." He returned to his room and lay down on the floor, his eyes staring straight up at the ceiling. He couldn't eat anything. Though tired, he could not sleep. "Where does the One return? *I don't know* . . ." One day passed. Two days. Three days. And still, from morning to night and morning again, Man Gong Sunim remained in the grip of this question. It would not let him go, even for an instant. "This little boy asked me a question, and I cannot answer. How terrible!"

Meanwhile, the temple abbot was beginning to wonder about him. Man Gong Sunim had not eaten or slept for several days. His face had become a pasty yellow and the skin lay in thick folds under his hollow eyes. The abbot called Man Gong Sunim into his room. "What is wrong with you lately? Are you thinking about money? Have you fallen in love with a woman? If you get attached to women or money, you must leave this temple!" But Man Gong Sunim would not answer him and only stared at the floor. This made the abbot even angrier. "What is wrong with you? Answer me!"

After a few moments, Man Gong Sunim slowly opened his mouth to speak. "I don't like money. I am also not interested in any woman. Nowadays I don't care about anything . . ."

"Then why haven't you eaten or slept for the last couple of days?"

"Sir, I have a big question, and it won't let me go, even for a moment."

"What's your question? Ask me! Any kind of question is no problem."

Man Gong Sunim said, "The ten thousand Dharmas return to the One. Where does the One return?"

The abbot laughed hard at Man Gong Sunim's words. "I don't care where the One returns! These words are not necessary. Why do they upset you so?" But try as he could, the abbot's speech did not change Man Gong Sunim's heavy expression. The abbot stared at the young monk sitting so disconsolate before him. "Ah ha, already one good monk is broken," the abbot said, shaking his head. "Now he must become a hippie monk." In Korea there is a saying that goes, "A garbage person becomes a monk. A garbage monk becomes a Zen monk. And a garbage Zen monk becomes Buddha." Man Gong Sunim was worth nothing to society, so he became a monk. But this little boy's question gripped him so fiercely that he was no longer worth anything to a busy ceremonial temple. The abbot now knew that there was only one path left open for his young student: the Zen meditation hall.

So the next day Man Gong Sunim moved to a Zen temple. From morning to night, he only kept this question: "The ten thousand dharmas return to the One. Where does the One return? I don't *know* . . ." For days on end, Man Gong Sunim would sit in meditation, only keeping this question. He ate once a day. He would not sleep but sat in meditation all night. He would not speak with anybody. Then one day, while sitting in meditation, a hole appeared in the wall in front of Man Gong Sunim. It was as if the wall suddenly became glass. He could see everything outside: there were rocks and trees and birds and clouds. He could see Mr. Lee working out in the temple garden, and Mrs. Kim walking toward the Main Buddha Hall. He saw people drinking water out of a stone cistern.

"Waaahhh!" Man Gong Sunim thought. "I got enlightenment! I got enlightenment!" When he looked up at the ceiling, all he could see was sky, the white clouds moving from left to right, birds flying here and there. When he turned to look behind him, there were only the pine trees that covered the back wall of the Zen room. "Waaahhh! I got enlightenment! I got enlightenment!" Man Gong Sunim jumped up from his cushion, an indescribable happiness spreading out of his mind.

The next day, he visited a Zen master who was staying at the temple. "I have realized the nature of the universe. I attained enlightenment!"

"Oh, that's wonderful," the master said. "Then I have a question for you: what is the nature of the universe?"

Man Gong Sunim replied, "When I look at the roof and the wall, there's nothing there. Everything disappears."

The Zen master smiled. "Hmmm. Is this really the truth?"

"Of course! I have no hindrance whatsoever. Ha ha ha ha ha!"

In one sudden burst, the master hit Man Gong Sunim on the head with his Zen stick.

"Owwwww!"

"Where is no-hindrance now?" Man Gong Sunim winced under the blow. His eyes bulged, his face flushed, and the walls became solid again. The master laughed. "Where is truth now?"

Man Gong Sunim was crestfallen. "I don't know . . . Please teach me."

"What kong-an are you working on nowadays?"

"The ten thousand Dharmas return to the One. Where does the One return?"

"So, Man Gong Sunim, do you understand One?"

"No, sir. I don't know . . ."

"You must first understand One. What you saw was just illusion. Don't touch it. You say 'I don't know.' This don't-know is your true master. Only keep a don't-know mind, always and everywhere, and soon you will understand."

Man Gong Sunim returned to his practice with even fiercer determination. He strongly kept don't-know mind, always and everywhere, no matter what he was doing. All his questions came together in one immovable mass. He practiced like this for three years, never straying from this great doubt that hung in his gut like a rock. Then one morning, he was chanting the daily Morning Bell Chant. One phrase in the chant says, "If you wish to understand all buddhas of the past, present, and future, then you must perceive that the whole universe is created by mind alone." As he chanted these words, he hit the great bell. The sound radiated out in waves that completely swallowed all notions of self and other. In that moment, Man Gong Sunim's mind suddenly shot open like lightning. He understood, in one vast, infinite moment, that all buddhas dwell in a single sound.

Man Gong Sunim was overwhelmed with joy. He ran into the Dharma Room and kicked the monk who used to sit next to him. "Ouch!" the monk cried. "Are you crazy?!"

"This is Buddha-nature!" he replied.

"Have you attained enlightenment?"

"Yah! The whole universe is One! I am Buddha! I am One!"

For the next year, Man Gong Sunim traveled the countryside, kicking and hitting more than a few monks. Soon, word spread about his actions, and

Man Gong Sunim became very famous. He believed in himself very strongly, so many monks were afraid of him. "Oh, Man Gong Sunim is a free man," they would say. "He has no hindrance at all!"

The next year, Man Gong Sunim decided to visit Ma Gok Sah temple on Buddha's Birthday. Many of his dharma brothers gathered from all over the country for the big ceremony. Zen Master Kyong Ho was also there. When he heard that his teacher would be present, Man Gong Sunim was very happy.

He went to Kyong Ho Sunim's room. As Man Gong Sunim adjusted his robes before bowing to his teacher, he looked at Kyong Ho Sunim and thought to himself, "I got enlightenment. Also you got enlightenment. Zen Master and I are the same, so I don't really need to bow. But since you were my first teacher I will bow like any other monk would have to do . . ." Man Gong Sunim believed in himself too much!

Kyong Ho Sunim only smiled as Man Gong Sunim bowed—he completely perceived his young student's mind. "Oh, welcome! Everybody says that you attained enlightenment. Is that really true?"

"Yes, I did."

"Oh, that's wonderful! Then let me ask you a question or two." Kyong Ho Sunim proceeded to ask Man Gong Sunim several kong-ans, and he answered without hindrance. Then the Zen master pointed to a fan and a calligraphy brush and said, "Are this fan and this brush the same or different?"

Man Gong Sunim replied, "The brush is the fan, and the fan is the brush." This answer surprised Kyong Ho Sunim a little. Man Gong Sunim had been able to answer several other questions quite easily, but this answer was not very clear. So for the next hour, with grandmotherly compassion, Kyong Ho Sunim tried to teach Man Gong Sunim his mistake. But Man Gong Sunim was too proud of his attainment and would not listen. Finally Kyong Ho Sunim said, "In the funeral chant, there is a verse that says, 'The statue has eyes, and tears silently drip down.' What does this mean?"

Man Gong Sunim was completely stuck and could not answer. He opened his mouth, but no words came out. Suddenly, Kyong Ho Sunim shouted at him, "If you don't understand this, how can you say that the fan is the brush and the brush is the fan?"

In great despair, Man Gong Sunim bowed and said, "I am sorry. Please forgive me."

"Do you understand your mistake?"

"Yes, Master. What can I do? Please teach me . . ."

"The Buddha said that all things have Buddha-nature. But when a monk once asked great Zen Master Joju if a dog has Buddha-nature, Joju said, 'No!' Do you understand?"

"No, I don't know . . ."

Kyong Ho Sunim said, "This don't-know is your true master. Always keep the mind that doesn't know and soon you will attain enlightenment."

For the next three years, Man Gong Sunim practiced very, very hard. He kept don't-know mind with great courage, always and everywhere. Then one day, when he heard the great temple bell being rung—*b-bong bong!*—Man Gong Sunim's mind shot open like lightning striking. In a single instant he attained Joju's "*Mu!*" and the teachings and kong-ans of all the eminent teachers.

In profound gratitude to his teacher, Man Gong Sunim wrote to Kyong Ho Sunim: "Now I understand why the bodhisattva faces away: Because sugar is sweet and salt is salty." Upon reading these words, Zen Master Kyong Ho gave Man Gong Sunim *inka* and Transmission.

The story of Zen Master Man Gong's enlightenment is very famous. What does this story teach us? First, it teaches us about the importance of keeping a try-mind, no matter what. It teaches us about one monk's Great Question, Great Faith, and Great Courage. But more importantly, this story shows us the different levels of attainment in Utmost Vehicle Zen. There are many people who can get some kind of enlightenment, some kind of deep insight into the nature of the universe. But how deep is their attainment? How *complete* is their attainment? Man Gong Sunim's first big experience was that he attained the realms of complete emptiness and of magic and freedom: when he looked at the walls and ceiling, there was only clear space. He could see everything coming and going before him without any hindrance. This means attaining freedom and the interpenetration of all universal substance. Attaining this is very wonderful. Many people will stop here in their practice, especially since it is very easy to attain some kind of magic power or special energy as a result.

But a keen-eyed Zen master will show you that one more step is necessary. Yes, the ten thousand Dharmas return to the One. Man Gong Sunim attained that very deeply. He attained that "form is emptiness, and emptiness is form." Then he attained "no form, no emptiness." But "Where does the One return?" It is wonderful to attain that everything is ultimately One: but how does the One *function* from moment to moment in each and every individual thing? That is a very important point. Where does the One *return*?

Even if you completely attain the realm of magic and freedom-thinking, you cannot stop there. That is because attaining complete enlightenment means returning to the realm of things as they really are. It means attaining that "form is form, emptiness is emptiness." The sky is blue. The tree is green. A dog is barking outside, "Woof! Woof!" Salt is salty. Sugar is sweet. Everything, just-like-this, is the truth. It is not special. When you see, when you hear, when you smell, when you taste, when you touch, everything is the truth, just as it is. Take away your Small I, and you attain Nothing I, or empty mind. If you keep practicing and don't attach to this place of complete emptiness, then the whole universe and you completely become one. You see clearly, hear clearly, smell clearly—everything is clear! That is because there is no longer subject or object, inside or outside. At this point, subject and object completely become one. Inside and outside completely become one. Sky and you become one: then there is just blue. Sugar and you become one: there is just sweetness. Dog and you become one: then just "Woof!" Another name for that is complete world, the place where the One returns. This is the highest teaching of the highest vehicle of all the Buddhas and eminent teachers. Everything is the truth, just-like-this. We sometimes call the teaching that describes this point the realm of Patriarchal Zen.

Nonattachment to Language

不 立 文 字

The path of scriptural study

看 經 門

The path of reciting the name of the Buddha

念 佛 門

The path of the mantras

真 言 門

The path of Zen practice

參 禪 門

THERE ARE MANY misconceptions about the nature of Zen teaching and practice. Zen teaching simply means not attaching to language. If you want to attain the Buddha's way, then don't attach to speech and words. There is a famous Zen verse that says: "Not depending on speech and words, a special transmission outside the Sutras: pointing directly to mind, see your true nature, and become Buddha." This is very interesting teaching. It expresses how the practice of Zen is not dependent on understanding, or on knowledge of books, or on having some high-class college degrees. It has nothing to do with the level of anyone's intelligence or cleverness. Zen meditation points directly to our minds so that we attain our true nature. Because of this emphasis on attaining mind over mere conceptual understanding, people sometimes think that Zen is anti-intellectual. Actually, that view is not correct. Zen teaching means, how do you *use* words, how do you *use* speech correctly to help all beings? That is a very important point. To do this, first you must do very hard training and attain your true nature before thinking arises. You must attain the nature of mind. Then the correct *function* of speech and words appears by itself. Only in this way can you use language without being attached to it. But how do we practice?

There are many different ways to practice. There are many different styles and techniques. We have already spoken about this. When American people eat, they use a knife and fork. When Korean people eat, they use a spoon and chopsticks. Japanese people use only chopsticks. And many people in India and Africa don't use chopsticks, spoons, or forks at all. They just pick up the food with their fingers and put it in their mouth—*puunnkk*! These are all just techniques for eating. The most important thing to consider about these styles is not the technique itself—whether it is "correct" or not—but did you get a full stomach? The techniques may all be different, but a full stomach is the same. That is the reason why we use these different tools for practicing Zen. The tools may all have different styles, but if used with the proper direction in mind, each can help us find our way.

In Buddhist practice we can say that there are four main techniques for studying the Buddha's teaching: reading sutras, invoking the name of the Buddha, mantra practice, and meditation. Even though meditation is known to be the most direct way of realizing the Buddha's teaching, each of these can help you very much. But if you become attached to the sutras, or to invoking the Buddha's name, or to mantras, or even to certain aspects of formal sitting meditation, then any one of these techniques will hinder you and drag you off the path. So the important thing to remember is not to become attached to anything, but rather to use each practice or technique correctly to find your true nature.

The Buddha sat under the Bodhi tree to realize his true nature and cut off the endless stream of suffering. After getting enlightenment, he gave many, many dharma talks. The talks were later written down and called sutras. These written records of the Buddha's speech only *point* at this attainment that he had and that we are all capable of experiencing. But by themselves these sutras cannot give us this attainment directly. Since Buddhism is not a dogma or theology, reading the sutras is never meant to be a substitute for actual practice. If we read the sutras with a don't-know mind, however, and don't attach to their words and speech, then the sutras can help our practice. They make our faith-mind strong and keep our cognition clear. They also give our minds a large and wide view, because the sutras often talk about many, many other universes and worlds spontaneously coexisting with our human realm.

If you read the sutras with a not-thinking mind, then the sutras can help; but if you are thinking, and checking, and holding, and wanting, then even the sutras can send you straight to hell. We have already seen several situations where great sutra masters were so attached to the sutras that they could not understand what the sutras were pointing to. "Nonattachment to language" means that attaining the Buddha's teaching does not depend on speech and words. More importantly, it means how do we *use* speech and words to help our practice? If you become even a little bit attached to any kind of speech or words, to anything that is said or written, then you will have a difficult time understanding the bone of the Buddha's teaching. The bone of his teaching can only be gotten through meditation. So that is why we say "Put it all down": ideas, beliefs, and philosophies cannot help your life, even Buddhist ones. When reading a sutra or reciting a mantra, don't become attached to any kind of special meaning in the words. As you read the sutras, you must look for the behind-meaning at which the words are pointing. Many people become quite strongly attached to the ideas or expressions themselves in the sutras. They believe that this or that idea is true, or correct, or a complete teaching. Then maybe they will develop strong reactions toward people or traditions that don't agree with this teaching. "You don't understand this sutra, you don't understand Buddha's speech!" "No, you don't understand Buddha's teaching!" This is a number-one bad Buddhist sickness. The Buddha's teaching is about not being attached to anything, keeping a mind that is clear like space so you can function from moment to moment to help all beings. So why be attached to the sutras? Find the clear meaning *behind* the words, and just do it. Just practice.

The same is true for reciting the Buddha's name. Some people go to the Dharma Room every day and chant *Kwan Seum Bosal, Kwan Seum Bosal, Kwan Seum Bosal* or *Om mani padme hum*. This kind of practice is not good and not bad. Simply do not allow yourself to become attached to Kwan Seum Bosal. "Ah, Kwan Seum Bosal will give me money." "Kwan Seum Bosal will give me happiness." "Kwan Seum Bosal will help my son get into a good college." With this kind of mind, your practice is going in the wrong direction, and it cannot help your life. But while chanting, just keep a Great Question. Always ask yourself, "Who is chanting Kwan Seum Bosal? What is the 'thing' that is trying this, over and over and over again? What is hearing this, right now?" When you keep a great doubt your chanting is true meditation practice, because any practice that keeps the Great Question is don't-know practice. "What am I?" cuts off all thinking and returns us to our original nature which is *before* thinking.

People will often do mantras in order to get some special experience or thing. If you do a mantra with this kind of wanting mind, it is no longer true meditation. People who practice like this have already lost their way. Some people chant and do mantra using the title of the *Lotus Sutra*, *Namu myoho renge-kyo*, to get a good car or good job or good relationship. But that is not even the point of the *Lotus Sutra*'s teaching! People only do this to get some kind of good situation for themselves. We sometimes call this want-something practice. Any practice that has some object will actually be a hindrance. It cannot get such people out of the ocean of suffering; it will never cut off birth-and-death in their minds. But if they used the same mantra with a different direction in mind, deeply asking themselves, "*Who* is doing this? *Where* does this come from?" then they have returned to true meditation, in that instant. The mantra itself doesn't really matter, but the direction and the question are of very great significance.

Zen meditation is not special. The path of Zen can include any of these practices, as well as eating, standing, walking, lying down, playing tennis. What is not Zen? But many people have certain strong ideas about meditation, and they become attached to these ideas. People hear about Zen Master Nam Cheon's "Everyday mind is the true way," and they use his words as an excuse for not doing strong practice. Meanwhile other people teach that Zen has to be a difficult physical experience for you. Many Zen students think that Zen must be some kind of extreme samurai training. They believe only in strong sitting meditation—one posture, never moving. One of my students is a monk who broke both kneecaps while practicing in Japan because a famous roshi told him that, unless a student breaks his kneecaps while sitting in the full lotus position, he will never have the will to attain enlightenment. This kind of teaching is a number-one bad Zen sickness! It is an attachment to form and attachment to suffering. We also call this an attachment to body-sitting.

Many years ago in China, there was a certain young monk who was renowned for always doing very hard training. He sat in meditation from morning to night in the temple of his teacher, the Seventh Patriarch. It was said he wouldn't even lie down to sleep. Everybody believed that of all the monks in the temple, this young monk was clearly the most earnest, because he only sat in meditation, no matter what.

One day the Patriarch decided to see for himself this ardent young monk's practice. When he visited the monk's cell, he found him absorbed in deep meditation. "What are you doing?" he asked.

The young monk replied, "I am sitting Zen."

"What is the purpose of sitting Zen?"

"I want to become a buddha."

"Oh, that's wonderful," said the Patriarch. Without saying anything, the Patriarch went to the garden and brought back a rock and a piece of roofing tile and began rubbing the rock against the tile.

The grating sound shattered the young monk's peace and quiet. He tried to ignore the sound, but the Patriarch kept on rubbing the two together. The sound was horrible! After a few minutes, he could not take it anymore. "Teacher, what are you doing?"

The Patriarch replied, "I am trying to make a mirror."

"That is impossible. How can you make a mirror by grinding a tile?"

"In the same way, how can you become a buddha by sitting Zen?"

These words shocked the young monk, and he bowed to his teacher. "Where is the mistake in my practice? Please teach me."

"When a horse does not pull the cart, do you whip the cart or the horse to make it go?"

"Sir, it would be foolish to whip the cart."

"You should view meditation practice the same way. The cart is your body, and the horse is like your mind. If you want to understand your true self, you must put effort into finding your mind, and not just pushing your body."

At these words, the young monk was enlightened. From that point on he practiced meditation correctly, and later got enlightenment and received Dharma Transmission from the Seventh Patriarch. He is now known to us as Ma Jo, one of the greatest Zen masters who ever lived.

True Zen means mind-sitting. It means keeping a not-moving mind, always and everywhere. This is not dependent on any particular posture. In many zendos, there is too much emphasis placed on getting some sort of intense energy out of sitting. "I am a Zen student! *Huuuhhhhh!*" The students in such Zen centers are taught to seem very strong and hard, you know? "I must become strong! Baaaaahhhhhhhh!" During interviews with the teacher, if the student doesn't shout loudly enough, the roshi will say, "No good! More energy is necessary!"

"Yaaahhhhhhhh!"

"Stronger!"

"Yaaahhhhhhhh!"

That style shows an attachment to some idea about Zen. If you keep any idea about Zen, it is no longer Zen. If you are attached to Zen, you will have a problem, because holding any special idea about meditation is already not Zen, but some kind of samurai or kendo training. Zen means completely relax. The great Chinese Zen Master Nam Cheon said, "Everyday mind is the true way." Don't make Zen special. By making Zen special in any way, you create many hindrances in your mind.

When the Buddha was alive, he only gave talks about the Dharma. He never taught sutras, or gave special mantras, or taught the recitation of his name. People would listen to his talks and then return to their homes to meditate. They would sit in meditation under trees or up on high rocks. The most important thing that characterized their practice is that they simply looked inside, very deeply inside, to find their true nature. This is how the Buddha's first students attained his teaching, preserved it, and passed it down to us. This is how they attained their own nature and truth. This is how they attained the correct way and correct life. After all, the path of meditation was the way that the Buddha himself had attained enlightenment. So if you want to practice Buddhism, then you should never become attached to any speech or words. Do not become attached to any one technique. That is the first course in the Buddha's teaching.

The Special Transmission

教 外 别 伝

Three occasions of transmission from mind to mind:

三 處 伝 心

1. Sharing the cushion with Mahakashyapa in front of the Pagoda of Many Children

多子 塔前 分半座

2. Holding up the flower on Vulture Peak

靈山 會上 拳拈花

3. Buddha's feet appear through the coffin

泥蓮河畔 示 雙趺

TWO PEOPLE SEE something funny happen, and so they both laugh at the same time. Or a man gives his wife a birthday present. She unwraps it and discovers her favorite kind of scarf, so she is very happy and smiles. When some action occurs and two minds completely connect through this experience, we call this a transmission from mind to mind. For one moment, at least, two minds stand on the same point and share the same complete understanding. It needs no speech or words. Explanation cannot deliver this experience or understanding.

We have already talked about how our true nature is beyond all speech and words. Language cannot describe it. All thinking and language splits the world into pairs of opposites: good and bad, high and low, birth and death, coming and going, happiness and sadness, and so forth. But our true nature is universal substance, and universal substance is the Absolute. In the Absolute, there are no words or speech. When he got enlightenment, the Buddha attained the Absolute, which is before all speech and words. He already realized that this point could not be expressed with words, but rather through some actions that would transmit the teaching more directly. So this "special transmission" means just three particular occasions when the Buddha transmitted his teaching to Mahakashyapa and other students directly, without relying on the use of speech or words.

1. Sharing the cushion with Mahakashyapa in front of the Pagoda of Many Children

A long time ago in India, men from certain higher castes were allowed to have several wives at any one time. When the husband died, of course he left behind many, many children and grandchildren. So in this particular story, all the children of one man and several of his widows got together and built a beautiful pagoda in his memory. That is how this place was named the Pagoda of Many Children.

One day, the Buddha sat down in front of this famous pagoda to deliver a dharma speech. There were about twelve hundred monks already sitting there in a vast assembly, waiting for him to speak. "What kind of dharma speech will he give? What kind of teaching?" Everyone sat there—waiting, waiting, waiting—but the Buddha did not open his mouth. After a little while, in walked the Venerable Mahakashyapa, one of the Buddha's most senior disciples. He was at that time about eighty years old, but he had just recently become a monk. Before ordination, he was a very high-class Brahmin in Indian society. In Buddhism there is a universal rule regarding the seating arrangements of monks. The longer you have been a monk, the closer you sit to the front of the assembly; new monks sit in the back, arranged strictly according to when they took the precepts. Even if your body is very old, or you were once a respected member of society, if you were only recently ordained, then you would have to sit in the back, behind any young men or boys who had been ordained before you. This was always a very important rule, devised by the Buddha himself to indicate the rarity and significance of the monk's decision to leave home and family for the Dharma. The rule continues to the present day, even in Western temples. That is how strong this particular rule is. Everybody in the monks' sangha understands this rule, and no one ever challenges it. So in the Buddha's lifetime especially, it was understood by all that Mahakashyapa would soon seat himself near the distant back of the assembly, in consideration of his very recent ordination.

Meanwhile, the whole assembly was still waiting for the dharma speech to begin. "Why is the Buddha waiting?" "What kind of teaching will he give us today?" But the Buddha would not open his mouth: it seemed as if he were also waiting for somebody. When Mahakashyapa walked in, at a point far in the back, the Buddha looked right at him, and Mahakashyapa looked right at the Buddha. In that instant, their minds completely connected with one another—*puunnk*! At this, Mahakashyapa walked up the main aisle toward the Buddha. The monks were confused. "He's a new monk. How dare he sit right up in the front rows near the Buddha!" But Mahakashyapa didn't sit in front of the Buddha, with the most senior and respected monks—he sat right *next* to the Buddha! Without any words or signal, the Buddha moved over to give him some space on his cushion, and—*puunnk*!—Mahakashyapa sat down. Then all the monks in this large assembly were very surprised. They all started to suffer inside: "Ahhh, this new monk doesn't understand his correct situation!" "How can he possibly sit next to the Buddha?" "That's not correct, you know?" They were all very angry. But a transmission had already taken place.

This was an important event in the Buddha's teaching career. It marks the occasion of the Buddha's First Transmission to Mahakashyapa. Their minds completely connected and became one. Teacher and student shared the same complete view. In this first transmission, the Buddha and Mahakashyapa taught everyone gathered at the Pagoda of Many Children about the equality of all substance: not only our human substance, but the sun, the moon, the stars, trees, dogs, cats, rocks, mountains, rivers. Everything is the same, because everything has the same universal substance. So originally the Buddha's substance, Mahakashyapa's substance, this table's substance, this book's substance, your substance, my substance, the air's substance, the floor's substance, and everything's substance is the same universal substance. Your true self and the Buddha's true self are the same, not different. The Buddha did not open his mouth, but his great dharma speech in front of the Pagoda of Many Children still teaches all of us about the equality of Dharma-nature, what we sometimes call substance.

2. Holding up the flower on Vulture Peak

On another occasion, the assembly of monks gathered at Vulture Peak to hear the Buddha give a dharma speech. There were more than twelve hundred monks in attendance. The Buddha sat on the peak but did not open his mouth to speak. One minute passed. Two minutes passed. Three minutes passed. Almost five minutes passed, but still the Buddha would not open his mouth. Some of the monks began wondering, "What is wrong with the Buddha? Why is he not talking? Maybe he's a little sick today . . . ?" Then after some time, the Buddha reached down and picked a flower. Without a word, he held the flower aloft. In that vast assembly, nobody understood what he meant. But seated in the far back, only Mahakashyapa smiled—"Ahhhhh!" This caused the Buddha to say, "I have the Eye of the True Law, the secret essence of nirvana, the formless form, and the ineffable realm of Dharma. Without depending on words or letters, a special transmission beyond all teaching, this I pass to Mahakashyapa." With this, Mahakashyapa was recognized as the Buddha's first successor in a teaching lineage that stretches all the way down to us.

In this simple gesture, the Buddha taught everything we need to know about truth. He showed us that understanding truth does not depend on learning some complicated philosophy. It certainly does not require a Ph.D. In fact, ultimate truth does not even need words or explanation. That is because this whole world is already truth. Just see. Just hear. Just smell. From moment to moment, the universe is always giving us a very wonderful Dharma speech about the nature of truth. The sky is blue. The trees are green. Salt tastes salty; sugar is sweet. When you see, when you hear, when you smell, when you taste, when you touch, when you *think*—everything, just-like-this, is the truth. What is one not-true thing? Can you find that? The Buddha was silent: that is truth. All students were confused: that is truth. The Buddha raised a flower: that is truth. Mahakashyapa smiled—"Ahhhh!" That is also complete truth. None of this truth depends on words or speech. In the First Transmission, the Buddha teaches us about the nature of "substance." In this transmission, he points directly at "truth." This is a very important point.

But perhaps this teaching on Vulture's Peak has a little problem. The Buddha did not open his mouth, and only raised a flower. Mahakashyapa saw that and smiled. Everything is finished. The Buddha and Mahakashyapa have shown truth without the use of words and speech. They have made a wonderful Dharma show together. But then maybe the Buddha made a little mistake when he said, "I transmit my true Dharma to you." Why does he need to say that? Mahakashyapa smiled: he already has the same mind, the same Dharma as the Buddha. How can the Buddha ever possibly give him something now? How can he possibly give Mahakashyapa his Dharma? Just seeing the flower and understanding the Buddha's teaching is already a transmission from mind to mind: when the Buddha announces he is giving his Dharma to Mahakashyapa, it is like painting legs on a snake.

Let's say you were the Buddha at that time, and you said to Mahakashyapa, "I transmit my true Dharma to you." Then suppose Mahakashyapa had replied, "No, thank you, Buddha. I already have Dharma. Your Dharma is not necessary." If you were the Buddha, what could you do? Because when the Buddha picked up the flower, Mahakashyapa's smile means that he already got enlightenment and shared the Buddha's mind. He already got the Buddha's Dharma. Adding "more" of the Buddha's Dharma is already a very big mistake! So if you were the Buddha, and Mahakashyapa had answered you this way, how would you respond?

3. Buddha's feet appear through the coffin

The Buddha died when he was eighty years old. At that time in India, it was not unusual for many people to live well past one hundred. Many yogis and other spiritual teachers in India had ways of extending life for a much longer period than that. So when the Buddha died, many of his students were very, very upset. "The Buddha has power, magic, and special energy. Why did he die so soon?" "He died so early, maybe he was not a real sage . . ." This kind of checking-mind appeared among some of his students. Nowadays, if someone dies in their fifties or sixties we say, "Oh, that's too early, yah? Why not die in their seventies or eighties?" The Buddha's early death caused some of his students to check all of his teaching; many began to doubt what the Buddha had shown them about the nature of life and death. "The Buddha taught that there's no life and no death. But now he's dead, and so early. So we cannot believe the Buddha's speech! We cannot believe his teaching!" This kind of checking could have become a big problem for the community so soon after their leader disappeared. The Sangha was very confused.

Meanwhile a huge funeral pyre was built for the cremation. Dry wood was stacked very high, and the coffin containing the Buddha's body was placed on top. This coffin was made of gold donated by a wealthy layman, and very strong. The funeral ceremony was to be led by Mahakashyapa, the Buddha's most prominent disciple and Dharma successor. But Mahakashyapa did not show up! One day passed. Two days, three days, four days passed, and yet there was still no Mahakashyapa. Everyone was starting to worry, because it was very hot out and soon a bad smell would appear from the Buddha's coffin. "Where is Mahakashyapa?" "Why doesn't he come?" At the time of the Buddha's death, Mahakashyapa was teaching in a remote mountain district, and the news took some time to reach him. When he heard the news of his teacher's death, he came right away. But it took several days to get back.

After seven days, Mahakashyapa finally arrived. When he entered the burning grounds, he immediately perceived his dharma brothers' and sisters' minds. He saw that many people were having trouble with the Buddha's death. He saw their confusion and thinking. He also saw that some of the monks were now having difficulty believing in the Buddha's teaching. Mahakashyapa approached the coffin and bowed to it three times. Then he slowly began to circumambulate the immense pyre. Because he walked so slowly, it took him a long time to go around even once. Many people started to get nervous. "What is he doing? We must soon make a fire!" Everybody thought like that. But Mahakashyapa simply kept on walking.

After circling the coffin three times, Mahakashyapa bowed to it three times. Suddenly, there was a loud sound—*boom!*—and the Buddha's feet broke through one end of the coffin. Everybody was very surprised and jumped back. In an instant all their thinking, checking, and sadness completely disappeared. "Whaaa! The Buddha never died! Only his *body* died! Only his *body* died! But the Buddha's true self never died!" Everyone was very, very happy.

On this occasion, the Buddha was showing his students that although this body may have life and death, our true nature is never born and never dies. It never comes or goes. That is a very important point. If you only go straight, and try, try, try, then you can do anything. From moment to moment you can function only to help other people. This is the teaching of our great function to help other beings.

So when Mahakashyapa sits next to the Buddha, that teaches us about *substance*, our original nature: all universal substance is completely equal. This was a very high-class teaching in India at that time, because all Indians believed in caste. They believed that the people in some castes were of a purer substance than others. So the Buddha was making a very radical point with this. All substance is the same substance. After his students had been practicing for a few more years, and their minds developed, he gave them even more high-class teaching: everything is *truth*, just as it is. You don't need words or some higher intelligence to perceive truth. What you see, what you hear, what you smell, what you taste, what you sense through touch, and what you think are all truth. Without the use of speech or words, the Buddha taught us, "My silence is truth. This flower is truth. Your confusion is truth. Mahakashyapa's smile is truth. Wake up!" This whole world is already a world of complete truth, and it is teaching us all the time. That is a very important point.

Then after he died, the Buddha taught everyone about correct *function*. In that situation, with all the students' minds so moved by his death, the Buddha showed them some kind of "do-it" action. This tells us that when we just completely do something, there is no life and no death. The name for that is Great Function. Attain that everything is the same universal substance, and then you can attain that everything in this world is truth. If you attain these things, you can then perceive how to use this perception of truth to function clearly and compassionately for others, from moment to moment.

Pointing Directly to Mind

直 指 人 心

Master Dong Sahn:	"Three pounds of flax."
洞山禪師	麻三斤
Master Un Mun:	"Dry shit on a stick."
雲門禪師	乾屎橛
Master Joju:	"The cypress tree in the garden."
趙州禪師	庭前柏樹子

ZEN DOES NOT EXPLAIN anything. Zen does not analyze anything. It merely points back directly to our mind so that we can wake up and become Buddha. A long time ago, someone once asked a great Zen master, "Is attaining our true self very difficult?"

The Zen master replied, "Yah, very difficult!"

Later someone else asked the same Zen master, "Is attaining our true self very easy?"

"Yah, it's very easy!"

Some other people asked him, "Is attaining our true self very easy or very difficult?"

The Zen master replied, "Yah, it's very difficult, and also very easy."

Someone later asked him, "How is Zen practice? Very difficult or easy?"

The Zen master said, "When you drink water, you understand by yourself whether it is hot or cold."

The point of this is that your mind makes everything. If you think something is difficult, it is difficult. If you think something is easy, it is easy. If you think that something is not easy, but also not difficult, then it's not difficult or easy. Then what is it really like? Go drink some water, and then you will understand, on your own, whether it is hot or cold. Don't make difficult or easy. Don't make anything: when you are doing something, just *do* it. That is Zen.

We all have questions about this life. That is why we practice. "What is Buddha?" "What is mind?" "What is consciousness?" "What is life and death?" If you want to understand the realm of buddhas, first you must keep a mind that is clear like space. That is already every buddha's mind. Keeping your mind clear like space means your mind is clear like a mirror: when red comes before the mirror, red appears; white comes, white. The name we sometimes give to this is reflect mind. You just reflect the universe exactly as it is. That is already truth. The following three situations are very simple examples of how Zen teaching points directly to mind.

Master Dong-Sahn: "Three pounds of flax"

One morning in China, many years ago, Zen Master Dong Sahn was weighing flax. The scale was simply pointing at three pounds. In that moment, he was not thinking anything. He was not holding some concept or idea. This means that his mind was clear like space. Clear like space means his mind was clear like a mirror. Just three pounds of flax. You could say he had three-pounds-of-flax mind. Just then a monk asked him, "Master, what is Buddha?" "Three pounds of flax." That's all! Just reflect: when red comes, red appears; when white comes, white. When three pounds of flax comes, three pounds of flax appears in your mind-mirror. Truth is very easy! If you are thinking, this kind of teaching seems difficult. When you are not thinking, then everything is already Buddha. Which one do you like?

Master Un Mun: "Dry shit on a stick"

In many old Chinese temples, the monks compost human and animal wastes together for several weeks before using them as fertilizer in the gardens. The wastes have to compost together for a long time to eliminate toxic poisons. The monks pee and defecate in large buckets placed under wooden benches, and sometime during the day collect the wastes for composting. A long, flat paddle is used to mix the wastes together with ashes and remove them from the buckets. At the end of the day, the stick would be left leaning in the sun near the outhouse to dry. Then one day, the great Zen Master Un Mun had just relieved himself, and was walking out of the privy adjusting his pants. At that moment, a monk approached him and said, "What is Buddha?" While he was being asked this question, the Zen master's eyes simply happened to catch sight of the long shit-stick, leaning against a wall drying in the sun. "Dry shit on a stick!" Un Mun replied, and continued on his way. In that moment, the Zen master's mind was only dry shit on a stick. Dry shit on a stick was his whole mind.

Master Joju: "The cypress tree in the garden"

Bodhidharma is regarded as the First Patriarch of Zen. Before he came to China, Buddhism was already well established there. There were already many temples, many monks, and many people studying the Sutras. Other great masters came from India and built beautiful pagodas and sutra schools. Buddhism received imperial favor and became the national religion in some dynasties. When Bodhidharma arrived in China, he realized that everybody only understood the Buddha's speech. No one, it seemed, had yet grasped the Buddha's mind, because they didn't understand correct meditation. Everybody was just using Buddhism to pray for things. So Bodhidharma decided he had to hit Chinese Buddhism and wake it up from its good situation.

When Bodhidharma arrived in China from India, he was already recognized as a great meditation master. The emperor Wu of Liang heard of his arrival and invited Bodhidharma to a private audience. During their meeting, the emperor said, "The Buddha teaches that if you give a robe and bowls to even one monk, you will go to heaven. But I have donated food and clothing and bowls to countless monks. I have sponsored the copying of sutras. I have also founded many, many temples. Tell me, sir, how much merit have I made?"

Bodhidharma replied, "None at all."

The emperor got a puzzled look on his face: perhaps he had just misheard the great master from India. "Then what is the highest meaning of the holy truths of Buddhism?"

"No holiness, only vast, clear space."

Now the emperor was completely baffled. "How dare you say such things! Who are you?"

Bodhidharma answered, "Don't know."

Then Bodhidharma left, and went to northern China where there were many famous temples, but he avoided them all, preferring instead a dank cave near Shaolin. He sat facing the wall. For nine years, only go straight, don't know. . . .

So Bodhidharma came to China to teach us truth. He taught us how to use meditation correctly to find our true self. He always pointed to mind, to how we could attain our own mind. This is the beginning of the mind school in Chinese Buddhism, or Zen. But this is only an explanation of Bodhidharma's teaching. Even one thousand wonderful explanations cannot give you the experience of enlightenment. When we are hungry, if we only look at pictures of good food—even a thousand pictures—our hunger will never be satisfied. We're still hungry! These thinking-pictures cannot help our body, cannot help our stomach or our mind. It is necessary to eat something right through our mouth. That is why Zen practice appeared in this world. "Open your mouth. That's food! That's drink!" Zen does not teach nice words, but points directly to your own mind—*boom!*—so that you can directly attain your true nature. This is how Bodhidharma taught us truth.

When Zen Master Joju was alive, Zen practice had become attached to hidden meanings in questions and answers. Monks looked for secret teachings and strange explanations. One day Joju was walking around the temple grounds. A monk came up to him and asked, "Why did Bodhidharma come to China?" This was another way of asking what was the teaching of Buddhism. Joju replied, "The cypress tree in the garden." Instead of giving the monk some secret teaching, Joju was showing him that everything is already the truth. When you look at the cypress tree in the garden, you get the Buddha's teaching. You attain Bodhidharma's teaching and the teaching of all the eminent teachers. The cypress tree in the garden *is* true Buddhism. When the monk asked his question, Joju did not reply by giving him another beautiful picture of food. Joju's answer says, "Open your mouth! That is food! Now *you* can taste it!" Ha ha ha ha!

See Your True Nature, Become Buddha

見 性 成 佛

1. The willow is green; the flowers are red.

柳 綠 花 紅

2. The crows are black, the cranes are white.

烏 黑 鷺 白

3. Do you see? Do you hear?

還 是 麼. 還 聞 麼.

ZEN TEACHING is very clear and simple. It points directly at our true nature so that we can wake up and help this world. When you see, when you hear, when you smell, when you taste, when you touch, when you think—everything, just-like-this, is the truth. Everything is Buddha-nature. Everything is your true nature. Your nature and the nature of everything in this universe are never separate. The willow is green, and the flower is red— that is correct. The crow is black, the crane is white—that is correct. The wall is white. This tablecloth is yellow. That is correct. Outside it's dark; inside it's bright—that is correct. Don't think anything, and this universe is already yours. Your mind is clear like space, which means it is clear like a mirror. Everything is reflected just as it is: when red comes, red appears in the mirror; white comes, white. The sky is blue. The tree is green. A dog is barking, "Woof! Woof!" Sugar is sweet. When you see something, that is your true nature. When you hear, smell, taste, touch, and think, that is also your true nature, your original substance and Buddha. Everything is already the truth. Everything is your nature, and everything is Buddha. That is not special teaching. It is very clear!

Kong-an and All Cases

古 則 公案

One thousand seven hundred kong-ans		(Chogye)
千七百公案 （拈頌）		曹溪宗
The Pi-yen Lu *(Hekigan Roku)* 碧岩錄	one hundred cases 百 則	(Rinzai) 臨濟宗
The Tsung-jung Lu *(Shoyo Roku)* 從容錄	one hundred cases 百 則	(Soto) 曹洞宗
The Wu-men-kuan *(Mumon Kan)* 無門關	forty-eight cases 48 則	(used by all) 諸 般

Since ancient times, there has been a special way in China, Korea, and Japan to authenticate important documents. Two versions of the document are laid side by side, and a red ink seal or "chop" is marked on the documents. Later, when someone wants to be sure that some title or document is not a forgery, they just match up the seals. If the seals match, the document can be believed. Similarly, when a Zen student practices hard and claims to have attained some insight into his or her true nature, how can this be proven or shown? This is the meaning of kong-ans (Ch. *kung-an*; Jap. *koan*) and kong-an practice. In the Zen tradition, kong-ans are used the same way. A student brings his or her understanding to the teacher. The student's understanding of a question is one half, and should match the teacher's understanding, which is the other half. When the teacher and the student share the same understanding, it is called transmission from mind to mind.

Originally there was no kong-an practice in Buddhism. The Buddha was born and attained enlightenment. He taught his students that everything is impermanent. He taught that the desire, anger, and ignorance in our minds create suffering, and that these are created by thinking. He taught how to actually attain freedom from suffering, or nirvana. There were no writings and not much discussion, only meditation practice. After the Buddha died, his disciples had several meetings to write down what he had taught. In the years that followed, the disciples debated about various points of the Buddha's teachings. Studying Buddhist texts often became more important than the actual practice of meditation. Also, some sects within Buddhism argued with each other over different interpretations of the Buddha's teaching.

About fifteen hundred years ago, Bodhidharma crossed the Himalayas into China. Buddhism had already been flourishing in China for some three hundred years at that time, but it was mostly academic and devotional Buddhism: there was not so much emphasis placed on meditation. Bodhidharma saw that the people were only using Buddhism to pray for the things they wanted, so he began to teach them correctly.

We have already talked about Bodhidharma's first visit with the Chinese emperor Wu of Liang. The emperor proudly told Bodhidharma that he had built many temples, supported the copying of many sutras, and given robes, begging bowls, and food to countless monks and nuns. According to the Buddha, someone who does even one of these things would earn immeasurable good karma. So the emperor asked Bodhidharma:

"I have done all these things, so how much merit have I made?"

Bodhidharma replied, "None at all."

This confused the emperor. "Then what is the highest meaning of the holy truths of Buddhism?"

"No holiness, only vast, clear space."

Now the emperor was completely baffled. He shouted, "How dare you say such things! Who are you?"

"Don't know."

Then Bodhidharma left and went to northern China, where there were many famous temples. But Bodhidharma avoided them all, because they were only interested in performing ceremonies and ritual. Instead he sat in a cave high above Shaolin Temple, facing the wall. Only don't know. After nine years, a monk named Hui K'o came to his cave. He stood all night in the falling snow before Bodhidharma even acknowledged his presence. Finally Hui K'o said, "Master, please teach me the Dharma."

Bodhidharma replied, "Even if I told you, you would not believe me."

To demonstrate his sincerity and try-mind, Hui K'o cut off his own arm and offered it to Bodhidharma, who still did not move. "Oh, Master," Hui K'o cried out, "the pain is unbearable. Please put my mind at rest!"

"Give me your mind, and I will put it at rest."

"I cannot find my mind . . ."

Bodhidharma replied, "So, I have already put your mind at rest." Upon hearing this, Hui K'o suddenly attained enlightenment and later became the Second Patriarch. This was the first teaching of Zen, and an important example of early dharma combat: transmission from mind to mind.

The next major change in Zen teaching came with the Sixth Patriarch, who taught, "If you don't make the cause, you have no effect. So don't make anything." He became well known for this very simple kind of teaching. One day he came upon two monks arguing over a flag that was flapping in the wind. One monk said it was the wind that was moving, not the flag; the other said that the flag was moving, not the wind. Overhearing them, the Sixth Patriarch said, "Neither the flag nor the wind is moving. It is your mind that is moving." So this new question—"What is mind?"—became an inspiration for Zen monks. Many questions came out of stories such as these: What is life? What is death? What is mind? All these questions became kong-ans, and people started to use them in their own practice. When a student came to him, the Sixth Patriarch asked him, "Where are you coming from? What kind of thing comes here?"

"Don't know," the student replied.

This is where the "What am I?" kong-an originated. It was the same question that the Buddha practiced with for six years. The Buddha, Bodhidharma, and the Sixth Patriarch all had the same question, "What am I?" and all answered, "Don't know." This was the original kong-an practice.

Up until the Sixth Patriarch, there were no schools. There was only the practice of meditation. The Sixth Patriarch produced many great students: after a big rain, many great mushrooms appear. So each of his students had a slightly different style and flavor to their teaching. The five schools of Zen appeared. Though emphasizing different aspects of the training with different expedients, the bone of their teaching was the same. Zen flourished during the T'ang and Sung Dynasties in China. During this period, many great Zen masters appeared. The stories of their enlightenment experiences, dharma combat, and dharma speeches were written down and eventually gathered into collections. These situations, or "cases," were then used by other masters to test the minds of their students. If some monk thought he got enlightenment, a master could test him by presenting him with the story or teaching of another monk's enlightenment experience. Any monk who truly had some sort of realization would hear the kong-an and instantly understand its true meaning. If you didn't really get enlightenment, you wouldn't understand the kong-an, and your teacher could perceive that. "A monk once asked Zen Master Dok Sahn, 'What is Buddha?' Dok Sahn replied, 'Dry shit on a stick.' What does this mean?" If you attain that, you attain the meaning of kong-ans. This is the origin of kong-an practice. A monk once asked Zen Master Ma Jo, "What is Buddha?" Ma Jo answered, "Mind is Buddha, Buddha is mind." Later he answered, "No mind, no Buddha." Whereas before, the teaching had been simple, now there were many intellectual styles of teaching, and so a kind of word-fighting, or dharma combat, also appeared. Thus we have *The Blue Cliff Record* and the *Mumon Kan*, two famous collections of Zen kong-ans.

Zen began to look more and more cryptic to ordinary people. The practice of Zen and people's ordinary lives grew farther apart. People couldn't understand esoteric sayings like, "The wooden chicken cries, the stone tiger flies in the sky," or "Do you see the rabbit's horn?" Zen practice became a practice only for the elite. One always had to look for the hidden meaning, because the words themselves didn't make any sense. This style went on for a while, until more direct teaching returned. "What is Buddhism?" was answered with "Spring comes, the grass grows by itself." So although Zen had developed many kinds of answers to these fundamental questions, all along they were pointing to the truth.

Different Zen traditions and schools sometimes use different kong-ans. But inside, their teaching is always the same. How do we *use* the kong-an to wake up and help this world? That is the most important part of kong-an practice. So, some kong-ans' speech is correct and some is not correct. Zen masters always use words and speech freely to lay traps for their students' thinking minds. It is like putting a worm on a fish hook. If a fish is too hungry, he swallows the whole worm and is caught by the hook! But if the Zen student has just enough mind—if their mind is clear and they are not attached to their thinking—then they can get the worm and not be caught by the hook. So this is why we say, "Enough-mind fish never touches the hook."

Whether a kong-an's speech is "correct" or not doesn't matter, because this "not correct" language is meant to cure the Zen student of his attachment to thinking.

There is a very famous example of this. The Buddha had always taught that everything has Buddha-nature, which means that everything has the same capacity to get enlightenment. This was a very important teaching. Then one time, a monk asked Zen Master Joju, "Does a dog have Buddha-nature?" Joju said, "*Mu!*" This means "No." That is a very big mistake! But Joju was deliberately making this mistake to cure the monk's attachment to ideas and conceptual thinking. Like most everyone else at that time, this monk was too attached to the Buddha's speech, too attached to the Buddha's verbal teachings, to the words recorded in books. He hadn't yet attained the Buddha's mind. He was attached to the realm of this and that, yes and no, Buddha-nature and no Buddha-nature. He thought maybe some things can have Buddha-nature, while others cannot. We say that this monk was stuck in dualistic thinking. Zen Master Joju perceived that, and said "No!" This "No" hit that monk's mind, hit all monks' minds, and continues to hit people's minds, even today. "Why does Joju say 'No'? Is he correct or not? Maybe Buddha is not correct? Does a dog really have Buddha-nature? I don't know . . ." This is how, when used properly, the "*Mu!*" kong-an and all kong-ans employ words and speech to cure us of attachment to thinking.

This is a very famous kong-an. When a teacher gives us this kong-an, we use Joju's "mistake" and make it correct. Actually, kong-ans have no mistake or not-mistake. If we are thinking, the kong-an has a mistake. But if we cut off all attachment to thinking, the kong-an is very clear, and is neither right nor wrong. Its teaching point is already beyond the realm of mistakes. Because kong-ans are used to cut off our attachment to thinking, we must also not become attached to the kong-an itself. Many people, for example, are attached to this "*Mu!*" kong-an. Joju made this kong-an to cure all peoples' minds. If a patient becomes attached to the medicine, sometimes an even worse sickness appears. We will talk more about this later.

As we mentioned before, different Zen schools may use different collections of kong-ans. The Chogye school of Korean Buddhism, for example, uses a collection of one thousand seven hundred kong-ans from Indian, Chinese, and Korean sources. The name for this is *yom sang*. Students of the Rinzai school train with the one hundred kong-ans of the *Hekigan Roku*, known in English as *The Blue Cliff Record*. The Soto school uses the one hundred cases of the *Shoyo Roku*. The *Mumon Kan*, or "the No Gate Checkpoint," is a collection of forty-eight kong-ans that are part of all other major kong-an collections. They are used by all schools of Zen that use kong-an practice.

Sitting in Zen Meditation

坐　禅

To control body, breathing, mind

調身. 調息. 調心.

Sitting in meditation

坐 禅

Walking Zen

行 禅

Lying-down Zen

臥 禅

ZEN MEANS MEDITATION, and meditation means keeping a not-moving mind from moment to moment. It is very simple. When we meditate, we are only using certain techniques to control our body, breathing, and mind so that we can cut off all thinking and realize true nature. Many people think that in order to do this, we must be sitting rigidly on the floor with both legs tightly crossed in a half- or full-lotus position, completely unmoving. Yah, that style of meditation is not good, not bad. In some zendos they teach that if you don't sit in full lotus, you cannot get enlightenment. But only teaching that method is an attachment to some posture alone as a form of meditation. It is making Zen special. We call that an attachment to body-sitting.

True meditation is not just dependent on how you keep your body: from moment to moment, how do you keep your *mind*? How do you keep a not-moving mind in every situation? Thus, true meditation means mind-sitting.

Keeping a not-moving mind in any situation or condition is the true meaning of meditation. That is a very important point.

Of course, for any kind of practice or study, it is important in the beginning to use some form or posture. If you want to keep a not-moving mind, at first you must control your body. You learn a certain posture to hold while sitting. Your legs are crossed, if possible, and your back and head are lined up straight. Your eyes are partly open, gazing at the floor in front of you. Your hands are holding a *mudra* position just above your lap. You learn to slowly breathe in and breathe out of your *tan t'ien*, the energy center located just below your navel. Breathe in for a long time, and breathe out for a longer time. Breathe in, breathe out; breathe in, breathe out; breathe in, breathe out. This is how you control your body and breath.

If you can control your breath, then you can control your mind. As you slowly breathe in and slowly breathe out, your thinking slowly goes down, down, down. Your thinking becomes less complicated as your energy begins to settle out of your mind, into your *tan t'ien*, your *hara* or center. In Zen practice, this is where you "keep" your mind—in your center. This is a very important technique. Most people keep their thinking up in their head, or in their chest area. Actually, this is not so good. Your head is your intellectual center, and your chest is your emotional center. Keeping your attention in your head makes your thinking complicated, and your energy goes up. If you keep your thinking and concern in your chest, you will naturally be pulled around by your emotions. Simply let your thinking come down out of your head and out of your chest. Your *tan t'ien* is your will, your "do-it center." As your thinking naturally settles down in your center, your thinking and your emotions become clear.

Sitting meditation means formal seated Zen meditation. Everybody understands what that is. But we must always keep a very wide view of meditation. If you keep a mind that is clear like space, then everything is meditation. There is walking meditation, chanting meditation, eating meditation. When your mind is clear like space, then your mind is not moving as situations constantly change. At that point, when you see, when you hear, when you smell, when you taste, when you touch, and when you *think*, everything is meditation, because everything is clearly reflected in your not-moving mind, just as it is. Then driving is meditation, and so is playing tennis. Only keep a don't-know mind, and everything becomes clear. Cutting off all thinking means there is no thinking, which means attaining your mind *before* thinking arises. The name for this is clear mind. Clear mind means just do it. So when you drive, just do it—just drive. That has no inside and has no outside. Inside and outside completely become one: that is driving meditation. When you eat, just eat. That is eating meditation. But most people, while their bodies eat, let their minds go here and there, wandering from New York to Los Angeles, or go to 1978, or some good time, or some bad experience. The food is going into their mouth, and their mouth chews, but they are not aware of it. Their mind is thinking about their girlfriend, or their problem, maybe their job or their friend, and their girlfriend again. That is attachment to thinking, and it always creates suffering both for yourself and for this whole world. But when you just do it, do it, do it, from moment to moment, then everything is already meditation.

Sometimes people have some injury or are too sick to do formal meditation practice. We once had a student who had a very, very serious back problem. He could not sit up straight for more than five minutes. But he also wanted to do a ninety-day intensive meditation retreat with everybody. He wanted to do together-action meditation in the Dharma Room. So of course we let him join the retreat. For three months, he lay down in the Dharma Room while everyone else was sitting. They faced the wall, and he faced the ceiling. Ha ha ha ha! During interviews, he would come in and sit up for a few minutes, and then return to his cushion in the Dharma Room with everybody else and lie down again. So lying-down Zen is also no problem.

Nowadays, there are more and more people who want to do meditation. But they have this idea that meditation means only sitting in a straight posture. "Oh, my body has much pain. So meditation is not possible." That is not a correct view. If you have some body difficulty, then it is possible to use a chair, or remain standing, or lie down during meditation. Any kind of position is no problem. The most important point is to keep a not-moving mind, from moment to moment. How strong is your don't-know practice? That should be the true posture and focus of your effort in meditation.

The Great Enlightenment

大　悟

Sky is earth, earth is sky—sky and earth revolve.

天 地 地 天 天 地 轉

Water is mountain, mountain is water—water and mountain are empty.

水 山 山 水 水 山 空

Sky is sky, earth is earth—when did they ever revolve?

天 天 地 地 何 曾 轉

Mountain is mountain, water is water—each is already complete.

山 山 水 水 各 琭 然

GREAT ENLIGHTENMENT means becoming completely independent. It means completely attaining a Great Love and Great Compassion for this world. This is known as the Great Bodhisattva Way. It means attaining our correct human job, from moment to moment, so that we can always function to help all beings. This kind of speech is very wonderful; everybody already understands something about this kind of direction. But how do we actually *do* this?

Human beings are completely deluded by attachment to thinking, and this delusion causes extraordinary suffering for humans and for many, many other kinds of beings. This results from humans' attachment to desire, anger, and ignorance, to their opinions, their conditions, and situations. Since most people are attached to their thinking, they constantly suffer because their thinking is always changing, changing, changing. Human beings do not understand truth; they only follow their constantly changing thinking minds. This is a wrong view.

Zen Buddhism means going from the world of ignorance and delusion and attaining the perception that everything is truth, just as it is. This world is already complete, and never moving. If you want to attain that point, first you must let go of your opinions, your condition, and your situation. You can see clearly, hear clearly, smell clearly, taste clearly, touch clearly, and think clearly. The name for that is truth. The next step in our practice is learning how to *use* this clear perception of truth to make our life correct. From moment to moment we can maintain a correct situation, correct relationship to this situation, and correct function with regard to this situation.

This old Zen poem is often called "The Great Enlightenment." It teaches us about how human beings can attain truth to help this world. When we first look at this world, we are attached to name and form. We see that everything is impermanent, because everything is always moving, moving, moving, changing, changing, changing—nonstop. So "Form is emptiness, and emptiness is form." Many people understand with their thinking-minds that the sky is earth, and earth is the sky. This is this, and that is that. They are the same and yet also different. Because it is still attached to name and form, however, this kind of understanding sees that everything is always moving, around and around and around. Everything is always changing. So therefore this first line says, "Sky is earth, earth is sky—sky and earth revolve." The one point follows from the other. "Form is emptiness, emptiness is form." This view is somewhat correct, but it is still only thinking, and not true attainment, so it is not complete.

The second line says, "Water is mountain, mountain is water—water and mountain are empty." As we practice meditation, a more correct view appears. We attain our minds before thinking appears. We attain substance, which means we perceive that everything is the same substance. This substance is without name and form, and it is completely empty. "No form, no emptiness." At this point, we attain what it means to be attached to name and form. "Ahhhh, everything is always changing. But universal substance is never changing. Until now I have been attached to the outer appearance of things. But the outside is only name and form. If I am attached to name and form, then everything is always changing, changing, changing. I can see how this view makes everything: time and space, cause and effect, name and form. That just comes from my thinking mind! Now I see that this mind is completely empty, this world is empty, everything is empty!" So how can anything ever come or go? How can original substance ever change? This is the meaning of the lines, "Sky is sky, earth is earth—when did they ever revolve?" In complete emptiness, nothing ever comes or goes. Sky is just sky; earth is just earth. Your mind is not moving, and never attaches to names and forms. This is a state of complete stillness.

As you attain true emptiness, your mind can completely reflect this world as it is. "Sky is sky, and earth is earth—when did they ever revolve?" The view of the *Mahaparinirvana-sutra* shows how "when appearing and disappearing disappear, this stillness is bliss." The meaning of this third line can be found in that teaching. When we experience no more appearing or disappearing, we see that the sky and earth have never revolved around each other, not once. Originally there is no coming or going. This is very interesting, but it is still not a complete view.

Practice more, and you attain the complete view: "Mountain is mountain, and water is water." Sky is sky. Water is water. Ground is ground. Just reflect this world. Another name for this is moment world. We sometimes describe it as a mind that is one divided by infinity. Moment world is truth, because in one moment, everything is already complete. "Form is form; emptiness is emptiness." Mountain is just mountain, and water is water. This truth.

But here is a very, very important point: in itself, truth has no function. Zen died out in China because many masters attached to words like these and could not perceive how this view of truth must function, from moment to moment, to help other beings. Zen lost its bodhisattva function, and became a word game for the elite. Many Zen teachers still say, "Yah, mountain is mountain, water is water. That is truth." And they are right: this is truth. But if you stop here, this is still an abstract view. It can remain a purely metaphysical truth. One more step is necessary: What is the correct function of truth? How does this truth connect with you and all other beings? How does this truth function in your life? The answer is very easy: "Mountain is blue, and water is flowing."

There are four difficult things in this life. The first is to receive a human body. The second is to encounter the Dharma. The third is to meet a keen-eyed Zen master. The fourth is to attain enlightenment. Number three is very important. A Zen master may not be deeply enlightened; he may not be a good teacher. If you meet the wrong Zen master, you will go the wrong way. It is like one blind man leading another blind man into a ditch.

Some people study Zen for five or ten years without attaining enlightenment. They become very attached to their teacher, and this teacher cannot help them understand. If you study with only one teacher, even if he is a great teacher, it is difficult to finish your study. So Zen students should travel from teacher to teacher until they find a keen-eyed Zen master. This is very important.

At first you may not know how to recognize a keen-eyed teacher. But if you practice Zen for a while and listen to many Zen masters, you will soon understand what is correct teaching and what is not. If you don't taste sugar, you can't understand sweet; if you don't taste salt, you can't understand salty. No one can taste for you. You have to do it yourself.

Many teachers may claim that they are enlightened, but there are different levels of enlightenment. There is first enlightenment, original enlightenment, and final enlightenment. First enlightenment is attaining true emptiness. Original enlightenment is attaining "like-this." Final enlightenment is "just like this."

Here is an apple. If you say it is an apple, you are attached to name and form. But if you say it is not an apple, you are attached to emptiness. So is this an apple or not? If you hit the floor or shout *katz*! this is a first-enlightenment answer. If you say, "The sky is blue, the tree is green," or "The apple is red, the wall is white," you are giving a "like this" answer. But if you take a bite of the apple, your answer is, "just like this." So first enlightenment, original enlightenment, and final enlightenment all have different answers. Some Zen masters do not make these distinctions. Some only understand *katz*! or silence. Some distinguish between *katz*! and "like this," but don't understand "just like this." The "just like this" answer is the complete answer. It is not some dry metaphysical truth: "just like this" is everyday life. A keen-eyed Zen master distinguishes among the three kinds of enlightenment. But he uses all three kinds with perfect freedom.

It is very important that you not become attached to enlightenment. "Enlightenment" is only a word. Many people practice meditation with this strong desire, "I want to get enlightenment! I want to get enlightenment!" Yah, that is not good and not bad. But the Buddha said, "All things are already enlightened." And an eminent teacher said, "Without thinking, just like this is Buddha." Without thinking is clear mind. So if you keep a clear mind, then any action is just like this. To even say that you attain enlightenment—or that you can attain "more and more" enlightenment—is thinking. Thinking is desire. Desire is suffering. So Zen Master Nam Cheon said, "Everyday mind is the Way." Everyday mind is already the Great Enlightenment. If you look for anything more, it is like painting legs on a snake.

Methods of Meditation

参究法

Sitting in silent meditation
(*Shikantaza*)　　　　　　　　　　(in Soto Zen)

只管打坐

Hit—all become one

打成一片

Muk Jo
Perceive silence

Illumination, calming
(looking into words)　　　　　　(in Rinzai Zen)

惺惺寂寂

If you understand "don't know,"
just this is enlightenment.　　　(in Chogye Zen)

但知不知 是即見性

Kwan Hwa
Perceive kong-an

Shi Shim Ma
What is this?
Perceive don't know

O
UR ZEN MEDITATION tradition comes from Bodhidharma. His robe and bowl were transmitted down through the Sixth Patriarch, Hui Neng. After the Sixth Patriarch, the Zen tradition separated into five teaching streams, or "schools": the Soto school, the Rinzai school, the Wei-Ahn school, the Poep Ahn school, and the Un Mun school. All of them may have had different styles and techniques, but the bone is the same. Most of the schools were not preserved for long, so their lines are not so long. But the Soto and Rinzai schools continue to this day, so their transmission lines are very long.

Before Zen separated into the five schools, the Sixth Patriarch taught for many years on Chogye Mountain. Many Korean monks traveled to seek out the great teachers in China, and several practiced with Hui Neng himself. The Sixth Patriarch's lineage was planted in Korea by Korean monks who received formal transmission from Hui Neng's immediate Dharma heirs. That is how we have the Chogye school in Korea. The lineage of Korean Zen is a direct transmission from the Sixth Patriarch's lineage, predating the historic five schools.

Every school has a kind of technique. Every school has a different kind of teaching style. In the Soto school, the main teaching form is *shikantaza*. This means "just sitting." When you sit, not only your body sits: mind is also "sitting." Your mind is not moving at all. Completely cut off all thinking, and just become one. The name for that is *ta sot il pyon*: hit—everything becomes one. If you cut off all thinking, then your mind is not moving. Your mind is clear like space, which means it's clear like a mirror. Inside and outside completely become one. When a mountain appears before you, the mountain and you become one: "Ahh, the mountain is blue." When you see the trees, the trees and you become one—there is only green. When you see this wall, the wall and you become one—there is only white. Inside and outside—*pung!*—become one. This is the point of *shikantaza* practice, the central technique of Soto Zen.

Originally the Soto school didn't use kong-ans, though nowadays some Soto teachers are using them. Soto practice means completely putting everything down and just sitting. If you cut off all thinking for one minute, then for one minute you become Buddha. If you're not thinking for one hour, then for one hour you become Buddha. One hour not thinking means one hour is clear like space, which means that for one hour your mind is clear like a mirror: The tree is green. This wall is white. A dog is barking, "Woof! Woof!" Everything—*boom!*—becomes one. When somebody is hungry, give them food. When somebody is thirsty, give them something to drink. That is all.

The Rinzai school teaches "Clear clear, stillness stillness." In many ways, it is the same teaching as in Soto Zen. Only the teaching words are different, and some of the techniques. In Rinzai practice, too, if you cut off all thinking, then your mind is not moving. That is stillness. Your stillness mind is clear like a clear mirror, which means that everything is reflected: The mountain is blue. Water is flowing. A dog is barking, "Woof! Woof!" Your mind just reflects this world as it is. That is all. The difference between Soto and Rinzai teaching is mainly one of technique, but all along the bone is the same: your mind becomes still and clear, reflecting this world's truth like an empty mirror.

One important teaching tool that the Rinzai tradition uses is kong-an practice (Jap. *koan*). We have already spoken a little about this before. Kong-an practice is what is known as "Looking into words," or using words to cut off all thinking. To use a kong-an, you must *perceive* the kong-an's true meaning, what it is *pointing* at. A kong-an is like something pointing at the moon. It could be a finger, or a stick, or this watch. "There's the moon! It's over *there*." You don't examine the finger that guides your eyes to the moon. You don't stare at the stick. You don't analyze the watch. The point of these things are, Do you see the moon, or not? That is a very important point. The same is true of this Zen teaching tool: the kong-an itself is not important; rather, what is it *pointing* to? But many, many people become attached to the kong-an and miss the moon. This is a very bad Zen sickness. There is a very well-known example of this.

Everyone is familiar with the *"Mu!"* kong-an. The Buddha taught that everything has Buddha-nature, which means that everything can get enlightenment. But a monk once asked Zen Master Joju, "Does a dog have Buddha-nature?" Joju replied, *"Mu!"* This is a very famous kong-an. The Chinese character *mu* means "no." But *mu* only means *"mu,"* OK? Don't attach to Zen Master Joju's speech. Don't attach to the finger. Don't attach to the moon. Zen Master Joju's speech is a big mistake. But he was using this mistaken speech to take away his students' thinking. Nowadays many people sit meditating in the zendo, only keeping "Muuuuuuuuu!" very, very strongly. Everywhere they go, everything they do is only "Muuuuuu!" "What am I?" Only "Muuuuuuu!" "What is this?" "Muuuuu!" That kind of practice is not clear: it misses the point of Zen entirely. It is an attachment to *mu*. Joju's answer is not special. Joju was only using this "No" to break all his student's ideas about Buddha-nature or not-Buddha-nature. He was using *mu* to point at the moon, but many people hold this finger and miss the moon. That is too bad.

So *mu* means only *"mu."* The true point of *mu* is already clear like space, which means it is clear like a mirror. Perceiving the kong-an simply means that you and the kong-an completely become one. "Why did Zen Master Joju say '*Mu*,' or 'No'? Don't know . . ." Using the kong-an in this way completely cuts off all thinking, and you return to a mind before thinking arises. This don't-know is you; you *are* don't-know. But "don't know" is also only speech, like this *mu* or any other teaching words. Don't attach to "don't know." If you don't attach to these words and try to make some special meaning, then you can *use* these words to find your correct direction and your original nature. This is the meaning of kong-an practice: looking into words to cut off all thinking, and returning to a mind that is clear like space, which means it is clear like a mirror. Then you can reflect this universe just as it is. The sky is blue. The trees are green. Salt tastes salty, and sugar is sweet. This is the teaching of the Rinzai school, and it is also the teaching of the Soto school. Only the techniques are different.

The teaching of the Chogye school is, "What are you?" "Don't know . . ." This not-thinking mind is already your true self. It is already enlightenment and your true nature. People give this experience many names, but originally it has no name. We sometimes call it "don't know." So, Socrates used to walk around the bustling marketplaces of ancient Athens, saying, "You must understand yourself! You must understand yourself! You must understand yourself!" Then one day, one of his students said to him, "Teacher, you always say 'You must understand yourself.' So I ask you: Do you understand *your* self?" "I don't know," Socrates replied. "But I understand this don't know." This "don't know" is your true self, because it is mind before thinking arises. Don't know is your true nature.

Many people still don't understand this point, so we can explain it in this way: When you are thinking, your mind and my mind are different. When you cut off all attachment to thinking, then your mind and my mind are the same. If you only go straight, don't know, then your don't-know mind, my don't-know mind, and somebody else's don't-know mind are the *same* don't-know mind. This is because experiencing don't-know mind already cuts off all thinking, which means there is no thinking; not-thinking is an empty mind; empty mind is *before* thinking. Another name for this is your true self. That is your substance. Your before-thinking mind is your substance; my before-thinking mind is my substance. Then your substance, my substance, this stick's substance, universal substance, everything's substance is the same substance. When you keep a don't-know mind one hundred percent—only go straight, don't knowww . . . you and the universe already become one. You are the universe; the universe is you. For teaching purposes we sometimes call this primary point.

So don't know is not "don't know." Don't know is your primary point; primary point's *name* is "don't know." But sometimes people call this point mind, or Buddha, or nature, or absolutes, or holiness, or energy, or consciousness. There are many, many names that people use for this. But, originally, the true primary point has no name and no form. There is no speech and no words, because this point is *before* thinking. Only when you keep a don't-know mind one hundred percent—*don't knowww*—at that time, you and everything in this universe have already become one.

[*Holds up a Zen stick.*] So I ask you: When you keep a don't-know mind one hundred percent—*don't knowwwww*—at that time, are this stick and you the same or different? But be very careful. If you say they are the same, then this stick will hit you thirty times. If you say they are different, this stick will also hit you thirty times. If you say "don't know," this stick will still hit you. That is because primary point's substance is before thinking, which means at that point, there is no speech or words. Opening your mouth is already a mistake! Then how can you answer? Ha ha ha ha ha! It's very easy.

So Chogye Zen teaches that by cutting off all thinking and returning to don't-know mind, you already attain your true self. The great Korean Zen Master Ko Bong used to teach, "If you attain don't know, that is your original master." This is the same as Socrates' famous teaching. "Teacher, do *you* understand *your*self?" "No, but I understand this don't know." Chogye Zen teaches in this way.

The Three Essential Elements in Zen

禅 三 要 素

Great Faith

大 信 心

Great Courage

大 奮 心

Great Question

大 疑 心

Ｉf you want to attain your true nature, you must have Great Faith, Great Courage, and Great Question. It is like a three-legged stool. If you always have all three legs, then the stool will stand; but if even one leg is missing, or weak, then whoever uses this stool will fall down. So it is very important to have the three legs of Great Faith, Great Courage, and Great Question. With these supporting your practice, you can attain your true self. You can attain universal substance, and attain your correct way, and truth, and make your life correct. Then you can help all sentient beings get out of suffering. That is our job.

Great Faith means only keeping one-pointed effort, no matter what the conditions. We have all seen what happens when water continuously falls onto a rock for some time. In themselves, the individual drops of water are not strong, while the rock is very, very hard, and not moving. But if these drops continue to fall for a long time, eventually they can make a hole in the rock. This is the same as having Great Faith: all your energy is only keeping *one* point, no matter what. "I must attain my true self." Every day try, try,

try, for ten thousand years, nonstop. Then after some time, you can say, "Ahhhh! *That's* my true self!"

There is another way to describe the mind of Great Faith: A chicken sits on her eggs, keeping them warm so they will hatch. This may take three weeks, but during this time, she never has a lazy mind. She nudges the eggs around from time to time to make sure they are all warmed. She changes position every now and then. But she never lets the eggs grow cold. She knows that if she stays away too long, and the eggs become cold even once, then no baby chicks will appear. If some thinking appears, or if she follows her desire-mind—maybe the chicken goes away to look for a boyfriend, or to find some good situation—the eggs will grow cold; her babies will die. So the chicken only sits there, never moving, nonstop. She has only one direction. She has no "my opinion" and "my condition" or "my situation." After some time, the chicks appear, and gather around their mother, "Bee bee! Bee bee! Bee bee!" Then this chicken can believe in herself. "I made these chicks. I cared for them for twenty-one days." That is very wonderful! The mind that only goes straight like this is called Great Faith.

Having Great Courage is like a cat trying to catch a mouse. The mouse runs away and jumps into a hole in the wall—*piitchhuu!* The cat stays crouched outside the mousehole, shoulders hunched down and back legs loaded like springs, completely determined to get the mouse. All its energy is centered on the hole. Its whole mind is totally focused on just this one point. Even though someone may walk by and bump the cat's body out of the way, or try to play with it, the cat is not distracted at all. The cat's mind doesn't move from this hole. Its eyes never leave that one point. It holds the same position, no matter what the outside conditions.

Several hours pass. Eventually this mouse thinks, "OK, that's enough. That stupid cat is gone by now." He slowly sticks his nose out of the hole—just the tip of his nose. Then just as he sticks out enough of his head to have a look around—*piitchhuu!*—the cat has caught him!

That is a cat's mind. A cat always has complete courage in any situation. It always has total concentration that does not waver. All its energy is focused on just one point, no matter how its outside condition changes. Everybody understands something about this intense concentration. Sometimes you see a group of little children playing with a cat, throwing it up in the air. The cat goes up in the air, and its body may turn and spin and flip. But it comes down and lands on the ground safely, all four paws—*puunnk!*—correct. Human beings cannot do this! If a human being falls from some height, they spin and flail and have no control. "Oooooh! Aaaahh! Oooooh! Oooooh!" When they land, many things are broken; maybe they die. But that doesn't happen to a cat, because being a cat means strongly having Great Courage, all the time. This makes their concentration very strong. They fall through the air, their body may spin and turn, but they nearly always land correctly. Their mind does not lose its focus no matter how difficult the circumstances. "Oh, you threw me in the air. That's no problem! I landed correctly!" Ha ha ha ha! That is a cat's Great Courage. If you have this kind of cat-mind, then in any condition and any situation, your mind is not moving. Your practicing effort does not waver and fluctuate according to changes in your outside circumstances. If your body falls, it's no problem. And someday, when your body disappears, that is also no problem. This is a very important point.

I have another story about using Great Courage, this great determination, to focus all one's energy on just one point. When I was a young monk, I lived at Ma Gok Sah Temple in Korea. My job was housemaster: I was responsible for overseeing the kitchen supplies and the general living affairs of the temple. It was a very big job, so I was always very busy! Then one time we were going to have a very big ceremony at the temple. Many great monks and laypeople were traveling from great distances for this ceremony. So, many, many people worked very hard preparing various kinds of food. We spent several days just making tofu, since it is such difficult work. Now, anybody who uses tofu knows that to keep it from spoiling, you must store it under water so that it stays wet all the time. At Ma Gok Sah we had this very big tub filled with water, and we would stack the tofu at the bottom of the tub. Afterward, we could take it out and cook it.

Then three days before the big ceremony, my assistant noticed that two blocks of tofu were missing. Two days before the ceremony, two more were missing. What was happening? This was all the more strange because the storage room where they were kept was made of very big logs, and it was always locked. Sometimes people would steal from the temples, so we kept all the food in that building, and nobody could get in to steal anything. But these kitchen workers were very unhappy, because some of the tofu was missing! And not only that: Only a few blocks were missing, which was strange. If somebody was hungry enough to steal, they would steal a lot. Why only take four or five blocks? Everybody was very nervous. "Maybe a demon is taking our tofu!" There was lots of thinking, thinking, thinking. Then I had a plan.

The next day, I stayed in the storage room, only sitting, all night. I stayed behind a pole where I could see the big water tub. Several hours passed, and nothing happened. I was very tired, and wanted to sleep, but I did not take my eyes off the tub. Then at around midnight, something slowly came out of the corner of the room and moved over to the tub. It was like a shadow, you know? It was moving very, very slowly—not like a normal creature. But soon it became clear that this was a cat. There was a hole under the wall where the cat could come and go to catch mice.

The cat climbed up to the rim of the tub. He sat there for several minutes, only staring into the water. His shoulders were hunched, his head aimed low. A long, long time passed, but the cat's head never moved from that one position, looking straight into the water with great intensity. He only stared right at this tofu. After some time—*bup! bup! bup!*—a block of tofu floated up toward the surface! Then the cat swiped it out of the water, carried it in its mouth, and ran out of the room to eat. This was very strange, because normally tofu does not float and always sinks to the bottom. But this cat could focus his mind-energy strongly enough through his eyes to make it float up to him! After another two hours, the cat came in again. He climbed up onto the tub and stared into the water for a long, long time. All his concentration was completely riveted on the tofu at the bottom. And again—*bup! bup! bup!*—a single block of tofu floated up to the surface, and the cat swiped it out. That is very interesting! A cat's consciousness focuses on just one point. Then it can do anything. That is a cat's Great Courage.

So, this hungry cat has very great teaching for practicing people: if you cultivate that kind of mind, you can do anything. Our practice must be like that: all our energy is focused on one important point: "What am I? *Don't knowwww . . .*" One point, regardless of the coming and going of outside conditions. Then your mind is not moving, which means that being in any condition or situation doesn't matter. If you practice in this way, then someday this not-moving mind—*piitchhuu!*—explodes. You get enlightenment. The name for that is Great Courage.

Great Question means making this one-pointed mind continue, and continue, and continue, for a very long time. Some people can experience don't-know mind for a few moments. Other people can keep don't-know mind for a few minutes. But keeping don't-know mind for the whole day is usually not possible, yah? In the morning, a mother says to her child, "I'm going to the store. I'll be back in an hour. If you're thirsty, drink; if you're hungry, have something to eat." Then she leaves. One hour passes, but she doesn't return. Two hours pass. Soon it's lunchtime, so the child is a little bit hungry and has something to eat. But Mother hasn't returned! The child thinks, "Maybe she's never coming back!" The child waits for another four or five hours. By now it's nearly evening, and all the child's coming-and-going thoughts have massed together as one questioning mind: "Where is Mother? I want my mother! Why is she not coming?" Though hungry or tired, the child has only one question filling his whole consciousness: "Where is my mother? When will she come home?" He cries and cries and cries. "Mother, where are you? Where *are* you?" The TV is on, but the child doesn't see it: he only has a strong want-to-see-my-mother mind. All his energy is focused on just one question, one point to the exclusion of all else, and continues on this point very strongly.

Another example of having a Great Question is somebody who has not eaten anything for three days. They are very, very hungry. They cannot see the sky, cannot see the trees, cannot see anything. There is only one question filling their mind: "Where is food?" Or a man wanders in the desert for several days. The sun is beating down, and it's extremely hot! He is sweating heavily. His head is throbbing and pounding in waves. And all he wants is water. "Where is *water*? I must find water soon, or I will die." But this desert is very big, and there is no town nearby. The man is near death. So there is only one question in his mind: "Where is water?" He doesn't think about money, or sex, or fame, or sleep. He doesn't think about how nice his house is, or what kind of car he should buy. There is only one question filling his whole mind: "Where is water?"

Practicing with "What am I?" is called keeping a Great Question. We must practice with the mind of one who desperately wants to see his mother, or needs even one cup of water to keep from dying. All our energy is completely focused on one point and doesn't move at all. The child wants to see his mother. "Where's my mommy?" The hungry person wants food. "Where is food?" And the thirsty person craves water. "Where can I find water?" If you truly want to attain your true nature, then simply keep the question "What am I?" Continue practicing with this mind, and enlightenment is not far away. But in Zen, unlike these situations, our Great Question does not want anything. "What am I?" Only don't *knowww* . . .

What is most important in your life? Especially when you are young, many things seem important: sex, or money, or fame, or any kind of desire. You want many things. This pursuit goes around and around and around, and never stops. It is never fully satisfied for more than a short time. "I want this." "I want that." "I like her." "Now I don't like her. I like *her*!" "I want money." But very soon, you get old—this happens very, very fast. Then when you arrive at age sixty or seventy, what do you want then? What is your *life* then? If you ask people this question, many will answer, "Nothing." Is that answer correct?

But there *is* something. You say "Nothing," but there still is something. What is this thing which says "Nothing"? Where does it come from? Where does it go? Before we die, we must find that—that one point, that "something." The name for it is "What am I?" Another name is "Don't know." We also call it Great Question.

As was said at the beginning, to attain your true self you must have Great Faith, Great Courage, and Great Question. If any one of these is missing, your practice will be weak. If any one of these is too much stronger than the others, that is not a balance, and your practice will also have a problem. If you just have Great Courage, but your faith is weak and your question is not clear, then all you will have is a lot of energy. The most important way to bring these into harmony with one another is just to relax and harmonize with your situation. That is another name for don't know. When your mind is not loose and not tight, then Great Faith, Great Courage, and Great Question can come together and function clearly, from moment to moment. Just doing it from moment to moment means relax: When you drive a car, if your shoulders are tight, and you hunch up, then soon you will have a problem. You cannot respond as situations suddenly change. But relax doesn't mean just to go to sleep: When a red light appears, you just stop; when green light appears, you go. That is all.

In most zendos, the teaching is mainly about cultivating a great energy. They overemphasize the importance of having this Great Courage. The roshi will often check his student in interviews by testing how much energy he or she can concentrate in one point. The goal of much of the practice is in making a strong burst of energy from your *hara*, or center. "What is '*Mu*'?"

The student says, "*Muuu!*"

Then maybe the roshi says, "That's not loud enough! More power!"

"*Muuu!*"

"You still don't believe in yourself! *What is Mu?*"

"*Muuuuu!* Huuuuuunnnhhh!! Hwaahhh!"

"More become '*Mu*'!"

"*MUUUUUUUUUUUUUU!*" This is samurai-style training, and not Zen. Yah, cultivating a strong *hara* is very important. But placing this much emphasis on making a strong center leads to wrong ideas about the point and function of Zen meditation. So if you only emphasize Great Courage—"Hwaaaahhh!"—then there is no room for Great Faith and Great Question. If you only have a Great Question, it is like going somewhere very fast, but not having a clear direction. Where do you arrive? San Francisco? Tokyo? New York? Beijing? Paris? That is why you need Great Faith, because it provides our direction and our try-mind. So you can see why it is very important that three legs of this stool function together to support your practice.

There are many kinds of techniques, but the most important thing is just to practice: finding your true self and helping others. If you practice hard, your Great Faith becomes your life: we call that Great Vow. If you practice hard, your Great Courage becomes Great Energy. And one day, your Great Question opens up—you get enlightenment. We call that Great Wisdom. That is very wonderful!

So, today, *right now*, what do you want?

Effort in Zen

禅 精進

When walking, standing, sitting, lying down, speaking,
being silent, moving, being still

行住坐臥　　語默動靜

At all times, in all places,

一切時　　一切處

Without interruption—what is this?

無間斷　　是甚麼

One moment is infinite kalpas.

一念即是無量劫

ANYTIME, ANYPLACE you must not forget your true direction. Why do you eat every day? When you are born, where do you come from? When you die, where do you go? "Coming empty-handed, going empty-handed—that is human." Everybody comes into this world carrying nothing. Everybody leaves for some place, also carrying nothing. We cannot take anything with us. And yet in between, everyone wants things, everybody chases things, and everybody is attached to things very much. But when you are born, everything is already set. Your karma in this life has already been determined by the karma you made in your previous life. You cannot do anything.

But there is one way to change this. If you can control your mind from moment to moment, then it is possible to change your life, and prevent your life from being the automatic product of your karma. So you should focus your energy on how you keep your mind, right now: When moving, standing, sitting, lying down, talking, being silent, moving, or dwelling in complete stillness—anyplace, anytime—how do you keep your mind? Outside conditions and outside situations constantly take your mind and pull it around and around and around. It is possible to find your true nature in the midst of all of this coming and going, in the middle of your everyday activities. The name for this is keeping a not-moving mind.

This world is becoming more and more complicated every day. There are always many, many things happening around you all the time. Many airplanes and cars are constantly coming and going. New scientific and technological changes appear more rapidly than we can ever digest them. Also every day we watch TV, or go to the movies, or go dancing, or visit the bustling city. We meet many people, fly here, and then fly there. There are plans to be made and projects to be finished on deadline. All these things are not good and not bad. But they take your energy, so you cannot keep your center in the midst of your involvement with them. Then when you die, where does your true self go? That is something that should concern you above all else. So, watching TV is not bad. Going to the movie theater is not bad. Meeting friends in the city is not bad. Any kind of action is not good and not bad, and should not be a problem. The most important thing is that you must help your center to become strong so that you can digest all of these experiences and turn them into some kind of wisdom for others. That is very, very important.

We must practice every day. Our outside condition and situation will always change, but this should not confuse us. We should never forget our direction and our vow to get enlightenment for the sake of all suffering beings. The way to do this is to practice, every day. It is very simple.

In Korea, a woman's husband was once called to the northern part of the country to fight in the Korean War. Before he left, the woman became pregnant. Several months later, the woman learned that her husband had been killed in combat. A few months after that, their baby was born. So this baby was very, very important to her, because it was like retrieving a part of her husband from death. This baby boy was the most precious thing in her life. Every day the woman went out and worked very hard to earn money to support this baby.

The child grew up. He went to grammar school and high school. Then he was accepted at the university. His mother was so proud! But in those days in Korea, all boys his age had to do mandatory military service. Meanwhile, the Vietnam War was going on, and many young Korean men were sent there to fight alongside the Americans. So eventually this young man was sent to fight in Vietnam. Many Korean men were dying there, so the mother was very tearful as they parted.

The mother cherished her son very much. He was all she lived for. She loved her son even more than she valued her own life. For eighteen years, she worked very hard, and all of her energy had been poured into him, to give him a happy life. But now he was in Vietnam! So, maybe being in this position, she could think, "My boy had to go to Vietnam. My goodness, whatever shall I do . . ." Then perhaps she would be so sad that she would not be able to eat, or work, or live. Maybe she would become very, very sick. This is the reaction of many people who find themselves in this kind of situation. But this Korean woman was not that kind of a woman. "My son went to Vietnam. So, more hard work is necessary!" Then she worked even harder than before—cooking for other people, cleaning their homes, taking care of her little business. Every hour of every day, she kept very, very busy. She also cleaned her own house all the time, and washed the dishes, washed the cupboards, and washed the floors. She met with other women, and they sewed together. She got down on her hands and knees and tended her little vegetable garden behind the house. Every day she sold bean sprouts in the market, saving what she earned for her son's future home.

Day in and day out, this woman did many, many different things. But all along, she never forgot her son—not for one moment. "How can I help my son? How can I help my son?" She never let outside conditions affect this concern in the least. "Maybe I can save more money for him in this way or that. Then when he gets back, maybe he will meet a good girl, get married, and make a sweet home. So I will not keep anything for myself—that would not help him." She never forgot about her son. Also even when she was with friends, playing cards or having tea, or walking in the marketplace, she never forgot about her son. In the midst of any activity, on any day, her mind was only, "How is my son? How can I help my *son*?"

This woman's direction was always very, very clear, yah? In any situation, good or bad, her energy was always directed toward her son. Although situations constantly changed, and her own situation changed, one thing never changed: "How is my son? How can I help my son?" If you want to practice, it is very important to have this kind of mind. This woman was only, "My son . . ." There was nothing else. "My son, my son, my son, my son, my son . . ."

But everybody in this world always forgets about their true self. Where is your true self? How can you find your true self? Everyone is always losing themselves in the constant desire for food and sex and money and entertainment and social approval and sleep. We get one of these for a few passing moments, and then we think, "Oh, wonderful! Now I got it!" But in just that moment, we have forgotten our true self even as the pleasure of that desire is already passing. We have lost our way to our original home. Allowing ourselves to be pulled around by desire and anger is not correct practice, and it is not correct life, because it always leads directly to suffering. How you keep your mind in *this* moment makes your whole life. So be very careful! When you are watching a movie or eating, working very hard or sitting on the beach, don't ever forget your true self. "What am I? Where is my true self?" Don't *know* . . . You must have the same mind as this woman: never forget your son. And not only in this life; but life after life after life after life, only keep a don't-know mind. Yah, everybody must work and earn money. We have appointments and projects. We must all become involved in many, many activities. But no matter what you do, don't forget your son. "What am I?" Never forget your Great Question. This question is the key to your one true treasure, the only treasure that you can ever take with you when you go. Keeping this way is the key to Zen practice.

The Zen Circle

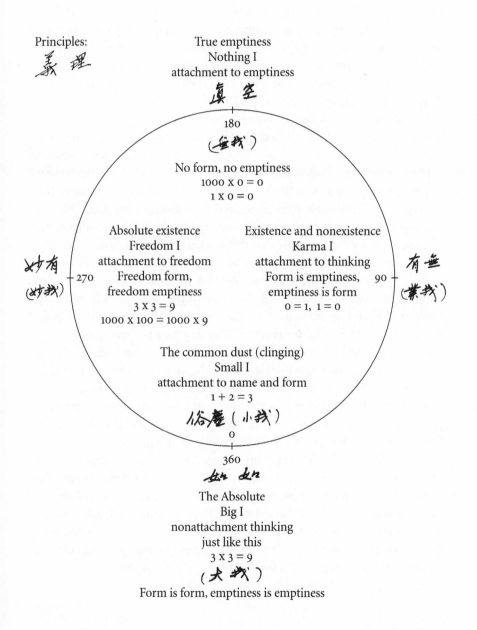

Principles:
義 理

True emptiness
Nothing I
attachment to emptiness

真 空

180

(無我)

No form, no emptiness
1000 X 0 = 0
1 X 0 = 0

Absolute existence
Freedom I
attachment to freedom
Freedom form,
freedom emptiness
3 X 3 = 9
1000 X 100 = 1000 X 9

妙有
(妙我)

270

Existence and nonexistence
Karma I
attachment to thinking
Form is emptiness,
emptiness is form
0 = 1, 1 = 0

有無
(業我)

90

The common dust (clinging)
Small I
attachment to name and form
1 + 2 = 3

俗塵 (小我)

0

360

如 如

The Absolute
Big I
nonattachment thinking
just like this
3 X 3 = 9

(大 我)

Form is form, emptiness is emptiness

O N THE DAY I graduated from primary school, my teacher gave us all a very important lesson. He drew a big white circle on the blackboard and said, "Today you are all graduating from school. That is very wonderful. From this day forward, I urge you to keep your minds like this circle. If you keep your minds in this way, your thinking will never become too tight. When good things come, you will know how to use them. When bad things come, you will know how to use them too. Nothing that appears will ever square your thinking. That is because this circle-mind can go anyplace with no hindrance. Anytime, anywhere it only follows its situation. With circle-mind you can serve other people, because a circle is completely empty and has no 'I, my, me' point. So you must all completely attain your circle-mind. This is keeping a true beginner's mind."

In Buddhism, the circle is a very important teaching tool. A long time ago, anytime someone would ask Zen Master Nam Cheon a question, he would only make a circle. Another time, Zen Master Nam Cheon and two other masters, Gui Jeong and Ma Gok, decided to pay a visit to the National Teacher, Chung, who was ill. After they had walked some distance, Nam Cheon stopped and drew a big circle on the ground with his stick. "Give me one word, and we will continue the journey," he said. "If you cannot, then it's not necessary for us to just visit this National Teacher's body!" Zen Master Gui Jeong just sat in the middle of the circle. Zen Master Ma Gok answered by curtseying like a woman. Neither of these answers was correct, and Zen Master Nam Cheon said, "We cannot go." So, Nam Cheon made a circle on the ground and said, "Give me one word!" If you were there at that time, how would you have answered? That is a very difficult question. This is another example of how many eminent teachers used the circle to test their students' minds. The circle itself is not special: it is only a teaching tool. We use it to explain the teaching simply and to test our students' minds.

Sometimes I explain Zen practice by means of a circle. This circle has five points: 0 degrees, 90 degrees, 180 degrees, 270 degrees, and 360 degrees. Three-hundred-sixty degrees is the same point as 0 degrees.

The circle begins in the area from 0 degrees to 90 degrees. This is the area of attachment and thinking. Thinking is desire, and all desire is suffering. This is also attachment to the realm of name and form. Because of that, we make opposites: good and bad, this and that, beautiful and ugly, like and dislike, mine and yours. I like this; I don't like that. This body has many desires, anger, and ignorance. I try to get happiness and avoid all suffering. So here life is suffering, and suffering is life. That is 0 degrees.

Proceeding along the circle past 90 degrees is the area of Karma I. Descartes said, "I think, therefore I am." This is consciousness-I: it is still only trying to understand yourself with thinking. "I think, so I exist." This means that my thinking makes "I." Everybody's thinking makes their "I." "I am a professor." "I am a father." "I am a mother." "I am a woman." "I am Chinese." "I am American." "I am Korean." "I am a Democrat." "I am holy." "I am a Zen student." Before this point, there is attachment to name and form. Here there is attachment to thinking. Before you were born, you were zero. Now you are one. In the future you will die and again become zero. So zero equals one, and one equals zero. At this point on the circle, all things are the same, because they are the same substance. All things have name and form, but their names and forms come from emptiness and will return to emptiness. "Form is emptiness, and emptiness is form." This is still just intellectual thinking.

At 180 degrees, there is no thinking at all. "I think, therefore I am. But if I am not thinking, what?" This is the experience of true emptiness, where "I" completely disappears. It is the realm of Nothing I. All substance completely becomes one. "No form, no emptiness." Some people would say this is the Absolute. But if you say "Absolute," that's no longer the Absolute. That is because this point is *before* thinking, and before thinking, there are no words and no speech. Opening your mouth is already a big mistake! Then how do you express this point? Anytime someone asked Zen Master Lin Chi, "What is Buddha?" he would shout "*Kaatz!*" Zen Master Dok Sahn would only hit the questioner. Zen Master Guji answered every question posed him by simply raising one finger. Only action expresses this point, because this point is universal substance. It cannot be shown with speech or words. So at this point there are no mountains, no rivers, no God, no Buddha, nothing at all. There is only . . ." [*Hits the table.*]

One day several years ago, I was sitting in my room at Hwa Gye Sah Temple in Seoul. There was an excited knock at the door, and one of my students burst in. "Zen Master! Zen Master! I attained emptiness!"

"You attained emptiness?"

"Yes, I attained emptiness—complete Nothing I!"

So I asked him, "*Who* attained emptiness?"

"Well, *I* attained emptiness!" That's not correct, yah? So I hit him with my stick—*piitchhuu!* Then he shouted, "Ouch!"

"If you truly attained emptiness, how can you possibly say 'Ouch'?" Then his face turned red, and he stared at the floor. He was very sad. This is because in true emptiness there is no speech and no words. He realized that.

A long time ago, while teaching in the United States, I was introduced to Werner Erhard, the founder of the est movement. He always gave these very long lectures that were attended by hundreds and hundreds of people. He had many thousands of students scattered all over the world. They all listened intently to his lectures about how they could believe in themselves. In his lectures he often talked about "true emptiness." "True emptiness is like this and this and this. It is also like this and this and this . . ." One day we were riding together in a car. I asked him, "You always talk about 'true emptiness.' Many people like your speech. But what is 'true emptiness'?"

"That's very easy," he said. "It's Nothing." I could not help myself and laughed out loud. He was very embarrassed. "Am I somehow mistaken . . . ?"

"Yah, no problem. You say 'Nothing,' but that's already something. So that is not true emptiness."

"Then what is true emptiness?" he asked.

I only sat there and didn't say a word.

So in emptiness there are no words and no speech. That is why we always show students how to demonstrate this point this way. [*Hits the table.*] We call this "hit." "Where are you coming from?" [*Hits the table.*] "Universal substance and your substance, are they the same or different?" [*Hits the table.*] "What is Buddha?" [*Hits.*] "What is Dharma?" [*Hits.*] "What is God?" [*Hits.*] Hitting at this point is a way of demonstrating complete Nothing I, that point of complete emptiness that cannot be explained with speech or words. That is 180 degrees.

If you keep this point for some time—only Nothing I, a complete stillness mind—and do not become attached to it, then you get universal energy. You reach the realm of magic and miracles. This is 270 degrees, or Freedom I. Here there is complete freedom, with no hindrance in space and time. This is also called live thinking. Children watch cartoons on television. A dog appears, a cat appears, a snake appears, a lion appears. Some of them are wearing clothes, or smoking a pipe. They dance with each other, fly through the sky, or drive a car. They sing songs and play the piano. "Wa wa wa wa wa! Wee wee wee wee!" Cats and birds talk with each other. A snake puts on a big top hat. Meanwhile children see this on TV and clap their hands, "Awwww, wonderful!" In a cartoon any kind of action is possible. We call that Freedom Thinking.

That is not only cartoons. Some kinds of Taoist and yoga practices cultivate this point, showing you how to strongly connect with universal energy and get some special powers. Actually, the energy that enables people to do such miracles and special actions is not special at all. It is natural energy. We can see it functioning in different forms in many everyday situations, but we're so used to it that we don't call it special. Here are three small magnets shaped like tiny doughnuts. If you slide one of them down a pencil, and then another, they will stick together, because the "plus" end of one is attracted to the "minus" end of another. Everybody understands this point. But if you take one off, turn it over, and slide it back down again, it only floats above the first magnet. The minus ends of both magnets represent the same kind of energy, so they push each other away. The top magnet seems to be floating in midair. What is more interesting is if you take another magnet, and slide it on top of the second magnet so that they stick together. Together they make a single magnet, and it's very heavy, yet they still float above the first magnet. If you push the bottom-most magnet up the pencil, the other two heavier magnets floating above it also move up at the same speed, and if you move it down, they also come down. Up and down, up and down, up and down. Meanwhile the space between the two groups of magnets remains the same.

These magnets show us something about how human beings can connect with basic universal energy. Magic and special powers are not different from the properties of these magnets. All things are made up of basic energies. You have all heard stories about yogis and martial arts masters who can fly through the air, or move or bend hard objects. This is just the result of some people being able to strongly control and manipulate this basic energy that is all things. Let's say that the earth represents "plus" energy, and the sky is "minus" energy. When you practice hard, and hold this completely empty mind for a long time, there is no thinking, so universal energy comes in. You return to "absolutes" energy, which means complete freedom to use and control your energy and any other energy at will. If earth is "plus" energy, for example, you can make your consciousness into "plus" energy. Then the earth's "plus" energy pushes you up in the air, just like these magnets. When you want to come down, you make "minus" energy, and the sky "pushes" you down.

When some yogis fly through the air, or lift things up with their minds, they are merely using their minds to channel the basic energies of which everything is composed. It is not special. Attaining this point, I can change my body into a snake's. I can ride a cloud to the Western Heaven. I can walk on water. If I want life, I have life. If I want death, I have death. In this area, the stone girl has a baby; the ground is not dark or light; the tree has no roots; the valley has no echo. On the Zen Circle, we call this point freedom thinking, or Freedom I. This is 270 degrees on the Zen Circle.

Zen practice is not about cultivating magic or special powers. Zen means attaining everyday mind; it is not about cultivating special practices. Yet there are stories about Zen masters sometimes using this special energy to hit their students' minds and wake them up. Some three hundred years ago lived Zen Master So Sahn, one of the most famous masters in Korea. He was a great scholar who practiced meditation, realized his true nature, and became the National Teacher and trusted advisor to the king. He founded many, many temples and had many students throughout the land. When the Japanese army invaded Korea in the sixteenth century, he gathered a vast army of monks against the heavily armored Japanese and defeated them in many battles. His actions protected the nation. He is a very famous monk.

One day, So Sahn Dae Sa was walking with one of his students, Sam Myong Sunim, high up in Myo Hyang Sahn Mountain, in what is present-day North Korea. On Myo Hyang Sahn Mountain there are two very famous waterfalls located right next to each other. One of the waterfalls is about 180 meters high, and the other is approximately 130 meters. Master So Sahn and Sam Myong visited the falls, enjoyed the view together in silence, and then headed back down the mountain on a narrow trail.

So Sahn Dae Sa had a very short body. He was also known for having a slight build and very soft features. But Sam Myong had formerly been a fearless general in the army before becoming a monk. He was tall and broad-shouldered, with a wide, rugged face and a strong brow. Sickened with the experience of suffering and war, he had cut his hair and searched for a teacher. He was recommended to So Sahn Dae Sa and became his student. Now, as they walked through the mountain pass, Sam Myong's mind was suddenly filled with confusing thoughts about his short, delicate teacher. "My teacher's face is not so good. His body is not so good. He walks like a woman . . ." He was very unhappy, you know? "The sky is wonderful," he thought to himself. "The mountain is wonderful! The waterfalls are wonder-ful! The trees are wonderful! But my teacher is *not* wonderful!" [*Loud laugh-ter*] "What kind of Dharma can he possibly have? How can he ever teach *me*?"

While thinking these things, Sam Myong suddenly heard a loud whoosh-ing sound. Turning his head, he saw that one of the great waterfalls had started flowing up! Wuuuhhhhh! The water jumped from the ground and ran up to the top of the cliff, turned at the edge, and flowed back into the mountain. Sam Myong was very surprised. "Teacher! Teacher!" he shouted, anxiously tapping So Sahn Dae Sa on the back as he walked ahead. "Teacher, what's happening?"

But So Sahn did not turn and only kept walking. "Why are you surprised?" the Zen master said over his shoulder. "This is just the same as your mind."

Sam Myong's mind opened, and he understood: "Ah, my teacher used magic to make this water go up! He is teaching me about my bad mind." Then he bowed to his teacher. "Zen Master! Zen Master! I am sorry! I am sorry! I had only bad thoughts about you. I made bad speech about you. I am very, very sorry."

So Sahn smiled and said, "If you truly understand your mistake, it is no longer a mistake."

"Yes, I do. I am sorry."

"Just keep your mind completely empty, and then your karma, too, is empty. Then these kinds of things will not appear in your mind again. But first you must keep your mind completely empty of all conceptual thought."

"Yes, sir. It is as if things have been set right in my mind for the first time, and I am beginning to find my true way." At these words, the waterfall just as suddenly returned to its former direction, cascading from the edge of the mountain cliff into the ravine below.

So this is a very important story. So Sahn Dae Sa perceived that his student had very strong ideas and opinions. He knew that words and speech alone could not hit or change this kind of especially strong mind. By using some kind of magic energy, So Sahn Dae Sa could penetrate Sam Myong's mind and open it up to clear teaching. The waterfall flowed up, and the student could only realize, "Oh, my teacher's body is small. But he has much power!" Then the student believes in his teacher and sees the foolishness of his own opinions and ideas. Keen-eyed teachers seldom resort to this style of teaching unless they absolutely have to. And if they do use this kind of candy to open their student's mind, they quickly take the candy away once the teaching has had its effect. A true teacher never lets his students become attached to the candy.

That is the use of 270 degrees for a keen-eyed teacher. A true master seldom, if ever, resorts to displays of magic and special energy. Students become easily attached to these qualities. If you often deal with a realm of magic, you are only a magic man and not a true teacher. That is because true teaching is about showing people how to take away their karma and help other beings, and not confusing people with magic and miracles.

But if you become attached to this point, you are only attached to freedom. And if you become attached to freedom, you cannot do anything. Since the French Revolution, everybody is free, yah? So nowadays everybody is free: there is no God, or Buddha, or anything at all that controls human beings. Human beings are the center of the universe. But this can be a problem for people who become attached to freedom. I was riding on a bus in New York City. In the bus there was a big "No Smoking" sign. But the man next to me lit up a cigarette and started smoking.

Suddenly another man shouted, "Hey, you! Can't you read? There's no smoking on this bus!"

But the man with the cigarette only smiled and said, "That's no problem. I am free!" and he kept smoking. Suddenly, there was a loud sound as the other man punched the smoker in the face—*piitchhuu!* The smoker wasn't smiling anymore! "Are you crazy? Why did you hit me?"

"I am also free to hit you!" Ha ha ha ha ha! So that is a very interesting story. If you stay at 180 degrees, you become attached to emptiness; if you stay at 270 degrees, you become attached to freedom. It is wonderful to be free. But when you become attached to freedom, you will always have a problem, and you will make a problem for others. You must pass this point.

At 360 degrees, all things are just as they are; everything is truth, and the truth is just like this. This point is actually the same as 0 degrees. We arrive where we started, where we have always been. The difference is that 0 degrees is attachment thinking, whereas 360 degrees is nonattachment thinking. There is no subject and no object. Inside and outside completely become one. When you see the sky, you and sky become one. When you see the trees, you and the trees become one. When you see, when you hear, when you smell, when you taste, when you touch, when you think—your mind and this whole universe completely become one. You are infinite in time and space. We sometimes call this moment life. In one moment, there is infinite time and infinite space. In moment there is always correct situation, correct relationship, and correct function. This is the Great Bodhisattva Way. It is not attached to anything.

For example, if you drive a car with attachment thinking, your mind will be somewhere else and you will go through the red light. Nonattachment thinking means that your mind is clear all the time. When you drive, you aren't thinking: you are just driving. So the truth is just like this. Red light means stop; green light means go. It is intuitive action. Intuitive action means acting without any desire or attachment. My mind is like a clear mirror, reflecting everything just as it is. Red comes, and the mirror becomes red; white comes, and the mirror becomes white. This is how a bodhisattva lives. I have no desires for myself. My actions are only for all beings. This is a complete life.

Zero degrees is Small I; 90 degrees is Karma I; 180 degrees is Nothing I; 270 degrees is Freedom I; 360 degrees is Big I. Big I is infinite time, infinite space. At this point there is no life and no death. I only wish to save all people. If people are happy, I am happy; if people are sad, I am sad.

Zen is reaching 360 degrees. When you reach 360 degrees, all degrees on the circle disappear. The circle is just a Zen teaching device. It doesn't really exist. It is only a tool we use to explain the teaching and to test a student's understanding.

[Holds up a book and pencil.] This book and this pencil—are they the same or different? At 0 degrees, they are different. At 90 degrees, since all things are one, the book is the pencil, the pencil is the book. At 180 degrees, all thinking is cut off, so there are no words and no speech. The best answer is only . . . [Hits the table]. At 270 degrees, there is perfect freedom, so a good answer is: the book is angry, the pencil laughs. Finally, at 360 degrees, the truth is just like this. Spring comes, the grass grows by itself. Inside it is light; outside it is dark. Three times three equals nine. Everything is just as it is. So the answer here is: the book is the book, the pencil is the pencil.

So at each point the answer is different. Which one is the correct answer? Do you understand?

Now here is an answer for you: All five answers are wrong. Why? [After waiting a few moments, he shouts] Katz! The book is blue, the pencil is yellow. If you understand this, you will understand yourself. But if you understand yourself, I will hit you thirty times. And if you don't understand yourself, I will still hit you thirty times. Why?

[After again waiting a few moments] Today it is very cold outside.

Once you attain this truth, you must perceive the correct function of truth. This is a very important point. At 360 degrees, your mind is clear like space, which means it is clear like a mirror. When red comes, the mirror is red; when white comes, the mirror is white. We already talked about this. But when a hungry person comes, what is your correct function? How do you help them? Do you also become hungry? When a thirsty person comes, do you become thirsty? Is that true compassion? Many meditation teachers only emphasize the importance of attaining an experience of reflecting truth; but they do not point out the correct function of truth, from moment to moment.

So, if a hungry person comes, give them food. When a thirsty person comes, give them something to drink. Only help other beings. That is sometimes called correct life. In the Bible, it says, "I am the Way, the truth, and the life." We are teaching the same thing. If you attain Nothing I, you attain your substance and everything's substance. Attaining that everything is the same substance means attaining the correct Way. When you attain 360 degrees, you attain that everything, just as it is, is the truth. The flower is red. The wall is white. You and this world's truth always become one. At this point, all degrees on the circle disappear, and you only function to help other beings, from moment to moment. Great Love and Great Compassion that only help other people are, we say, your correct life.

What Is Buddha-nature?

如何 是 佛性

Buddha said that all things have Buddha-nature.

佛說 一切皆有 佛性

Joju said that the dog does not have Buddha-nature.

趙州 狗子 無佛性

Which one is correct?

如何是 是耶

Which one is wrong?

如何是 非耶

The ten thousand Dharmas return to the One.

萬法 歸一

Where does the One return?

一歸何處？

Z EN MEANS not being attached to words and speech. If you are attached to words and speech, you cannot understand your true nature and the nature of this whole universe. You cannot understand Buddha-nature. You cannot understand anything. So, for people who are attached to words and speech, Zen Master Joju has made a big mistake, yah? Does a dog have Buddha-nature? Joju said, "*Mu!*" That is not correct! But *mu* is just a thinking word: it means "no." Yes and no are thinking words, since they represent opposites thinking. Then how can this great Zen master say that a dog doesn't have Buddha-nature, especially since the Buddha already taught that all things have Buddha-nature? That is a very big mistake on Joju's part.

But in that situation, Joju's answer was very necessary. The monks living at that time read many, many sutras. They became attached to the words and letters of the Buddha's speech, and lost touch with the spontaneous and living experience to which the Buddha's speech is always pointing. So they talked about things like enlightenment and Buddha-nature. They became wrapped up in matters and arguments over whether or not other beings can get enlightenment. They became attached to the Buddha's speech. "Ahh, everything has Buddha-nature. Then even a dog must have Buddha-nature. But if that's so, do they become buddhas, or not? And if that's so, why don't dogs need to do meditation like us?" These monks were always thinking, thinking, thinking, thinking about such things. They read too many sutras and didn't do much meditation, so their thinking was too clever. "Can a dog get enlightenment? Can a dog become Buddha? That's a difficult question . . ."

So one day, some monk decided to ask Zen Master Joju. "Ahh, Teacher. I have a question for you . . ."

"Yes?"

"The Buddha said that all things have Buddha-nature . . ."

"Yes . . ."

"Well, then, does a dog also have Buddha-nature?"

Joju replied, "*Mu!*" [No!] Then this monk was probably a little surprised, since this great Zen master's speech seemed to contradict the Buddha's speech. Because of this, a big question appeared in all of these monks' minds. "Zen Master said 'Mu.' Is that *correct*?" We call that Great Doubt. This is the meaning and function of a kong-an.

But as we said earlier, even today people become attached to eminent teachers' speech and words and make all sorts of terrible Zen sicknesses. Joju's "*Mu*" became a famous kong-an that is used even today. Yet many people look for some secret meaning in Joju's words. "What is *mu?*" "Are *mu* and I the same or different?" They think and think and think and think. Yet the correct use of this is to cut off all thinking and give you a don't-know mind. But many students sit in the zendo all day, "*Muuuuuuu!*" "I must become *muuuuu* . . ." That kind of practice is making-something practice. It is making *mu*. It is using Joju's very good medicine to make a very bad sickness.

A long time ago in Korea, someone said to Zen Master Man Gong, "Sir, I am trying to understand the meaning of Joju's '*Mu.*' Please, help me."

"Oh, that's very easy," Man Gong replied. "Go stand in the garden behind the meditation hall. There are many *mu* over there. They will teach you." In Korea, the word for radish is *mu*! This is very high-class teaching. Zen Master Man Gong was showing this monk that *mu* has no special meaning. "Go stand in the garden. There are many *mu* over there!" If you want to find some deep meaning in *mu*, then that's already a big mistake. It misses entirely the point of Joju's teaching. It misses the point of all the eminent teachers' teaching. We have another kong-an which says that in the *mu* kong-an there are ten kinds of sickness. If you don't understand why, only go straight with *mu*. Don't check *mu*. Don't think, "Why *mu*? What does *mu* mean?" If you check in this way, you will never understand *mu*. You will never understand your true self. Only go straight with *mu*. And if you *still* don't understand *mu* then take a plane to Korea. Find a temple and go stand in their garden. Many different *mu* will teach you. They are better than a Zen master. Ha ha ha ha ha!

The ten thousand Dharmas return to the One. Where does the One return?

Here is another one of Joju's mistakes. A monk once asked Joju, "The ten thousand Dharmas return to the One. Where does the One return?" Joju replied, "When I was in Chonju, I made a robe. It weighed seven pounds." That answer is not so clear. Why does Joju make such a long answer? "The ten thousand Dharmas return to the One. Where does the One return?" If at that time you answer by hitting the floor or shouting, that is a good answer. If you say, "This is a pencil," that is also a good answer. "The ten thousand Dharmas return to the One. Where does the One return?" The sky is blue. The tree is green. These answers are all possible. But Joju gave a very long answer. If he had just said, "This robe is seven pounds," perhaps even that would have been enough. But he added a long tail when he said, "When I was in Chonju I made a robe. It weighed seven pounds." That is very long speech: is it really necessary?

But Joju was using this long speech to hit his student's mind. Perhaps this student had some special idea: "Oh, 'the ten thousand Dharmas return to the One.' There must be some special meaning to this. 'Where does the One return?' What is the hidden meaning? I want to find that." So Joju wanted to cut his "special" mind, and gave him a Great Doubt. "When I was in Chonju, I made a robe. It weighed seven pounds." Everybody knows that there's no robe that weighs this much—that's too heavy! But the student with a "special" mind gets a Great Doubt from this, just as he would from the "Mu" kong-an. "Oh, seven pounds! That's a very big robe! Why did this great master make such a big robe?" This is Joju's teaching technique: he used words and speech to hit his students' ideas about special meanings. He used words freely to cut through thinking and give his students a big question. If you attach to the teaching technique—if you say that Joju made a mistake or didn't make a mistake—you are already dead. Joju has already hit you thirty times. If you want to escape Joju's blows, then don't attach to Joju's speech. That is true of all kong-an practice.

Then "What is Buddha-nature?" There are many ways to point at it. You can say that a dog has no Buddha-nature. You can say "The ten thousand Dharmas return to the One." You can ask "Where does the One return?" Or someone can say that they have a seven-pound robe. All these kinds of answers are not good and not bad ways of pointing to Buddha-nature. But there is also another way.

Everybody has heard the famous story about the Buddha's best disciples inquiring into Vimalakirti's health. Vimalakirti was a deeply enlightened layman who lived during the time of the Buddha. Once he got very sick, and the Buddha sent all his highest students to convey the Buddha's greetings to Vimalakirti. So many, many arhats and bodhisattvas gathered together in Vimalakirti's house. Then they all tried to express the Dharma of not-two, to show that point which is not made by dualistic thinking. One great bodhisattva said, "The sky and ground are not two." Another great bodhisattva said, "Good and bad are not two." Another one said, "Coming and going are not two." They all had many different explanations of what is not two. It was a very interesting exchange.

Finally Manjushri said, "If you speak or don't speak, it's still not two." Everybody thought, "Oh, that's a wonderful teaching." Then Manjushri turned to Vimalakirti and said, "What is your view of the Dharma of not-two?" And Vimalakirti only sat there. He did not open his mouth at all. This was the best answer of all! It is the complete answer, and the deepest answer. That is because if you open your mouth, it's already *not* not-two. Opening your mouth to express it is already making two things. If you want to understand Buddha-nature, don't open your mouth: speech and words cannot touch it. If you close your mouth, you and the whole universe have already become one. That is the true not-two. This is why in the Bible it says, "Be still, and know that I am God."

Buddha-nature is also like this. So someone asks, "The ten thousand Dharmas return to the One. Where does the One return?" If you want to understand Buddha-nature, first you must understand where this One comes from. Remember: opening your mouth is already a big mistake. This is the first course. Then with mouth closed, how do you answer? Here is a hint: A long time ago, anytime someone asked Zen Master Lin Chi any kind of question, he would shout, "*Katz!*" Zen Master Dok Sahn would just hit the questioner—*piitchhuu!* And whenever anyone asked Zen Master Guji a question, his answer was just to raise one finger. To truly express this point, you cannot say *anything*. If you open your mouth, you already make opposites. Only demonstrating that point is possible, because speech and words cannot touch it.

Three Prajna Things

三 般 物

The ground that is not dark or light.

無 隱 陽 地 一 片

The tree that has no roots.

無 根 樹

The valley that has no echo.

無 叫 響 山 谷

DURING THE BUDDHA'S lifetime, there were seven sisters who always did everything together. They always practiced together. They regularly visited the temple together. They bowed together, chanted together, and did meditation together. One day, a common acquaintance died, and there was to be a big funeral. On the way to the ceremony, the sisters passed a skeleton lying in the dust. Its bones were bleached white. One of the sisters said to the others, "When this body was alive, it had flesh, blood, a good face, and good clothes. But now all that remains are whitened bones decaying in the dust." Another of the sisters asked, "Where did the master of this body go?" One sister tapped her finger on the skull and said, "Like this." And yet another pointed to the sky and said, "Like this." As soon as she spoke these words, all seven sisters suddenly got enlightenment.

Far up in the sky lived Indra the Heaven King. He saw a bright light fill the universe below when the seven sisters got enlightenment. Struck with amazement, he descended to earth and approached the women. "You all got enlightenment," he said. "I want to give you a present. Ask me for anything in this world, and it is yours."

Then the sisters asked for three things: "We want the ground that is not dark or light. We want the tree that has no roots. We want the valley that has no echo."

But Indra was only a mere god. He had never gotten enlightenment and could not understand what they meant. "Every ground has shadows. Every tree has roots. Every valley has an echo. How can I find that?" He traveled all over the world, searching for these three things. He looked in the highest heaven and then descended into the lowest hell. But he could not find them anywhere, so he went to the Buddha for teaching. After bowing to the Buddha, he said, "These sisters got enlightenment, and I promised them anything they wanted. They asked for these three *prajna* things, but I cannot find them anywhere. What can I do?"

The Buddha replied, "A tenth-class bodhisattva understands their request. Manjushri, Jijang Bosal, Kwan Seum Bosal, and Dae Sae Ji Bosal all understand these things. But you are just a low-class bodhisattva, so you don't yet understand. If you practice harder, you will soon find these three kinds of *prajna* things. Then you can save all beings from suffering."

Indra bowed deeply. "Thank you very much. Now I understand my true job. Just being a god is not enough if I don't understand my true nature."

The Three *Prajna* Things point to the realm of magic and "freedom I." We have already talked about the 270-degree point on the Zen Circle. "The stone dog is barking every day." Does anybody understand that point? The stone dog goes "Woof! Woof! Woof! Woof!" Ha ha ha ha! Is that possible? "A wooden chicken flies in the sky, coming from the east and heading west." "The steel snake drills into the eye of a diamond." Perhaps many people have heard these words in dharma talks by Zen masters and eminent teachers. But what do they mean? If you want to attain that, first you must attain the experience behind the Three *Prajna* Things.

The Three *Prajna* Things point to an area of spiritual attainment between 180 degrees and 270 degrees, from complete emptiness to the realm of magic and freedom-thinking. These are only teaching words. If you are attached to the words, you won't understand their true meaning. They merely point to our true self and help us find our original nature. In our true nature there are no opposites: there is no high or low, no good or bad, no man or woman, no this or that. So there is also no name and no form. At that point, you cannot say anything. If you say something, it is already not true speech. These Three *Prajna* Things use words to point at that experience.

But even after having this explained to them, many people still don't understand how these three sentences function. Actually they are not special. So I often describe it this way: Somebody goes to the stock exchange, pays some money, and buys a few shares of stock. At the same time, their friend is standing very far away, in the midst of a bustling crowd of traders. There are many, many people in the room, and it is very loud. So as the trades are being made, these two friends need to communicate with each other about the sale. They need to advise each other when it is a good time to buy and when it is the right time to sell the shares. Shouting might work, but then everyone else will hear them. They must do it secretly, so no one else will understand their strategy. So one man raises his hand, or points a rolled-up newspaper in some direction. Maybe he makes a fist and then raises three fingers. Other people may see this happening, but nobody understands its meaning. Only the two men understand each other. "Oh, he is saying I should wait before selling, and then unload half. The price will soon change." We say that their minds connect. If you truly attain your true nature, and then you hear the words "The tree with no roots," or "The valley has no echo," you instantly attain the meaning of these words. "Ah, I understand that experience!" So that is the function of these "secret" Zen words.

Another example goes like this: Korea is still divided into North and South. There is a line drawn on the map at the Thirty-eighth Parallel. Above the line is Communist North Korea, and below the line is South Korea. Every so often, North Korean spies secretly cross this line and come down into South Korea. Then they want to meet with one of their agents who is secretly gathering information in South Korea. Maybe this other spy is South Korean! If they want to meet, they must do it secretly. Also it is likely that the two spies have never met before. So how do they recognize each other, and how are they sure that they are not walking up to a South Korean policeman? This is a very important point!

So, the North Korean government instructs its spy: "You must go to Seoul, to the Great South Gate. Stand on the north side of the gate, and at exactly one PM, take out a cigarette and light it. Don't smoke the cigarette—just light it. Then drop it on the ground, and crush it into the ground three times with your right heel. Then wait, and somebody will soon appear and talk to you. If he hands you a card that has the Chinese characters for *sky* and *one*, then he is our man. You can talk with him."

The spy secretly goes to South Korea. He has no idea of who he will meet or even what this person will look like. But he finds the Great South Gate and stands on the north side. At one PM, he takes out a cigarette. He lights it and then drops it on the ground. He crushes it three times with his right heel. Just at that moment, someone steps out of a car and walks over to him. He hands the North Korean man a card that has the Chinese characters for *sky* and *one*. Then the two shake hands and start talking.

This is all secret language. Everything is hidden. But when these two see this language—*boom!*—their minds connect. The North Korean spy and the South Korean spy instantly understand each other, and they understand their job together. But no one else can understand their secret language. Anyone who looks at this man dropping the cigarette on the ground and crushing it under his right heel three times thinks that these actions have no meaning. They don't pay attention to it. But the other spy is looking closely, and when he sees these things, it is not a secret. This is what the Three *Prajna* Things point to. We call them our true nature's secret words. If you attain your mind, then you will understand what these Three *Prajna* Things are pointing to.

The Realm of Like-This

如 如 地）

Spring comes, grass grows by itself.

春來草自生

The blue mountain does not move.

一青山 自不動

White clouds float back and forth.

白雲自去來

THE THREE *PRAJNA* THINGS point to an attainment of the realm described at 270 degrees on the Zen Circle. The Realm of Like-This is the
experience at 360 degrees. It is the realm of truth. Actually, we are always
living in truth. But everyone is attached to their thinking, so they only keep
their ideas and opinions about truth and do not see this world's actual truth.
When you cut off all thinking, however, your mind is clear like space. When
it is clear like space, it is clear like a mirror. Red comes before the mirror,
and the mirror shows red; white comes, white. When you see, when you
hear, when you smell, when you taste, when you touch, when you think,
everything, just like this, is the truth. All things are reflected just as they are.
The sky is blue. That is truth. The trees are green. That is truth. A dog is
barking, "Woof! Woof!" That is also truth. Spring comes, and the grass
grows by itself. The blue mountain is never moving. White clouds float back
and forth. This is all truth.

The clear mirror reflects truth because it never holds anything. Originally
the mirror has no blue, no green, no white clouds, no blue mountain—there
is nothing at all contained in its empty face. But when clouds appear before

the mirror, clouds are reflected; and when the clouds are no longer before the mirror, they disappear from the mirror. This means that there is no hindrance of any kind: the empty mirror doesn't hold anything or push anything away. It is not attached to anything, so it always has complete freedom. Whether anything appears or disappears in the mirror doesn't matter. And yet everything that appears and disappears is truth.

The same is true of our minds. When we don't keep a clear and empty mind, we cannot reflect this world's truth. We normally just follow our thinking and let it drag us into some suffering realm. And because we are attached to the names and forms of things in this world, our minds get pulled hither and thither by the constant coming and going of things. When you don't become attached to name and form, then you already return to your true self. Our original nature is complete emptiness, infinite in time and space. Only habitual thinking and conceptual thought cloud its surface. By completely cutting off all thinking, your mind is like the clear mirror. As clouds come, the clouds and you become one. "Ah, the clouds are white." When spring comes and the grass grows, the spring and you become one. "The grass is green." When you see the mountain, the mountain and you become one. "Ohh, the mountain is blue." Your mind becomes one with the appearing and disappearing of everything. The name for that is truth. If you find truth, you have already attained the correct way. That is the Realm of Like-This.

Looking Within, You Perceive
Mind's True Light

廻　光　返照

Go drink tea.

喫茶去

Watch your step.

照顧脚下

A T THIS POINT on the Zen Circle, all degrees disappear. We return to just a circle. If you make one point, you make 0 degrees, then 90 degrees, 180 degrees, 270 degrees, and 360 degrees all appear. If you don't make anything in your mind, there are no degrees. There is just a circle, which means returning to your true self: everything is already complete. This is our everyday life—it is not special. It is our correct way, and truth, and our correct life.

For many years, anytime someone asked Zen Master Joju a question, he would always answer, "Go drink tea." Many people still don't understand what Joju meant with these words. But it is actually very, very simple. Even a child understands this point. Yet everybody makes something special, so they cannot see Joju's true meaning. With these words, Joju taught about how we attain correct function and correct life. It is very high-class teaching because it points directly to the functioning of our everyday mind. A monk once asked Joju, "What is Buddha?"

Joju replied, "Go drink tea!"

"But Zen Master, I have already drunk tea."

Joju said, "If you have already drunk tea, then why do you come here with such questions?" The monk was stuck and could not answer. Perhaps he hadn't correctly drunk his tea, yah? When you correctly drink tea you attain something, and when you attain something then any kind of dharma combat is possible.

If you had been there, and Joju asked you this question, how would you have answered? What could you say? The most important thing is not to let yourself become attached to the Zen master's speech. Then when Joju said, "Why do you come here?" perhaps you could bow to the Zen master and say, "Oh, how are you, Zen Master?" Or you could say, "Zen Master, your face is yellow!" This kind of answer is no problem. The main point is not to hold the Zen master's speech. Don't become attached to any kind of situation or teaching technique. When your center is strong, you never hold on to any kind of dharma speech or teaching. Then you can digest all dharma speeches and any situations that appear before you, and attain truth. When you see, when you hear, when you smell, when you taste, when you touch, when you think, everything is truth. Then by continuing to practice, this truth can function correctly to make your life clear and compassionate. When you're thirsty, drink tea. If somebody else is hungry, give them food. That is the correct Way. That is truth. That is your correct life. Everything becomes Bodhisattva Action. This is why Joju's "Go drink tea" means Great Love, Great Compassion, and the Great Bodhisattva Way. It means from moment to moment when you are doing something, just do it. That is all.

There is another way to express this. One day, a long time ago, the great Zen Master Ma Jo was out walking with one of his students. The monk asked Ma Jo, "What is Buddha?"

Ma Jo replied, "The sky is blue. The trees are green."

"I understand this point," the monk said.

Just then, Ma Jo pointed to the ground in front of the monk and said, "Watch your step!" At that moment a poisonous snake was moving across the monk's path. He was very surprised and jumped back. In that moment, all his understanding completely disappeared. His "sky is blue" mind disappeared. In that instant, understanding "The trees are green" was of no use.

Ma Jo's "Watch your step" is very high-class teaching. This incident shows how understanding cannot help you. It cannot save your life. Rather, from moment to moment, what are you *doing*, right now? Always keep a clear mind, and then when you are doing something, you just *do* it. Even if you understand that the blue sky is truth, and the green tree is truth, when you don't keep a clear mind from moment to moment, this understanding cannot function correctly to help your life. So moment-to-moment do-it mind is very important. Just-now mind. It has no subject and no object. You only function clearly in this moment to help all beings. That is also Great Love, Great Compassion, and the Great Bodhisattva Way.

The Human Route

人生線

Coming empty-handed, going empty-handed—that is human.

空手來 空手去 是人生

| When you are born, | When you die, |
| where do you come from? | where do you go? |

生從何處來. 死向何處去.

Life is like a floating cloud that appears.

生也一片浮雲起

Death is like a floating cloud that disappears.

死也一片浮雲滅

The floating cloud itself originally does not exist.

浮雲自體本無實

Life and death, coming and going, are also like that.

生死去來亦如然

But there is one thing that always remains clear.

獨有一物常獨露

It is pure and clear, not depending on life and death.

湛然不隨於生死

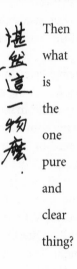

Then what is the one pure and clear thing?

湛然這一物麼.

THIS POEM IS all about finding our original face. It is a very famous Zen poem. Our body is like a floating cloud that appears and disappears in the sky. Here is my hand. Here is my head. This is my body. My body is not I. Yet whenever people's bodies have some kind of sickness or problem, they always think that they have a problem. They think that this body is I. "Oh, I am sick! I am sick!" That kind of thinking is actually not correct. My body is sick, yah? "I am suffering. I am suffering." That is also not correct. This poem shows how the body may appear and disappear like a cloud in the sky. But one thing never appears and never disappears. "It is pure and clear, not dependent on life and death." What is this? Can you find it?

Everybody knows the story of the Buddha. He had a very good situation. He had lots of money, power, food, women, music, drink—whatever he wanted for his enjoyment. He was a prince! He had lots of beautiful clothing, shining jewels, and property. And someday he would inherit his father's kingdom, with its land and titles and power. We say he had a very good situation.

But inside the young prince was unhappy because he saw all the suffering of the world. He could not understand why there was so much torment and agony, and why all beings eventually had to get sick and die. "Why do human beings live? Why must they die? What is life? What is death? What is this *world*?" A big question grew up inside him, and he was very unhappy. Nothing could make him feel any better: food, money, sex, and any other pleasant thing coming in front of him would not take away the agony that he experienced in the face of this question. In fact, the question only got bigger and bigger all the time. "What is life? What is death?" he thought. "Not only me, but all beings constantly appear and disappear, appear and disappear, appear and disappear in an endless cycle of suffering. Why do we appear in this world? Why must we and all that we love eventually disappear?" This kind of Big Question completely filled the young prince's mind, from morning to night. The pleasures of palace life certainly could not take away this question.

He could not stay in his good situation. The palace, with all its superficial beauty, made him even sicker. He went to the mountains and gave all his beautiful clothes to his attendant. "Take these back to the palace," he said. "I don't need them anymore." "Yes, sir," the attendant replied, and left. Next the prince took a sword and cut off the big topknot that symbolized his high-class rank. Then he only stayed in the mountains, wearing yellow robes. He did many kinds of ascetic disciplines, like eating only a single grain of rice a day, and breathing in and out once an hour. He practiced very, very hard for six years. He only kept the Big Question, "What am I?" always and everywhere.

Then one morning, under the Bodhi tree, he was only keeping complete don't-know mind. He saw a star in the eastern sky and got enlightenment. We say that the young prince woke up, and became a Buddha. BOOM! The Buddha attained "the one pure and clear thing." He got freedom from life and death. My body has life and death, but my true nature is never born and never dies. Perhaps my body is my thing for some time, but it is not I. The Buddha attained that point. So, what is the "one pure and clear thing"? If you want to find it, only keep a Great Question. Only go straight, *don't know* . . .

You must always remember that your body is not your true I. Sometimes your body suffers, is sick or has some kind of pain. But I is never sick. Your true I is never suffering or in pain. That is because your true I never comes or goes. It cannot be moved by your body's pain.

There are many different kinds of water. There is clear water, dirty water, rainwater, tap water, spring water, Coca-Cola, and Seven-Up. Water takes many different forms, and they all seem completely different. Each has a different taste and look, but inside—deep, deep inside—they are all the same. If you analyze all these things, eventually you will find H_2O. The names and forms are different, so the tastes and uses are different, but inside they are all the same. The flavor and color and use simply can never affect the fact that, inside, it is ultimately all just H_2O. The same is true of the flowers in spring. As the season advances, many very beautiful flowers appear. But before the flowers appear, there is only some bare tree, or a naked stalk. Then the flowers appear in all of these wonderful colors. Before the flowers come, there is no color. Now they have color. In several days someone will throw them all away. "Aww, these flowers are too old. They're no good!" They will be thrown away because they are shrivelled and ugly. So all the colors eventually disappear, no matter how wonderful they are. Where does this color come from, and where does it go?

If you view this world as it is, you see that everything happens like these flowers. Everything appears out of emptiness, remains for a time, and then returns to emptiness. So "form is emptiness, and emptiness is form." Any kind of thing has this substance: water, flowers, color, smell, mountains, rivers, trees, and your mind. That substance never appears or disappears. Your substance, my substance, universal substance, this robe's substance, a mountain's substance, and anything's substance is the same substance, and it never appears or disappears. On the outside, everything is constantly moving around and around and around—changing, changing, changing. But there is one thing that never changes and never moves. Everybody *already* has it. It comes from you! That "thing" is always clear and bright, and it helps all beings. What is it? We must find that. The most important thing we can do with our lives is to find the one pure and clear thing. When you find it, you can control everything. Then even if this world were to explode tomorrow, it would not matter. It could not touch the one pure and clear thing in the least.

Just Seeing Is Buddha-nature

即是　如來

If you want to understand the realm of Buddhas,

若人欲識佛境界

Keep a mind that is clear like space.

當淨其意如虛空

Let all thinking and external desires fall away.

遠離妄想及諸趣

Let your mind go anyplace with no hindrance.

令心所向皆無碍

Then what is keeping a mind that is clear like space?

還當淨其意如虛空麼

If your mind is not clear, listen to the following:

其或未然　　更聽註脚

It is enlightenment nature.

此正覺之性

Above is the dwelling place of all Buddhas;

上至諸佛

Below are the six realms of existence.

下至六凡

One by one, each thing is complete;

一一當當

One by one, each thing has it.

一一俱足

It and dust interpenetrate.

塵々上通

It is already apparent in all things.

物々上現

So, without cultivation, you are already complete.

不得修成

Understand, understand. Clear, clear.

了了 明明

(*Holding the Zen stick:*) Do you see?

（指柱杖云） 還見麼.

(*Hitting with the Zen stick:*) Do you hear?

（打柱杖云） 還聞麼.

Already you see clearly. Already you hear clearly.

既了了見　　既了了聞

Then what are this stick, this sound, and your mind?

畢竟 是仁甚麼

Are they the same? Or different?

同耶. 別耶.

If you say "same," I will hit you thirty times.

同也　打三十棒

If you say "different," I will hit you thirty times.

別也　打三十棒

Why?　　　　　　　　*Katz!*

何以故　　　　　喝

3 × 3 = 9

三 三 九

WANTING TO UNDERSTAND the realm of Buddhas means wanting to understand your true self. "What am I?" This is because mind is Buddha, and Buddha is mind. When you completely attain your own mind, you attain the mind of all the Buddhas and all the eminent teachers. It is the same mind. We may understand this kind of speech intellectually, but we don't understand what it actually means. People always like to talk about mind, mind, mind, mind, mind. But what is our mind? How big is it? What color is it? Is it hard or soft? Round or square? Is it green or yellow or blue? We don't understand this thing that we use every single moment of every day. We only understand this word, this name: *mind*. Yet despite hundreds of thousands of books on philosophy, we still aren't exactly sure where this mind is! Is it here, or in my arm, or in my stomach—where is my mind? What makes it stay, and where does it go? Do we really have a mind, or do we actually have no mind? What *is* mind? If you truly ask this question, very deeply, the only thing you can answer is *don't know* . . .

It is very easy to test this point. [*Raises Zen stick overhead.*] If you say you have mind, then are this stick and your mind the same or different? If you say they are the same, this stick will hit you thirty times. And if you say they are different, this stick will also hit you thirty times. That is because *stick* and *mind* are only empty names. These names have no self-nature. When you don't understand your true self, you don't understand anything, because you only remain stuck in this provisional realm of names and forms. Then you cannot answer.

Human beings have a great deal of understanding. We understand that the sky is blue, and that trees are green. We understand that this is a river, and that is a mountain. Here is a dog, and there is a cat. We understand everything. But actually we don't understand anything, because the understanding that everybody takes for the truth is only somebody else's idea that was given to them. It is not their own true idea. We say, "The sky is blue." But the sky never said, "I am blue." It never even said, "I am sky." You say, "The tree is green." But the tree never said, "I am green." A dog never said, "I am a dog." Cats never say, "I am a cat." Human beings make all these names and forms and then become attached to them. For example, how do you describe a dog's barking? Korean people say a dog barks "Wong! Wong!" In China, it's "Wo! Wo!" In America, "Woof! Woof!" Polish people say that a dog barks "How! How!" They're all different sounds! Which one is the correct barking dog? The correct bark is not "Wong! Wong!" It is not this Chinese style "Wo! Wo!" or the American "Woof! Woof!" or "How! How!" Different human beings make different sounds. But that is still not the correct sound of a dog barking. This is a human's bark: no dog has ever said any of these. In fact, a dog never even calls itself "dog." Sometime go and ask a dog, "Are you a dog?" Maybe he will have a good answer for you.

The point of this is to show that all human beings make these names and forms themselves. They make *sky* and *blue* and *tree* and *green* and *dog*. We all know that the sky is blue, right? American people say, "Ah, the sky is blue!" But a Korean person looks up at the same thing and never says, "The sky is blue." A Korean says, "*Hannulun purumnida.*" A Japanese person would say, "*Sora wa aoidesu.*" They're all different sounds, yah? So this shows how we have many different kinds of understanding inside. But that understanding is only somebody else's idea that was given to you: it is not your own true idea. It is not this world's idea. It is not the real idea, which actually has no idea.

If you want to find your own true idea, you must return to primary point. Returning to primary point means that point where everything is clear like space. When your mind is clear like space, then you and the universe completely become one. There is no separation, and no idea, no subject, and no object. Then slowly your eyes open, your ears open, your nose opens, your tongue opens, your body opens, and your mind opens. You can see clearly, hear clearly, smell clearly, taste clearly, touch clearly, and think clearly. Everything is clear, just as it is. Then the sky and you become one. The tree and you become one. The dog and you become one. Sugar and you become one. The name for that experience is truth. It is very simple. Truth means that everything becomes yours. Jesus said, "I am the Way, the truth, and the life." Our practice means actually attaining our true self, and then attaining our correct Way, and truth, and correct life. This is our own true idea. It is already inside each one of us, right now.

So if you want to understand the realm of all the Buddhas—"What is Buddha?"—first your mind must become clear like space. At this point, there is no thinking and no desire. From this point, your mind simply reflects the universe, exactly as it is. Your mind can go anywhere with no hindrance. That is our practice: returning to this point, what we often call primary point. How can you return to primary point? Only ask yourself, very deeply, "What am I?" Only *don't knowwww* . . . Keep a don't-know mind, and then all your thinking becomes clearer and clearer. Eventually your mind becomes clear like space. It is very interesting! But what exactly does it mean to say your mind is clear like space? If you don't understand that point, then it is necessary to explain a little more.

We call that clear-like-space mind enlightenment nature. All Buddhas, bodhisattvas, and demons come from just that point. So we say, "One by one, each thing is complete. One by one, each thing has it." For some people, this is very difficult speech, but actually it is quite easy and clear. Everything is the same universal substance, and this substance is our true nature. For example, here is a cookie factory. In this cookie factory there is a lot of dough. There is a very big room filled with cookie dough. Then the cookie makers take this dough, and one by one they make various forms. They make airplanes, cars, human beings, tanks, demons, and bodhisattvas. They make dogs and cats and birds. They make many, many different cookie shapes. These cookies all have different names and forms. But they all come from the same substance, the same dough. Most people in the world say, "No, that's an airplane cookie, and this is a dog cookie. They're really not the same." But put them both in your mouth, and soon you understand, "Ahh, that's the same taste . . ." So the mountain's taste, the sky's taste, Buddha's taste, bodhisattvas' taste, God's taste, demons' taste, and your mind's taste are all the same taste. Everything in this universe is the same substance.

This poem is making the same point. This whole universe—the sun, the stars, the moon, the trees, your mind, my mind, *everything*—comes from the same universal substance, the same point. The names and forms of everything are all different, but the substance is the same. The sun, the moon, the mountain, this stick, this sound, and you are all the same substance. We describe that with the words, "One by one each thing is complete. One by one, each thing has it." Everything is the same substance. This means that heaven and hell both have the same nature. God and demons share the same nature. "At the same time, everything becomes Buddha. All beings enter nirvana at the same moment." When the poem says, "Above is the dwelling place of all buddhas; Below are the six realms of existence," it is making this point, that even buddhas and the hellish six lower realms are ultimately all of the same substance. They are of the same dough, and the same taste, and fundamentally not different from one another. They are also not different from your own mind. Only the names and forms are different, and all of this just comes from thinking.

If you are not attached to name and form, you can perceive that everything is the same. "One by one, each thing is complete. One by one, each thing has it. It and dust interpenetrate. It is already apparent in all things." Substance and name and form interpenetrate. Boom! Our substance and everything's substance are already one. They are the same, so our own substance is already apparent everywhere. The sky is blue. The tree is green. A dog is barking, "Woof! Woof!" Nirvana and hell are the same dough, the same substance. [*Hits the table.*] That point. This sound's point [*hits the table*] is sound's substance, your substance, my substance, the sky's substance, the tree's substance, nirvana's substance, hell's substance, and everything's substance. This sound [*hits the table*] is universal substance. In Japanese they say *kensho*, which means see nature, and become Buddha. [*Hits the table.*] Already you hear this clearly. [*Hits.*] It is very clear, already apparent. Then what is this cup's nature? See the cup. What is *not* Buddha-nature? Can you find that? Everything has it. The blue mountain. The flowing water. The incense smell. The sound of my voice. Seeing, hearing, smelling, tasting, touching, thinking—everything is Buddha-nature.

A student once said to me, "Zen master, I have a problem . . ."

"What is your problem?"

"My thinking never stops. How can I stop my thinking?

"Oh," I said. "That is very easy."

"No, no, no. It is very difficult. I sit retreats, and do practice, but my thinking never stops. I cannot stop my thinking. I cannot realize my Buddha-nature. I cannot do anything."

So I asked him, "Do you have five dollars? Five dollars will take away your thinking."

"What? How can five dollars take away my thinking?"

"If you have five dollars, you go and buy a movie ticket . . ."

"A movie ticket? That's crazy!"

So I said to him, "You listen to me. Have you ever seen the movie *E.T.*?"

"Yes."

"Then when these children were riding bicycles in the sky, were you thinking and worrying then?"

He said, "No . . ."

"So, go watch a movie, and you will experience no-thinking. During a movie, you never think about last week, or your problem, or how much money you have in the bank. During movies you don't worry about your job, your life, your problems. When the children ride their bicycles in the sky, everyone goes, 'Ahhh, wonderful!' This movie-mind is like a completely clear mirror. Movie-mind is completely nonattached thinking. Nonattached thinking is no-thinking, OK? When the good guy is happy, you are happy. When the woman is dying, everyone is sad. When the bad man is beating up the good guy and is about to kill him, everyone in the theater shares the same mind: 'Get up! Get up and get the bad man!' "

This is a wonderful example of nonattachment thinking. Just see. Just hear. Just smell. Just taste. Everyone can keep this kind of mind while watching a movie, but the minute they leave, their minds are again attached to thinking and fear and checking and feelings going around and around and around. Watching a movie is nonattached thinking: it is *just* thinking. Art, beautiful music, and beautiful pictures can all give us the same experience of no-thinking, for a short period. That is one way we "let all thinking and all external desires fall away." "So, without cultivation, you are already complete." If you completely put it all down and keep an empty mind, then when you see, when you hear, when you smell, when you taste, when you touch, you and everything are never separate. You and everything always become one. "Without cultivation, you are already complete." When you see the sky, the sky and you become one. When you taste sugar, the sugar and you become one. Outside a cow goes, "Mooo!" And in that instant, "Mooo" and you completely become one, because that "Mooo" is your own substance. The sweetness of sugar is your own true nature. You and the universe always become one. The most important thing is completely believing in your true self. And the only way to that point is to just put it all down, right now. Putting it all down simply means not making "I," and then you are never separate from anything else. "Without cultivation, you are already complete."

"Understand, understand. Clear, clear." Attaining our true self is not difficult. Some people think that it must be difficult. But what is our true self? The wall is white. The floor is brown. The sound of those birds outside right now—*cheep-cheep, cheep-cheep, cheep-cheep!* "Do you see? Do you hear?" This *is* your true self; your true self is not different from this in any way. So when your mind is clear like space, everything is already very clear, yah?

But no matter how wonderful this kind of speech may be, even understanding these words about true nature cannot help us, if we don't actually attain their true meaning. So any good Zen speech always has a test. "Already you see clearly. Already you hear clearly. Then what are this stick, this sound [*hits the table*], and your mind? Are they the same? Or different?" If you say they are the same, this stick hits you. And if you say they are different, this stick also hits you. How can you answer? How can you actually *show* your true nature, in this moment, instead of just trying to explain it? That is a very important point. This point is already clear like space, which means that there are no speech or words that can possibly describe it. There are no opposites; it is the realm of absolute experience. Saying "same" or "different" is using opposites thinking, so if you open your mouth to explain this point, it's already a big mistake. Some kind of demonstration is necessary. Then how do you demonstrate it?

A long time ago, anytime someone asked Zen Master Lin Chi any kind of question, he would shout, "*Kaaaaaatz!*" Anytime someone asked Zen Master Dok Sahn something, he would hit the questioner with his stick: *piitchhuu!* Zen Master Guji would answer by simply raising one finger. So now I ask you again: Are Lin Chi's "*Katz!*", Dok Sahn's *hit*, and Guji's finger the same or different? [*No one answers.*] Same? Different? If you say "same," I hit you. If you say "different," I also hit you. What can you do? Some kind of demonstration is necessary! "*Katz!*" [*Hits the table.*] Only that! [*Hits.*] It's very simple, and very clear. But human beings have complicated ideas, so they cannot attain that point.

The last line of this poem is very interesting: "3 × 3 = 9." This line means that you cannot stop at "*Katz!*" or [*hits the table*]. One more step is necessary. Attaining the realm of the buddhas means attaining truth, that everything is just as it is. The wall is white. The sky is blue. My robe is gray. That is all. This point returns us to a perception of a complete world. Salt is salty. Sugar is sweet. 3 × 3 = 9. This is truth, the world just as it is. It is not special. If you truly attain this poem, you attain everything. You are already complete. That is the realm of the buddhas.

Where Are You Going?

去甚麼處

Ancient buddhas went like this.

古佛也 伊麼去

Present buddhas go like this.

今佛也 伊麼去

You go like this.

汝亦是 伊麼去

I also go like this.

我亦是 伊麼去

What is the thing that is not broken?

何物不敗壞

Who is it that is eternally indestructible?

是誰長堅固

Do you understand?

諸人還知麼

(The Zen stick is held overhead, and hit on the ground:)

（打 柱杖云）

In the three worlds, all buddhas of past, present, and future simultaneously attain enlightenment.

與三世諸佛 一時成道

On the ten levels, all beings on the same day enter into nirvana.

共十類群生 同日涅槃

If you don't understand this, check the following:

其或未然 著眼下句

The statue has eyes, and tears silently drip down.

有眼石人 齊下淚

The boy sniffles wordlessly in the dark.

無言童子 暗嗟噓.

A NCIENT BUDDHAS and present buddhas all have the same substance. [Hits the table.] You and I also have this same substance. [Hits.] That point [hits] means universal substance. We have already talked about that. It is your substance and the substance of everything. [Hits.] It is ancient Buddhas' substance, present Buddhas' substance, Bodhisattvas' substance, animals' substance, your substance, my substance, a car's substance, a rock's substance, water's substance. [Hits.] It is also God's substance and the Devil's substance. [Hits.] So this just demonstrates that there is no coming and no going. "Go like this" means just that point. [Hits.]

"What is the thing that is not broken?" Time and space control everything in this world. Everything has name and form, so it is always changing, changing, changing, changing, changing, nonstop. The sky and ground and trees, mountains, rivers, human beings, animals, and cars all have names and forms, so they are constantly coming and going. They appear and disappear: some of them quickly, and some of them only over vast kalpas of time. Some insects last only a few days, and the blue mountains last for many millions of years. But ultimately all of them appear, remain for some time, decline, and return to emptiness, because they all have names and forms. Eventually this earth will also disappear and be burned up by the sun. "If mind appears, Dharma appears; if Dharma appears, then name and form, coming and going, time and space, and cause and effect all appear. But if mind disappears, Dharma disappears; if Dharma disappears, then name and form, coming and going, time and space, and cause and effect all disappear." This teaches the same point.

So there is one thing that never changes. It never appears or disappears, and it is never broken. It is "eternally indestructible." What is this "thing" that never changes? What is this "thing" that is never broken? [Hits the table.] It never moves and never changes. This is your substance and the substance of everything. You must find that, you must attain it, and then you are free.

"In the three worlds, all buddhas of past, present, and future simultaneously attain enlightenment." Everything becomes Buddha at the same time. [Hits the table.] Actually, past, present, and future do not really exist. Time and space only come from thinking. Where is the "past"? Where do you keep it? Can you show me your past? Do you have your past somewhere, and I have my past somewhere? The past is just a dream, yah? It does not exist, except in our thinking-minds. The same is true of the future. Where is it? Everybody thinks about things in the past and the future, and they treat them as if they were real. We think about something that happened in the past, or that will happen tomorrow, and we can get angry or happy or sad. But this is only thinking, because you cannot show any of these things, right now. The present is the same. Everybody thinks that at least the present exists, even if the past and future do not. But I ask you, where is it? If you say "present," it is already passing. By the time you say "present" again, it is also in the past. You have no present! Our thinking *makes* present, just as it makes past and future. If you are thinking, you have time and space, and then time is always moving, nonstop. But where does time come from, and where does it go? It only comes from thinking. Time does not exist apart from our own thinking minds.

We only have this moment. Our life happens from moment to moment to moment. This moment is infinite time and infinite space, which is just another way of saying that it has no time or space. This is how "All buddhas of the past, present, and future simultaneously attain enlightenment." [*Hits the table.*] That is moment-mind. In a moment there is past, present, and future, which means there is no time and no space. Having no time and no space means infinite time and infinite space. In a moment there is everything. [*Hits.*] So if you attain this moment, you attain everything. You are moment, and moment is you.

But this next line is very interesting. "On the ten levels, all beings on the same day enter into nirvana." The ten levels are just a symbolic representation of all beings. It means this whole world, so it points to the dimension of space. In the Buddhist worldview, there are ten levels that compose the ordering of all beings in the universe, from buddhas to bodhisattvas, *arhats*, *sadahan*, heavenly beings, *asuras*, human beings, animals, hungry ghosts, and hell beings. Actually, the ten levels are not ten levels. The ten levels are created entirely by our thinking. Inside every mind there is the capacity for being a hell being, a hungry ghost, an animal, a human being, an *asura*, a *sadahan*, a bodhisattva, and a buddha. The ten levels are inside everyone's mind. The ten levels are inside every buddha's mind, too! Every buddha has hell, hungry ghosts, animals and every other being. Everybody has the same levels.

So how much do you have Buddha-mind? How much do you have an animal mind? How much do you act like a hungry ghost in your life? That is a very important point. If you look at this world, you will see that this kind of speech is not just some Buddhist idea. Walk down the street and look at the faces you pass. All the people may have human features. But just below the surface, many people nowadays have some kind of animal consciousness.

If your mind is clear, you can easily perceive that. This is not just a metaphor. The outside form may be human, but inside, their consciousness is dominated by some animal-consciousness. Perhaps they are only twenty percent human and eighty percent dog, or snake, or lion. Some people have a very strong hell-consciousness, so their actions are always making some hell experience for themselves and others in this world. One example of this is people who do things that put them in prison. Some people have just heavenly consciousness, or bodhisattva consciousness. How much Buddha mind do you have, and how much hell mind? Some people have fifty percent "I want something" mind, and their Buddha mind is only one percent of their consciousness. What kind of mind do you keep longer: Buddha mind, or bodhisattva mind, or *arhat* mind, or human mind, or animal mind, or hell mind? This makes your life, right now, in this very moment as well as in the next life. So these ten levels, as we can see, all just come from our own minds.

All beings on all these ten levels enter nirvana at the same time. Buddhas and hell beings, bodhisattvas and hungry ghosts, humans and all animals enter nirvana in the same moment. [*Hits the table.*] Time and space disappear; the whole universe becomes one. You return to moment-mind, just now [*hits*], this point. Name and form, time and space, and cause and effect all become one. [*Hits.*] Everything returns to moment. All buddhas of past, present and future (time) and the ten levels (space) completely become one, in this moment. [*Hits.*] It is very clear!

Does everybody understand what this means? As the poem goes on to say, "If you don't understand, check the following: The statue has eyes, and tears silently drip down. The boy sniffles wordlessly in the dark." Once you attain that time and space are completely empty, and that they don't exist—once you attain moment—you must come back to the correct functioning of this moment-mind, which is nothing other than compassionate action for suffering beings.

We have already talked about 270 degrees on the Zen Circle. If you want to completely attain the correct *function* of this [*hits the table*], first you must attain the realm of magic thinking. So, everyone hears stories about someone seeing some bodhisattva appear before them. "Oh, I did a chanting *kido* and saw Kwan Seum Bosal. She said I must do this and this and this." Experiences such as this come from the realm of 270. If you believe in Kwan Seum Bosal strongly enough, Kwan Seum Bosal will appear before you. Somebody thinks, "I need Kwan Seum Bosal's help. I want to see Kwan Seum Bosal! I want to see Kwan Seum Bosal!" Then they do a lot of bowing and chanting, maybe they also do a lot of Kwan Seum Bosal mantra. After some time, people will see Kwan Seum Bosal appear before them. "Ahh, Kwan Seum Bosal!" This comes from their mind.

And this is not limited to Buddhists. There are many, many stories nowadays about Jesus or the Virgin Mary appearing to people and giving them special teaching. Maybe a statue of Jesus will seem to bleed, or a statue of Mary will look like it is crying. Then many, many people will travel from all over to see if they can also witness it. It does not happen again, but meanwhile many people are cured of their diseases. Though they don't realize it, all miraculous cures associated with such sites are simply caused by their consciousness. They have "I want to see Mary" consciousness, and strong faith-mind, so these things occur. They get "I want to see a miracle" consciousness, or "I want to be healed," and some experience appears in their consciousness that might help them a little. It is the realm of magic thinking, the realm of complete freedom-thinking. "The statue has eyes, and tears silently drip down." This line points to that experience. If you attain this experience, you understand this teaching technique. But this point is not complete function: it is only a technique. If you become attached to this technique, it becomes a karma demon. One more step is necessary.

What is the correct *function* of this moment? How do you *use* this moment to make your life correct? First, we understand that "Ancient buddhas went like this. Present buddhas go like this. I go like this. You also go like this." It has past, present, and future. It has "I" and "you." Those lines represent 90 degrees on the Zen Circle. The next point is, "What is the thing that is not broken? Who is it that is eternally indestructible? Do you understand?" Then the Zen stick is hit. [*Hits the table.*] This point has no name and no form, and returns us to everything's substance. That represents 180 degrees on the Zen Circle. Then, "In the three worlds, all buddhas of past, present, and future simultaneously get enlightenment. On the ten levels all beings on the same day enter into nirvana." If you attain that point [*hits*], all name and form disappear. Past, present, and future buddhas getting enlightenment at the same time means the dimension of time. All beings of the ten levels represent the dimension of space. These lines show how time and space do not exist. From 0 degrees to 180 degrees there is time and space. But if you pass 180 degrees, you experience that there is actually no time and no space. That is the Absolute world. Holding that point for a long time, you attain that "The statue has eyes, and tears silently drip down." This is 270 degrees on the Zen Circle, the realm of magic and miracles.

"The boy sniffles wordlessly in the dark." That point is 360 on the Zen Circle. How does moment-mind function? If a hungry person appears before you, what do you do? If a thirsty person comes to you, how do you respond? When your mind is clear, it can function to help others, from moment to moment. That is Great Love, Great Compassion, and the Great Bodhisattva Way. Helping other people is enlightenment's job. "The boy sniffles wordlessly in the dark." When we see a suffering person or hear that someone is suffering, our compassion naturally connects and wants to help them.

So this teaching begins at 0, and passes 90, 180. At 180, there is no speech and no words. Opening your mouth is already a mistake. Then we advance to 270, where any kind of speech appears. "The statue has eyes, and tears silently drip down." When you keep practicing and digest this experience, you take one more step. The name of that step is 360, which is the realm of things as they are. It is the same as 0. At this point, all degrees on the Zen Circle disappear, and the circle disappears. The circle only means that the sky is sky, and the tree is the tree. But a keen-eyed teacher will encourage you to take one more step, that point where there is no longer any kind of circle or teaching point. Then the sky is blue. The tree is green. A dog is barking, "Woof! Woof!" Sugar is sweet. When you see, when you hear, when you smell, when you taste, when you touch, when you think, everything, just like this, is complete. There is no subject and no object at this point. There is also no inside and no outside. Everything completely becomes one, and your every action is only for other people. "My life is only for all beings." This is the Great Bodhisattva Way.

Zen Master To Sol's Three Gates

兜率三關

1. Cutting ignorance grass and sitting Zen is wishing to see true nature.

   撥草參玄　　只圖見性

   Then where is your true nature now?

   即今上人　　性在甚處

2. You already understand your true nature and pass beyond life and death.

   識得自性　　方脫生死

   When you die, how then will you be reborn?

   眼光落地　　作麼生脫

3. You already have freedom from life and death, and also understand where you return to.

   脫得生死　　便知去處

   When the four elements disperse, where do you go?

   四大分離　　向甚麼去

333

A LONG TIME AGO in China, Zen Master To Sol used to test all his monks with these three questions. "Cutting ignorance grass" means shaving your head and becoming a monk. In Buddhism we call hair ignorance grass because it represents attachment to appearance, attachment to this impermanent body and your love of appearance. When you cut your hair, you are cutting your ignorant ideas that this impermanent body is something worth following and suffering needlessly over. That is why monks and nuns shave their heads. "I don't want to just follow my karma. I want to understand my true nature and help this world." We have already talked about how everything is your nature. [Hits the table.] This is not special. So if I ask you, "Where is your true nature now?" how can you respond? If you can answer this, you understand your nature, and you get freedom from life and death. That is the first gate.

If you pass this gate, then you arrive at the second gate. "When you die, how will you be reborn?" Your true self has no life and no death. And it never comes or goes. Of course, your *body* has life and death. This is my hand. That's my head. That's my body. But that's not me. What is your true self? Your true self is only that point. [Hits the table.] In that point, the whole universe and you become one. That point has no life or death. [Hits.] Then I ask you again, when you die, how will you be reborn? But be careful! If you attach to these words, you will not be able to answer. You will only think and think and think. "You mean, there is no life and no death? Is that possible? Am I not alive right now? How will I be reborn?" But all of that is not important. If you keep this mind [hits], then whether your body disappears or not doesn't matter.

You have a car. When you arrive home, you get out of your car. The next morning, you get in your car again and drive somewhere. You get out again at the office. Then you get in again and go home. The next morning, you get in your car again and go to the office. You drive from here to there, back and forth, coming and going, always doing errands. But perhaps one day someone suddenly hits your car, and it is all broken. It is completely totaled, and you cannot use it anymore. But even if this car is completely broken, you don't die. Before the accident you worked hard and paid money, and you have some good insurance. So a good car appears again! Ha ha ha ha! Before, your car was used and worn out anyway, yet now a new car appears. You get to drive a brand-new car.

So the car that all of you are driving now is already an old car. That car is the body that you now have. Maybe it was made in America, or Russia. My car was made in Korea. But maybe your next car will be made in China, or Korea, or Germany. The next time you do a trade-in, you could get a French car, or Spanish car, or Sri Lankan car. The most important thing is, Who is the *driver* of this car? You must answer that. When it is time for you to get a new car, what kind of car will you get? This is what the second gate asks. Someday you will have to answer this question with your own life.

But this car's appearing and disappearing doesn't matter. What is your driver? Does everybody understand their driver? [*Hits the table.*] That is your driver. The universe and you become one point—your true driver appears very clearly.

When we die, where do we return to? We have already seen how the body has life and death, but our true self has no life and no death, no coming or going. So our body is composed of four elements: earth, air, fire, and water. When our body dies, these four elements are all dispersed. Then your master—this thing that controlled your body—goes where? Remember, there is no coming, no going, and also no staying. Universal substance and your substance always become one. [*Hits.*] Speech and words cannot describe this point. Only demonstration can express it. If you attain that point, it is always possible to keep this [*hits*] mind. So you must practice every day, for at least ten minutes a day. "What am I?" Don't know . . . "Where is my true nature?" Don't know . . . "How will I be reborn?" Don't know . . . "When the four elements disperse, where will I go?" Don't know . . . Answer this clearly and you can walk with no hindrance through the last of To Sol's three gates.

Which of the Following Four Sentences Is Freedom from Life and Death?

如何是　能死能活 之一句癰

Under the sea, the mud cow eats the moon.

海底泥牛啣月走

In front of the cliff, the stone tiger sleeps, holding a baby in his arms.

岩前石虎抱兒眠

The steel snake drills into the eye of a diamond.

鉄蛇鑽入金剛眼

Mount Kun-Lun rides on the back of an elephant pulled by a little bird.

崑崙騎象鷺鷥牽

IN CHINA THERE ARE many Taoist and even Confucian masters who do special kinds of practice in the mountains and get special energy. They can fly in the sky. They can transform their body into a tiger. They can make smoke appear. This is what we call magic. If you practice very hard, then universal energy and your energy become one. Our human energy is called, in Sino-Korean, *won gi*. Every day we breathe in and breathe out. Breathe in and breathe out. Breathe in, breathe out. That is called *kong gi*. Then the energy of the sun and the moon, the orbiting of planets and the stars is called *hap gi*, or universal energy. If your energy (*won gi*), concentrated breathing (*kong gi*), and universal energy (*hap gi*) become one, then you get *dae gi*, or great energy. With this energy you can do anything. You can transform your body. You can levitate, or fly in the sky. You can do magic and miracles. But the most important thing is to completely take away "I, my, me" in your mind. If you have "I, my, me," you cannot get strong human energy. You cannot connect with space energy. You cannot attain great energy. When there is no "I, my, me," and you just continue to practice, practice, practice, however, then great energy, space energy, and your own energy—*boom!*— become one. Then it is possible to experience this realm of magic and complete Freedom I.

These four lines all point to that realm. It is located at 270 degrees on the Zen Circle. Each of these lines has some kind of behind-meaning that is impossible to understand unless you have actually attained this realm of absolute existence. "Under the sea, a mud cow eats the moon." This is very crazy speech, yah? How can a mud cow eat the moon? But everybody already understands something about this point. We have all seen children's cartoons, where animals talk and laugh and sing songs and dance or fly through the air. All children understand this point, but adults don't get it. So that means that as we get older our minds become set and become tightly attached to fixed ideas about name and form. But this realm at 270 degrees is "freedom name and form." It is freedom thinking. "In front of the cliff, a stone tiger sleeps, holding a baby in his arms." Can a stone tiger sleep? "The steel snake drills into the eye of a diamond." But diamond is stronger than steel: how can steel drill into a diamond? "Mount Kun-Lun rides on the back of an elephant pulled by a little bird." Mount Kun-Lun is the biggest mountain in China. This huge mountain is riding on the back of an elephant, and the elephant is being pulled by a little bird. How is that possible? All children already understand that kind of freedom realm that always exists in our minds. If you practice hard, you can also attain it.

Original Face

Sitting in silence in a mountain temple in the quiet night:

山堂静夜坐無言

Extreme quiet and stillness are our original nature.

寂々寥々本自然

Why then does the western wind shake the forest?

何事西風動林野

A single cry of the cold-weather geese fills the sky.

一声寒鴈唳長天

THIS IS A VERY GOOD example of a typical Zen poem. It was written many years ago by Zen Master Ho Am and is chanted every day in Korean temples. True Zen poems are not decorative-style poems. Their purpose is not to just use some beautiful language for the sake of art. A Zen poem uses words and speech to point to an experience that cannot be expressed in words. They are always used for teaching. They often express a student's enlightenment experience.

Many Zen poems have a certain form that is used to cognitively lift the reader's mind from the realm of name and form to the view of things as they are. The teaching is revealed step by step. Each line has a special "job" in this form. The first lines show how "Form is emptiness, emptiness is form." They explain our nature. They explain primary point. "Sitting in silence in a mountain temple in the quiet night. Extreme quiet and stillness are our original nature." These lines use opposites thinking to express some sense of opposites, a dualism.

The third line asks, "Why then does the western wind shake the forest?" You must *attain* your nature. Explanation is not necessary. Taken together, these three lines give you some question, to lead you to directly experiencing don't-know mind. There is another poem that says, "This whole world is complete stillness. The sun, the moon and stars come from where?" But if you are complete stillness, where can the sun and moon and stars possibly come from? That is opposites thinking making a Great Question. Those lines make the same point as this section of our poem. "Extreme quiet and stillness are our original nature." Why does the wind come in and move things around, making sound and disturbing the stillness? Where does wind come from? Why does it appear? This gives you a Big Question.

If you attain your Big Question, then your mind is clear like space. Keeping your mind clear like space means your mind is clear like a mirror. Everything is reflected, just as it is. The sound of a bird flying through the air, beating its wings and crying out—*Gaa! Gaa Gaa! Gaa!*—that is your nature. Just hearing is Buddha-nature. Just seeing is Buddha-nature. Just-like-this is truth. Everything is complete.

So this is how a Zen poem usually teaches. Although the numbers of lines may vary, the ordering is usually the same. The first lines express some opposites view or idea. The next part gives a Big Question, or sometimes it expresses some stillness point. The third line in many Zen poems will express the view of the realm of magic and miracles, what we refer to as 270-degree teaching. But none of these views is the final truth; that is why the last sentence is a just-like-this sentence. It brings the reader back to the realm of things just as they are.

Zen Master Ko Bong's Three Gates

室 中 三 関 (高峰禅師)

The sun in the sky shines everywhere. Why does a cloud obscure it?

杲日當空 無所不照 因甚被片雲遮却

Everyone has a shadow following them. How can you not step on your shadow?

人人有箇影子 寸步不離 因甚踏不著

The whole universe is on fire. Through what kind of samadhi can you escape being burned?

盡大地是箇火坑 得何三昧 不被燒却

A LONG TIME AGO in China, Zen Master Ko Bong made three kong-an gates for his students to pass. The first Gate is: "The sun in the sky shines everywhere. Why does a cloud obscure it?" So you must understand this point: why does a cloud cover the sun? This is a kind of problem. When a cloud appears and covers the sun, then the sun is no longer shining someplace. A shadow appears. Why does a cloud appear and cover the sun? If you think about it, you won't understand. But if you completely cut off all thinking, then you will understand.

Perhaps this will help you: We have two eyes, two nostrils, and two ears. Why do we have only one mouth? There is two of every other opening on our face, so two mouths are necessary. That's natural! If you have only one mouth, you always have a big problem. Your two ears have only one job. Your two eyes have only one job. Your two nostrils have just one easy job. It's very simple: your ears just hear; eyes just see; and nostrils just smell. But this one mouth has four important jobs. It must talk, taste, breathe, and eat. That is a very complicated situation. If you had a mouth on each side of your head and one in the back, it would be a lot easier. One side could eat while the other side talks. The front could breathe, and the back could taste. But there is only one mouth, so it is always very, very busy. And this mouth has another problem: It makes a lot of karma and suffering for us. It makes bad speech about other people, it craves tasty food, and then sometimes it has too much desire, so you end up overeating and getting sick. If you were to have two mouths, maybe it would be an even bigger problem. So maybe this is why God and Buddha only gave human beings just one mouth.

That is our nature. That is the way things are. The sun hangs in the sky. Clouds appear and pass in front of it. But why? That is what this kong-an asks. That is nature. We have two eyes, two ears, two nostrils, and only one mouth. That is nature. But do you understand this nature?

Then the next gate asks, How can you not step on your shadow? The sun is shining, so you have a shadow following you, all the time. But how can you not step on your shadow? Zen means don't check anything. As we have said before, if you attach to speech and words, you will always have a problem. If you are thinking about some possible answer to this, you are a thousand miles away from the truth.

Finally, the whole world is on fire. Through what kind of samadhi can you escape being burned? Samadhi means very deep meditation. But more importantly, it is mind that does not move, in any situation. Many people have special ideas about meditation in general and samadhi in particular. People try to attain some special samadhi so that they can get special powers. But when the whole world is a sea of fire, what kind of meditation practice will keep you alive? Here is a clue: Zen means that when you are doing something, you must just do it. When you're hungry, eat. When you're tired, sleep. When you're thirsty, drink. It is very, very clear.

Just-Like-This Is Buddha

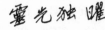

The spirit remains clear and bright. The six roots (senses) and six dusts (perceptions) fall away.

靈光獨曜　　　　迥脫根塵

The original body remains clear constantly. Speech and words cannot hinder it.

体露眞常　　　　不拘文字

True Nature has no taint, and is already a perfect sphere.

眞性無染　　　　本自圓成

Not attached to any thinking, just-like-this is Buddha.

但離妄緣　　　　即如如佛

The four elements [earth, fire, water, air] disperse as in a dream.

四大各離如夢中

The six dusts [perceptions], roots [senses], and consciousnesses are originally empty.

六塵心識本來空

If you want to understand the Buddha and the eminent teachers, return to your original light:

欲識佛祖迴光處

The sun sets over the western mountains. The moon rises in the east.

日落西山月出東

THIS IS A VERY famous poem. A long time ago in China, there was a monk named Shin Chang. When he was very young, he began study at a famous sutra temple. After three years of study, and still just a boy, Shin Chang passed all the highest examinations in the school. He was regarded as one of the most outstanding students of the temple's master, Kye Hyon. He was also the one hundredth monk to be ordained by Kye Hyon, so Shin Chang was very special. The old master was not so interested in meditation, so he taught Shin Chang only sutras and expected the young monk to one day become a great sutra master and succeed him in the long lineage. In a few years, it was said that Shin Chang even surpassed his teacher and started to become a great scholar with a promising future. Master Kye Hyon had bright hopes for Shin Chang! However, the more Shin Chang read the sutras, the more he realized he didn't understand himself. Gradually his mind grew attracted to the study of Zen.

One day, on the day the monks were graduating from sutra school, master Kye Hyon picked his three best students and offered them traveling money to pursue further studies for a period of three years. They could study whatever they wanted, anywhere in China. After the three years, they would come back and report on what they had learned. Then, Kye Hyon would give each of them transmission and they would teach in his school. The first student accepted the money and promised to study Confucianism. The second student promised to study Taoism. Finally it was Shin Chang's turn. Though renowned as by far the most brilliant student in his class, Shin Chang waited until last.

"Master," he said, "I don't like learning anymore. I don't want to learn anything."

The master was taken aback by his bright student's words. "What? But that won't get you anywhere. You are already well versed in the Sutras. I beg you to pursue more fruitful studies . . ."

But Shin Chang was very determined. "I am sorry, sir. But I don't want to study anything. I will only accept this three-year vacation that you offer."

The master, though sad, gave Shin Chang his consent and a small bag of traveling money. "Though it is not my wish, you may take a vacation. But you must learn something that you can bring back and teach to other people."

"Yes, sir," Shin Chang said. "I will not let you down."

Shin Chang soon arrived in the community of the great Zen Master Pai Chang. He did very hard training. He already understood the Sutras. Now he only kept don't-know mind, with one hundred percent determination. After three years of hard practice, day and night, Shin Chang was finally enlightened. Though tempted to stay on in Pai Chang's temple, he remembered his indebtedness to his old teacher who had ordained him and cared for him since childhood. He also remembered that his two classmates would be coming back to report to their teacher, as they had all agreed. So he packed his sack and returned to his master's temple.

The three students all returned on the appointed day. After receiving them in his private quarters, the master began to ask after their studies. He asked the first student, "Did you study Confucianism?"

"Yes, I studied Confucianism."

"What did you learn from Confucianism?"

"I learned always to keep a correct relationship to others. I learned about my obligation to my parents, my teachers, and this whole world."

"Oh, that's wonderful," the teacher said. "Congratulations on your study." Then he asked the second student, "Did you study Taoism?"

"Yes, I studied Taoism."

"What did you learn from Taoism?"

"I learned about this whole universe's substance."

"Oh, that's wonderful. Congratulations on your study."

Then the master came to Shin Chang. "What did you get these last three years?"

"Originally there is nothing, so I cannot get anything."

"What?" his teacher shouted. "Are you crazy? What did you do for the last three years while your two brothers studied so hard?"

"When I was tired, I slept. When I was hungry, I ate."

His teacher shouted at him, "You're no good! Your two brothers both studied something, so they will become teachers. But you have done nothing but waste our money. So you must become my attendant!"

"Yes, sir," Shin Chang replied. "I am sorry. I am sorry."

Every day, Shin Chang cleaned his master's quarters. He prepared food, washed his teacher's clothes, and did a lot of heavy work. He was always exhausted as night drew near, but he still found energy to do meditation long into the night. One day, the master ordered Shin Chang to prepare the bath for him, and asked him to scrub his back. While Shin Chang was scrubbing his teacher's back, he muttered to himself, "The Buddha hall is wonderful, but its Buddha is not clear . . ."

At these words, his teacher slowly turned his head to look at Shin Chang.

Seeing this, Shin Chang continued, "Buddha is not clear, but he sure emits light!" With these words the master could feel something strike deeply into his heart, and he perceived dimly that Shin Chang was no longer an ordinary man. Something in this young monk had *changed* . . .

One morning a few days later, the master was in his room, intently studying a sutra. Shin Chang quietly swept the floor in the background, careful not to make any noise lest he disturb his teacher. Suddenly a bee flew into the room. It began loudly knocking itself against the rice-paper window beside his teacher's desk, trying to get out, even though the door was wide open beside it. Looking up from his work, Shin Chang said to himself, "The world is vast and wide. Why drill into this old paper?" After a few more moments, he composed the following lines aloud:

> Ah, foolish bee! Why use all your energy
> Bouncing off rice paper like that,
> When you can easily penetrate the empty gate?
> Though you may drill rice paper for a hundred years,
> Still you will never get out of the ocean of suffering.

Bent over his moldy sutra, the old master heard these words and was struck motionless. He slowly put the rice-paper sutra back on the table next to his tub. His eyes met Shin Chang's eyes: teacher and student remained like this in wordless contemplation of each other for several long minutes. After some time, the master said, "And here I thought you'd just squandered those three years . . . Please, during the time you were gone, what kind of study did you do?"

Shin Chang lowered his head. "Teacher, forgive me. I am sorry for my bad speech. In fact, while studying with Zen Master Pai Chang, I got something. Upon returning, I only felt pity for you still being engrossed in mere words and letters, without any interest in true study of the Great Matter. I knew you would not listen to my advice, so I decided to arouse your interest and desire for enlightenment with such crude words as these. Please forgive me."

"No, it is I who have been mistaken," the master replied. "Though for years you have been only my pupil, you are now a teacher to me in the study of Buddha-Dharma. From now on you will teach me what you have learned." The master made this request while assuming a prayerful gesture. He ordered the great temple bell to be struck and had all the monks gathered in the Main Dharma Hall for a talk.

346   THE COMPASS OF ZEN

Shin Chang climbed the high rostrum. All the great monks and novices bowed to him three times, and then he gave a dharma speech. "Zen Master Pai Chang always instructed us with these words," he said.

The spirit remains clear and bright.
The six roots and six dusts fall away.
The original body remains clear constantly.
Speech and words cannot hinder it.
True nature has no taint and is already a perfect sphere.
Not attached to any thinking, just-like-this is Buddha.
The four elements disperse as in a dream.
The six dusts, roots, and consciousnesses are originally empty.
If you want to understand the Buddha and the eminent teachers,
    return to your original light:
The sun sets over the western mountains. The moon rises in the
    east.

At these words, the old master was enlightened. With tears in his eyes, he bowed to his student for the profound teaching that he had received only now, at such an old age.

This important poem is originally the teaching of the great Chinese Zen Master Pai Chang. He says, "The spirit remains clear and bright. The six roots [senses] and six dusts [perceptions] fall away." These lines clearly describe the experience of emptiness, our original nature. "No eyes, no ears, no nose, no tongue, no body, no mind." The next lines "hit" sutra learning and all academic knowledge: "The original body remains clear constantly. Speech and words cannot hinder it." Intellectual understanding is not enough—you must find your original body, your true nature, which remains clear constantly. It has no life and no death. If you attain this experience of emptiness, then you see that everything is already complete; therefore, "True nature has no taint and is already a perfect sphere." No matter what we ever do—good or bad—our original nature is always completely free of impurity and complete. There is no such thing here as original sin. Like a perfect sphere, our true nature has no beginning and no end. At this point, you see things exactly as they are. So, "Not attached to any thinking, just-like-this is Buddha."

The second half of this poem is very, very interesting. It contains the whole teaching of Hinayana Buddhism, Mahayana Buddhism, and Zen. It is like the Zen poem style which we talked about a little earlier. The first line says, "The four elements [earth, air, fire, and water] disperse as in a dream." This is Hinayana Buddhism's teaching. We are living in a suffering world, a suffering dream. If you attain emptiness, or nirvana, all your suffering disappears. The next line expresses the bone of Mahayana Buddhist teaching: "The six dusts [perceptions], roots [senses], and consciousnesses are originally empty." Everything is created by mind alone. Everything comes from your mind, which is already fundamentally empty and without self-nature. Whereas Hinayana Buddhism stops at this point of emptiness, or nirvana, emptiness is where Mahayana teaching begins. Everything is empty. Everything is without self-nature. Everything comes from your mind. The first two lines are merely an explanation of this point.

The third line is an important question. It can be rephrased as, "Where do the Buddha and all the eminent teachers return?" When you deeply ask this question, you get a don't-know mind. The experience of your mind before thinking is the place where the Buddha and the eminent teachers return! It is not somewhere other than your own mind. Then the last line expresses the complete view of truth, just as it is. "The sun sets over the western mountains. The moon rises in the east." The truth is just like this. That is all. If your mind is completely empty, it is like a clear mirror. Just reflect the sun and moon. By just reflecting, you attain moment-world, which is simply truth. Just reflect. Your eyes reflect this world just as it is. That is the Buddha's teaching. It is our true self. It is truth, correct Way, and correct life.

This whole poem explains our true nature, our primary point. [*Hits the table.*] Our true nature means Buddha-nature. Yet that is just a provisional name for something that has no name. We can change these words quite easily. When I used to lead meditation retreats for the monks at the Gethsemani Monastery in Trappist, Kentucky, I never said the name "Buddha." That is a famous Catholic monastery, so why would we just talk about Buddha? During kong-an interviews with the monks there, I always read this poem as "Just-Like-This Is God-Nature." We changed the words. The lines "True nature has no taint . . ." became "Our God-nature has no taint . . ." And the last line, which says, "Not attached to any thinking, just-like-this is Buddha," became ". . . just-like-this is God-nature." The Gethsemani monks were very happy, and we could all connect together. Because this point [*hits the table*] doesn't depend on these words, we can change them. So these words are only an explanation of something which cannot be explained with any words or speech.

CONCLUSION
Only Go Straight, Don't Know

THERE ARE MANY, MANY teaching words in this book. There are Hinayana words, Mahayana words, and Zen words. There are Buddhist and Christian words. We use American, Polish, Korean, Chinese, and Japanese words—too many words! But all of these words are not necessary. Words and speech are only thinking, and thinking makes suffering. You must throw them all in the garbage! The reason for this is that our true nature is not dependent on understanding. This is why I only teach "don't know." This teaching has no East or West, Korean or Japanese or American. "Don't know" is not Buddhist or Christian or Zen or anything.

Several years ago, after I had been teaching in the West for some time, some of my American students were having a meeting to discuss the use of certain practice forms in the Kwan Um School of Zen. During the meeting, one of the students asked, if everything is One, why I had to teach Asian-style Buddhism, why I taught Mahayana style and Zen. "Doesn't this make 'same' and 'different'?" she asked. This is a very interesting question.

I answered, "Yah, I don't teach Korean or Mahayana or Zen. I don't even teach Buddhism. I only teach don't know. Fifty years here and there teaching only don't know. So only don't know, OK?" Only don't know, always and everywhere. Our don't-know mind can do anything.

So we have talked a lot about Hinayana Buddhism, Mahayana Buddhism, and Zen. We have seen how they all have different meditation techniques and styles. But while the speech and words may be different, all along, the bone of their teaching is the same: How do we wake up and help this world, right *now*? No matter what the tradition, the point of any meditation practice is to help you realize your own original nature so that you can help all sentient beings get out of suffering. Meditation is not about making something special. It is not about having some peaceful experience of stillness and bliss. Yah, it is possible to experience this sometimes during meditation. But what are *you*? When you were born, where did you *come* from? When you die, where will you *go*? Can you tell me?

Most human beings cannot answer these basic questions. Instead they spend all their energy chasing desire, anger, and ignorance. Day in and day out they crave impermanent things; they become attached to things, to fame and feelings, and suffer when these things change or disappear. They make suffering, and then keep this suffering like a precious treasure. Human beings should be the very highest of animals. But instead, they spend their whole lives wandering around and around and around the ocean of suffering. That is not the correct way for human beings.

So if you do not control your karma, you cannot do anything in this life. Then when you die—when your body disappears—what can you do? The force of your karma will pull you somewhere. Where you go, you don't understand. Maybe you will be reborn in a suffering place, or have many problems with your body. Only if you completely cut off all thinking can you return to your original nature, which is beyond life and death. That point's name is "don't know." It is very important to attain that and then help this world: then life and death cannot touch you. This is why meditation is so important.

A long time ago, there was a Zen master who lived on a small mountain. Every day, the Zen master only stayed in his hermitage, always practicing meditation. As is customary, the monk's lay students brought him food, medicine, and clothing. Sometimes the Zen master was invited down to the village at the bottom of his mountain to give a Dharma speech. He didn't like to leave his mountain, but these laypeople wanted some teaching, so he would go. At the end of the Dharma talk, they would prepare a big meal for him. They set out rice and soup and vegetables. Although poor, these simple farmers would also prepare wonderful rice "medicine" wine for their teacher. Now, this Zen master never drank alcohol—he only kept a clear mind. But the villagers did a lot of work to prepare this special wine, because they said it would help his body. So when they asked him to, he drank it. It was very, very strong! He was not sick; he didn't want any medicine drink. Nevertheless, the Zen master had cup after cup of the wine for as long as they asked him to stay, and so the villagers were very, very happy.

Then one day, the Zen master was returning to his hermitage after a visit to the village. Night was setting in as he walked up the steep mountain trail. He had to walk past an old cemetery. The moon was full that night, and he could see the old burial mounds clearly in the blue light, their rounded tops rising like waves in a little mountain sea. As usual, the Zen master stopped at the front wrought-iron gate and did a short bow to the ancestors, and turned to continue on his way. This rice wine was very, very strong, so his head had a special feeling!

Suddenly, there was a loud sound and the earth shook. *Ba-boom!* The Zen master looked up, and towering above him, high above the trees, was a great fearsome ghost! He was of a massive size, arrayed in what seemed to be military clothing, with a great breastplate and a massive broadsword. "Hey, you!" the terrible ghost thundered down on him. "Old monk! I don't like *you.*" The ghost was very, very angry!

But this old monk's center did not move. He only looked up at the big ghost.

"You don't like *me?*" He couldn't help the little smile spreading on his lips as he tottered back and forth.

"Yes, I don't like you!"

"Oh, that's too bad. I never made any problem for you. Why don't you like me?"

"You are a number-one bad monk! Every week you go down to the village, and you have alcohol to drink. Then when you come past here you leave a very bad smell! The Buddha said no drinking for monks, but every week you drink rice wine. I don't like bad monks, so I don't like *you!*"

"And who, may I ask, are you?"

"I was the highest general in the land. I served the king himself. I killed many people in war, so when I died, I got this ghost body. Now I will kill you, because you are a bad monk!"

"OK, OK," the Zen master said. He was completely unafraid. "You killing me is no problem. But you are such a great general. Why only kill me? That is too easy! I have a much better idea."

"Better idea? How dare you . . . !"

The Zen master continued, "We'll make a bet. I will hide three times. If you can find me by the third time, I will be your slave. If you cannot find me, then you must become my student."

The ghost general grew livid at this. This monk believed in himself too much! "Maybe this old monk is just crazy," he thought. But he saw that the Zen master was completely unafraid. The Zen master's mind was not moving. There was something interesting about this old monk.

"OK," the general thundered. "You can try to hide! I will find you anywhere—in heaven or in hell, you cannot hide from me!"

"Wonderful!" the Zen master said. "You are surely a great man. Now, you must close your eyes and take three deep breaths, and then you can open your eyes and try to find me."

Now this old monk was a Zen monk. He had practiced for many, many years, so he had many kinds of special energy. He could change his body into any kind of animal at will, disappear, or travel around the whole world in the blink of an eye. So when the ghost general closed his eyes, the Zen master suddenly disappeared and went to the meditation room of an old Zen temple in the southern mountains. Landing on the floor and quickly crossing both legs in full lotus, he put all of his energy strongly into his *hara*. Then he called up the *Mu* kong-an. With great determination, focusing one hundred percent of his energy on *mu*, the old monk fell into the *mu* samadhi—only "*Muuuuuuu . . .*" Everything completely became "*Muuuuuuu.*"

Suddenly a deafening sound shattered the old monk's samadhi.

"Ahaaa!" a great voice boomed. "I found you!" Looking up, the monk saw the ghost general leaning into the meditation room, whose tile roof he had torn off like a little toy. "You cannot hide from me, you bad old monk! Ha ha ha ha ha!"

"Oh, you found me," the monk said. "You are surely a great general. But I was just testing you. Close your eyes again, and I will try harder."

When the ghost closed his eyes, the Zen master immediately disappeared again. This time when he reappeared, he had transformed himself into a wild tiger. But this was not all. He sat deep in a cave at the top of a high, snowy mountain in the farthest reaches of China, somewhere near the border with Tibet. He was high above the cloudline, where even grass could not grow: surely no one would think to find any living thing there!

But within one minute, there was loud thunder from the back of the cave. "Ha ha ha ha ha! You stupid rice-worm of a monk! I found you again!" The ghost general reared his head out of the shadows, and in an instant the tiger became an old Zen master again.

"Oh, you are a very high-class ghost," the Zen master said. "You can almost find me anywhere!"

"Yes, there is no place for you to hide in this whole universe. Soon you will be my slave!"

"That is *your* idea," the Zen master said. "Now close your eyes, and we will try again." The ghost put his hand over his eyes, and started to breathe in and out slowly. Instead of making his body disappear again, the Zen master stepped behind a nearby tree, and simply cut off all thinking. He returned to complete don't-know mind. This mind has no thinking, because it is the mind before thinking arises. It is empty mind, our clear original nature.

The ghost general stopped counting and removed the hand from his eyes. He did not know where the Zen master was. He looked everywhere, but could not find him. From the highest heaven to the deepest hell state, the ghost searched every place in the universe. Looking over clouds and under mountains, he searched everywhere. But he could not find the Zen master anywhere! And not only that: this general was dead, so he was no longer bound by time and space. He could check the three periods of past, present, and future. He searched the three realms of form, the formless, and desire. But this old monk could not be seen anywhere! This was very stange, because the ghost could see anything, anyplace. Yet when the old Zen master completely kept a don't-know mind, the ghost could not find him anywhere.

"Oh, Zen master, I cannot find you!" the ghost said. "Surely you are a great man. Please come out so that I may bow to you and become your student."

The Zen master stepped out from behind the tree. "Here I am." The ghost did three full prostrations to the old monk. "Before you were a number-one bad ghost; now you are my student. From now on, don't scare anyone. Only help other people, OK?"

"OK, OK! I said many bad things about you. I am very sorry. From now on I will only follow you!" From that day on, the ghost was the Zen master's attendant.

So this story shows us something about don't-know mind. If you keep a don't-know mind one hundred percent, then your demons cannot find you. Suffering cannot find you. Karma, problems, life, death, coming and going, good and bad—nothing can touch you when you only keep a don't-know mind. This don't-know mind is your most important treasure; it can do anything. It is not dependent on God or Buddha, Hinayana, Mahayana or Zen. It is not dependent on life or death.

If you want to get out of the ocean of suffering, only one kind of compass is necessary: your don't-know compass. It is always inside you. When you use this, then you find that your correct direction always appears clearly in front of you, from moment to moment.

So I hope from moment to moment you only go straight, don't know, which is clear like space, try, try, try for ten thousand years, nonstop, get enlightenment, and save all beings from suffering.

APPENDIX
The Ten Gates: "Mind Meal"

THERE ARE SEVERAL major kong-an collections available to Zen students. The Rinzai school picked out one hundred kong-ans, or "cases," for use by Zen monks. That is called *The Blue Cliff Record.* The Soto school also uses one hundred cases. This collection is called the *Shoyo Roku.* The Rinzai school's collection is a very complicated selection of kong-ans, whereas the Soto school has a very simple collection. Zen Master Un Mun chose forty-eight essential kong-ans and called that the *Mumon Kan,* sometimes translated as the "Gateless Gate" or "No-Gate Checkpoint." Any Zen school uses that collection. Finally, the Chogye school of Korean Buddhism has developed a collection of seventeen hundred important kong-ans. All these kong-an collections, when taken together, can present a somewhat daunting arrangement of kong-ans that every Zen student must master. So in the Kwan Um School of Zen, we have distilled the wisdom of the most essential kong-ans into the Ten Gates.

The Ten Gates is a succinct collection of ten kong-ans that represent the major teaching points or "styles" touched on by all the major kong-an collections. Passing each one of the ten gates is equivalent to passing a corresponding level of kong-an practice covered by each of the major collections. Of course, students of this lineage work on more than just the kong-ans of the Ten Gates. However, if you pass the ten gates, you understand the nature of all kong-an practice. If you understand what is a kong-an you understand what is correct practicing. But intellectual understanding is not enough. You cannot perceive a kong-an's inner wisdom through merely conceptual thought. You must *attain* the kong-ans. This is what we mean by "understand."

There are some people who can pass many kong-ans without attaining them. We call this ability dry cognition. Also there are some people who, though they may pass certain kong-ans, still don't try hard in their practice.

If you don't try, if you constantly check yourself, and if you don't digest this kong-an's meaning, the kong-an does not become yours. It is only dry cognition. So this kong-an should give your practice a direction. That direction is called "don't know." Answering the kong-an is not enough: you must completely do it, and then you attain this kong-an's wisdom.

Let us say that someone tells you, "If you go south ten miles, you will come to a big mountain with a peak shaped like an eagle's head. Go up the south side and find the valley with the stream in it. One mile up the valley, there is a cave. Inside this cave, there is a pot of gold. You must go over there, and then you can get this gold." You may *understand* these directions. You may *understand* where the gold is. You may *understand* how high the gold is located and where. But no matter how much you understand this point, if you do not walk over there yourself, you cannot get the gold. Nearly everyone says, "Yah, I understand this gold. Ten miles south there is a mountain with a peak shaped like an eagle's head. I understand that. If you go up the south side, you can find a valley with a stream in it. I understand that. I also understand that one mile up the valley there is a cave, and inside the cave there is a pot of gold. I understand all this very, very well." If you understand it, but do not go and get the gold, you cannot *attain* this gold. You only understand the gold's location. Understanding money and actually having some in your pocket are completely different, right? The same is true of kong-ans: Only understanding kong-ans cannot help you. Many people have good answers during interviews, but their daily life is not such a good answer. Their backseat driver always controls them. When you truly attain the kong-an, however, the kong-an becomes *yours*.

Understanding kong-ans is not so good. Whether your kong-an answers are correct or not does not matter. The most important practice is your everyday life. If your everyday life is clear and is correct from moment to moment, then all kong-ans are not a big problem. That is the point. In some zendos kong-an practice is made into an overly special experience. It is very hard to connect this kind of practice with actual everyday-life situations. The students are taught to only follow this *Mu* kong-an very strongly, in a very strange manner. Every day, every action, they just make *"Muuuuuuuuuu!"* But how does *mu* connect your before-thinking mind with everyday life in a complicated world? This teaching point is seldom made clear.

In the Kwan Um School of Zen, traditional kong-an practice in both East and West has been undergoing a revolution. The point of kong-an practice is to show you how to connect your don't-know mind with everyday life.

How does your meditation on the cushion find its correct function, from moment to moment, to help other people? Nowadays this world is moving very quickly, and there are always new situations in which you must function clearly and meticulously to help others. If you only hold on to *mu*, attach to old poetic commentaries, and make some special experience out of Zen practice, you will lose your way. When you step out onto the street keeping "*Muuuuuu*," maybe you will be hit by a car because you are only holding One Mind. However, our style of kong-ans means using kong-ans as practice to instantly perceive your correct situation, your correct relationship to that situation, and your correct function in that situation. All three points— *boom!*—instantly and intuitively become one. Then you can save all beings. This is our correct direction: using meditation spontaneously from moment to moment only to help other people.

Another important aspect to the kong-ans in this tradition is that they all have questions. The questions provide the kong-an with its basic direction. They point to the wisdom of your original mind, and how it functions, right *now*. Most other teachers who use kong-ans do not provide this question; the student cannot find their direction with the kong-an. So the kong-an does not connect to everyday life. This does not help the student become independent.

Another name for the Ten Gates is "Mind Meal." This means that if you study these kong-ans, your mind has enough food. When your mind has enough, then not so much desire and thinking appear, and your mind remains clear. Only in this way can it function clearly from moment to moment and from situation to situation to help all beings.

The First Gate: Joju's Dog

A monk once asked Zen Master Joju, "Does a dog have Buddha-nature?"

Joju answered, "*Mu!*"

1. The Buddha said that everything has Buddha-nature. Joju said that a dog has no Buddha-nature. Which one is correct?
2. Joju said, "*Mu!*" What does this mean?
3. So I ask you, Does a dog have Buddha-nature?

This is a very interesting kong-an. The Buddha taught that everything has Buddha-nature. The sun, the moon, the stars, the mountains, and you all have the same substance. So Buddha-nature is not special. Your nature, my nature, and a dog's nature are all the same. The name for Buddha-nature is substance. The Buddha taught that everything has this universal substance, even if everything's names and forms are different.

But a monk once asked Joju, "Does a dog have Buddha-nature?" Joju replied, "*Mu.*" Everybody knows that *mu* is the Chinese character for "no" or "nothing." Buddha-nature is originally empty and is complete nothingness. So does a dog have Buddha-nature? "Nothing." Does Buddha have Buddha-nature? "Nothing." "Nothing" is the correct answer, but this is still just metaphysical-style speech. It is only an explanation of some point and is a kind of abstraction to many. However, if you want to express the true point, it is important to make some concrete expression. For example: Here is a watch. Now I ask you, Does a watch have Buddha-nature? If you just answer, "Big," or "Heavy," or "Gold-colored," that is not enough. Perhaps those answers are in some way true—they may express some partial truth about the watch—but they are still not correct answers. While true in some way, they are not the *complete* answer. If you answer, "The sky is blue, the trees are green," you are also making a valid truth-statement, but that is also not enough. Those answers are what we call metaphysical-style answers. Then what is a concrete demonstration of this watch's Buddha-nature? [*Picks up the watch and reads.*] Now it's seven-thirty PM. What is your correct situation with regard to the watch? Then what is your correct relationship to it? And what is the correct function of this watch? That is your everyday life. Every kong-an points to that. It is very clear, and not so special as people make it out to be.

Zen teaches us how to make a correct life in this very moment. So a monk asked Joju, "Does a dog have Buddha-nature?" Joju said, "*Mu.*" That answer is a big mistake. But sometimes Zen masters use "mistake speech" to teach their students, because Zen teaches the importance of cutting off all attachment to thinking. It means cutting off dependence on speech and words. It means showing how speech and words and ideas and thinking and understanding are only provisional and have no self-nature. So a Zen master uses language freely, because he is not attached to whether it is "correct" or "not correct." Here is an example: During the Japanese occupation of Korea, the colonial rulers maintained the highest positions in Korean society. They had the most beautiful houses and beautiful clothes. When they ate fruit, they peeled away the skin and threw it away and ate only the fruit itself. This was considered high class. It was not considered good to eat fruit with the peel still on. At the end of the Second World War, Japan surrendered, and the Japanese army had to leave Korea and return to Japan. For the Japanese people who remained in Korea, life suddenly became extremely difficult. They were removed from their high positions. Most lost all their jobs and wealth. The Japanese people lost their wonderful possessions, their wonderful clothes and houses. The Russian army was particularly severe on the Japanese. Many Japanese people had no food to eat and had to pick through garbage to survive.

After the war, the Russian and American army people would peel fruit and throw away the skins. But the Japanese would find these peels and say, "Oh, wonderful! Food!" They would pick up the peels, clean off the dust, and eat them. Why did this happen? The Japanese people's situation changed, so their thinking also changed. Thinking has no fixed place. So in the new situation, all their ideas about good and bad—ideas that seemed so fixed and permanent before—were completely exchanged for one another. Now they only saw those peels, that before were considered garbage, and they thought, "Food! How wonderful!" They only believed this hungry mind and not their previous conventions about what was proper or improper. In that new situation, correct and incorrect didn't matter anymore.

The same is true of the *Mu* kong-an. The monk who asked Joju whether a dog has Buddha-nature had lots of thinking about different Buddhist ideas. He thought about the Buddha's teachings about Buddha-nature. He thought about dogs having the same substance as him, a human being. He thought that if dogs have Buddha-nature, then they too can get enlightenment. "Maybe the Buddha is wrong? Maybe Zen Master Joju has some different teaching from the Buddha. Perhaps then a dog can get enlightenment without having to do so much meditation practice." The monk had lots and lots of thinking going around in his head. So how do you cut this monk's thinking? Joju answered *"Mu"* because in that situation this "wrong" speech could completely cut off the monk's thinking. Just this little "No" would jam up his whole conceptual mind! This is why the *"Mu"* kong-an is so important: It is an excellent case of some Zen master using speech and words—whether correct or incorrect—to cut through a student's thinking mind and give him a Big Question. "Hmm. Why did Joju say 'Mu'? Everything has Buddha-nature. But a dog has no Buddha-nature . . . That's strange . . ." A big question appears.

But since Joju opened his mouth, some Zen traditions have become overly attached to Joju's medicine. It must be said that just using *mu* to attain some samadhi state of mind is not the correct use of this kong-an. Many people use *mu* in the zendo because they have been taught that you must hold this *mu* very strongly and attain a kind of *samadhi* with it. The teacher says, "You must keep *mu* in your *hara*, always and everywhere, OK?"

The student shouts, *"Muuuuuuuuuu!"*

"Stronger!"

"MUUUUUUUU!"

"Good!" This is only *mu* samadhi; it is not correct Zen practicing at all. This kind of practice is not even true *samadhi*. Zen means from moment to moment keeping a clear mind. This cannot be emphasized enough. Keep a mind that is clear like a mirror: when red comes, the mirror becomes red; when white comes, white. You reflect the universe exactly as it is. But *mu* samadhi means that everything in your mind just becomes *mu*. When red comes before your mirror, there is only *mu*; when white comes, only *mu*. Then if a hungry person comes, *mu*. If a thirsty person comes, *mu*. This is an attachment to some special kind of *samadhi* practicing. It cannot function clearly to help other people. It is a very, very bad Zen sickness. Actually, true

Zen practice is not very concerned with samadhi at all. Yah, maybe you experience samadhi, but you don't become attached to it. Zen means always keeping a clear mind, from moment to moment.

Many people like to combine meditation with some psychotherapeutic practices, like the use of samadhi practice. This is because *samadhi* meditation makes a good feeling for those who try it. For some period their problems and suffering all seem to have gone away. "Oh, samadhi! Wonderful!" But this is like opium: you only want more and more and more. And when you practice in this way, everyday mind doesn't feel so interesting anymore—all you want is to continue your wonderful samadhi experience. You are making a special experience that is separate from everyday-life-mind. If you do samadhi, or *mu* samadhi practice, then you are making Zen somehow "special." You are heading east when you want to go west. Then when do you get enlightenment? But Zen is not so special. From moment to moment, what are you *doing* now? This is true Zen mind.

So with this kong-an, we test how clearly a student perceives substance, truth, and their correct function. The first question in this kong-an reveals original substance. For example, here is some gold. You can make many different things out of this gold: earrings, necklaces, watches, and glasses. The *forms* are all different. And if the forms are all different, then the *function* of each thing is also different. But all along the *substance* is the same: everything is still gold. Sky and clouds, mountains, rivers, human beings, airplanes, buddhas, demons, and hells all have different names. All their forms are different, so their functions are also all different. But the substance of all these things is exactly the same. The correct use of this kong-an is to demonstrate that point. How do you express everything's substance? The next step is, how do you express truth? And lastly, what is the proper function of universal substance and truth in each individual thing?

The Buddha taught that everything has Buddha-nature. So Buddhas and dogs are the same. Their *substance* is the same universal substance, but their form and function are quite different. The Buddha is gold and sits on the altar; the dog is white and lives in a little doghouse. This is their form, their *truth*. Also, though their substance is exactly the same, their *function* is altogether different. The Buddha sits on the altar, and people bow to it. The dog stays outside: when good people come, he wags his tail; when bad people or strangers come, he barks, "Woof! Woof! Woof!" If you just do *mu* samadhi practice, you cannot perceive this different function so clearly, so you, too, cannot perceive your correct function and the correct function of everything in this universe. You cannot help other people in different situations according to their particular need. You only see *mu*.

In this kong-an, we test a student's attainment of substance, truth, and function. The first question is: "The Buddha said that everything has Buddha-nature. But Joju said a dog has no Buddha-nature. Which one is correct?" Buddha-nature? No Buddha-nature? Buddha-nature? No Buddha-nature? Buddha-nature? No Buddha-nature? That is only thinking. Whether there is or is no Buddha-nature doesn't matter: Joju already demonstrated that point when he answered *"Mu!"* Rather, what *is* Buddha-nature, right now? Let go of your thinking, and don't attach to words and speech. You must simply attain your nature, which means attaining your substance. That is the point of this first question: what is your *substance*? If you attain your nature then everything is no problem. That is the meaning behind this first question.

The second question is: "Joju said '*Mu!*' What does this mean?" If you completely cut off all thinking in your mind, then the meaning of this question is very clear. Everything is reflected, just as it is. Red comes, and the mirror becomes red; white comes, it becomes white. This is truth. Remember: *mu* has no special meaning. Some people make *mu* special, but originally it is not special. So somebody once asked Zen Master Man Gong, "What is the meaning of Joju's '*Mu*?' " Man Gong replied, "Go into the garden behind the meditation hall. There you will find many radishes [in Korean, *mu*]." How do you reflect *truth*? That is very important.

The third question is: "I ask you, does a dog have Buddha-nature?" This question is very, very clear. If you correctly perceive this question, then you also see Joju's big mistake. This last question tests your perception of correct *function*. If you want to answer all these questions, the most important thing you should do is not hold Joju's "mistake." You must learn the correct *function* of Joju's "mistake," and then you can learn how to use it to help other people. Substance, truth, and their correct function: that is the *mu* kong-an.

The Second Gate: Joju's "Wash Your Bowls"

A monk once asked Zen Master Joju, "I have just entered the mon-
astery. Please teach me, Master."
Joju said, "Have you had breakfast?"
"Yes, I have," replied the monk.
"Then," Joju said, "go wash your bowls."
The monk was enlightened.

1. What did the monk attain?
2. If you were the monk, and Joju said, "Go wash your bowls," what
   could you say?

This kong-an teaches us that everyday mind is truth. Everyday mind is very
important, but it is not special. Everyday mind is the correct way, and truth,
and the correct life. So someone asked Zen Master Joju, "Please teach me,
Master." "Have you had breakfast?" "Yes, I have." "Then go wash your
bowls." The monk heard that and—*piittchuuu*—he got enlightenment. This
means he attained that everyday mind is the true way.

But if we check this kong-an a little more closely, we see something interesting happening. Zen Master Joju sometimes hit his students in a very interesting way. "Did you have breakfast?" "Yes, I have." If we stop at this point,
we can see that breakfast is already finished, perhaps long finished. Joju said,
"Then go wash your bowls." But this is not correct! Breakfast is already
finished. Why does Joju answer this way? But that is Joju's style: he uses
speech—whether correct or not—to hit his students' minds. His answer already changes the student's mind. Whether the speech is mistaken or not
doesn't matter: How do you wake up the student's mind?

So Joju is always testing his students. He does not expect the answer to be
accepted as some final truth. If you were there at that time, how would you

reply to Joju? Washing your bowls after breakfast is indeed correct mind, but in this case breakfast is long ago finished, and the bowls are already clean. Would you go and wash your bowls again? If your mind is clear, you must respond to him. So for beginning students, a very simple kind of answer is possible. But as you advance in your practice, you are asked to hit Joju back. You must keep a clear mind, and then you can perceive the way to talk to Joju.

Zen means from moment to moment intuitively perceiving how to keep a correct situation, correct relationship, and correct function. Any kind of speech coming from the Zen master doesn't matter. You must digest the Zen master's speech and from moment to moment make it correct. Make it *yours*. That is wisdom. But it is very important that you not let yourself become attached to any Zen master's speech.

The Third Gate: Soeng Am Calls "Master!"

Master Soeng Am used to call to himself every day, "Master!"
And he would answer, "Yes!"
"You must keep clear!"
"Yes!"
"Never be deceived by others, any time, any place!"
"Yes! Yes!"

1. Soeng Am used to call to himself and answer himself—two minds.
Which one is the correct master?

You often see little children talking to themselves while they play. They have very simple minds. They hold a little doll and say [*assumes a singsong voice*], "Oh, you like me? I like you." They make a little singsong. "Oh, ho, ho, ho, la la la la la la!" Yah, this toy doesn't seem to answer or say anything, but the child keeps talking to it as if they are talking together. "Oh, you like me? I like you! La-lee, la-la-la!!" Does this child have one mind or two minds? Zen Master Soeng Am is the same as these little children. He has a very simple and pure mind. In Sino-Korean we call that *yu ju sam mae*, or "play samadhi." I make two, and play.

But this kong-an asks about the correct master. Can you find it? One master calls and another master answers: which one is the correct master? Remember: Soeng Am made the call-master and he made the answer-master. Where is the true master? You must find your true master. Here is a hint: If you keep a mind that is clear like space, then everything is your master. The sky is your master. The trees are your master. The barking dog is your master. Everything is your master, because your master is always right in front of you. That is a very important point.

However, this is just a metaphysical-style answer. "Your true master is always in front of you." That is only a kind of explanation. You must digest your experience and make it yours. Then your master appears very clearly in front of you. How do you find your concrete master? Attain that, and then you can answer this kong-an.

The Fourth Gate: Bodhidharma Has No Beard

Master Hok Am used to ask his students, "Why does Bodhidharma have no beard?"

1. What is Bodhidharma's original face?
2. I ask you, Why does Bodhidharma have no beard?

Somebody takes a nap in the middle of the day. He dreams that somebody cuts his neck, and he wakes up in a cold sweat. "Where is my head? Where is my head?" He cannot find his head anywhere! He cannot see his head, so he runs around and around and around looking for his head. He looks in the closet and under the table. "Where is my head? Somebody took my head!" He opens the door and shouts, "Where is my head? Please! Somebody help me find my head!" Slamming the door, he looks in a cabinet. He opens the window and shouts, "Somebody please help me find my head!"

Then suddenly his friend appears and says, "Hey, hey! Calm down. What are you looking for?"

"Where is my head? Somebody took a knife and cut off my head! Oh, goodness—now my head is gone! Where is my head?" Then the friend hits him hard. "Ouch!"

"That is your head!" [*Laughter from the audience.*]

This is an attack kong-an. This means that if somebody hits me, I must attack and defend. Zen teaches, don't make anything in your mind. But Master Hok Am makes something with this question, "Why does Bodhidharma have no beard?" If you want to attain this question, you must first completely attain the true Bodhidharma. What is the true Bodhidharma? The true Bodhidharma has no eyes, no ears, no nose, no tongue, no body, and no mind, so he also has no beard. That is correct. You must attain this point, and then you attain the first question. If you don't attach to name and form, anything is possible. That is the first course.

But the next course means that if form appears, you must perceive the correct function of form. Some people remain in this samadhi-like stage and claim, "I don't know form. I don't bother with names." If you keep this mind, you have fallen down into emptiness. You are attached to voidness, and even Buddha cannot help you. So don't attach to name and form, and don't try to take away name and form. If name and form come, how do you use them correctly? What is their correct function? If you find the correct function of name and form, then maybe there is a beard. Which one do you like?

So some Zen masters will ask, "Why does Bodhidharma have no beard?" Then if their students give a strong, "*Muuuu!*" they are very happy. This way of teaching does not point out the correct function of name and form. Some students will say, "My beard is very wonderful." That kind of answer is better, but it is still not the complete answer. This is clearly an attack kong-an, so if you don't strike back, you haven't perceived the true point of Master Hok Am's question.

Perhaps this kong-an will help: In Korea there is a very famous mountain range called the Diamond Mountains. On the top of these mountains is the Maha Yon Zen Center, where up to one thousand monks would practice meditation at any one time. At the bottom of the mountain was a famous sutra temple called Yu Jom Sah. Located halfway up the mountain was the famous Diamond Mountain Hot Springs. The owner was a devout Buddhist laywoman who let monks use the hot springs free of charge.

One day, a sutra master from Yu Jom Sah named Sol Hae came to use the hot springs. He was the most famous sutra master in Korea. After he finished bathing, the woman said, "Oh, Master, how do you feel?"

"Oh, very wonderful! Your hot springs are the best in the whole country."

Then the owner said, "Master, I have a question for you. You cleaned your body in the hot tub; how do you clean your mind?" The sutra master was stuck and could not answer.

That is a very important question, an attack question: "How do you clean your mind?" If you have mind, you must clean it all the time. But if you have no mind then cleaning is not necessary. That is the point of this kong-an. If you say you have mind, I will hit you thirty times. If you just say you have no mind, I will also hit you thirty times. What can you do? That is also the point of Master Hok Am's question.

The Fifth Gate: Hyang Eom's "Up a Tree"

Master Hyang Eom said, "It is like a man hanging by his teeth from a branch high up in a tree. His hands and feet are tied, so his hands cannot touch the branch, and his feet cannot touch the tree. Another man standing under the tree asks him, 'Why did Bodhidharma come to China?'

"If he opens his mouth to answer, he will lose his life. If he does not answer, he evades his duty and will be killed."

1. If you are in the tree, how do you stay alive?

This is known as a *kyon jol mun* kong-an, a "no-way-out kong-an." If you open your mouth, you die. If you remain silent, you die. Someone once asked Zen Master Joju, "Why did Bodhidharma come to China?" This is another way of asking, "What is truth? What is Buddhism's teaching?" So Joju replied, "The cypress tree in the front garden." But if you are in the tree, you cannot do anything, or else you will die. Then how do you stay alive?

If you completely cut off all thinking, you attain don't-know mind. This point is before thinking. There is no life and no death. Don't-know mind is freedom from life and death. If you think "life," you have life. When you think "death," you have death. But when you don't think anything, you are already beyond that point. So in this kong-an, if you want to stay alive you will die. At that time, hanging in the tree, what is your correct situation? What is your correct relationship to that situation, and then what is your correct function? Put it all down, and then they appear very clearly right in front of you.

The Sixth Gate: Dropping Ashes on the Buddha

Somebody comes to the Zen center smoking a cigarette. He blows smoke and drops ashes on the Buddha.

1. If you are standing there at that time, what can you do?

This is a very important teaching kong-an. The Buddha taught that everything has Buddha-nature. In Korea and China, we hang long vertical boards with Chinese characters carved and painted on them on the columns of temple buildings. One well-known phrase that many temples have says, "Buddha's body is the whole universe." This is a very wonderful teaching. Buddha's body is everywhere—what is *not* the Buddha's body? So a man comes into the temple, smoking a cigarette. He walks up to the Buddha statue and blows smoke in its face, and drops ashes on the Buddha's head. The abbot comes running in. "You are crazy! Why are you dropping ashes on the Buddha?" But the man points to the board with Chinese characters on it and says, "It's written right here. 'Buddha's body is the whole universe.' Everything is Buddha. Where could I possibly throw away my ashes? Also these ashes have Buddha-nature. Everything has Buddha-nature. How could I ever throw them away and have them not land on the Buddha?" This man is attached to one side. He understands one, but he doesn't understand two. And he believes, "I already got enlightenment. I understand everything." He is only attached to his view.

There is another kong-an that teaches this point: A devout Buddhist laywoman supports a monk's meditation practice for ten years. She has a hermitage built for him and continually sends him food and clothing and medicine. There is an old saying in Asia that if you practice hard for ten years, surely you will get something. If you cannot get anything, it is because you have not been practicing correctly. So after ten years, she wants some word about the progress of his efforts. She has one daughter who is very young and very, very beautiful. She has her daughter dress in wonderful clothing and then loads her up with all kinds of delicious food and fresh new monk's clothes.

She says to her daughter, "Give these gifts to the monk. Then embrace him strongly and ask him how he feels." The daughter is very excited and heads up the mountain to find the monk.

When she arrives, she places all the fine food and clothing in front of the monk, who is meditating with fierce determination. "You are a great monk. You have been practicing very hard for ten years, so my mother wanted you to have this."

"Oh, your mother is a great bodhisattva," the monk says. "Thank you very much."

Just at that moment, the young girl grabs the monk, embraces him strongly, and says, "Now how do you feel?"

The monk is completely expressionless. He says, "Rotten log on cold rocks. No heat in winter." He has no feeling or warmth at all.

The daughter is struck with admiration. "Oh, you are a great monk! Your center is completely not moving, very strong." She bows to him and heads back down to her mother, very happy.

When she gets back, her mother asks, "Well, what did he say?"

"Oh, Mother. He is surely a great and holy monk. His center is very strong. It is not moving. His face didn't change, his color didn't change. Nothing moves him!"

"I don't care how strong his center is," her mother says. "All I want to know is, what did he say?"

"He said, 'Rotten log on cold rocks. No heat in winter.'"

At these words, the woman flies into a rage. She grabs a stick and runs straight up the mountain and beats the monk. "I have only been helping a demon for ten years! Get out, you devil!" She kicks him out and burns the hermitage to the ground.

What happened here? Where is the monk's mistake? This monk is the same as the cigarette man in the Dropping Ashes kong-an: he is only attached to his idea. He is attached to his practicing experience. He only wants a quiet and peaceful not-moving mind. In America there are many, many people who teach this kind of practice. People do meditation to get a quiet, peaceful, not-moving mind so that they can have some good feeling. But where is wisdom in such teaching? How does your wisdom grow up if you just keep a peaceful mind? If you practice in this way your wisdom will not grow up very well, and you will not be able to perceive the correct situation, correct relationship, and correct function of your life, from moment to moment. This monk's correct situation is that he is a monk, so his correct situation is monk's situation. His correct relationship is as a monk with this woman's daughter. So what is his correct function? If you are a monk, your correct function is to give clear and compassionate teaching to this young girl. That is very clear.

So somebody comes to the Zen Center, blows smoke in the Buddha statue's face, and drops ashes on its head. He does not understand truth. He does not understand the real nature of his present situation, or his correct relationship to that situation, and therefore he doesn't understand his correct function in that place, at that time. How do you teach him? How do you fix his mind? Be careful! This man is very strong, and no matter what you say he will hit you. And if you just hit him, he will hit you back even harder.

The Seventh Gate: Ko Bong's Three Gates

1. The sun in the sky shines everywhere. Why does a cloud obscure it?
2. Everyone has a shadow following them. How do you not step on your shadow?
3. The whole universe is on fire. Through what kind of samadhi can you escape being burned?

This is a complete-action kong-an. Don't check anything and just do it. In one moment, on one point, what is your correct situation, your correct relationship to that situation, and your correct function? If you have do-it mind, this kong-an is no problem.

There is another kong-an that points at this: Someone asked Zen Master Dong Sahn, "When cold or hot comes, how can we avoid them?"

Dong Sahn replied, "Why don't you go to the place where there is no cold or hot?"

The monk asked, "What is the place where there is no cold or hot?"

Dong Sahn said, "When cold, cold kills you. When hot, hot kills you." What does that mean? If you check these words, you will have a big problem. This is the same as Ko Bong's Three Gates.

"The sun is shining everywhere. Why does a cloud obscure it?" At that time, what is your correct situation? And then what is your correct relationship to that situation? How do you connect your situation with the sun and cloud? What is your relationship to that situation, and then what is your function? All these come together in this kong-an.

"Everybody has a shadow following them. How can you not step on your shadow?" What is your correct situation, correct relationship, and correct function with regard to your shadow? If you check it, you lose it.

"The whole universe is on fire. Through what kind of samadhi can you escape being burned?" When fire engulfs the whole universe, how do you make it correct? What is your correct situation, your correct relationship, and your correct function? When you want something fear rises up, and if you are afraid of something, you freeze and cannot do anything. Whenever you have "I, my, me," there is fear and confusion. But when this "I, my, me" disappears, when they are revealed as empty, then there is no longer any situation or condition. I have no self, so inside and outside become one. That is the point of this only-do-it kong-an.

There is an interesting story that should help you: Many years ago in Japan there was a famous actor who was well-known for his portrayal of samurai fighters. The actor was a seventh *dan* in *kendo* sword-fighting and had trained for twenty years before he ever became an actor. He had won all the major *kendo* competitions in Japan several times, so everybody knew that he was the best. He was very handsome, and his acting was also very good. This man was a very popular actor in Japan.

He was chosen to be the star of an epic samurai film with the greatest director in Japan. They were backed by the best movie company in the country. The company spared no expense in bringing together in this film the best camera people, the best sound people, the best technicians. The lighting people, costume designers, and music directors were all the best in Japan.

Like all samurai movies, the story was very simple: when bad men appeared, the star would fight them. Not a complicated movie at all! He had starred in many, many samurai movies, so acting in this one would be no problem. A few weeks of easy work, and it would be on to the next one. The actor already knew, "I am the best. Nobody can do these movies better than me." The director already understood his mind too.

Then the first battle scene was arranged. The director got everything carefully prepared. Then he said, "Lights? Camera? *Actionnnnn!*" The camera started running—*hrrrrrrr*!! At that moment, the bad man came out from behind a rock, and the star jumped up, swung his sword around in the air, and killed him. But the director only shouted, "*Cut!* No good! No good!"

The star had a strange look on his face. "Hmmm . . . no one has ever told me my acting was 'no good' before. I am the best one. What does he mean?" He had a little strange feeling. But meanwhile the scene was redone, and everything was carefully prepared. The director said, "Lights? Camera? *Actionnnnnn!*" The camera started running—*hrrrrrr*!!—and the bad man leapt out from behind the rock. The star jumped up, swung his sword in the air perfectly, and killed him.

"*Cut!* No good! No good!"

The star got very angry. "No *good?* Nobody has ever told me that even once before, much less twice. This is getting ridiculous." A very angry mind appeared. The director said, "We must do it again!" The cameras were readied, and the sound people got prepared.

Though very angry, the star took a deep breath, calmed down and just completely focused his mind. "Maybe he is right. Maybe there is some mistake I am making. If so, this time it will *not* appear." Everyone was silent on the set. "Lights? Camera? *Actionnnnn!*" The cameras were rolling—*hrrrrrr!!* The bad man came out on cue, and the star jumped up just at the right moment. He swung the sword with greater precision than he had ever done; it was like magic. He flew through the air and killed the bad man perfectly. Landing squarely on both feet, he was in an ideal position, facing into the camera lens.

"*Cut!* *Cut!* No good! No *good!* Do it again!" The star heard these words and *really* raged inside. He had never been this angry in his whole life. "I am the best samurai actor in Japan! I am also seventh *dan* in kendo. Nobody has ever told me 'No good' three times. Even twice is too much." His mind was very, very angry. He glowered at the director, a short, pudgy man not half his size. The director saw this, but his mind did not move. He already understood something . . .

The cameras were readied again. The big lights went on, and soundmen watched their dials. The director said, "Lights? Camera? *Actionnnnn!*" The cameras rolled—*hrrrrrr!!*—and the bad man appeared, on cue, brandishing his sword. The star jumped up—and immediately ran at the director with his sword!! "Yaaaaaaaahhhhh!! I'm gonna *kill* you!" He toppled the director's chair and grabbed the director by the throat, pinning him to the ground.

But the director was not afraid. He laughed and shouted, "*Correct! Correct!* Excellent!" Ha ha ha ha! He was very happy: his star completely attained do-it mind.

When he saw this, the star immediately understood. He lifted up the director, brushing him off. "Oh, I am sorry! I am sorry! Thank you very much for your teaching. I am sorry!"

"Oh, no problem," the director said. He was laughing. They shot the scene over again, and every scene thereafter was done in just one or two takes. The star acted with complete do-it mind, not checking his reputation or his feeling or idea. The movie later became a number-one film in Japan because the action scenes were so completely lifelike to people.

So this was a very keen-eyed director. He already understood this actor's mind. He knew that this star believed too much that he was number one. "I am the best! No one can touch me!" This kind of mind was a problem. It is a checking mind, so even when it does something, that action is always not complete. By pushing his star, the director forced his one hundred percent do-it mind to appear. "*Yaaaaahhhhh!* I'm gonna *kill* you!"

When you are doing something, only do it. Then you and this whole universe completely become one. That is the nature of Ko Bong's Three Gates.

The Eighth Gate: Dok Sahn Carrying His Bowls

One day, Zen Master Dok Sahn came into the Dharma Room carrying his bowls. The housemaster, Seol Bong, saw this and said, "Old Master, the bell has not yet been rung, the drum has not yet been struck. Where are you going, carrying your bowls?" Dok Sahn returned to the master's room.

Seol Bong told the head monk, Am Du, who said, "Great Master Dok Sahn does not understand the last word."

Dok Sahn heard of this and sent for Am Du. "Do you not approve of me?" he demanded. Then Am Du whispered in the master's ear. Dok Sahn was relieved.

The next day, making his dharma speech from the high rostrum, Dok Sahn was really different from before. Am Du went to the front of the Dharma Room, laughed loudly, clapped his hands, and said, "Great joy! The old Master has understood the last word! From now on, no one can check him."

1. What was the last word?
2. What did Am Du whisper in the master's ear?
3. How was the master's speech different from before?
4. If you were Dok Sahn, and Seol Bong told you that the bell had not yet been rung and the drum had not yet been struck, what could you say to Seol Bong?

This is a very important and difficult kong-an. But if you keep a clear mind, it is actually not so difficult. It teaches us how to perceive correct situation, correct relationship, and correct function.

The "last word" is just a term for correct situation, correct relationship, and correct function. The first question asks about this. They have not yet rung the bell and have not yet struck the drum to signal the beginning of mealtime. Yet Zen Master Dok Sahn comes into the Dharma Room carrying his bowls for the meal. The housemaster sees that, and questions the master, who only turns and heads back to his room without explaining anything. That is very strange, you know? So the housemaster tells all this to Am Du, the head monk. Am Du answers, "Our great Zen master doesn't understand the last word." This is another way of saying, "Our teacher does not understand his correct situation, correct relationship, and correct function," because he comes at the wrong time. He does not follow his situation. That is what these words mean. So at that time, what was the last word? What is the master's correct situation, correct relationship, and correct function? That is the first question.

The next question asks, "What did Am Du whisper in the master's ear?" When Am Du hears the housemaster's report, he says about his teacher, "Dok Sahn doesn't understand the last word!" So the Zen master hears of this, and he gets very angry, because the head monk must always obey and respect the Zen master. Why does the head monk make this bad speech about his own teacher? So Dok Sahn calls Am Du into his room. "You! Why are you making this bad speech about me? Do you not approve of me?" Am Du whispers something into Dok Sahn's ear, and Dok Sahn is very happy. "Oh, OK, OK. I am happy." It is like a wife who gets into a tiff with her husband and perhaps says some bad things about him to others. "My husband is like this, nya, nya, nya, nya, nya . . ." When he learns of this he gets very angry. "You don't believe in me?" But the wife says, "No, no, no. Such and such and such. You are my husband. This and this and this. How could you ever doubt me?" Then the husband says, "Oh, you are a good wife." There is no problem after that.

This second question points to that. First of all, what is the problem between them? That is the first question. The Zen master gets angry and demands an explanation, which Am Du delivers. What is the nature of his response? What does he whisper in the master's ear? This addresses the matter of the master's correct situation, correct relationship, and correct function. But exactly what does the head monk, Am Du, whisper in the Master's ear to appease his angry mind? There is an interesting point to be raised here: This kong-an requires a clear answer that demonstrates the student's grasp of correct situation, correct relationship, and correct function. Some Zen schools only want to see you answer this question by going up to the teacher and making a whispering sound in the teacher's ear. "Psss, psssssss, psssss, pss . . ." This is not enough. This is only the outside *form* or appearance of Am Du's response. It is not *clear*. An answer like that has no bone, and it contains no wisdom. What is that, a snake talking? "Psss, pssss, psssssss, psss . . ." It could be the sound of somebody urinating. What exactly did Am Du say to take away his teacher's angry mind? Someday someone will become very angry with you, and if you only make a pissing sound in their ear it will not assuage their anger in the least. Perhaps they will even get angrier and hit you! So a kong-an like this shows us how to perceive our correct situation, correct relationship to that situation, and correct function in that situation. The name for this is wisdom.

Then the next day, Master Dok Sahn ascends the high rostrum to deliver a dharma speech. He is different from before. He gives a very good talk. Am Du claps his hands and laughs in the front of the room. "Now our great master understands the last word. From now on no one can check him." So the third question asks, How is his dharma speech different from before? If you want to understand how his dharma speech is different from before, you must first understand what his Dharma speech was before . . . That is very important. That is a very big question.

If you answer these three questions, that is wonderful. But then we have one more question for you. It is very difficult homework. Dok Sahn is carrying his bowls into the Dharma Room. The housemaster Seol Bong says to him, "Old Master, the bell has not yet been rung and the drum has not yet been struck. Where are you going, carrying your bowls?" If you are the Zen master in that situation, you must respond in some way. You have made a big mistake in front of many students. Making a mistake is not a problem, but how do you make it correct? Maybe your students will doubt you from now on. Perhaps they will check you and not believe in your teaching. Dok Sahn makes an even bigger mistake when, instead of simply responding to Seol Bong, he just turns on his heel and abruptly returns to his room. If Dok Sahn opens his mouth and says something appropriate to Seol Bong, then perhaps the head monk, Am Du, won't make that bad speech about the Zen master. The master won't have reason to get angry with the head monk, and there won't be any need to have this whispering in the Master's ear. There will be no bad talk going on in the temple, because, as we see, all the problems in this kong-an come from the Zen master's mistake. If he speaks to Seol Bong, however, the matter will be completely finished.

The point of this fourth question is, how should Dok Sahn correct his own mistake? There is a well-known story that shows how this might be possible.

One night many years ago, before he became a great Zen master, my teacher, Ko Bong Sunim, went out and had a lot to drink. He came back to the temple very late. By that time the monks had already gotten up and started morning chanting. But Ko Bong Sunim only stayed in his room, lying on his bed and shouting all sorts of bad things about his teacher, the great Zen Master Man Gong. "Man Gong doesn't understand Dharma! He's low class! His teaching is complete bullshit! Nya nya nya!" This went on for quite a while. All the other monks were a little frightened, because Man Gong Sunim was the greatest Zen master in Korea, and he was also a very large and power-fully built man too! Man Gong Sunim was on his way to the Main Buddha Hall when he heard these terrible things being shouted in Ko Bong Sunim's room. "Ko Bong Sunim is making bad speech about me! That is no good." All the other monks stood around, watching, wondering what would happen.

Zen Master Man Gong went up to Ko Bong Sunim's room and whipped open the door. "Ko Bong! Why are you saying all these bad things about me?" Ko Bong Sunim straightened up on his bed. The great Zen master had come to his room: now he was in *really* big trouble. He had already made a big mistake. Now how would he make it correct? His teacher stood over him, glaring. Everybody was watching very closely outside.

Anyone else in this situation would have cowered in fear, maybe stam-mered or been too ashamed to say anything. But not Ko Bong Sunim. He did not hesitate in the least. He simply smiled and said, "Zen Master, I haven't made any bad speech about you!"

This got Man Gong Sunim even angrier. "What? You have just been saying bad things about me. Everyone heard you! I heard it myself."

"No, I was not saying anything bad about you. I was only saying bad things about that good-for-nothing Man Gong."

Then Zen Master Man Gong said, "Are Man Gong and me the same or different?"

"*Katz!*" Ko Bong Sunim shouted.

Man Gong Sunim smiled broadly. "You've had a little too much to drink," he said. "Now get some sleep."

So whether you make a mistake or not does not really matter. Everyone makes mistakes, even Zen masters like Dok Sahn. The most important thing is how you make it correct. "I wasn't saying bad things about you. I was only saying bad things about that good-for-nothing Man Gong." Ko Bong Sunim always kept a clear mind from moment to moment and in any situation. So his mistake was not a mistake: it is still teaching us, because he was able to instantly turn it to some clear purpose. Zen Master Dok Sahn has made a mistake, and the whole temple is disturbed if he just goes back to his room without making his mistake correct. His eyes, ears, nose, tongue, body, or mind have made a mistake. How does he fix it? That is the point of this fourth question.

The Ninth Gate: Nam Cheon Kills a Cat

One day, the monks of the Eastern and Western halls were disputing over a cat. Seeing this, Master Nam Cheon held up the cat in one hand and a knife in the other and said, "You! Give me one word and I will save this cat. If you cannot, I will kill it!" No one could answer. Finally Nam Cheon killed the cat. In the evening, when his student Joju returned from outside, Nam Cheon told him of the incident. Joju took off his shoe, put it on his head, and walked away. Nam Cheon said, "If you had been there I could have saved the cat."

1. Nam Cheon said, "Give me one word!" At that time what could you do?
2. Joju put his shoe on his head. What does this mean?

This is a Great Love and Great Compassion kong-an. If you have Great Love and Great Compassion, you love and you act with no condition. Unconditional love means not having "my" opinion and "my" condition and "my" situation. Only help other people. So how do you save this cat?

There is a story in the Bible that may teach you. A long time ago lived King Solomon. He was admired all over Israel for his profound wisdom. One day, there was a great commotion, and two women were brought into the palace, fighting over a baby.

"It's my baby!"

"No, it's my baby!"

"My baby!"

"No, my baby!" All the great judges in the land of Israel could not resolve this difficult matter, so it was brought before the king.

"This matter is actually quite simple," the king said. Picking up the baby in one hand, he held a sword in the other hand and declared, "Since both of you cannot decide on your own, one of you can get half, and the other can get the other half." Just as he was about to cut the baby in two, one woman shouted, "No! That's not necessary. You keep the baby," and offered it to the other woman. The woman who spoke up was the baby's real mother.

The situation is nearly the same as the situation that Nam Cheon creates for the monks of the Eastern and Western halls. But in the particular situation that Nam Cheon creates, you cannot do just that. You cannot answer merely as this mother answers. It requires a more meticulous response. There are two hundred and fifty monks in each hall. Each side believes the cat is rightfully theirs. So Nam Cheon holds up the cat and a knife. If some monk steps forward and says, "OK, you take it," perhaps someone else will come forward and say, "No! You can't give it away. That's my cat." And the fighting will begin all over again. So in this situation only true, unconditional love will save the cat. If you want to attain this kong-an, you must go to a cowboy movie. Those types of movies have very simple teaching because they are only concerned with two things: love and money. When you learn the kind of love they show in cowboy movies, then this kong-an is no problem whatsoever. [Laughter from audience.]

There is another way to view this kong-an. We separate the various ways of perceiving reality into four expressions: without like-this, become-one like-this, like-this, and just-like-this. Without like-this means primary point. That point is before thinking, so words and speech cannot express it. It is the complete nothingness and stillness point, without anything whatsoever.

Become-one like-this means that everything becomes one. "Where are you coming from?" [Hits the table.] "When you die where do you go?" [Hits.] "Does the sky have Buddha-nature?" [Hits.] This point demonstrates how everything becomes one. It does not attempt to explain that point, because that point cannot be shown with speech or words. How do you demonstrate primary point? How can I teach you primary point? [Hits the table.] Only hit, or hold up one finger, or shout "Katz!" Something like this that literally demonstrates everything becoming one.

The next point is like-this. It is very interesting. If you truly attain primary point—this point [hits the table]—then your mind is clear like space. When your mind is clear like space it is clear like a mirror: if red comes before the mirror, the mirror is red; if white comes, the mirror is white. Everything is simply reflected in your clear-mirror mind exactly as it is. You perceive that the sky is blue. The trees are green. Salt is salty. Sugar is sweet. Everything is already the truth, just as it is. We call this like-this, because it means that everything, like-this, is the truth.

Like-this is truth, but it is still a metaphysical way of answering. "What is Buddha?" "The sky is blue." "What is Dharma?" "Outside right now the wind is howling." "What is Dharma-nature?" "The wall is white." "What is God?" "The floor is brown." All these answers point directly to truth. But they still just *explain* truth, so we sometimes call them metaphysical-style answers. The answers are very wide. So if you have a wide question like "What is Buddha?" these answers are sufficient.

Sometimes, however, we are in situations that ask a much more specific or one-pointed question. In that case, this concrete question requires a concrete answer, something that points directly at the situation. Every single day we encounter situations that can only be answered with some clear, intuitive action: words alone are not enough. For example: Here is a cup. If you call it a cup, you are attached to name and form. If you say it is not a cup, you are attached to emptiness. So I ask you, is this a cup or not? Some people will answer, "The sky is blue." Or "The tree is green." They will express some truth, but that truth, while true in and of itself, is not the correct answer to this question. That answer does not connect directly your true nature and the nature of this cup. This is a very one-pointed question: Is this a cup or not? If you answer with some truth, you are not expressing the true nature of this cup. You are not expressing the true nature of this particular situation and your relationship to the cup and the correct function of the cup.

[*Turning to somebody next to him*:] So I ask you, is this a cup or not? [*The person lifts the cup and drinks from it.*] Correct! That is the correct situation you are in: you and this cup. It expresses your correct relationship to that situation, and your correct function, which is to just drink from the cup. The point of this view is to show how you use the perception of truth to function correctly to make a correct life. Making a correct life means function. A one-point question demands a one-point answer. That is truth just-like-this. Without like-this is nothing, only stillness. Become-one like-this is cutting off all thinking, the demonstration of primary point, universal substance. [*Hits the table.*] Like-this is truth: when you see, when you hear, when you smell, when you taste, when you touch, and when you think, everything is truth, only like this. And next, how does this *perception* of truth *function* in your life, from moment to moment, to help all beings? Yah, the sky is blue. The tree is green. That is truth. But if someone is suffering in front of you, how do you take this perception and make it function clearly for them? That is the point of just-like-this.

A long time ago, anytime someone asked Joju a question, he would just answer "Go drink tea." "Master, I want to understand Buddha. What is Buddha?" "Go drink tea." "Teacher, I want to understand the highest teaching of all the eminent teachers. What is Dharma?" "Go drink tea!" This answer is very, very deep. It contains correct situation, correct relationship, and correct function. If you correctly drink tea, you attain your correct situation with regard to tea. You attain your correct relationship to it and therefore your correct function. That is correct life.

But there are actually two different ways to express our correct function or response to situations that appear in this life. At this point we must meticulously separate the teaching of just-like-this for a very important reason, as we shall see. First, there is just "my" action from moment to moment, how I keep *my* correct situation, correct relationship, and correct function with this world. That is only pointing to my job of helping all beings. *My* correct action and correct life are subject just-like-this. Someone asked Zen Master Joju, "Master, I have just entered the monastery. Please teach me."

Joju said, "Have you had breakfast?"

"Yes, I have."

"Then go wash your bowls." *Piitchhuu!* The monk got enlightenment. He attained his own everyday life job, his own mind. This means he attained subject just-like-this.

But the kong-an about Nam Cheon holding up the cat demands a much more meticulous response. It is not a subject just-like-this kong-an. Zen Master Nam Cheon held up the cat in one hand and a knife in the other and said, "You! Give me one word and I will save this cat. If you cannot, I will kill it." At that time, if you were there, what could you do? Many prominent Zen traditions teach that in order to answer Master Nam Cheon, you just "become one" with the cat, and that is all you can do. Roshi asks you the question and you say, "Meow! Meow! Meow!" That answer is not so good. It does not bring the student to attain any kind of wisdom or bodhisattva action. There is no compassionate function connecting your true self with the cat caught in *that* particular situation. Like the "Pssss, psssss, pssssss" sound that some teachers want you to make in Zen Master Dok Sahn's ear, saying "Meow" just *reflects* things as they are—truth—but does not make truth *function* compassionately for others. It is a dead answer. That kind of answer is not clear, because it does not help the cat. This is what Nam Cheon is looking for, after all. He does not want some reflection of the cat he is holding under a knife. Nam Cheon wants one monk to come forward and save it. He is looking for a bodhisattva among them. That is a very important point. If Nam Cheon asks you this question and you just say, "Meow," you are nothing more than a parrot. Then maybe he will kill the cat *and* you! Ha ha ha ha ha!

Let us take that style of answering and go back to the situation with the baby. King Solomon held up the baby in one hand and a sword in another and said, "Whose baby is this? Answer correctly, and it is yours. If you cannot decide, I will give you each half a baby." At that time, if the women had only cried like a baby—"Waaahhh! Waaaahhh! Waaaahhh!"—the story would not have ended the way it did: each woman would have received half a baby. That is not so wonderful. But one woman did not just "become one" and photographically reflect the truth of this situation as it is: she completely *connected* the king's question with the baby's situation and condition in that moment. Then a correct answer spontaneously appeared. This is true wisdom and compassion. This is called object just-like-this. What is your correct situation, relationship, and function with regard to the object of this kong-an?

Is this a cup or not? The only complete answer available to you is to demonstrate your correct function with regard to the cup. That is subject just-like-this. But if you have a true bodhisattva mind and direction, you must be able to clearly and spontaneously perceive your correct situation and function with regard to this object. That is why we separate this teaching view into subject just-like-this and object just-like-this, to demonstrate how you can function meticulously in any situation. Here is a simpler way to express it: When you are hungry, what do you do? You eat. When you are thirsty, what do you do? You drink. This is subject just-like-this. It is subject's correct situation when hungry, correct relationship to hunger, and correct function in that situation.

But a hungry person comes to you, so what can you do? Do you pretend to be hungry? Do you eat something yourself? No, that doesn't help them: Give *them* some food. If a thirsty person comes to you, should you act like you're thirsty, or get yourself something to drink? Does that really help them? No, you get *them* something to drink. If someone is suffering, what can you do? You must help them. The name for that is object just-like-this. Some Zen teachers ask, "A baby has wet its pants. What is the meaning of this?" Then if you assume the position of a crying baby in wet diapers, the teacher says, "Oh, wonderful! That's correct!" Yah, such an answer is possible for a beginning student, but from an older student a more high-class perception is required. Becoming the baby in wet diapers doesn't help the baby. In this school, if you are asked this question, the answer is clear: How does your clear mind connect with this baby, from moment to moment? You change the child's diapers. That is bodhisattva mind. It is object just-like-this. It is the whole point of sitting down to do Zen practice.

Separating these ways of teaching represents a kind of revolution in Zen kong-an practice. Years ago, a monk would take one kong-an into the mountain and hold it for many, many years until he got enlightenment. That was possible because a monk's life does not always need to be involved with changing situations in a hectic world. But nowadays many people must connect their practice with life in a very fast and complicated society. If you only hold this samadhi-style and become-one style of using kong-ans, you are attached to an old and dead tradition. Then your kong-an practice does not have some practical and spontaneous application to life in the modern world. This is how Zen died out in China. Zen practice and kong-an practice there could no longer connect with everyday life, so they both died. Zen became an esoteric practice based on secret words and behind-meanings. Zen practice after the T'ang and Sung dynasties lost all of its bodhisattva direction. Our Zen style means intuitively perceiving how you use these kong-ans to connect meditation practice to bodhisattva action in a complicated world. That is the point of separating this way of viewing kong-an practice. It is a Zen revolution.

The second question in this kong-an asks: Joju put his shoe on his head and walked away. What does this mean? Joju's reply is based on an old tradition of China and Korea. When somebody dies, a pair of grass shoes and a plate of food and fruit are kept outside the front door. This is done so that when the dead person's spirit comes to visit, it can eat something and have a pair of shoes to walk to heaven. Keeping these shoes outside means that somebody has died. A long time ago, at ceremony time you would pick up the shoes and go put them outside. That is the meaning of this question. At that time, what is the nature of the situation, your proper relationship to it, and therefore your correct function? All three points—*boom!*—come together in one point. It is very clear. . . .

The Tenth Gate: The Mouse Eats Cat Food

The mouse eats cat food, but the cat bowl is broken.

1. What does this mean?

This kong-an is a complete expression of subject just-like-this attainment. In subject just-like-this there are no opposites, and everything completely becomes one. The mouse eats cat food, but the cat bowl is broken. Let us say that someone doesn't feel so well. She says, "Oh, I want some ice cream." She checks her pocket and finds a quarter. "Where is the ice-cream store? Ah, there is an ice-cream store over there." The sign says, "One ice cream: twenty-five cents." She goes over and hands the man a quarter, and the man gives her some ice cream. The ice cream goes into her stomach, and she feels good again. "Ah, wonderful!" So the key to this kong-an is that a quarter is twenty-five cents. Twenty-five cents buys ice cream. The ice cream goes into your stomach. "Ah, wonderful!"

This kong-an is very high-class. But it is too easy. Everybody is too clever, so they don't understand. If you become completely stupid, then it is very easy to attain this kong-an. How do mouse, cat food, the cat bowl, and broken combine? Every child understands this!

Three Men Walking

Three men are walking. The first one makes a sword sound, the second man waves his hands, and the third takes out a handkerchief. What does this mean?

1. If you were there, what would be your correct function?
2. What is the relationship?
3. What is the situation?

This is a complete object just-like-this kong-an. It is like a TV game—only that. The announcer says a few things and asks the contestants, "OK, now, what does this mean?" Or it is like watching a movie in a theater. Something funny happens on the screen. One person in the audience laughs like this, another laughs a different way, and one person laughs still another way. The situation is the same, but three people react in somewhat different ways. What does it mean? If you finish the *Ten Gates* you get this as special homework. And if you pass this, the Zen master checks your center, and you can get *inka*.

GLOSSARY

BODHISATTVA (Sanskrit)   A being whose actions promote unity or harmony; one who vows to postpone one's own enlightenment in order to help all sentient beings realize liberation; one who seeks enlightenment not only for oneself but for others. The bodhisattva ideal is at the heart of Mahayana and Zen Buddhism.

BUDDHA (Sanskrit)   An awakened one; refers usually to Siddhartha Gautama (sixth century BC), historic founder of Buddhism.

BUDDHA-NATURE   That which all sentient beings share and manifest through their particular form; according to Zen, the Buddha said that all things have Buddha-nature and therefore have the innate potential to become Buddha.

CHOGYE ORDER   The major order in Korean Buddhism, formed in 1356 by the unification of the Nine Mountains Schools of Zen.

DAE SOEN SA NIM (Korean)   Title used by Zen Master Seung Sahn's students in referring to him; "great honored Zen Master."

DHARMA (Sanskrit)   The way or law; the path; basically, Buddhist teaching, but in a wider sense any teaching or truth.

DHARMA ROOM   In Zen Master Seung Sahn's centers, the meditation/ceremony hall.

HARA (Japanese)   The vital energy center of the abdomen; in many Zen traditions considered the seat of the heart-body-mind.

INKA (Korean)   "Public seal"; certification of a student completion of, or breakthrough in, kong-an practice.

KALPA (Sanskrit)   An endlessly long period of time.

KARMA (Sanskrit)   "Cause and effect," and the continuing process of action and reaction, accounting for the interpenetration of all phenomenon.

Thus our present thoughts, actions, and situations are the result of what we have done in the past, and our future thoughts, actions, and situations will be the product of what we are doing now. Individual karma results from this process.

KASA (Korean)   Brown piece of cloth worn around the neck or over the shoulders, symbolic of Buddhist vows and precepts.

KIDO (Korean)   "Energy way"; a chanting retreat.

KONG-AN (Korean, Japanese *koan*)   A paradoxical or irrational statement used by Zen teachers to cut through students' thinking and bring them to realization.

KWAN SEUM BOSAL (Korean, Sanskrit *Avalokitesvara*, Chinese *Kwan Yin*, Korean *Kwan Um*, Japanese *Kanzeon*)   "One who perceives the cries of the world" and responds with compassionate aid; the bodhisattva of compassion.

MAHAYANA (Sanskrit)   The Buddhism practiced in northern Asia; encompasses schools in China, Korea, Japan, and Tibet.

MANTRA (Sanskrit)   Sounds or words used in meditation to cut through discriminating thoughts so the mind can become clear.

PATRIARCH   The founder of a school and his successors in the transmission of its teaching.

SAMSARA (Sanskrit)   The cycle of birth, death, and rebirth.

SANGHA (Sanskrit)   In the Mahayana and Zen traditions, the community of all practitioners; may refer to a family of students under a particular master.

SUTRA (Sanskrit)   Buddhist scriptures, consisting of discourses by the Buddha and his disciples.

TRANSMISSION   Formal handling over of the lineage succession from teacher to student.

ZEN (Japanese, Korean *Son*, Chinese *Ch'an*, Sanskrit *Dhyana*)   Meditation practice.

ZEN CENTER   Meditation communities which may include a residence. All the Zen centers in the Kwan Um School of Zen are under the spiritual direction of Zen Master Seung Sahn, and each offers regular practice and periodic retreats.

Zen Master Seung Sahn's Lineage

歷代傳燈

Indian

The Buddha
1. Mahakashyapa
2. Ananda
3. Sanakavasa
4. Upagupta
5. Dhrtaka
6. Miccika
7. Vasumitra
8. Buddhanandi
9. Buddhamitra
10. Parsva
11. Punyayasas
12. Asvaghosa
13. Kapimala
14. Nagarjuna
15. Kanadeva
16. Rahulata
17. Sanghanandi
18. Gayasata
19. Kumarata
20. Jayata
21. Vasubandhu
22. Manorhita
23. Haklena
24. Aryasimha
25. Basiasita
26. Punyamitra
27. Prajnatata
28. Bodhidharma

Chinese

29. Hui K'o
30. Seng Ts'an
31. Tao Hsin
32. Hung Jen
33. Hui Neng
34. Huai Jang
35. Ma-tsu Tao-i
36. Pai-chang Huai-hai
37. Huang-po Hsi-yün
38. Lin-chi I-hsüan
39. Hsing-hua Tzun-chiang
40. Nan-yüan Hui-yü
41. Feng-hsüeh Yen-chao
42. Shou-shan Hsing-nien
43. T'ai-tzu Yüan-shan
44. T'zu-ming Ch'u-yüan
45. Yang-ch'i Fang-hui
46. Pai-yün Shou-tuan
47. Wu-tsu Fa-yen
48. Huan-wu K'o-ch'in
49. Hsü-ch'iu Shao-lung
50. Ying-an T'an-hua
51. Mi-an Hsi-chieh
52. P'o-an Tsu-hsien
53. Wu-chuan Shih-fan
54. Hsüeh-yen Hui-lang
55. Chi-an Tsung-hsin
56. Shih-shih Ch'ing-kung

Korean

57. Tae-Ko Bo-Wu
58. Whan-Am Hon-Su
59. Ku-Gok Gak-Un
60. Byeok-Ke Joung-Shim
61. Byeok-Song Ji-Eom
62. Bu-Yong Yeong-Kwan
63. Cheong-Heo Hyu-Jeong
64. Pyeon-Yang Eong-Ki
65. Pung-Joung Heon-Shim
66. Weol-Dam Seol-Je
67. Hwan-Seong Ji-An

68. Ho-Am Che-Jeong
69. Cheong-Bong Keo-An
70. Yul-Bong Cheong-Kwa
71. Keum-Heo Beop-Cheom
72. Young-Am He-Eon
73. Yeong-Weol Bong-Yul
74. Man-Hwa Bo Seon
75. Kyong Ho Seong-Wu
76. Man Gong Weol-Myeon
77. Ko-Bong Gyeong-Uk
78. Seung-Sahn Haeng-Won